BENCHMARK LITERACY™

Grade **3** | Volume **1**

D1788484

TRS

Teacher's Resource System

Benchmark Education Company

145 Huguenot Street • New Rochelle, NY 10801

©2011 Benchmark Education Company, LLC. All rights reserved. Teachers may photocopy the reproducible pages for classroom use. No other part of the guide may be reproduced or transmitted in whole or in part in any form or by any means, electronic or mechanical, including photocopy, recording, or any information storage or retrieval system, without permission in writing from the publisher. Printed in Guangzhou, China. 4401/0117/CA21700028

ISBN: 978-1-4509-0537-4

For ordering information, call **Toll-Free 1-877-236-2465** or visit our website at **www.benchmarkeducation.com.**

Table of Contents

Volume 1

Unit 1: Ask Questions/Identify Main Idea and Supporting Details

Week 1: Model and Guide Strategy Practice Using Comprehension Anchor Posters
Week 2: Apply Strategies Using the Genre Anchor Poster–Biography
Week 3: Integrate Skills and Strategies through Reader's Theater–*Harriet Tubman and the Underground Railroad*

Unit 2: Visualize/Analyze Character

Week 1: Model and Guide Strategy Practice Using Comprehension Anchor Posters
Week 2: Apply Strategies Using the Genre Anchor Poster–Personal Narratives
Week 3: Integrate Skills and Strategies through Reader's Theater–*Our New Home*

Unit 3: Determine Text Importance/Identify Sequence of Events

Week 1: Model and Guide Strategy Practice Using Comprehension Anchor Posters
Week 2: Apply Strategies Using the Genre Anchor Poster–Historical Fiction
Week 3: Integrate Skills and Strategies through Reader's Theater–*Cesar Chavez Comes to Visit*

Unit 4: Summarize and Synthesize/Analyze Story Elements

Week 1: Model and Guide Strategy Practice Using Comprehension Anchor Posters
Week 2: Apply Strategies Using the Genre Anchor Poster–Realistic Fiction
Week 3: Integrate Skills and Strategies through Reader's Theater–*The Great Lemonade Standoff*

Unit 5: Make Connections/Make Inferences

Week 1: Model and Guide Strategy Practice Using Comprehension Anchor Posters
Week 2: Apply Strategies Using the Genre Anchor Poster–Trickster Tales
Week 3: Integrate Skills and Strategies through Reader's Theater–*Kanchil Outsmarts the Crocodile*

Volume 2

Unit 6: Fix-Up Monitoring/Distinguish and Evaluate Fact and Opinion

Week 1: Model and Guide Strategy Practice Using Comprehension Anchor Posters
Week 2: Apply Strategies Using the Genre Anchor Poster–Persuasive Letters
Week 3: Integrate Skills and Strategies through Reader's Theater–*The Food Pyramid Disaster*

Unit 7: Make Inferences/Make Predictions

Week 1: Model and Guide Strategy Practice Using Comprehension Anchor Posters
Week 2: Apply Strategies Using the Genre Anchor Poster–Fairy Tales
Week 3: Integrate Skills and Strategies through Reader's Theater–*Rough-Face Girl*

Unit 8: Determine Text Importance/Compare and Contrast

Week 1: Model and Guide Strategy Practice Using Comprehension Anchor Posters
Week 2: Apply Strategies Using the Genre Anchor Poster–Tall Tales
Week 3: Integrate Skills and Strategies through Reader's Theater–*How Davy Crockett Moved the Sun*

Unit 9: Make Connections/Identify Cause and Effect

Week 1: Model and Guide Strategy Practice Using Comprehension Anchor Posters
Week 2: Apply Strategies Using the Genre Anchor Poster–Pourquoi Tales
Week 3: Integrate Skills and Strategies through Reader's Theater–*Why the Sky Is Far Away*

Unit 10: Make Inferences/Draw Conclusions

Week 1: Model and Guide Strategy Practice Using Comprehension Anchor Posters
Week 2: Apply Strategies Using the Genre Anchor Poster–Fables
Week 3: Integrate Skills and Strategies through Reader's Theater–*The Ant and Grasshopper Show*

Introducing Benchmark Literacy for Grades K–6

Benchmark Education Company is known for its pedagogically sound, research-proven literacy solutions. Now Benchmark Education is proud to put these carefully developed, scientifically tested components into one easy-to-implement comprehensive reading program for Grades K–6.

Benchmark Literacy supports all the daily components of high-quality reading instruction, with a particular emphasis on the development of comprehension. You will find:

• **Assessment** to drive instruction and help teachers monitor progress

• **Interactive read-alouds** to model good-reader strategies with award-winning trade literature

• **Shared reading mini-lessons** to explicitly model comprehension, vocabulary, and fluency

• **Differentiated small-group reading** that builds seamlessly on shared-reading instruction and addresses the needs of above-, on-, and below-level readers, as well as English learners and special-needs students

• **Independent reading** to encourage the transfer of skills and strategies

• **Phonemic awareness, phonics, and word study** to build strong decoding and word-solving strategies

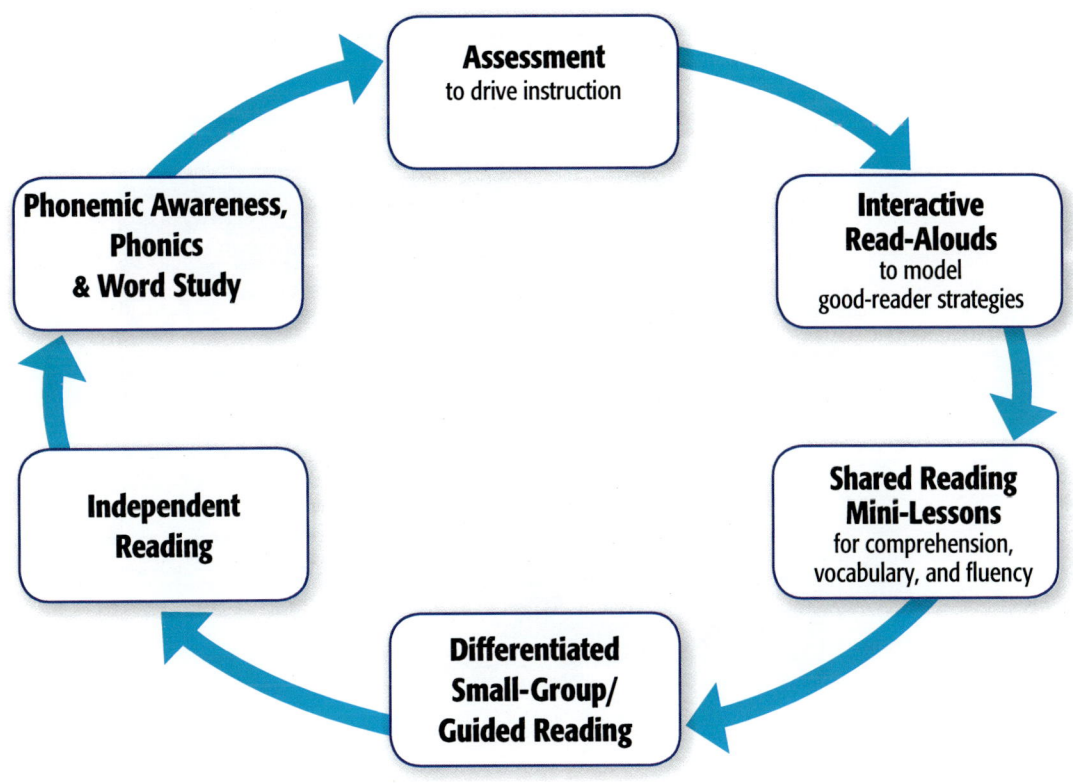

What Makes Benchmark Literacy Different–and Better?

- **Ten comprehension-focused units** per grade with three distinct weeks of instruction that build developmentally and eliminate boredom

- **Seamless, spiraling, whole-to-small group comprehension instruction** across K–6 that supports your curriculum standards

- **Grade-specific leveled text collections** organized by comprehension strategy

- **Phonics and word study kits** that provide a complete K–6 continuum of phonological awareness, phonemic awareness, phonics, spelling, and word study for vocabulary development

- **Short mentor texts** for whole-group skill and strategy instruction

- **Motivation for all students** through trade literature connections, big books, genre texts, and reader's theater

- **Pre-, post-, and ongoing assessment** to drive the instruction

- **Research-proven instruction** that fits both comprehensive literacy and reader's workshop models

The Research Behind Benchmark Literacy

Benchmark Literacy is an integrated literacy program designed around the principles of apprenticeship. This approach suggests that students acquire literacy through assisted instruction with a sensitive and knowledgeable teacher. Students are provided with meaningful and functional materials and experiences according to their developmental needs. Teachers activate new learning through the use of focused mini-lessons, demonstrations, and discussions that promote problem solving and reflective thinking. A complete bibliography of the research underlying Benchmark Literacy can be found at the back of this overview.

Principles of an Apprenticeship Approach	
Principles	**Description**
1. Observation and responsive teaching	Teachers observe how students respond to print and they design instruction according to students' strengths and needs.
2. Modeling and coaching	Teachers use clear demonstrations and explicit language.
3. Clear and relevant language for problem solving	Language prompts help students initiate problem-solving actions during reading and writing events.
4. Adjustable scaffolds	Varying degrees of support and interactions in the classroom setting help students reach higher levels of literacy development.
5. Structured routines	Structured routines and interactions in the classroom setting help students reach higher levels of literacy development.
6. Assisted and independent work	Students are provided balanced opportunities to work with teachers and to work independently.
7. Transfer	When students acquire knowledge of skills and strategies, they are able to use these flexibly in all types of text for varying purposes.

In addition to having a solid research base, Benchmark Literacy is made up of whole-group, small-group, phonics/word study, and assessment components that have been proven effective in multiple year-long classroom studies. These studies were conducted by independent research firms. Teachers can be confident that these resources can make a significant academic difference in real K–6 classrooms. Details of this research are available at www.benchmarkeducation.com.

Components at a Glance–Grade 3

Teacher Resources

❏ **2 Spiral-Bound Teacher's Resource Systems**

❏ **1 Benchmark Literacy Toolkit** that contains a getting started guide, comprehensive assessment resources, and professional development tools

Read-Aloud Support

• **Recommended Trade Books for Read-Aloud**

• **Read-Aloud Strategies**

Shared Reading

❏ **20 Genre Posters** (with matching small books)

❏ **20 Comprehension Anchor Posters** with clings

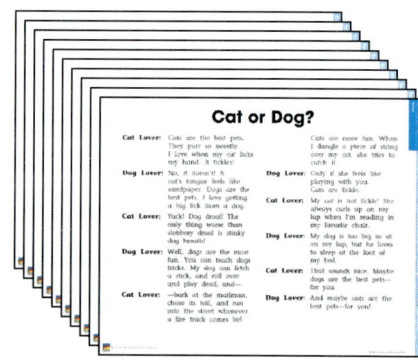

❏ **10 Fluency Posters**

❏ **10 Reader's Theater Scripts** (6-packs)

Small-Group/Guided Reading

80 leveled text titles packaged in 6-packs by comprehension focus:

☐ **5 Titles** at level J/18 ☐ **5 Titles** at level K/20 ☐ **10 Titles** at level M/28

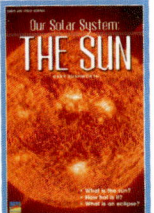 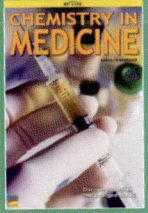 

☐ **14 Titles** at level N/30 ☐ **13 Titles** at level O/34 ☐ **13 Titles** at level P/38

☐ **10 Titles** at level Q/40 ☐ **10 Titles** at level R/40

☐ **Explicit 12-Page Teacher's Guide** for every title ☐ **Comprehension Question Card** for every title

☐ **Teacher Comprehension Flip Chart** and **Student Book Marks** ☐ **Responsive Prompts Flip Chart**

Word Study & Vocabulary Resources

32 Systematic, Explicit, 5-Day Lessons

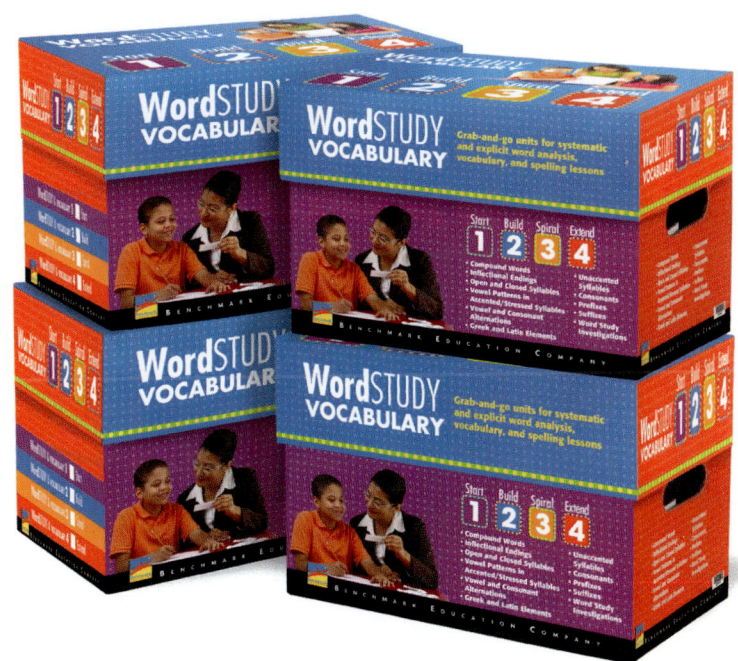

☐ **32 Units** per grade for developing syllables and affixes and derivational constancy.

BenchmarkUniverse.com Technology Resources

Teacher Resources: Preview and download Teacher's Guides, Comprehension Question Cards, blackline masters, and assessments.

Subscription-Only Resources
- Interactive Whiteboard Resources for whole-group components
- Talking E-Books for small-group reading titles
- Online Comprehension Strategy Assessments with immediate reporting to support data-driven instruction
- Independent Text-Dependent Comprehension Activities

Ask Questions/Identify Main Idea and Supporting Details

Unit 1/Week 1 at a Glance

Day	Mini-Lessons
ONE	• Introduce the Comprehension Strategy: *Identify Main Idea and Supporting Details* • Think Aloud and Use the Metacognitive Strategy: *Ask Questions* • Find the Main Idea in a Picture • Connect Thinking, Speaking, and Writing • Reflect and Discuss
TWO	• Review the Metacognitive Strategy: *Ask Questions* • Use the Comprehension Strategy: *Identify Main Idea and Supporting Details* • Connect Thinking, Speaking, and Writing • Reflect and Discuss
THREE	• Extend the Comprehension Strategy: *Identify Main Idea and Supporting Details* • Observe and Prompt for Strategy Understanding • Reflect and Discuss
FOUR	• Read and Summarize • Answer Text-Dependent Comprehension Questions: *Identify Main Idea and Supporting Details (Level 2: Look Closer!)* • Reflect and Discuss
FIVE	• Metacognitive Self-Assessment • Constructed Written Response • Ongoing Comprehension Strategy Assessment

Colonists at Home

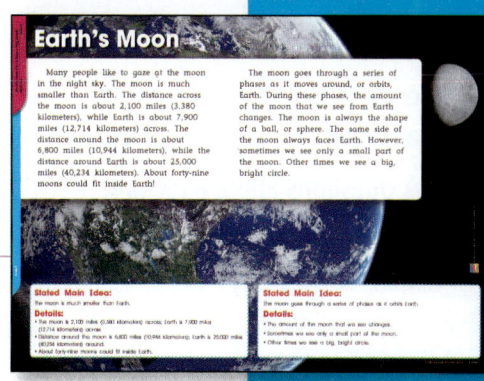

Earth's Moon

Living Off the Land

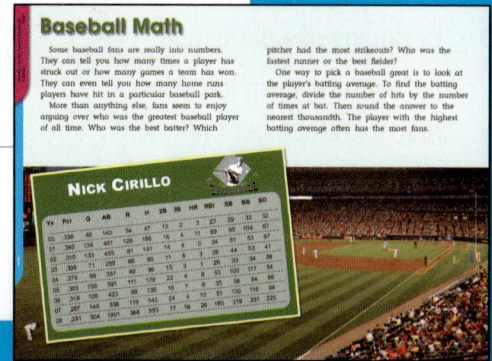

Baseball Math

Day One

Comprehension Anchor Poster 1

Lesson Objectives

Students will:

- Identify the main idea of a picture.
- Identify details that support the main idea.
- Ask questions about a picture.
- Use academic sentence frames to discuss strategies.

Related Resources

- Home/School Connections (BLM 1)
- BenchmarkUniverse.com

About the Strategy

- The main idea is what a paragraph, passage, or story is about.
- Supporting details describe or explain the main idea.
- A main idea is often stated at the beginning of a paragraph.
- Recognizing main ideas helps readers remember important information.
- Recognizing supporting details helps readers understand the main idea.

Read-Aloud (10 MINUTES)

Select a favorite fiction read-aloud from your classroom or school library with which to model the metacognitive strategy "Ask Questions." Use the sample read-aloud lessons and suggested titles in the Getting Started Guide.

Mini-Lessons (20 MINUTES)

Introduce the Comprehension Strategy: Identify Main Idea and Supporting Details

Say: *To be healthy we need to be physically active. Exercise helps make and keep our hearts, muscles, and bones strong. We have more energy and stamina, and the more we exercise, the stronger we get. When we exercise regularly, we sleep better, and we feel better. Exercise will help us keep our weight at a safe level, too.*

Ask: *What do you do to get the exercise you need?*

Turn and talk. Ask students to turn to a partner and share things they do that help them get exercise. Ask a few students to share with the whole group.

Explain: *The importance of being physically active is the main idea. The benefits of exercise are details that support that main idea. Sometimes when we talk, first we state the most important point we want to make, and then we tell details about that point. Writers do this, too. Good readers know how to recognize a main idea and supporting details in fiction and nonfiction texts. We're going to practice recognizing main ideas and supporting details this week.*

Think Aloud and Use the Metacognitive Strategy: Ask Questions

Display Poster 1.

Draw students' attention to the people, their actions, and the setting. (Whiteboard users can use the highlighter tool.)

Explain: *When I look at this picture, the first thing I need to do is figure out what it's trying to show me. One way I can do that is by asking myself questions. I ask questions to make things clearer in my mind. Let me show you how I do it.*

Think aloud: *The picture shows a scene from long ago. People are doing chores in their home. What chore is each person doing? Asking and answering questions helps me recognize a main idea as well as identify details to support, or tell more about, that idea.*

Write your questions on chart paper. Ask students to generate other questions they could ask about the picture, and add these to your list. Explore possible answers together.

Post these questions on the wall as an Ask Questions anchor chart, or have students write them in their reading journals or notebooks to use in the future.

Find the Main Idea in a Picture

Ask students what this illustration is mostly about, or what the main idea is. Point out that the title of the poster, "Colonists at Home," can help them figure out the main idea.

Ask students to tell which details in the illustration helped them figure out the main idea. Remind them that details tell more about the main idea.

Provide the following academic sentence frames to support ELLs and struggling students:
The main idea is _____.
One detail that supports the main idea is _____.
Clues that help me identify the main idea and details are _____.

Connect Thinking, Speaking, and Writing

Write down the main idea that students identify and reread it as a group. Then write the details they found that support the main idea. Give students the opportunity to expand on their shared writing.

Reflect and Discuss

Ask and discuss the following questions:
- *Why is it important to identify the main idea and details?*
- *How does this help you?*
- *How did asking yourself questions help you understand the illustration?*
- *How does the title help you identify the main idea?*

Connect and transfer. Say: *Remember, you can look for main ideas in texts, too. Tomorrow, we will read a text to find main ideas and details.*

Make Content Comprehensible for ELLs

Use the following strategies to help ELLs understand the poster content and acquire academic language.

Beginning
Read the title of the poster. Demonstrate the concept of doing chores by role-playing classroom chores. For example, **say:** *This is one chore we do in the classroom. We clean off the chalkboard.* Erase chalkboard.

This is another chore we do in the classroom. We put away the books. Put books on shelves.

Point to and name the colonists' actions in the illustration: cooking, spinning, churning butter, making pastry, peeling apples. Ask ELLs to repeat the words and pantomime the actions.

Beginning and Intermediate
Draw and label, or ask ELLs to draw, chores they do at home.

Comprehension Quick-Check

Observe whether students are able to articulate the main idea and details in the poster. If they have difficulty, use the following additional explicit instruction.

Draw a main idea/supporting details graphic organizer on chart paper.

In the Main Idea box, write *Colonists had many chores to do at home.*

Say: *This is the main idea. The main idea gives the most important information.*

In the first Detail box, write *The father is peeling apples.*

Say: *I looked at the picture, and I identified one chore that a colonist is doing. I write that chore as a detail that supports the main idea.*

Say: *Now you find another detail in the illustration that I can write in a Detail box.*

Support Special Needs Learners

Support visual learners and students with attention issues by projecting the whiteboard versions of the posters. Allow students to come to the whiteboard and circle, underline, or highlight the main idea and details in the text. Invite them to label what they see.

Access the graphic organizer provided on the whiteboard. Record main ideas and details with students.

Provide opportunities for active involvement. For example, assign posters to pairs of students. Ask them to write the main idea and details of their poster's content on index cards.

Access the image bank for enlarged images that students can use to practice asking questions, determining main ideas and supporting details, and retelling facts.

Home/School Connections

On Day 1, distribute copies of Home/School Connections (BLM 1). Each day during the week, assign one of the six home/school connection activities for the students to complete. Ask them to bring their completed assignments to class the next day. Make time at the beginning of each day for students to share their ideas.

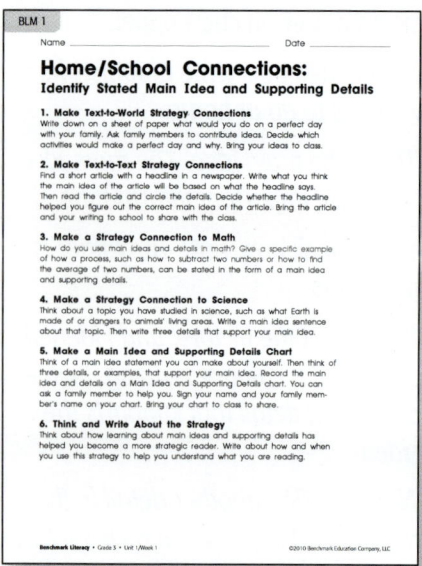

Home/School Connections (BLM 1)

Small-Group Reading Instruction (60 MINUTES)

Based on students' instructional reading levels, select titles that provide opportunities for students to practice identifying stated main ideas and details. See the Leveled Text Titles chart provided at the back of this Teacher's Resource System.

Use the before-, during-, and after-reading instruction provided in the Teacher's Guide for each text.

Individual Student Conferences (10 MINUTES)

Confer with individual students on their text selections and applications of strategies. Use the Individual Reading Conference Form on page 32 of Informal Assessments for Reading Development to help guide your conferences.

Word Study Workshop (20 MINUTES)

Use the Day 1 instruction provided in Word Study Unit 1.

Read-Aloud (10 MINUTES)

Select a favorite fiction read-aloud from your classroom or school library with which to model the metacognitive strategy "Ask Questions." Use the sample read-aloud lessons and suggested titles in the Getting Started Guide.

 ## Mini-Lessons (20 MINUTES)

Review the Metacognitive Strategy: Ask Questions

Display Poster 2 with annotations hidden and/or distribute BLM 2 and read aloud the title.

Read aloud the text with students.

Explain: *Yesterday when I looked at the "Colonists at Home" poster, I asked myself questions to help me understand. When I ask questions, I think about what I want to know so that I can look for answers as I read on. I'll show you how I do this.*

Reread the first two sentences. **Think aloud:** *In the second sentence, I learn that the moon is much smaller than Earth. How much smaller than Earth is the moon? I will look for an answer as I read on.*

Write your question on chart paper.

Reread the rest of the paragraph. **Think aloud:** *The next three sentences tell three facts about the moon's and Earth's relative sizes. These sentences answer my question.* Write the answers on the chart paper next to the question.

Ask students to generate other questions. Add their questions to the list on the chart paper. Ask students to write the questions in their reading journals to use in the future.

Build academic oral language. Reread the second paragraph. Encourage students to ask themselves what the main idea of this paragraph is and what details support that main idea. Invite students to describe how asking questions helped them identify the main idea and details in this paragraph. Reinforce the idea that good readers ask questions and look for answers to help them understand what they are reading. Support ELLs and struggling readers with the following sentence frames:

> *The main idea of this paragraph is _____.*
> *The supporting details are _____.*
> *Asking questions helped me _____.*

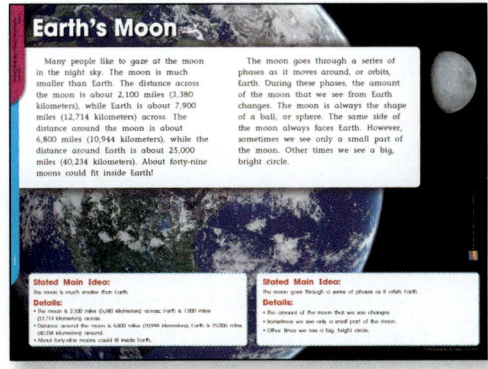

Comprehension Anchor Poster 2 (BLM 2)

Lesson Objectives

Students will:

- Identify the stated main idea of a paragraph.
- Identify the details that support the main idea.
- Ask questions to understand a text.
- Use academic sentence frames to discuss strategies.

Related Resources

- Home/School Connections (BLM 1)
- Comprehension Anchor Poster 2 (BLM 2)
- BenchmarkUniverse.com

Stated Main Idea:
The moon is much smaller than Earth.

Details:
- The moon is 2,100 miles (3,380 kilometers) across; Earth is 7,900 miles (12,714 kilometers) across.
- Distance around the moon is 6,800 miles (10,944 kilometers); Earth is 25,000 miles (40,234 kilometers) around.
- About forty-nine moons could fit inside Earth.

Stated Main Idea:
The moon goes through a series of phases as it orbits Earth.

Details:
- The amount of the moon that we see changes.
- Sometimes we see only a small part of the moon.
- Other times we see a big, bright circle.

Comprehension Anchor Poster 2
Sample Annotations

Make Content Comprehensible for ELLs

Use the following strategies to help ELLs understand the poster content and acquire academic language.

Beginning
Read aloud the poster title and passage. Point to the pictures of Earth and the moon as you say their names.

Beginning and Intermediate
Use realia such as a small ball and a large ball to show the locations of Earth and the moon relative to each other and to demonstrate how the moon orbits around Earth.

If you have students whose first language is Spanish, share these English/Spanish cognates: **distance/la distancia, phase/la fase, ball/la bola, circle/el círculo, kilometer/el kilómetro.**

Use the Comprehension Strategy: Identify Main Idea and Supporting Details

Reread the poster text with students, annotations still hidden.

Say: *Now think about the content of the first paragraph. What is this paragraph mostly about?*

If necessary, explain that the paragraph is about the moon being much smaller than Earth. The author provides specific examples, or details, about the sizes of the moon and Earth.

Say: *Let's look closely to find the sentence that tells what the paragraph is about. Which sentence states the main idea?*

Write the sentence that students identify. Then reveal the first Stated Main Idea annotation. **Ask:** *Did we find the stated main idea? Let's compare sentences.*

Build academic oral language. Say: *Details give more information about a main idea. Let's think about details in this paragraph that tell about the main idea that the moon is much smaller than Earth. What is the first detail the author gives about their sizes?* (distances across the moon and Earth) *What does the author tell us about the distances around them?* (about 6,800 miles for the moon; about 25,000 for Earth) *How many moons could fit inside Earth?* (49) *How do these details support the main idea?* (They tell three ways in which the moon is smaller than Earth.) Reveal the first Details annotations and let students compare the details they identified to those listed on the poster.

Connect Thinking, Speaking, and Writing

Prompt students to identify the stated main idea and supporting details in the second paragraph on the poster. Students should understand that some details in a paragraph may not support the paragraph's main idea directly, but they must add something to the discussion of the main idea.

Record students' main idea and details on chart paper. Then reveal the second Stated Main Idea and Details annotations.

Say: *Let's compare our list to the list on the poster.* Allow time for discussion.

Reflect and Discuss

Ask and discuss the following questions:
- *How does identifying the main idea help you understand what you are reading?*
- *How does finding the supporting details help you understand the main idea?*

Connect and transfer. Say: *How will you use what we have practiced today when you read on your own?*

Small-Group Reading Instruction (60 MINUTES)

Based on students' instructional reading levels, select titles that provide opportunities for students to practice identifying stated main ideas and details. See the Leveled Text Titles chart provided at the back of this Teacher's Resource System.

Use the before-, during-, and after-reading instruction provided in the Teacher's Guide for each text.

Individual Student Conferences (10 MINUTES)

Confer with individual students on their text selections and applications of strategies. Use the Individual Reading Conference Form on page 32 of Informal Assessments for Reading Development to help guide your conferences.

Word Study Workshop (20 MINUTES)

Use the Day 2 instruction provided in Word Study Unit 1.

Comprehension Quick-Check

Take note of which students can or cannot contribute to the discussion of Poster 2 stated main ideas and supporting details. Use the following activity to provide additional explicit instruction for these students.

Use another real-world example to help students understand the difference between main ideas and details, for example:

Our school has many different sports. (main idea)

These include _____, _____, and _____. (details)

After students name school sports, draw a main idea and details graphic organizer and ask students to tell you what to record in the boxes.

Oral Language Extension

During independent workstation time, pair students and ask them to construct oral main ideas and supporting details related to science topics they have studied. Partners work together to state a main idea and two or more details that support the main idea. Encourage them to use their science textbook to check their work. Tell students to be ready to report on their main idea and details during individual conference time.

Home/School Connections

At the beginning of the day, make time for students to share their ideas based on the activity they completed the previous night.

At the end of the day, ask students to complete another home/school connection activity from BLM 1 and to bring their assignment to class the following day.

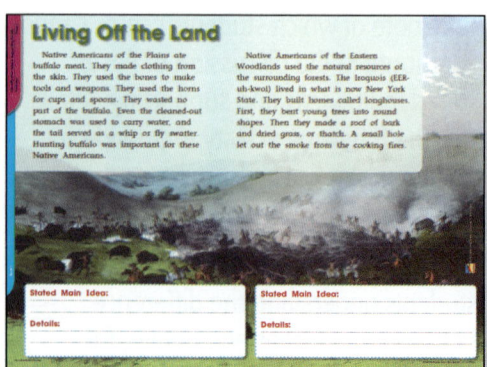

Comprehension Anchor Poster 3 (BLM 3)

Lesson Objectives

Students will:

- Identify the stated main idea of a paragraph.
- Identify details that support the main idea.
- Ask questions about a text.
- Use academic sentence frames to discuss strategies.

Related Resources

- Home/School Connections (BLM 1)
- Comprehension Anchor Poster 3 (BLM 3)
- BenchmarkUniverse.com

Comprehension Quick-Check

The responsive prompts on pages 8–9 are designed to help you meet the needs of individual students. Based on your observations, identify students who may need additional explicit reinforcement of the strategy during small-group instruction or intervention time. Use similar responsive prompts during small-group instruction to scaffold students toward independent use of the strategy.

Home/School Connections

At the end of the day, ask students to complete another home/school connection activity from BLM 1 and to bring their assignment to class the following day.

Read-Aloud (10 MINUTES)

Select a favorite nonfiction read-aloud from your classroom or school library with which to model the metacognitive strategy "Ask Questions." Use the sample read-aloud lessons and suggested titles in the Getting Started Guide.

Mini-Lessons (20 MINUTES)

Extend the Comprehension Strategy: Identify Main Idea and Supporting Details

Display Poster 3 and/or distribute BLM 3.

Say: *Today you're going to practice reading and identifying stated main ideas and details in a text. Remember to use what you've learned. You can ask yourself questions about the text to help you understand.*

Based on students' needs and abilities, ask them to read each paragraph independently or with a partner. Tell them to locate and write the main idea under Stated Main Idea and the details under Details in the box below each paragraph. Encourage students to underline, circle, or flag key information as they read.

Invite individual students or pairs to share the main ideas and details they identified. Record students' findings on the poster or on chart paper. See the sample annotations.

Observe and Prompt for Strategy Understanding

While using the poster, note students who demonstrate understanding of the concepts and those who seem to struggle. Use appropriate responsive prompting to help students who need modeling or additional guidance or to validate students who demonstrate mastery.

Goal Oriented

- *I am going to read slowly and reread if necessary to find the stated main idea.*
- *I am going to think about which details tell more about the main idea.*
- *The details _____ support the main idea that _____.*

Directive and Corrective Feedback

- *Does that sentence tell the most important idea of the paragraph?*
- *Which details in this paragraph are important? How can you tell?*
- *What do the details tell you about the main idea?*

Self-Monitoring and Reflection

- *What could you do to help yourself identify the main idea?*
- *What questions could you ask yourself?*
- *Did you try to identify the most important details? How?*

Validating and Confirming

- *You identified the main idea. Great job!*
- *You found all the details that tell more about the main idea.*
- *I like the way you asked yourself questions about the text to clarify your understanding.*

Reflect and Discuss

Ask and discuss the following questions:

- *What kinds of texts have you read include a main idea and details?*
- *Does a fictional story have a main idea and details? Why or why not?*
- *How does finding a main idea and details help you understand a persuasive essay? A how-to article? A news report?*

Connect and transfer. Say: *Remember that all nonfiction texts have main ideas and details that support the main ideas. Look for the main ideas and details today when you read in small groups. Ask yourself questions to help you identify the main ideas and details.*

Small-Group Reading Instruction (60 MINUTES)

Based on students' instructional reading levels, select titles that provide opportunities for students to practice identifying stated main ideas and details. See the Leveled Text Titles chart provided at the back of this Teacher's Resource System.

Use the before-, during-, and after-reading instruction provided in the Teacher's Guide for each text.

Individual Student Conferences (10 MINUTES)

Confer with individual students on their text selections and applications of strategies. Use the Individual Reading Conference Form on page 32 of Informal Assessments for Reading Development to help guide your conferences.

Word Study Workshop (20 MINUTES)

Use the Day 3 instruction provided in Word Study Unit 1.

Stated Main Idea:
Hunting buffalo was important for Native Americans of the Plains.

Details:
They ate buffalo meat, made buffalo skin clothing, weapons and tools from buffalo bones, used buffalo horns as cups and spoons, and wasted no part of the buffalo.

Stated Main Idea:
Native Americans of the Eastern Woodlands used the natural resources of the forests.

Details:
They bent young trees into round shapes to make their homes, and made a roof of bark and dried grass for their homes.

Comprehension Anchor Poster 3 Sample Annotations

Make Content Comprehensible for ELLs

Use the following strategies to help ELLs understand the poster content and acquire academic language.

Beginning
Point to the poster illustration and provide the language for what you see. For example: Native Americans, horses, herd, buffalo, dust, hunting. Invite ELLs to repeat the words with you.

Intermediate
Describe what is happening in the illustration. For example, **say:** The buffalo are running. The Native Americans are riding their horses. The Native Americans are hunting the buffalo. Ask students to describe other things they see happening in the illustration.

All Levels
If you have students whose first language is Spanish, share these English/Spanish cognates: **buffalo/el búfalo, natural/natural, resource/el recurso, stomach/el estómago, part/la parte.**

Pair ELLs with fluent English speakers during partner discussions and activities.

Day Four

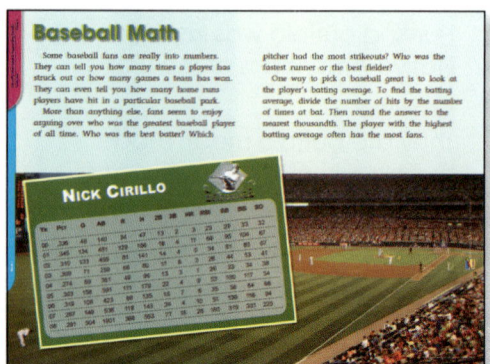

Comprehension Anchor Poster 4 (BLM 4)

Lesson Objectives

Students will:

• Learn strategies for analyzing questions and finding answers, clues, and evidence.

• Identify stated main ideas and their supporting details in a text.

• Answer text-dependent main idea and supporting details questions.

• Use academic vocabulary to discuss strategies.

Related Resources

• Home/School Connections (BLM 1)

• Comprehension Anchor Poster 4 (BLM 4)

• Comprehension Questions (BLM 5)

• BenchmarkUniverse.com

Read-Aloud (10 MINUTES)

Select a favorite nonfiction read-aloud from your classroom or school library with which to model the metacognitive strategy "Ask Questions." Use the sample read-aloud lessons and suggested titles in the Getting Started Guide.

Mini-Lessons (20 MINUTES)

Read and Summarize

Display Poster 4 and/or distribute BLM 4.

Based on students' needs and abilities, ask them to read the passage independently or with a partner. Remind students to ask themselves questions to help them understand what they read.

Build academic oral language. When students have finished, ask individuals or pairs to tell what the passage was mostly about. Encourage ELLs or struggling readers to use this academic sentence frame:

This passage was mostly about _____.

Answer Text-Dependent Comprehension Questions: Identify Main Idea and Supporting Details (Level 2: Look Closer!)

Say: *Sometimes you need to answer questions about a passage you've read. Some questions require you to identify main idea and details. Today we're going to read and answer questions. Some of the questions will ask you to identify a main idea and supporting details.*

Distribute BLM 5 and read Question 1 together. ("What is this passage mostly about?")

Ask: *What is the question asking us to do?* If students can't tell you, **ask:** *Is the question asking us to make predictions? Is it asking us to identify facts and opinions? What strategy will we need?* (identify main idea and supporting details) *How do you know?* (The main idea is what a text is mostly about.)

Say: *To find the main idea, I will have to think about what most of the details in the passage are about and then see if I can find an answer that the details tell about, or support. I'm going to read this question carefully again to be sure I understand what I need to do.*

Say: *Now we're ready to answer the first question. We know we need to find an answer that states what the passage is mostly about. The first choice is "how to find a baseball player's batting average." That may be the main idea of the last paragraph, but I don't think it's the main idea of the whole passage, so I'll keep reading. The next choice says, "why fans argue over who was the greatest baseball player of all time." I know the passage doesn't give reasons for that. The last choice says, "how some baseball fans are really into, or keep track of, numbers." That goes with the first sentence in the passage, and the details in the passage support that idea. That must be the answer. It was right in the text, and I figured it out by looking at the text. The answer makes sense. So I'll choose C.*

Have students work independently or with a partner to answer additional text-dependent questions on BLM 5.

Review students' answers and use the poster as needed to model analyzing questions and rereading to find answers in the text.

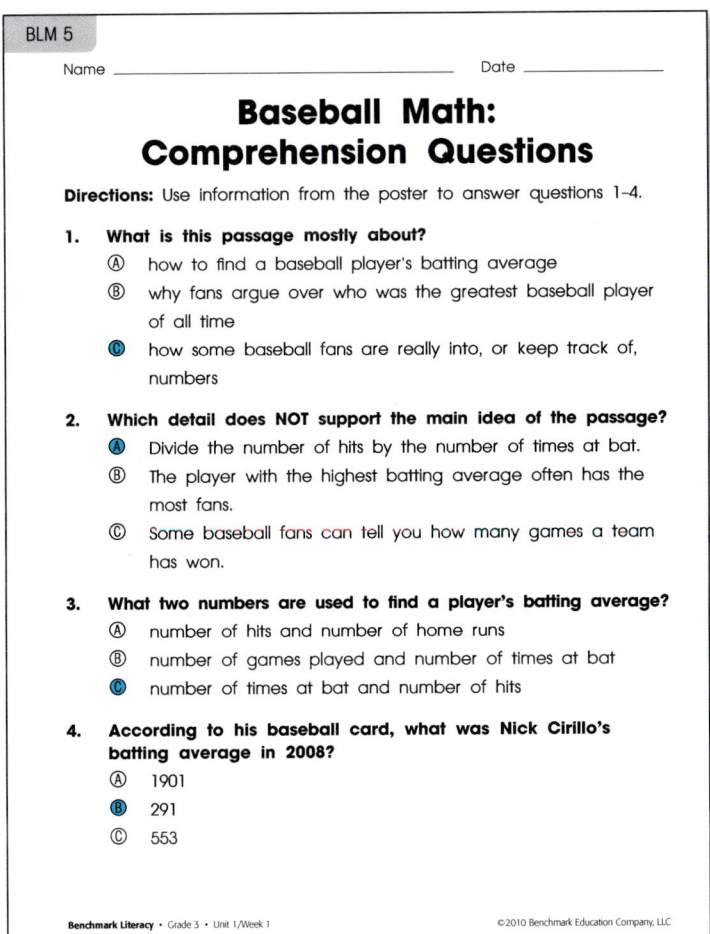

Comprehension Questions (BLM 5)

Stated Main Idea:
Some baseball fans are really into, or keep track of, numbers.

Details:
• These fans can tell you how many times a player has struck out or how many games a team has won.
• They can even tell you how many home runs players have hit in a particular baseball park.
• They enjoy arguing over who were the best baseball players.
• The player with the highest batting average often has the most fans.

Comprehension Anchor Poster 4
Sample Annotations

Make Content Comprehensible for ELLs

Use the following strategies to help ELLs understand the poster content and acquire academic language.

Beginning
Support the concept of baseball by pantomiming pitching, catching, throwing, and batting and using the words pitch, catch, throw, and bat as you explain what you are doing.

Beginning and Intermediate
Point to the poster photograph and **say:** *The fans are watching a baseball game. The home team is on the field.* Encourage knowledgeable students to name the positions on a baseball team.

Point to the card showing the statistics for Nick Cirillo and **say:** *These numbers show how this baseball player has played for nine years.* Read aloud some of the numbers and explain what they mean.

All Levels
If you have students whose first language is Spanish, share these academic English/Spanish cognates: **baseball/el béisbol, math/las matemáticas, park/el parque.**

Comprehension Quick-Check

Note whether students are able to analyze each Level 2 text-dependent comprehension question and return to the text to find the information they need to answer the question correctly. If students have difficulty, use small-group reading time for additional practice answering these kinds of questions, which appear on standardized reading assessments. The Comprehension Question Card for each leveled text provides practice questions at four levels of comprehension. The Comprehension Through Deductive Reasoning Flip Chart helps you model the strategies students need to master.

Oral Language Extension

Display Comprehension Anchor Poster 4 during independent workstation time. Invite pairs of students to read and talk about the poster together. Encourage students to generate a list of other sports that use numbers and to develop a main idea statement based on their list. Remind students to be prepared to share their lists and main idea statements during independent conference time.

Home/School Connection

At the beginning of the day, make time for students to share their ideas based on the activity they completed the previous night.

At the end of the day, ask students to complete another home/school connection activity from BLM 1 and to bring their assignment to class the following day.

Reflect and Discuss the Comprehension Strategy

Ask and discuss the following:
What strategy did we use to answer questions about the text?
Notice how we looked for the main idea and details to understand and answer questions.

Connect and transfer. Say: *Practice identifying main idea and supporting details. This strategy can help you answer questions in all your subjects. It can also help you when you take tests.*

 ## Small-Group Reading Instruction (60 MINUTES)

Based on students' instructional reading levels, select titles that provide opportunities for students to practice identifying stated main ideas and details. See the Leveled Text Titles chart provided at the back of this Teacher's Resource System.

Use the before-, during-, and after-reading instruction provided in the Teacher's Guide for each text.

Use the Comprehension Question Card for each title and the Comprehension Through Deductive Reasoning Flip Chart to practice answering Level 2 text-dependent comprehension questions.

 ## Individual Student Conferences (10 MINUTES)

Confer with individual students on their text selections and applications of strategies. Use the Individual Reading Conference Form on page 32 of Informal Assessments for Reading Development to help guide your conferences.

 ## Word Study Workshop (20 MINUTES)

Use the Day 4 instruction provided in Word Study Unit 1.

Read-Aloud (10 MINUTES)

Revisit the week's read-alouds to make text-to-text connections and provide opportunities for reader response. Use the suggested activities in the Getting Started Guide, or implement ideas of your own.

Assessment (20 MINUTES)

Metacognitive Self-Assessment

Ask students to reflect on their use of metacognitive and comprehension strategies this week. What did they learn? How will they use the strategies in the future? What do they still need to practice, and how can they do this?

Invite students to share their reflections in one of the following ways: conduct a whole-class discussion; ask students to turn and talk to a partner and then share their ideas with the class; or ask students to record their thoughts in their journals or notebooks.

Constructed Written Response

Distribute copies of Constructed Written Response (BLM 6) and ask students to think about their favorite sport or game. In the Main Idea box, have them write what their favorite sport or game is. In the Detail boxes, have them write details that support their main idea—that is, sentences about why that sport or game is their favorite.

Ask students to write a paragraph based on the main idea and details on their graphic organizer. Remind them to state their main idea clearly in a sentence at the beginning or end of their paragraph.

Read aloud the checklist at the bottom of BLM 6 to help students evaluate their work.

Challenge activity. Students who are able to may write three paragraphs, one for each detail, in which they elaborate on each reason by giving more information.

Support activity. If students cannot write about their main idea and details, encourage them to tell you about their ideas instead. They can use the sentence frame: *My favorite sport (game) is _____ because _____.* Reinforce the idea that they are to give three reasons and that these reasons are details.

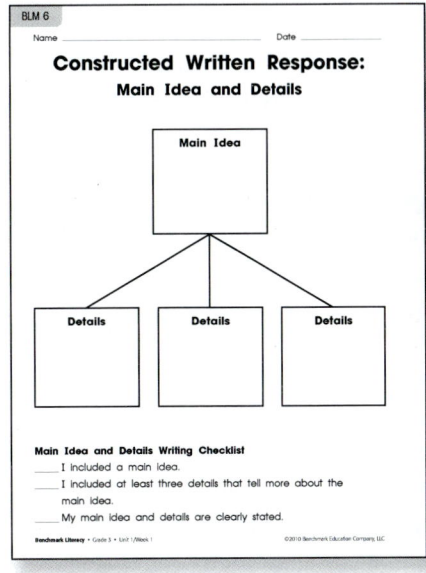

Constructed Written Response (BLM 6)

Lesson Objectives

Students will:

- Reflect orally on their strategy use.

- Create a main idea and supporting details graphic organizer and write a paragraph based on it.

- Answer multiple-choice and short-answer questions.

Related Resources

- Home/School Connections (BLM 1)

- Constructed Written Response (BLM 6)

- Comprehension Strategy Assessments, Grade 3

- BenchmarkUniverse.com

Make Assessments Accessible for ELLs

Use the following strategies to help ELLs demonstrate their understanding of the strategies.

Beginning
Work with beginning ELLs to complete Constructed Written Response (BLM 6). Allow ELLs to draw their ideas.

Beginning and Intermediate
Use the Comprehension Strategy Assessment as a listening comprehension assessment and scaffold students' understanding of the text. As an alternative, allow students to tell you about the main ideas and supporting details in one of the Comprehension Anchor Posters you have used during the week.

Intermediate and Advanced
Support ELLs with academic sentence frames during the metacognitive self-assessment. Possible sentence frames to use are:

I ask questions because _____.

I will look for answers to my questions when I _____.

All Levels
Pair ELLs with fluent English speakers during partner discussions and activities.

Home/School Connection

At the beginning of the day, make time for students to share their ideas based on the activity they completed the previous night.

Ongoing Comprehension Strategy Assessment

Distribute one of the Identify Main Idea and Supporting Details Comprehension Strategy Assessments from the Grade 3 Comprehension Strategy Assessment book ("The Great Pyramid," pages 74–75, or "Become a Cloud Watcher," pages 76–77). Ask students to read the passage and use the information to answer the questions.

Use the results of this assessment to identify students who need additional work with the strategy.

Record students' assessment scores on the Strategy Assessment Record (page 133) so that you can monitor their progress following additional instruction or intervention.

Provide additional modeling and guided practice during small-group reading instruction using the recommended titles in this Teacher's Guide.

Small-Group Reading Instruction (60 MINUTES)

Based on students' instructional reading levels, select titles that provide opportunities for students to practice identifying stated main ideas and details. See the Leveled Text Titles chart provided at the back of this Teacher's Resource System.

Use the before-, during-, and after-reading instruction provided in the Teacher's Guide for each text.

Individual Student Conferences (10 MINUTES)

Confer with individual students on their text selections and applications of strategies. Use the Individual Reading Conference Form on page 32 of Informal Assessments for Reading Development to help guide your conferences.

Word Study Workshop (20 MINUTES)

Use the Day 5 instruction provided in Word Study Unit 1.

Name _____   Date _____

Home/School Connections:
Identify Main Idea and Supporting Details

1. Make Text-to-World Strategy Connections

Write down on a sheet of paper what would you do on a perfect day with your family. Ask family members to contribute ideas. Decide which activities would make a perfect day and why. Bring your ideas to class.

2. Make Text-to-Text Strategy Connections

Find a short article with a headline in a newspaper. Write what you think the main idea of the article will be based on what the headline says. Then read the article and circle the details. Decide whether the headline helped you figure out the correct main idea of the article. Bring the article and your writing to school to share with the class.

3. Make a Strategy Connection to Math

How do you use main ideas and details in math? Give a specific example of how a process, such as how to subtract two numbers or how to find the average of two numbers, can be stated in the form of a main idea and supporting details.

4. Make a Strategy Connection to Science

Think about a topic you have studied in science, such as what Earth is made of or dangers to animals' living areas. Write a main idea sentence about that topic. Then write three details that support your main idea.

5. Make a Main Idea and Supporting Details Chart

Think of a main idea statement you can make about yourself. Then think of three details, or examples, that support your main idea. Record the main idea and details on a Main Idea and Supporting Details chart. You can ask a family member to help you. Sign your name and your family member's name on your chart. Bring your chart to class to share.

6. Think and Write About the Strategy

Think about how learning about main ideas and supporting details has helped you become a more strategic reader. Write about how and when you use this strategy to help you understand what you are reading.

Name ______________________________ Date ______________

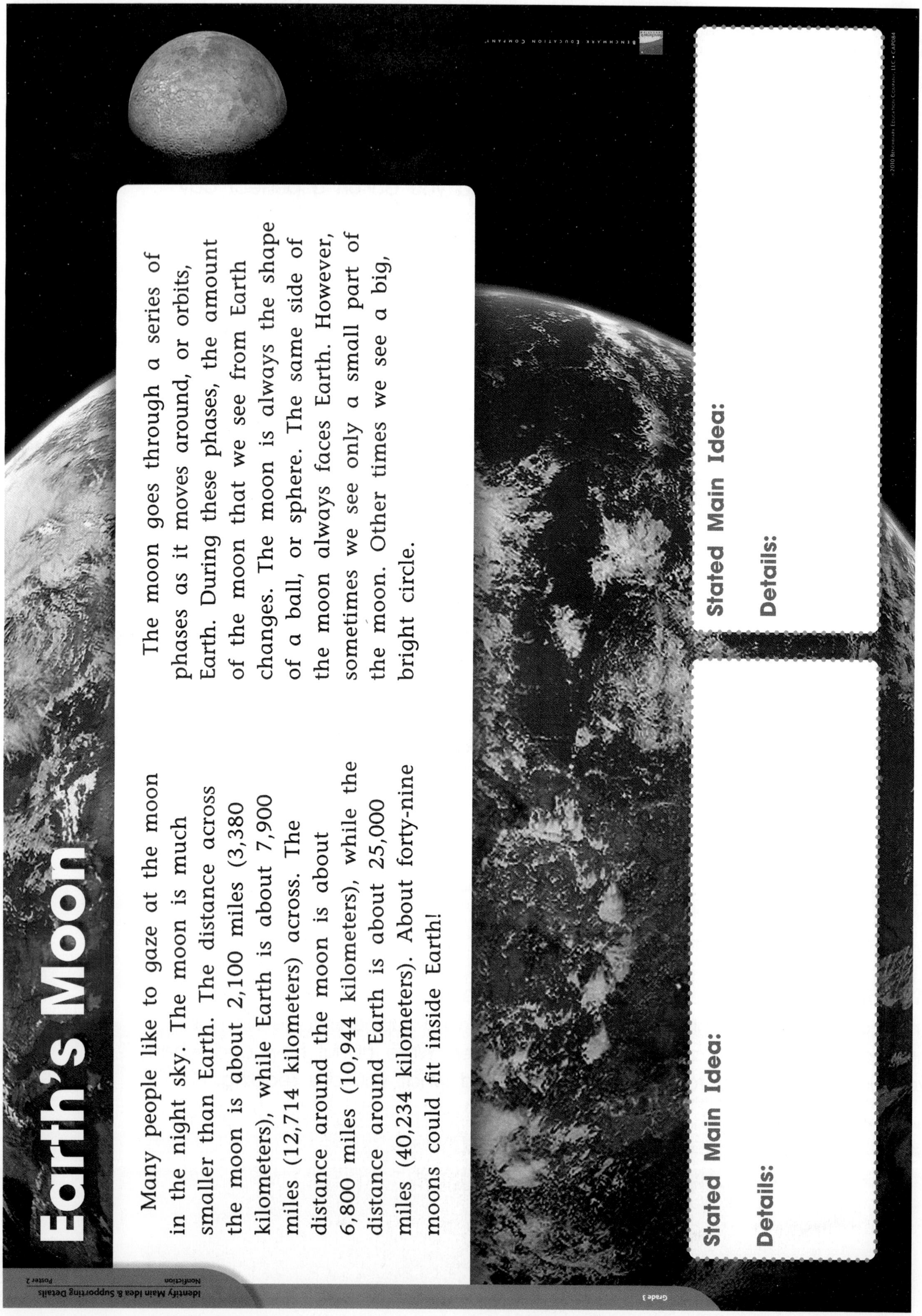

Earth's Moon

Many people like to gaze at the moon in the night sky. The moon is much smaller than Earth. The distance across the moon is about 2,100 miles (3,380 kilometers), while Earth is about 7,900 miles (12,714 kilometers) across. The distance around the moon is about 6,800 miles (10,944 kilometers), while the distance around Earth is about 25,000 miles (40,234 kilometers). About forty-nine moons could fit inside Earth!

The moon goes through a series of phases as it moves around, or orbits, Earth. During these phases, the amount of the moon that we see from Earth changes. The moon is always the shape of a ball, or sphere. The same side of the moon always faces Earth. However, sometimes we see only a small part of the moon. Other times we see a big, bright circle.

Stated Main Idea:

Details:

Stated Main Idea:

Details:

Identify Main Idea & Supporting Details
Nonfiction
Poster 2
Grade 3
Benchmark Education Company
© 2010 Benchmark Education Company, LLC • CAP084

Name _____   Date _____

Living Off the Land

Native Americans of the Plains ate buffalo meat. They made clothing from the skin. They used the bones to make tools and weapons. They used the horns for cups and spoons. They wasted no part of the buffalo. Even the cleaned-out stomach was used to carry water, and the tail served as a whip or fly swatter. Hunting buffalo was important for these Native Americans.

Native Americans of the Eastern Woodlands used the natural resources of the surrounding forests. The Iroquois (EER-uh-kwoi) lived in what is now New York State. They built homes called longhouses. First, they bent young trees into round shapes. Then they made a roof of bark and dried grass, or thatch. A small hole let out the smoke from the cooking fires.

Identify Main Idea & Supporting Details
Nonfiction
Poster 3

Stated Main Idea:

Details:

Stated Main Idea:

Details:

Name _____   Date _____

Baseball Math

Some baseball fans are really into numbers. They can tell you how many times a player has struck out or how many games a team has won. They can even tell you how many home runs players have hit in a particular baseball park.

More than anything else, fans seem to enjoy arguing over who was the greatest baseball player of all time. Who was the best batter? Which pitcher had the most strikeouts? Who was the fastest runner or the best fielder?

One way to pick a baseball great is to look at the player's batting average. To find the batting average, divide the number of hits by the number of times at bat. Then round the answer to the nearest thousandth. The player with the highest batting average often has the most fans.

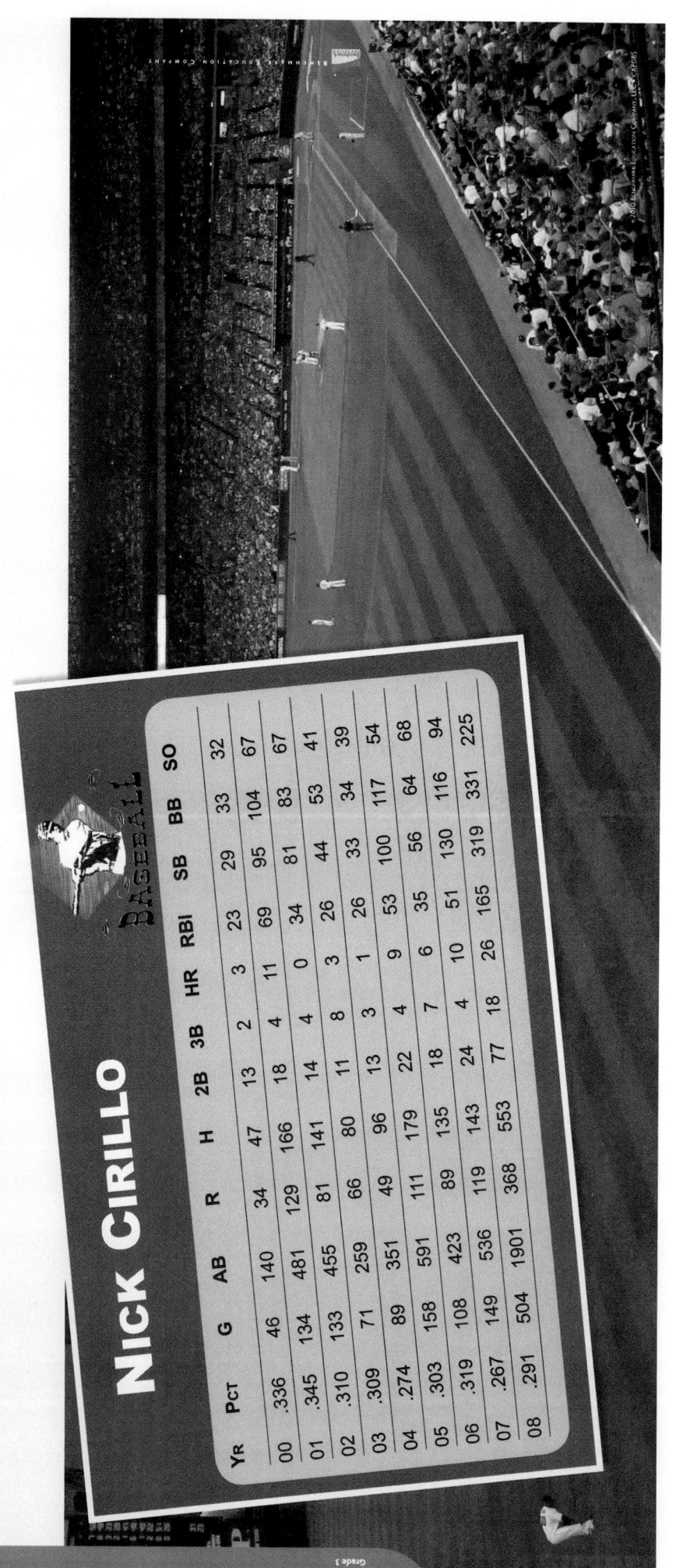

NICK CIRILLO

BASEBALL

YR	PCT	G	AB	R	H	2B	3B	HR	RBI	SB	BB	SO
00	.336	46	140	34	47	13	2	3	23	29	33	32
01	.345	134	481	129	166	18	4	11	69	95	104	67
02	.310	133	455	81	141	14	4	0	34	81	83	67
03	.309	71	259	66	80	11	8	3	26	44	53	41
04	.274	89	351	49	96	13	3	1	26	33	34	39
05	.303	158	591	111	179	22	4	9	53	100	117	54
06	.319	108	423	89	135	18	7	6	35	56	64	68
07	.267	149	536	119	143	24	4	10	51	130	116	94
08	.291	504	1901	368	553	77	18	26	165	319	331	225

Name _____   Date _____

Baseball Math:
Comprehension Questions

Directions: Use information from the poster to answer questions 1–4.

1. **What is this passage mostly about?**
   - Ⓐ how to find a baseball player's batting average
   - Ⓑ why fans argue over who was the greatest baseball player of all time
   - Ⓒ how some baseball fans are really into, or keep track of, numbers

2. **Which detail does NOT support the main idea of the passage?**
   - Ⓐ Divide the number of hits by the number of times at bat.
   - Ⓑ The player with the highest batting average often has the most fans.
   - Ⓒ Some baseball fans can tell you how many games a team has won.

3. **What two numbers are used to find a player's batting average?**
   - Ⓐ number of hits and number of home runs
   - Ⓑ number of games played and number of times at bat
   - Ⓒ number of times at bat and number of hits

4. **According to his baseball card, what was Nick Cirillo's batting average in 2008?**
   - Ⓐ 1901
   - Ⓑ 291
   - Ⓒ 553

Name _____   Date _____

Constructed Written Response:
Main Idea and Details

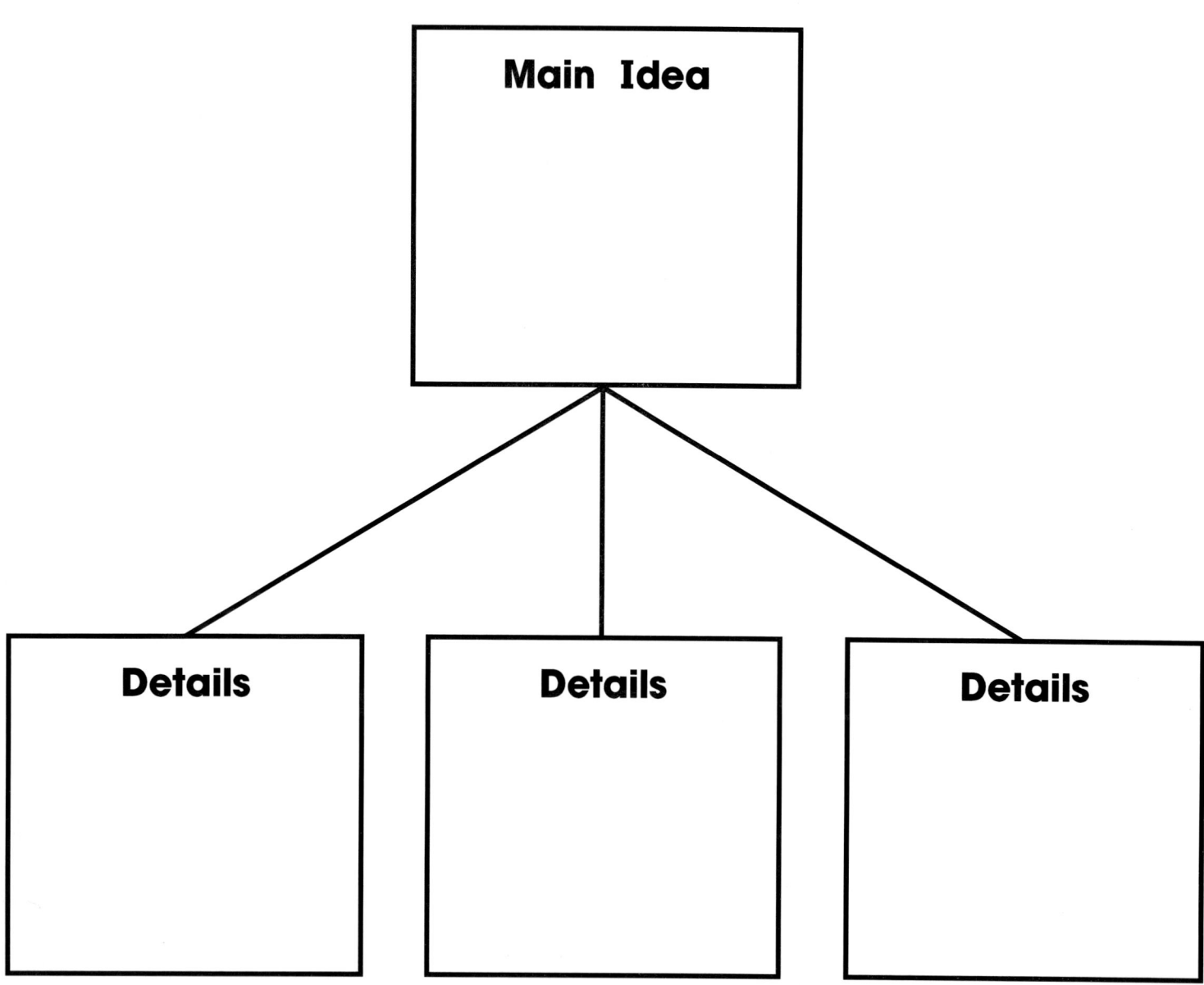

Main Idea and Details Writing Checklist

_____ I included a main idea.

_____ I included at least three details that tell more about the
main idea.

_____ My main idea and details are clearly stated.

Ask Questions/Identify Main Idea and Supporting Details

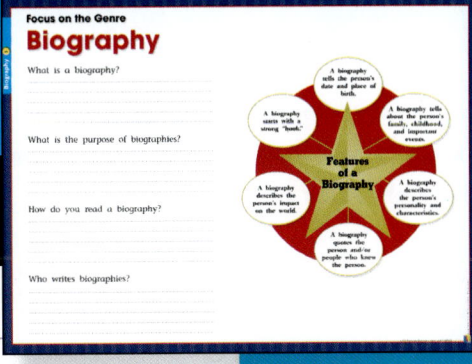

Unit 1/Week 2 at a Glance

Day	Mini-Lessons
ONE	• Build Genre Background • Introduce the Genre: *Biography* • Focus on Genre Features: *Biography*
TWO	• Model Metacognitive Strategies: *Ask Questions* • Introduce Main Idea and Supporting Details • Focus on Genre Features: *Biography*
THREE	• Ask Questions to Identify Main Idea and Supporting Details
FOUR	• Build Comprehension: *Analyze Character* • Build Tier Two Vocabulary: *Word Origins*
FIVE	• Synthesize and Assess Genre Understanding • Make Connections Across Texts

Day One

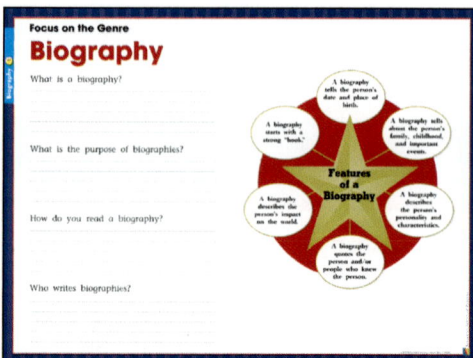

Biography Poster 1

Lesson Objectives

Students will:

- Review the concept of genre and previously studied genres.

- Create a Biography anchor chart to demonstrate prior knowledge.

- Build academic oral language and vocabulary as they engage in partner and whole-group discussion.

Related Resources

- Biography Poster 1 (BLM 1)
- BenchmarkUniverse.com

Read-Aloud (10 MINUTES)

Select a favorite fiction read-aloud from your classroom or school library with which to model the metacognitive strategy "Ask Questions." Use the sample read-aloud lessons and suggested titles in the Getting Started Guide.

Mini-Lessons (20 MINUTES)

Build Genre Background

Write the word **genre** on chart paper. **Ask:** *Who can recall what the word* **genre** *means?* Allow responses.

Review: *The word* **genre** *means "a kind of something." Things are grouped in genres because they are all alike in some ways. For example, one genre of music is rock music. Examples of rock music are alike because they are played on the same instruments. What are some other genres of music that you know?* (electronic, country, classical, hip-hop)

Say: *As readers and writers, we focus on genres of literature. As readers, we pay attention to the genre to help us understand. When we recognize the genre, we can predict what elements the text will have. We can predict how it will be presented. As writers, we use our knowledge of genre to help us choose a way of presenting our ideas.*

Ask: *What are some literary genres you have studied and read in the past? Let's make a list.* Allow responses. Post the list on the classroom wall as an anchor chart.

Introduce the Genre: Biography

Display Genre Workshop Poster 1 and distribute BLM 1.

Say: *This week we are going to focus on the biography genre. You will read a biography in our small reading groups, and you can select other titles from this genre to read independently, too. Let's spend some time thinking about this genre and create our own Biography anchor chart to record what we already know about biography. Later in the week, we can come back to our chart and reflect on how our understanding of the genre has changed and expanded.*

Display Poster 1 on an easel or use the interactive whiteboard version. You may also make a transparency from BLM 1. Show students several biographies from your classroom or school library and ask students to share any biographies they have read previously.

Read each question on the poster and encourage volunteers to share ideas they have related to the question. Based on students' prior knowledge, provide additional genre background information as needed to fill in the answers to each question. This poster can serve as an anchor chart that you and students can refer to throughout the week as you read and analyze biographies.

Support the academic language development of ELLs and struggling readers by providing the following sentence frames to use as they discuss the genre:

> A biography is _____.
> The purpose of a biography is to _____.
> When you read a biography, pay attention to _____.
> People who write biographies are _____.

Make Content Comprehensible for ELLs

Beginning and Intermediate

Show various biographies from your classroom or school library. Flip through the biographies with students. Use simple language to explain that a biography is a book about a real person's life. For example, **say:** *A biography tells about a person. Look at this biography. This biography tells about _____.*

All Levels

If you have students whose first language is Spanish, share the English/Spanish cognate **biography/la biografía**.

Model the academic sentence frames provided in this guide to help ELLs contribute their ideas to the discussion of biographies.

Support Special Needs Learners

Throughout the week, use these strategies to help students who have learning disabilities access the content and focus on genre studies and comprehension strategies.

Support students by projecting the posters on a whiteboard. Allow students to come to the whiteboard and circle, underline, or highlight features of the genre. Invite them to label what they see on the posters.

Provide opportunities for active involvement. For example, to understand how biographies reveal character, allow students to take the role of the subject in a biography and use details from the text to role-play their characters.

Provide repeated opportunities for students to analyze the features of biographies. Find features of biographies in text examples from read-alouds, small-group, and independent reading. Chart the features on graphic organizers and post them in your classroom as examples.

Find high-interest biographies that students can relate to. Use the recommended read-aloud titles provided in the Teacher's Guide, as well as other examples from your school library.

Focus on Genre Features: Biography

Point to the "Features of a Biography" web on the right side of the poster.

Say: *As we've discussed, every genre has certain consistent features. Based on our discussions so far, what do you think are the consistent features of all, or most, biographies? Let's work together to identify them.*

Invite volunteers to name features of biographies. As students generate suggested features, encourage other students to think about them and decide whether to add them to the web on Poster 1. As necessary, prompt students with the following questions and statements:

- *How far back in a person's life do you think a biography might begin? Would it tell about the person's birth? His or her childhood? What else?*
- *What information might the author include to help you get to know the person?*
- *How do you think an author might make you want to read the biography?*

Connect and transfer. Say: *This week we will read some biographies. We will look for these features in the books we read.*

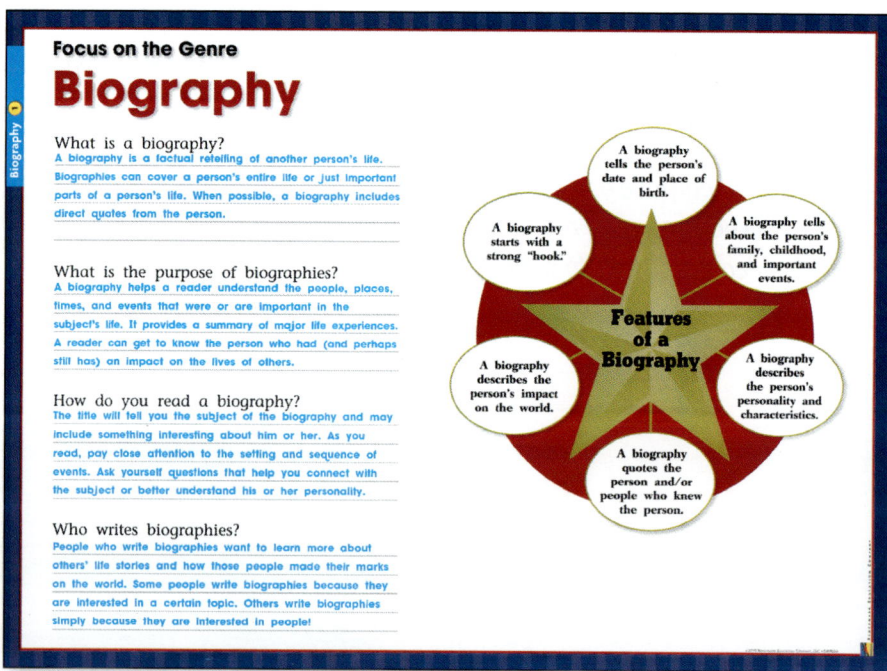

Biography Poster 1, sample annotations

Small-Group Reading Instruction (60 MINUTES)

Based on students' instructional reading levels, select titles that provide opportunities for students to focus on the biography genre or to practice identifying main ideas and supporting details. See the Leveled Text Titles chart provided at the back of this Teacher's Resource System.

Use the instruction provided in the Teacher's Guide for each title to introduce the text.

Individual Student Conferences (10 MINUTES)

Confer with individual students to discuss their understanding of the genre. Use the Individual Reading Conference Form on page 32 of Informal Assessments for Reading Development to help guide your conferences.

Word Study Workshop (20 MINUTES)

Use the Day 1 instruction provided in Grade 3 Word Study Unit 2.

Comprehension Quick-Check

Note which students do or don't actively participate in the discussion of genre. Ask some questions at the end of the lesson to confirm students' understanding. For example:

- *Can you tell me in your own words what a genre is?*
- *What do you already know about the biography genre?*

Home/School Connection

Ask students to think about someone whose biography they would like to read. Ask them to write a paragraph about why there should be a biography about this person.

Day Two

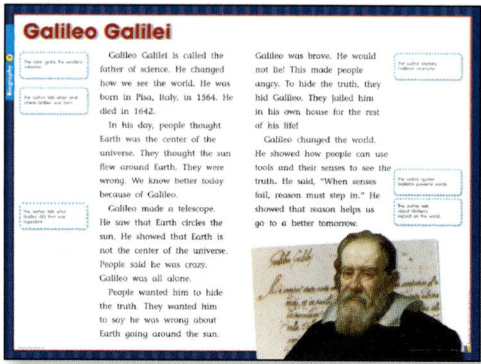

Biography Poster 2

Lesson Objectives

Students will:

- Ask questions about a biography text.

- Identify main ideas and supporting details using a graphic organizer.

- Use academic sentence frames to discuss strategies and features of a biography.

Related Resources

- Biography Poster 2 (BLM 2)

- BenchmarkUniverse.com

Read-Aloud (10 MINUTES)

Select a favorite fiction read-aloud from your classroom or school library with which to model the metacognitive strategy "Ask Questions." Use the sample read-aloud lessons and suggested titles in the Getting Started Guide.

Mini-Lessons (20 MINUTES)

Model Metacognitive Strategies: Ask Questions

Display Genre Workshop Poster 2 with the genre annotations concealed. Also distribute copies of BLM 2.

Read aloud the poster passage with students.

Explain: *Good readers ask themselves questions before, during, and after they read. Asking questions helps them understand what they are reading and clarifies words or information that is confusing. Let me show you how I ask questions about this biographical passage.*

Think aloud: *The title of this passage is "Galileo Galilei." I wonder about this title. I wonder who Galileo Galilei is or was. Is he alive now? I try to answer this question by looking at the illustrations, and they make me think he probably lived long ago. Why is there a biography about him? What did he do that was important? These questions help me focus my head to start reading the passage.*

Ask students to generate other questions based on the text. Write these questions on chart paper and reread them together. Encourage ELLs to use the sentence frame: *I wonder _____.*

Introduce Main Idea and Supporting Details

Explain: *Every biography that you read has main ideas about the life of its subject. It also has rich details that support the main ideas. Asking questions can help you figure out the main ideas in a biography.*

Reread "Galileo Galilei." Ask students to state the main idea of the whole passage in their own words and to share at least two details that support their main idea. Provide the following academic sentence frames to support ELLs and struggling students:

The main idea is that _____.
Two details that support the main idea are _____ and _____.

Record students' main idea and supporting details on a graphic organizer like the one shown below.

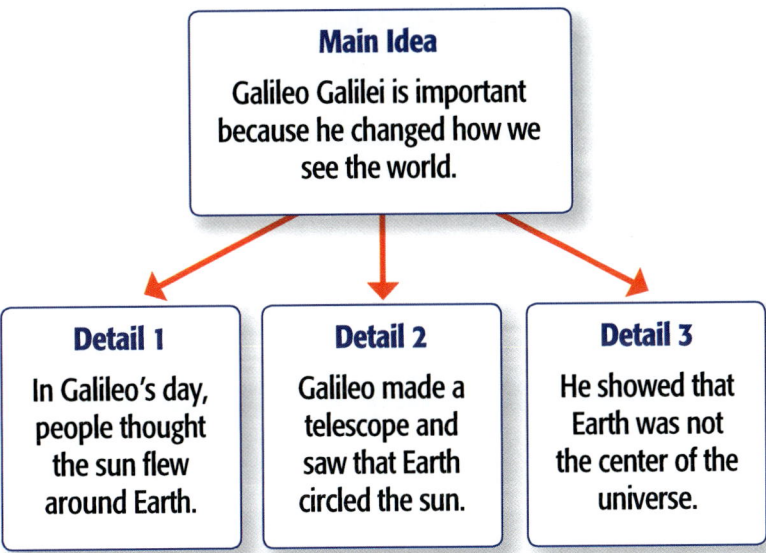

Sample Main Idea and Supporting Details Annotations
(Note: Your class graphic organizer may differ.)

Make Content Comprehensible for ELLs

Beginning
Point to the poster image of Galileo Galilei as you say his name.

Intermediate and Advanced
Model the academic sentence frames provided in this guide to help ELLs contribute their ideas to the discussion of biographies.

Explain the meaning of the phrase "the father of science" in the first sentence of the biography.

All Levels
Display images from the 1600s to build a visual context for the poster.

Display a map of the solar system showing Earth in its path around the sun.

If you have students whose first language is Spanish, share these English/Spanish cognates: **science/la ciencia; center/el centro; universe/el universo**.

Comprehension Quick-Check

Note which students are or are not able to generate main ideas and details. Use the following strategies to provide additional explicit instruction.

Use a Main Idea and Supporting Details graphic organizer such as the one shown on page 7.

Say: *Let's write the main idea of this passage. What is the passage mostly about? Why is Galileo important?*

Help students find details in the passage that support the main idea.

Say: *The details support the main idea. They help explain the main idea. What details help explain the main idea that we wrote in the box?*

Oral Language Extension

Display Poster 1 (your class Biography anchor chart) during independent workstation time. Have pairs of students work together. Partner A interviews Partner B about his or her life based on each feature of a biography on the class anchor chart. Then the partners switch roles. Tell students to listen carefully to their partners so that they can share details from their interview during independent conference time. Encourage them to take notes as they listen.

Home/School Connection

Have students turn in their homework from the night before. If time allows, invite them to briefly share the subjects they felt should have a biography.

Have students take home BLM 2, reread the text, and highlight and label the features of a biography present in the passage.

Focus on Genre Features: Biography

Ask students to name some of the features of a biography that you discussed yesterday.

Say: *Now let's reexamine "Galileo Galilei" and look for features of a biography. What do you notice?*

Work with students to identify the following genre features embedded in this passage:
- a strong hook that makes you want to read
- Galileo's date and place of birth
- information about Galileo's accomplishments
- information about his personality and characteristics
- a powerful quote from Galileo

Reveal the poster annotations so that students can confirm or revise their ideas. Reread them as a group.

Connect and transfer. Say: *As you read biographies, look for these features. The features of the biography are details that will help you understand the main ideas about the subject's life. As you read, remember to ask yourself questions to clarify information.*

 ## Small-Group Reading Instruction (60 MINUTES)

Continue small-group reading instruction from the previous day. Use the instruction provided in the Teacher's Guide for each text.

 ## Individual Student Conferences (10 MINUTES)

Confer with individual students to discuss their understanding of genre and comprehension strategies. Use the Individual Reading Conference Form on page 32 of Informal Assessments for Reading Development to help guide your conferences.

 ## Word Study Workshop (20 MINUTES)

Use the Day 2 instruction provided in Grade 3 Word Study Unit 2.

⏱ Read-Aloud (10 MINUTES)

Select a favorite nonfiction read-aloud from your classroom or school library with which to model the metacognitive strategy "Ask Questions." Use the sample read-aloud lessons and suggested titles in the Getting Started Guide.

⏱ Mini-Lessons (20 MINUTES)

Ask Questions to Identify Main Idea and Supporting Details

Display Genre Workshop Poster 3 and distribute BLM 3.

Read aloud the excerpt with students. **Say:** *We are going to identify the main idea of this passage together. To do that, we're going to ask questions about the text. I will ask the first question, and then I want you to ask questions of your own. Here is my question: How does the author compare Einstein to Galileo? What does that tell you about Einstein?*

Say: *Now you ask some additional questions.* Allow responses. If students are unable to generate questions, prompt them to think about the following:
- *How did Einstein's ideas about school change as he got older?*
- *What did Einstein study?*
- *What did he write?*

Say: *Asking these questions helped us focus on the details of the text. Let's write these details on a graphic organizer. Then we will use these details to develop a main idea statement about this text.*

Work with students to identify details about Albert Einstein from the passage. Reinforce how the details in a biography are related to the specific features of the genre. Record the details on a graphic organizer like the one shown on page 10.

Work with students to develop a main idea statement based on the details on your graphic organizer. Make sure that all of the details support the main idea. If one or more details do not support the main idea, remove the detail(s) from your graphic organizer, or reassess your main idea statement.

Albert Einstein

Albert Einstein was a famous scientist. He studied the nature of the universe. That type of science is called **physics**. Like Galileo, he changed the way we think about the world. Einstein was born in Germany in 1879. He died in New Jersey in 1955.

As a child, Einstein did not like school. Teachers said he was a lazy student. The problem was that he was bored. The lessons were too simple for him. Things got better as he grew older. He learned how new ideas can help the world.

As a young man, Einstein worked in an office. He studied physics when he wasn't working. He wrote reports about his studies. One of his reports gave new ideas about how time works. Like Galileo, he used reason to understand nature.

Einstein left Germany in 1933. He went to America. He became a well-known college professor.

Albert Einstein once said, "Look deep into nature, and then you will understand everything better."

Biography Poster 3

Lesson Objectives

Students will:
- Review features of the biography genre.
- Ask questions about a text.
- Use their understanding of genre features to identify details.
- Develop a main idea statement.
- Build oral language and vocabulary through whole-group and partner discussion.

Related Resources
- Biography Poster 3 (BLM 3)
- Main Idea and Supporting Details (BLM 4)
- BenchmarkUniverse.com

Make Content Comprehensible for ELLs

Beginning
Point to and name Einstein. Show Germany and New Jersey on a map.

Intermediate and Advanced
Explain that the word **nature** in the first paragraph means "the basic character or form of something."

All Levels
Group students with fluent English speakers during all whole-group and partner discussions.

Comprehension Quick-Check

Note whether students can generate details based on the passage. If they need additional support, review the features of a biography using Poster 1. Then highlight or underline specific details about Albert Einstein on Poster 3 using a write-on/wipe-off marker. **Say:** *In a biography, the details are the specific information about a person's life.* Have students underline or highlight additional details on the poster with you.

Home/School Connection

Have students take home the Main Idea and Supporting Details graphic organizer (BLM 4) and write three details that support a main idea statement about their own lives. Tell students that each of their details should reflect a feature of the biography genre.

Remind students that the main ideas may not be directly stated in the text of a biography. It is often up to readers to infer the main ideas based on the information provided.

Connect and transfer. Say: *This week as you read biographies, ask questions and look for the main idea about the subject.*

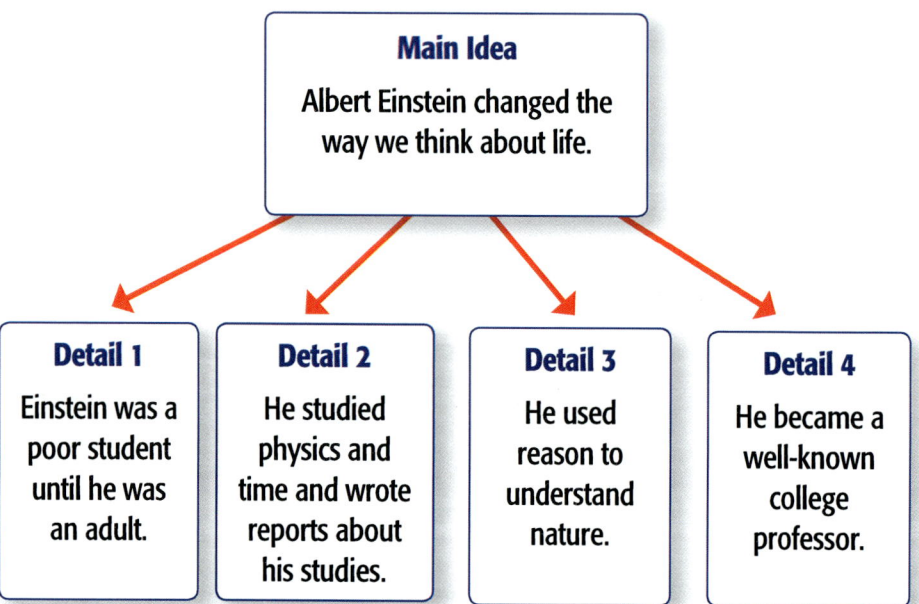

Main Idea
Albert Einstein changed the way we think about life.

Detail 1	Detail 2	Detail 3	Detail 4
Einstein was a poor student until he was an adult.	He studied physics and time and wrote reports about his studies.	He used reason to understand nature.	He became a well-known college professor.

Sample Main Idea and Supporting Details Annotations

 # Small-Group Reading Instruction (60 MINUTES)

Continue small-group reading instruction from the previous day. Use the instruction provided in the Teacher's Guide for each text.

 # Individual Student Conferences (10 MINUTES)

Confer with individual students to discuss their developing understanding of genre and comprehension strategies. Use the Individual Reading Conference Form on page 32 of Informal Assessments for Reading Development to help guide your conferences.

 # Word Study Workshop (20 MINUTES)

Use the Day 3 instruction provided in Grade 3 Word Study Unit 2.

Read-Aloud (10 MINUTES)

Select a favorite nonfiction read-aloud from your classroom or school library with which to model the metacognitive strategy "Ask Questions." Use the sample read-aloud lessons and suggested titles in the Getting Started Guide.

Mini-Lessons (20 MINUTES)

Build Comprehension: Analyze Character

Say: *When you read a biography, you learn about a person's life. The author gives you factual information and, based on this information, you can form an understanding of the person's character. Let's focus on analyzing Albert Einstein's character based on the information on this poster.*

Reread Biography Poster 3 with students.

Say: *We are going to make a character chart. We will put on our chart all the information from the text that helps us understand Albert Einstein's character. What kinds of information will you look for to understand his character?* Allow responses.

Engage students in a discussion to ensure they understand that they must pay attention to visual and text descriptions to learn about Einstein's personality traits and feelings, events in his life that helped to shape who he was, and how he responded to those events.

Biography Poster 3

Lesson Objectives

Students will:

- Analyze character.
- Extend Tier Two Vocabulary by focusing on word origins.
- Build oral language and vocabulary through whole-group and partner discussion.

Related Resources

- Biography Poster 3 (BLM 3)
- BenchmarkUniverse.com

Make Content Comprehensible for ELLs

Beginning

As you identify character information in the text, use pantomime or simple definitions to help ELLs understand the meaning of key words and traits on your chart. Then have them repeat the words. For example, **say:** *Someone who is hardworking works hard and does a good job. A person who is brave dares to try new things even when he or she is scared or afraid.*

Intermediate and Advanced

Provide sentence frames to help students use the scientific vocabulary:

> *Physics is _____.*
> *A physician is _____.*
> *Physical education is _____.*

All Levels

Pair ELLs with fluent English speakers during partner discussions and activities.

Comprehension Quick-Check

Take note of students who may need more support to identify facts and clues about the subject of a biography. Provide additional modeling during small-group reading, and have students practice during independent workstation time by analyzing the character based on another biography excerpt that you assign.

On chart paper, draw a two-column chart like the one shown below.

Think/Pair/Write/Share. Tell students they will complete this chart. **Say:** *Work with a partner to identify facts and personality traits. Make a chart like the one I just drew, and fill in your ideas. Then we will share them as a group. As partners share facts, traits, and evidence from the text, add them to the chart.*

Connect and transfer. Say: *Remember, when you read a biography, you need to analyze the character of the person you are reading about. You need to look for facts and clues in the text that help you understand the person.*

SUBJECT: ALBERT EINSTEIN	HOW DO YOU KNOW
Facts: • famous scientist • studied the universe • born in Germany in 1879 • died in New Jersey in 1955	Paragraph 1 gives this information.
Personality Traits: • willing to learn • hardworking	• teachers said he was a lazy student as a child • his attitude about learning changed when he grew older • studied physics in time off from work

Build Tier Two Vocabulary: Word Origins

On chart paper, write the word **physics**.

Say: *We know Einstein studied a type of science called physics. What do you think the word physics means?*

Turn and talk. Ask students to turn and talk with their neighbor for a moment to come up with a definition.

Ask students to share their definitions, and record them on chart paper. Explain that **physics** comes from an ancient Greek root, **phys**, meaning "nature." Physics is the study of nature, especially the study of time, energy, and matter.

Ask: *What other words can you think of that might be related to physics?*

Write the words **physical** and **physician**. Point out the word part **phys** in each and discuss how knowing the origin of one word can help students understand other unfamiliar words. Encourage students to generate other words using a dictionary. Circle the Greek root in each word and remind students to use this word part to help them figure out word meanings. Invite students to use the list of words they generated in meaningful sentences.

Small-Group Reading Instruction (60 MINUTES)

Continue small-group reading instruction from the previous day. Use the instruction provided in the Teacher's Guide for each text.

Individual Student Conferences (10 MINUTES)

Confer with individual students to discuss their developing understanding of genre and word-solving strategies. Use the Individual Reading Conference Form on page 32 of Informal Assessments for Reading Development to help guide your conferences.

Word Study Workshop (20 MINUTES)

Use the Day 4 instruction provided in Grade 3 Word Study Unit 2.

Oral Language Extension

During independent workstation time, ask pairs of students to tell their partners about themselves using the main idea and supporting details they brainstormed as homework on Day 3.

Home/School Connection

Have students take home BLM 3 and read it with a family member to practice fluent reading. Tell students to have their family member sign the page to indicate they have participated in the reading.

Day Five

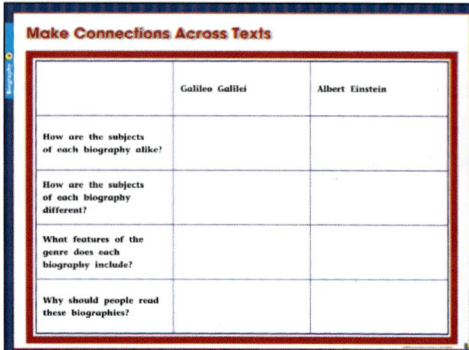

Biography Poster 4

Lesson Objectives

Students will:

- Summarize the main ideas and supporting details in biographies.
- Review features of the biography genre.
- Make text-to-text connections.
- Build academic oral language and vocabulary through small-group and whole-group discussions.

Related Resources

- Biography Poster 4 (BLM 5)
- BenchmarkUniverse.com

Read-Aloud (10 MINUTES)

Revisit the week's read-alouds to make text-to-text connections and provide opportunities for reader response. Use the suggested activities in the Getting Started Guide, or implement ideas of your own.

Mini-Lessons (20 MINUTES)

Synthesize and Assess Genre Understanding

Synthesize genre understanding. Ask students to work in teams to summarize what they now know about the biography genre. Tell students that each group member should contribute an idea to the discussion. Each group should appoint one member to be the group's recorder. Another student should be the group's spokesperson.

Give students five to seven minutes to discuss and record their ideas.

Have each group's spokesperson share his or her group's ideas.

Record key concepts from each group on chart paper.

Self-assessment. Display the class Biography anchor chart from Day 1. Ask each group to compare their group's ideas to the information they recorded on the anchor chart on Day 1.

Ask: *How has your understanding of the biography genre developed? What do you know now that you didn't know before?* Encourage individual students to share their personal insights.

Connect and transfer. Ask: *How can you use your new understandings of this genre as a reader the next time you read a biography? How do you think you can use your genre knowledge as a writer?*

Make Connections Across Texts

Display Biography Poster 4.

Say: *You have read biographies this week. Sometimes in school and on tests, you will be asked to make connections between different fiction and nonfiction texts. Today we are going to practice making connections between biographies.*

Ask each group to compare and contrast the poster passages. Ask them to answer the questions comparing and contrasting the two selections on BLM 5.

Give students about five minutes to record their ideas. Then bring the groups together and have them share their ideas.

Challenge students to express their own opinions on these subjects:
- *Which subject would they like to read more about? Why?*
- *Which biography did they find easier to understand? Why?*

Connect and transfer. Say: *When you compare and contrast two biographies, think about how each biography reflects the features of the genre. Did the writer give you a clear picture of the subject through the details that he or she provided? Did the writer help you understand why the subject is important to know?*

Small-Group Reading Instruction (60 MINUTES)

Continue small-group reading instruction from the previous day. Use the instruction provided in the Teacher's Guide for each text.

Individual Student Conferences (10 MINUTES)

Ask students to reflect on what they have learned about the biography genre. Use the Individual Reading Conference Form on page 32 of Informal Assessments for Reading Development to help guide your conferences.

Word Study Workshop (20 MINUTES)

Use the Day 5 instruction provided in Grade 3 Word Study Unit 2.

Make Content Comprehensible for ELLs

Beginning
Allow beginning ELLs to participate as active listeners in their groups.

Intermediate and Advanced
Provide sentence frames to help ELLs contribute to their groups' discussions. For example:

The biographies are alike because _____.

The biographies are different because _____.

This biography has the feature _____.

All Levels
Pair ELLs with fluent English speakers during all partner and group activities.

Encourage ELLs to revisit the books they are comparing and to find and read specific information in the text to help them communicate their ideas.

Name _____   Date _____

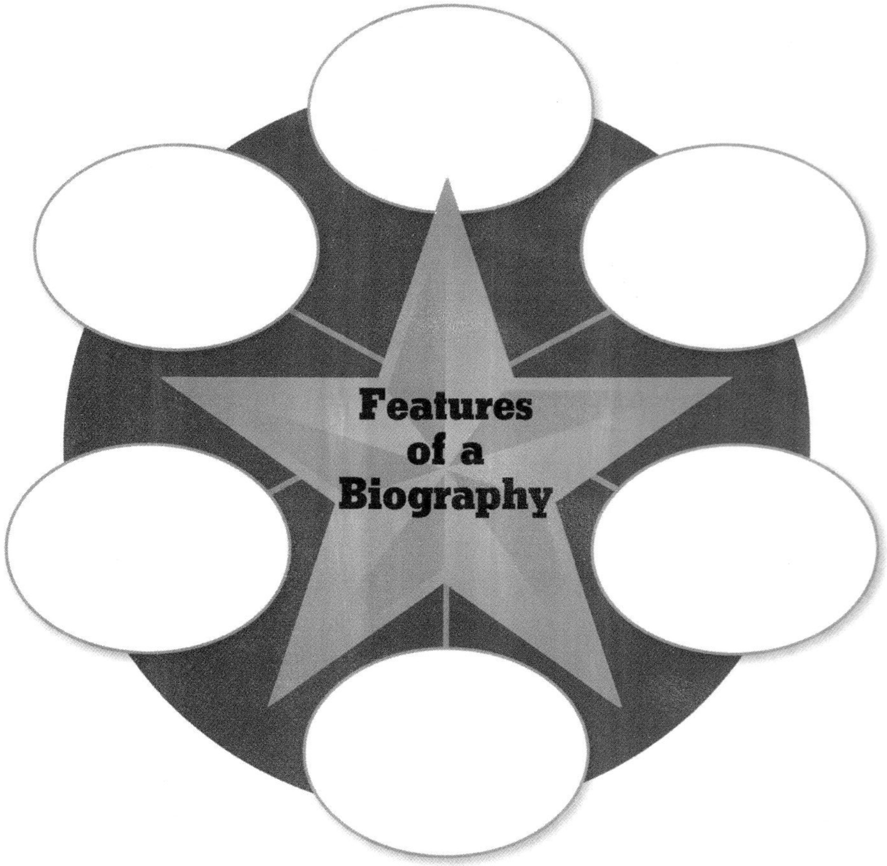

Features
of a
Biography

Focus on the Genre
Biography

What is a biography?

What is the purpose of biographies?

How do you read a biography?

Who writes biographies?

Biography ❶

Name _____   Date _____

Galileo Galilei

The hook grabs the reader's attention.

The author tells when and where Galileo was born.

The author tells what Galileo did that was important.

The author explains Galileo's character.

The author quotes Galileo's powerful words.

The author tells about Galileo's impact on the world.

Galileo Galilei is called the father of science. He changed how we see the world. He was born in Pisa, Italy, in 1564. He died in 1642.

In his day, people thought Earth was the center of the universe. They thought the sun flew around Earth. They were wrong. We know better today because of Galileo.

Galileo made a telescope. He saw that Earth circles the sun. He showed that Earth is not the center of the universe. People said he was crazy. Galileo was all alone.

People wanted him to hide the truth. They wanted him to say he was wrong about Earth going around the sun.

Galileo was brave. He would not lie! This made people angry. To hide the truth, they hid Galileo. They jailed him in his own house for the rest of his life!

Galileo changed the world. He showed how people can use tools and their senses to see the truth. He said, "When senses fail, reason must step in." He showed that reason helps us go to a better tomorrow.

Name _____ Date _____

Albert Einstein once said, "Look deep into nature, and then you will understand everything better."

Albert Einstein

Albert Einstein was a famous scientist. He studied the nature of the universe. That type of science is called **physics.** Like Galileo, he changed the way we think about the world. Einstein was born in Germany in 1879. He died in New Jersey in 1955.

As a child, Einstein did not like school. Teachers said he was a lazy student. The problem was that he was bored. The lessons were too simple for him. Things got better as he grew older. He learned how new ideas can help the world.

As a young man, Einstein worked in an office. He studied physics when he wasn't working. He wrote reports about his studies. One of his reports gave new ideas about how time works. Like Galileo, he used reason to understand nature.

Einstein left Germany in 1933. He went to America. He became a well-known college professor.

Name _____   Date _____

Main Idea and Supporting Details

Directions: Write a main idea statement about your own life. Then write three details that support your main idea. Each detail should relate to a feature of the biography genre.

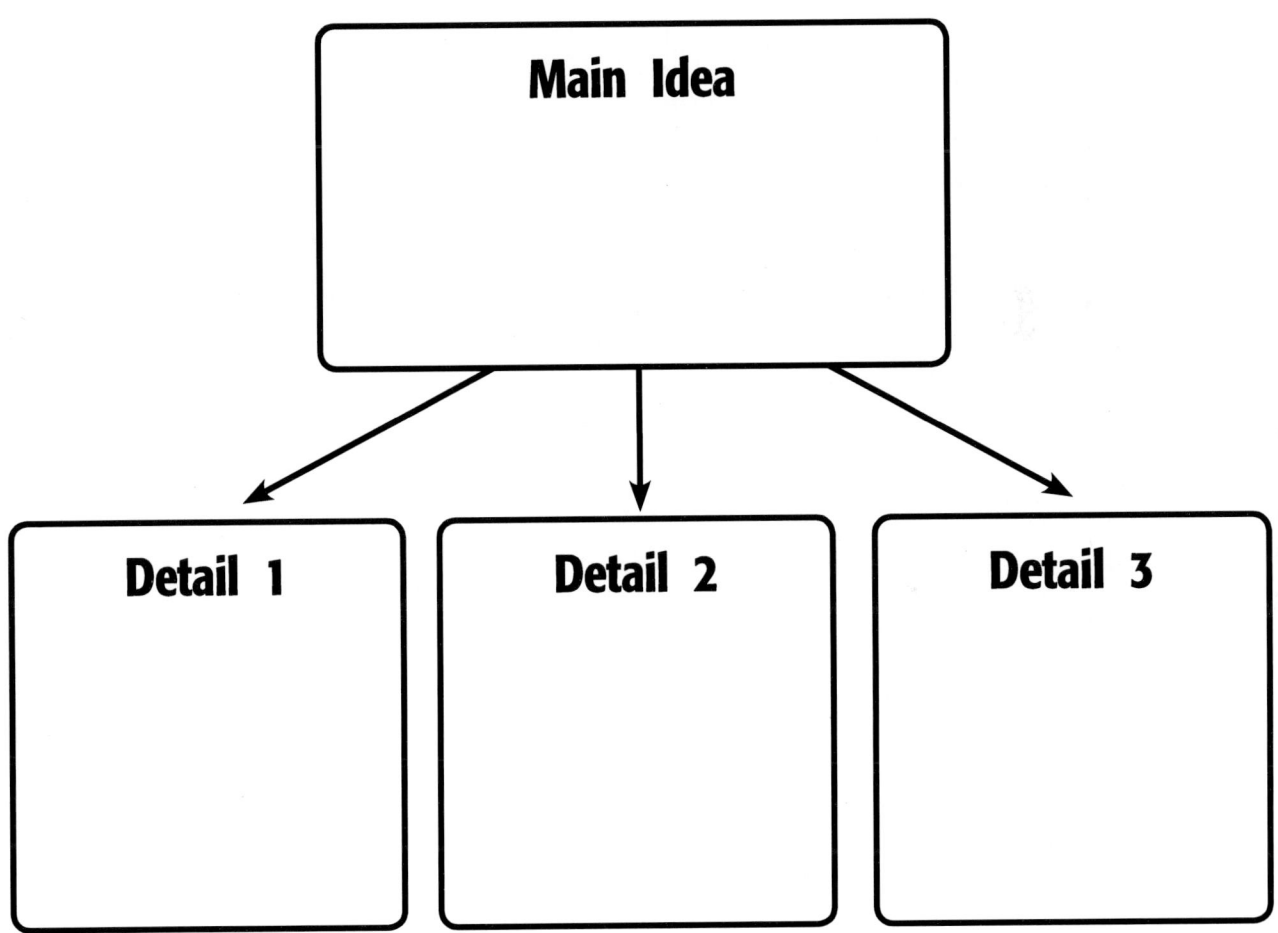

Main Idea

Detail 1

Detail 2

Detail 3

Name _____ Date _____

Make Connections Across Texts

Biography 4

	Galileo Galilei	Albert Einstein
How are the subjects of each biography alike?		
How are the subjects of each biography different?		
What features of the genre does each biography include?		
Why should people read these biographies?		

Ask Questions/Identify Main Idea and Supporting Details

Unit 1/Week 3 at a Glance

Day	Mini-Lessons
ONE	• Introduce Fluency Skills: *Speed/Pacing–Varied* • Model the Skill
TWO	• Practice and Self-Assess Fluency Skills: *Speed/Pacing–Varied* • Connect Fluency and Comprehension: *Analyze Author's Purpose*
THREE	• Apply Fluency Skills to Reader's Theater • Build Comprehension: *Analyze Author's Purpose*
FOUR	• Build Tier Two Vocabulary: *Adjectives That Describe People*
FIVE	• Prepare for and Manage Student Performances: *Audience and Performer Expectations* • Show Time! • Assess and Reflect

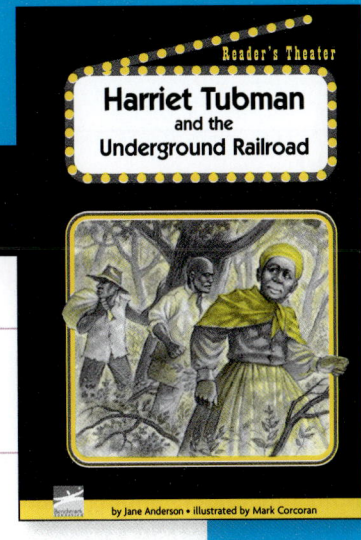

Cat or Dog?

Cat Lover: Cats are the best pets. They purr so sweetly. I love when my cat licks my hand. It tickles!

Dog Lover: No, it doesn't! A cat's tongue feels like sandpaper. Dogs are the best pets. I love getting a big lick from a dog.

Cat Lover: Yuck! Dog drool! The only thing worse than slobbery drool is stinky dog breath!

Dog Lover: Well, dogs are the most fun. You can teach dogs tricks. My dog can fetch a stick, and roll over and play dead, and—

Cat Lover: —bark at the mailman, chase its tail, and run into the street whenever a fire truck comes by!

Cat Lover: Cats are more fun. When I dangle a piece of string over my cat, she tries to catch it.

Dog Lover: Only if she feels like playing with you. Cats are fickle.

Cat Lover: My cat is not fickle! She always curls up on my lap when I'm reading in my favorite chair.

Dog Lover: My dog is too big to sit on my lap, but he loves to sleep at the foot of my bed.

Cat Lover: That sounds nice. Maybe dogs are the best pets—for you.

Dog Lover: And maybe cats are the best pets—for you!

Cat or Dog?

Cat Lover: Cats are the best pets. They purr so sweetly. I love when my cat licks my hand. It tickles!

Dog Lover: No, it doesn't! A cat's tongue feels like sandpaper. Dogs are the best pets. I love getting a big lick from a dog.

Cat Lover: Yuck! Dog drool! The only thing worse than slobbery drool is stinky dog breath!

Dog Lover: Well, dogs are the most fun. You can teach dogs tricks. My dog can fetch a stick, and roll over and play dead, and—

Cat Lover: —bark at the mailman, chase its tail, and run into the street whenever a fire truck comes by!

Cat Lover: Cats are more fun. When I dangle a piece of string over my cat, she tries to catch it.

Dog Lover: Only if she feels like playing with you. Cats are fickle.

Cat Lover: My cat is not fickle! She always curls up on my lap when I'm reading in my favorite chair.

Dog Lover: My dog is too big to sit on my lap, but he loves to sleep at the foot of my bed.

Cat Lover: That sounds nice. Maybe dogs are the best pets—for you.

Dog Lover: And maybe cats are the best pets—for you!

Fluency Poster

Lesson Objectives

Students will:

- Read a dialogue at a varied pace.
- Utilize punctuation cues.
- Demonstrate understanding of the text through purposeful pacing.
- Use effective pacing to make their reading sound like talking.

Related Resources

- BenchmarkUniverse.com

Read-Aloud (10 MINUTES)

Select a favorite fiction read-aloud from your classroom or school library with which to model the metacognitive strategy "Ask Questions." Use the sample read-aloud lessons and suggested titles provided in the Getting Started Guide.

Mini-Lessons (20 MINUTES)

Introduce Fluency Skills: Speed/Pacing—Varied

Explain: *We read different texts at different speeds. Sometimes we read slowly. Sometimes we read more quickly. How fast or slow you read depends on many factors. Can you think of what things might affect your reading speed?* Allow responses.

Reinforce the idea that what you are reading often determines the pace at which you read.

Ask:
- *Would you most likely read a tongue twister quickly or slowly?*
    (quickly, to keep the rhythm going)
- *How would you read a list of steps to follow to build something?*
    (slowly, to make sure you understand and don't miss any steps)
- *And how might you read a story?*
    (You would vary your pacing to keep it interesting and to reflect the mood and action of each moment.)

Say: *The speed at which we read is called pacing. Remember, good readers use pacing to help their reading sound right and to make sense to themselves and others.*

Model the Skill

Display the fluency poster "Cat or Dog?" and read aloud the title.

Say: *This is a dialogue. In this dialogue, the speakers say some parts faster and some parts slower. I'll have to pay close attention to their words and meaning to know how to read their parts. I'll also look for easy and hard words and pay close attention to the punctuation to know when to speed up or slow down.*

Ask students to listen and follow along as you read the passage aloud, varying your speed to match what the speakers are saying and utilizing punctuation cues. For example, in the opening, the cat lover might say the first and third sentences at a normal rate, the second sentence slowly, and the last sentence fast.

Say: *Now I will read part of the dialogue again. This time, I will read every word at the same speed.*

Read the first few lines of the dialogue in a slow, word-by-word manner.

Turn and talk. Have students turn to a neighbor and compare and evaluate your two readings. Ask them to think about how each reading affected them as listeners. Then have pairs of students share their ideas with the whole class. Reinforce the idea that varying the pacing of your reading keeps readers interested and engaged. If you read in a steady monotone, readers are likely to tune out.

Shared Writing. Invite students to help you create a class anchor chart to remind them how good readers use speed and pacing. (See the example below.) When you are finished, ask students to echo-read the entire chart. Display the chart in the classroom for future reference.

Speed/Pacing

- We read different kinds of texts at different speeds.
- We read easy parts faster and hard parts slower.
- We match our pacing to what the author is saying.
- Reading too fast makes the reading hard to understand.
- Reading too slowly does not sound natural.
- No matter what speed we use to read, we pay attention to punctuation.

Sample Anchor Chart

Make Content Comprehensible for ELLs

Beginning
Orally demonstrate fast and slow pace. Invite students to vary their pace, too, and tell you whether it was fast or slow.

Beginning and Intermediate
Engage ELLs in a discussion about pets. Ask them to tell why they like certain pets using the sentence frame: *I like _____ because they _____.* Record their sentences and reread them together.

All Levels
Before reading to model fluency, read to support comprehension of unfamiliar Tier Two words through explanation, gestures, and role-play, or by using props. Difficult words may include: **sandpaper**, **drool**, **fetch**, **fickle**.

Support Special Needs Learners

Throughout the week, use the following strategies to help students who have learning disabilities access the content and focus on skills and strategies.

During partner reading practice, pair special needs students with more fluent readers who can model fluency and support their development.

Group students heterogeneously for small-group reading of the script so that struggling students benefit from working with more fluent readers.

Assign multiple students to specific reader's theater roles so that they can support each other.

Fluency and Comprehension Quick-Check

Throughout the week, refer to the Fluency Rubric provided in the Benchmark Literacy Assessments to help you informally assess where students are in their development of key areas of fluency.

The end goal of all fluency practice is increased comprehension. Use the following questions to check students' comprehension of the passage they have read:

- *What was this dialogue mostly about?*
- *Why are Cat Lover and Dog Lover talking to each other? What is the purpose of their conversation?*

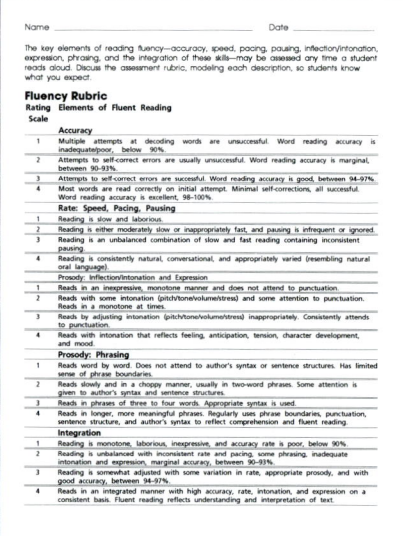

Fluency Rubric

Connect and transfer. Say: *Today during small-group reading, we will read a reader's theater script. As we read the script, one skill we will practice is varying our speed and pacing to make the script interesting and make the characters come to life.*

Small-Group Reading Instruction (60 MINUTES)

Introduce and read *Harriet Tubman and the Underground Railroad*. Use the before- and during-reading instruction in the Teacher's Guide for the script.

Individual Student Conferences (10 MINUTES)

Confer with individual students to discuss their understanding of the script. Use the Individual Reading Conference Form on page 32 of Informal Assessments for Reading Development to help guide your conferences.

Word Study Workshop (20 MINUTES)

Use the Day 1 instruction provided in Grade 3 Word Study Unit 3.

Read-Aloud (10 MINUTES)

Select a favorite fiction read-aloud from your classroom or school library with which to model the metacognitive strategy "Ask Questions." Use the sample read-aloud lessons and suggested titles provided in the Getting Started Guide.

Mini-Lessons (20 MINUTES)

Practice and Self-Assess Fluency Skills:
Speed/Pacing–Varied

Distribute copies of Cat or Dog? (BLM 1).

Divide students into Cat Lover and Dog Lover groups and ask them to choral-read their parts with you one or more times.

Next, allow the groups to choral-read their parts without your assistance.

Distribute the Fluency Self-Assessment Master Checklist (BLM 2) and review the assessment criteria for speed/pacing and integration. Ask students to give a thumbs-up or thumbs-down on each question based on the group's choral-reading. Discuss their responses.

Partner reading. Pair students, and then put two pairs together. Assign one pair as Cat Lover and one pair as Dog Lover, and invite them to read "Cat or Dog?" together one or more times.

Monitor students' partner rereading practice and provide responsive feedback using the prompts provided on page 6.

Ask students to rate themselves on specific fluency skills covered in this lesson using their Fluency Self-Assessment Master Checklist (BLM 2).

Connect and transfer. Ask students to reflect on their fluency practice, using the following prompts:
- *When did you read faster? What effect do you think that had?*
- *When did you read more slowly? Why did you slow down? What were you trying to do?*
- *Remember, you will need this skill as we practice and perform a reader's theater script this week.*

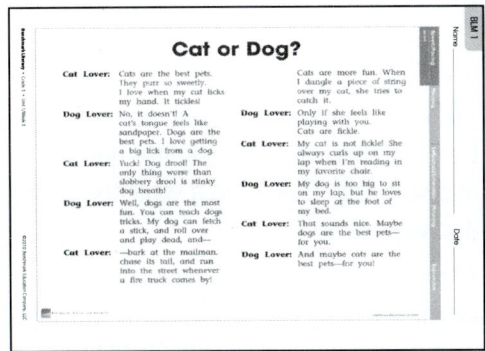

Cat or Dog? (BLM 1)

Lesson Objectives

Students will:
- Read a dialogue at a varied pace.
- Utilize punctuation cues.
- Demonstrate understanding of the text through purposeful pacing.
- Use effective pacing to make their reading sound like talking.

Related Resources
- Cat or Dog? (BLM 1)
- Fluency Self-Assessment Master Checklist (BLM 2)
- BenchmarkUniverse.com

Make Content Comprehensible for ELLs

Beginning

Make sure students understand the terms **fast** and **slow**. Read a sentence quickly and **say:** *fast*. Then read a sentence slowly and **say:** *slow*.

Allow ELLs to participate through active listening while other students demonstrate varied speed and pacing. Invite ELLs to indicate when the pacing is fast or slow.

Intermediate and Advanced

Read the Self-Assessment Master Checklist (BLM 2) with students to ensure understanding. Monitor understanding of academic vocabulary and provide examples of **appropriate** and **natural** as necessary.

All Levels

Pair ELLs with fluent English speakers during partner discussions and activities.

Fluency Self-Assessment Master Checklist (BLM 2)

Responsive Prompts for Speed and Pacing

As students work together, observe those who demonstrate understanding and those who struggle. Use appropriate responsive prompting to provide additional support or to validate students who demonstrate mastery.

Goal Oriented

- Listen to me read. Can you read it like I do?
- Listen to how I read this. I am going to read this faster.
- Listen to how I read this. I am going to read this slower.
- Listen to my voice as I read the next sentence. Am I reading at a fluent pace?

Directive and Corrective Feedback

- Read these words faster.
- Read these words slower.
- Try that again and read slower.
- Try that again and read faster.
- Try moving your eyes quicker so you can read more words together.
- Read the text again and make it sound like you are talking.

Self-Monitoring and Reflection

- How did you pace your reading?
- Did you read that too fast or too slow?
- What did you do to read that faster/slower?
- How did you vary your pace in that passage?
- What did you notice about your reading?
- What made you read slower or faster?
- Where did you read too fast/slow?
- Where did you read at the right pace?

Validating and Confirming

- I liked the way you read it faster that time.
- I liked the way you slowed your reading down that time.
- Good job at varying your pace in the passage.
- You read at an appropriate rate. Great job!

Connect Fluency and Comprehension:
Analyze Author's Purpose

Say: *If you don't understand what you are reading, you can't read at the correct pace and with the correct expression. However, when you understand why an author wrote a piece, you can use your voice to help your audience understand as well. What are some reasons, or purposes, authors may have for writing?* Allow responses. List the author's purposes that students identify on chart paper.

Say: *Now think about "Cat or Dog?" Why do you think the author wrote this dialogue?* Allow responses.

Discuss how scripts are usually intended to entertain and that this particular script has another purpose, too. It shows the many pros and cons of dogs and cats as pets.

Ask: *How does understanding the author's purpose of "Cat or Dog?" change how you sound when you read it aloud?*

Connect and transfer. Say: *Today during small-group reading, focus on understanding the purpose of the script. This will help you read with the right expression.*

Small-Group Reading Instruction (60 MINUTES)

Reread *Harriet Tubman and the Underground Railroad* to build comprehension and critical thinking using the After Reading Interpret the Script questions. Assign roles to individual students.

Individual Student Conferences (10 MINUTES)

Confer with individual students to discuss their script roles and how they plan to rehearse and read their part. Use the Individual Reading Conference Form on page 32 of Informal Assessments for Reading Development to help guide your conferences.

Word Study Workshop (20 MINUTES)

Use the Day 2 instruction provided in Grade 3 Word Study Unit 3.

Oral Language Extension

Have pairs of students practice the fluency passage during independent workstation time.

Home/School Connection

Have students take home Cat or Dog? (BLM 1) to read with a family member. Ask students to focus on reading smoothly and with good expression. Have them switch roles with their family member so that they practice both roles in the dialogue.

Ask students to have their family member sign the page to indicate they have participated in the reading.

Day Three

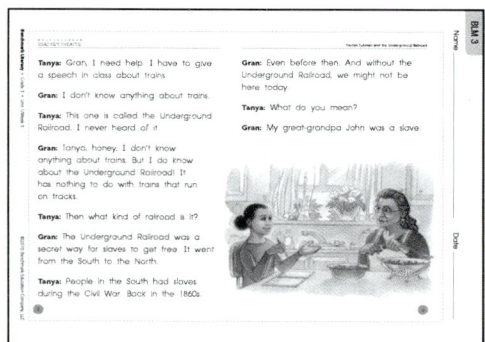

Harriet Tubman and the Underground Railroad, pages 2–3 (BLM 3)

Lesson Objectives

Students will:

- Read a script excerpt at a varied pace.

- Utilize punctuation cues.

- Demonstrate understanding of the text through purposeful pacing.

- Use effective pacing to make their reading sound like talking.

- Use metacognitive strategies to help them analyze the author's purpose.

- Build oral language and vocabulary through whole-group and partner discussion.

Related Resources

- *Harriet Tubman and the Underground Railroad*, pages 2–3 (BLM 3)

- BenchmarkUniverse.com

Read-Aloud (10 MINUTES)

Select a favorite nonfiction read-aloud from your classroom or school library with which to model the metacognitive strategy "Ask Questions." Use the sample read-aloud lessons and suggested titles provided in the Getting Started Guide.

Mini-Lessons (20 MINUTES)

Apply Fluency Skills to Reader's Theater

Distribute the first two pages of *Harriet Tubman and the Underground Railroad* (BLM 3), which students have completed during small-group reading time.

Say: *Yesterday you practiced varying your speed and pacing as you read a dialogue. Now I want you to apply what you learned to the script we will perform this week. Listen as I read these two pages to you.*

Read pages 2–3 of the script to model how you vary your pacing. Use the suggestions below or interpret the text in your own way:
  - Tanya: slow and unexcited at the beginning, faster when she realizes that the Underground Railroad is something interesting
  - Gran: varied, but slower at longer sections of explanation so that Tanya understands

Ask students to comment on how your reading affected them as listeners.

Partner reading. Have pairs of students practice reading these pages together. Monitor their practice and provide responsive prompting as needed to validate their efforts, give corrective feedback, or encourage them to self monitor. Use the responsive prompts provided on page 6.

Build Comprehension: Analyze Author's Purpose

Say: *Yesterday we discussed why the author of "Cat or Dog?" wrote that dialogue. Today let's think about why the author of Harriet Tubman and the Underground Railroad wrote about these events and characters. Understanding the author's purpose will help you interpret the script more effectively.*

Activate metacognitive strategies. Ask: *What strategies can we use to help ourselves understand the author's purpose?* Allow responses. If necessary, prompt students to use the following strategies:

Summarize and synthesize. Say: *How would you summarize this script? What important information does the author want you to remember? How does summarizing help you understand the purpose of the script?*

Fix-up monitoring. Say: *What parts do you need to reread? Are there dates or places you need to remember? Read those parts again.*

Support ELLs' and struggling readers' participation in the discussion by providing the following sentence frames:

> *A summary should include _____.*
> *I need to remember_____.*
> *I think the author's purpose is _____.*

Shared Writing. Make a list of students' ideas about the author's purpose. Post this on the wall.

Connect and transfer. Say: *Today, as you practice reading the script, think about what the author wants people to experience through the script. Use what you have learned about pacing to help you express her purpose.*

Small-Group Reading Instruction (60 MINUTES)

Have students rehearse their roles in *Harriet Tubman and the Underground Railroad* together as a group. Offer suggestions for voice, expression, and pacing.

Individual Student Conferences (10 MINUTES)

Confer with individual students to discuss their script roles and their rehearsal progress. Use the Individual Reading Conference Form on page 32 of *Informal Assessments for Reading Development* to help guide your conferences.

Word Study Workshop (20 MINUTES)

Use the Day 3 instruction provided in Grade 3 Word Study Unit 3.

Make Content Comprehensible for ELLs

Beginning
Allow ELLs to participate through active listening while other students demonstrate varied speed and pacing. Invite them to indicate when the pacing is fast or slow.

Intermediate and Advanced
Allow ELLs to read parts of the script chorally with you or other students as they demonstrate their varied speed and pacing.

All Levels
Pair ELLs with fluent English speakers during partner reading practice.

Model the use of academic sentence frames to support ELLs' academic vocabulary and language development. (See suggested sentence frames provided.)

Home/School Connection

Have students take home *Harriet Tubman and the Underground Railroad*, pages 2–3 (BLM 3) and read it with a family member to practice fluent reading. Ask students to have their family member sign the script page to indicate that they have participated in the reading.

Fluency Quick-Check

As students practice oral reading with a partner, note students who would benefit from additional repeated oral reading practice during independent workstation time.

Day Four

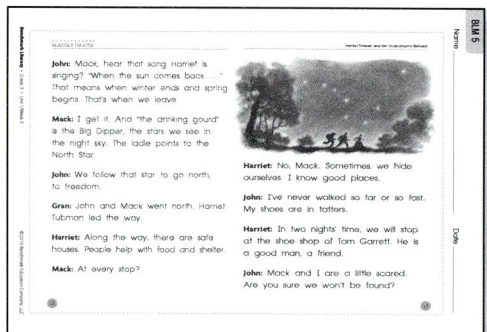

Harriet Tubman and the Underground Railroad, pages 10–11 (BLM 5)

 Read-Aloud (10 MINUTES)

Select a favorite nonfiction read-aloud from your classroom or school library with which to model the metacognitive strategy "Ask Questions." Use the sample read-aloud lessons and suggested titles provided in the Getting Started Guide.

 Mini-Lessons (20 MINUTES)

Build Tier Two Vocabulary: Adjectives That Describe People

On chart paper, draw a graphic organizer like the one below (BLM 4). Remind students that adjectives are words that describe people, places, or things. Today they will discuss words that describe people.

Think/Pair/Write/Share. Distribute the Adjectives graphic organizer (BLM 4). Ask students to work with a partner to list adjectives that describe people, including how they look, how they act, and how they feel. Give students approximately three minutes, and then bring them back together to share their answers. If students are unable to come up with adjectives, prompt them with the following questions:

- *How do you feel after a long day at school?*
- *What word might describe a person who smiles a lot?*
- *How might you feel if you were lost?*
- *What word might describe a person who takes up a lot of space?*

Record students' responses on the chart and work together to use several of the words in oral sentences.

Distribute *Harriet Tubman and the Underground Railroad*, pages 10–11 (BLM 5).

People look . . .	People act . . .	People feel . . .
tall	silly	unhappy
skinny	mean	frightened
old	kind	tired

Sample Adjectives That Describe People Annotations (BLM 4)

Say: *Writers use adjectives to help readers get a clear understanding of a character. Read the text with a partner. Find adjectives that describe characters.*

Have pairs add the adjectives they find in the text to the chart on BLM 4. Then have them share their answers with the class. Ask students to tell how the adjectives helped them understand more about the characters. Possible answers include: **scared** and **good**.

Discuss fix-up monitoring strategies. Ask students what they can do when they encounter an unfamiliar adjective and are confused about the meaning. Generate discussion of the strategies that help good readers. For example, students can read on to find out more about the character and find additional clues about the word's meaning. They can also stop and think about what they already know.

Connect and transfer. Say: *Several words in our script are adjectives that describe characters. In order to understand your part, you need to think about how your character is described. This will affect how you read and portray that character.*

Small-Group Reading Instruction (60 MINUTES)

Have students continue to rehearse their roles in *Harriet Tubman and the Underground Railroad* together as a group. Discuss and plan how students will stage their script performance tomorrow.

Individual Student Conferences (10 MINUTES)

Confer with individual students on sections of the script you would like them to work on before the performance. Use the Individual Reading Conference Form on page 32 of Informal Assessments for Reading Development to help guide your conferences.

Word Study Workshop (20 MINUTES)

Use the Day 4 instruction provided in Grade 3 Word Study Unit 3.

Make Content Comprehensible for ELLs

Beginning
Help ELLs understand adjectives that describe characters by naming characteristics of students: *Mario is tall. April is kind. Kim is happy.* Use gestures and pantomime to further understanding. Have students repeat the sentences.

Intermediate
Use this sentence frame to help students generate descriptive sentences:

[Student/Character] is _____.

All Levels
Pair ELLs with fluent English speakers during partner discussions and activities.

Oral Language Extension

Write several glossary words from the reader's theater script on chart paper and display the list during independent workstation time. Challenge pairs of students to use each word in meaningful oral sentences. Ask students to write down at least five sentences to show you during independent student conference time.

Home/School Connection

Have students take home *Harriet Tubman and the Underground Railroad*, pages 10–11 (BLM 5) and read it with a family member to practice fluency skills. Ask students to have their family member sign the script page to indicate that they have participated in the reading.

Day Five

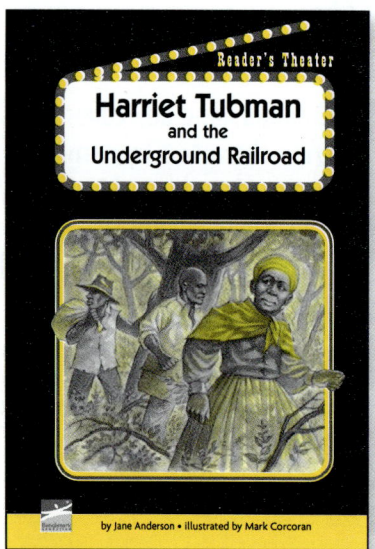

Reader's Theater Script

Lesson Objectives

Students will:

- Demonstrate their level of fluency development through an oral reading interpretation of the script.

- Demonstrate active listening skills.

- Reflect on and assess their own fluency development.

Related Resources

- Reader's Theater Self-Assessment (BLM 6)

- BenchmarkUniverse.com

Read-Aloud (10 MINUTES)

Revisit the week's read-alouds to make text-to-text connections and to provide opportunities for reader response. Use the suggested activities in the Getting Started Guide, or implement ideas of your own.

Mini-Lessons (20 MINUTES)

Prepare for and Manage Student Performances: Audience and Performer Expectations

Prepare students for their reader's theater performances by sharing your expectations of audience members and performers.

Audience expectations. Say: *While you are listening to the other groups perform, I expect you to do the following:*

- Give your classmates your full attention.
- Do not speak to your neighbors or make any noise.
- Enjoy their performance and show your appreciation by clapping when they are finished.
- Be prepared to give your feedback on the script, and always remember to make your feedback constructive, or helpful.

Performer expectations. Say: *While you and your group are performing the script, remember to do these things:*

- Read in a loud, clear voice and act out your role.
- Use expression and fluency to help everyone listening to understand your character.
- Remember to vary your speed and pacing.
- When it is not your turn to read, follow along in the script so you know when to come in.
- If one of your group members gets lost or forgets to come in, prompt him or her quietly.
- Accept both suggestions and praise from your audience.

Show Time!

Invite students to perform the script for an audience such as members of the class, students from other classes, school staff members, or parents.

Continue your performances during small-group reading time, giving each group the opportunity to perform.

Assess and Reflect

After all groups have completed their performance, use the following self-assessment activity to help students reflect on their performance, identify how they have improved as readers and performers, and determine what they will focus on as they participate in future reader's theater experiences throughout the year.

Draw a three-column reflection chart on chart paper. Include a column for **Reflection Questions** and columns to answer **Yes** or **No** in response. Use the following questions to guide the group's assessment of their performance, or use the Reader's Theater Self-Assessment (BLM 6). Place a check mark in the appropriate column, noting their responses.

- Did we make our reading sound smooth like talking?
- Did we make our characters sound and feel like real people (or animals/objects) with feelings?
- Did we act out our parts with our voices and body language?
- Were our parts at "just right" reading levels?
- Did we practice our reading many times before performing?
- Did we vary the pace of our reading to help our audience understand the characters and message of the script?

Connect and transfer. Discuss ways to improve future performances based on the self-assessment and reflections.

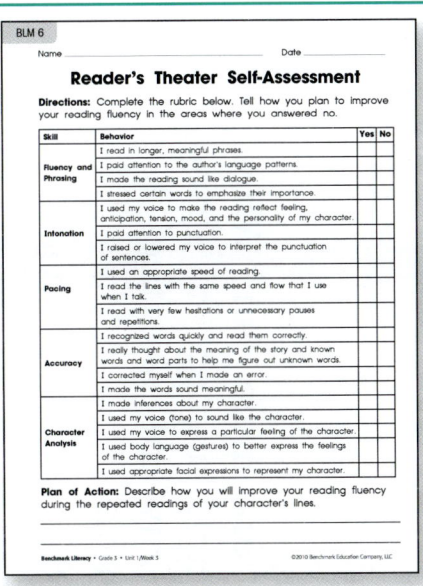

Reader's Theater Self-Assessment (BLM 6)

Make Content Comprehensible for ELLs

Beginning

Allow beginning ELLs to participate as active listeners. Do not overwhelm students with the entire script. Instead, partner students with fluent speakers and let them track print while the partner reads the lines.

Intermediate and Advanced

Pair ELLs with more fluent readers to chorally read their parts in the script.

Assessment Tip

During student performances, record anecdotal notes that focus on how students are developing fluency skills and how they are meeting performer and audience member expectations.

Small-Group Reading Instruction (60 MINUTES)

Use the small-group reading time to continue students' performances of *Harriet Tubman and the Underground Railroad.*

After all groups have performed, use the Assess and Reflect activity above.

Individual Student Conferences (10 MINUTES)

Have students use their self-reflection to show how they would read differently next time. Discuss how students plan to apply what they learned to future performances and independent reading.

Word Study Workshop (20 MINUTES)

Use the Day 5 instruction provided in Grade 3 Word Study Unit 3.

Name _____ Date _____

Speed/Pacing	Pausing	Inflection/Intonation	Phrasing	Expression
Varied				

Cat or Dog?

Cat Lover: Cats are the best pets. They purr so sweetly. I love when my cat licks my hand. It tickles!

Dog Lover: No, it doesn't! A cat's tongue feels like sandpaper. Dogs are the best pets. I love getting a big lick from a dog.

Cat Lover: Yuck! Dog drool! The only thing worse than slobbery drool is stinky dog breath!

Dog Lover: Well, dogs are the most fun. You can teach dogs tricks. My dog can fetch a stick, and roll over and play dead, and—

Cat Lover: —bark at the mailman, chase its tail, and run into the street whenever a fire truck comes by!

Cat Lover: Cats are more fun. When I dangle a piece of string over my cat, she tries to catch it.

Dog Lover: Only if she feels like playing with you. Cats are fickle.

Cat Lover: My cat is not fickle! She always curls up on my lap when I'm reading in my favorite chair.

Dog Lover: My dog is too big to sit on my lap, but he loves to sleep at the foot of my bed.

Cat Lover: That sounds nice. Maybe dogs are the best pets—for you.

Dog Lover: And maybe cats are the best pets—for you!

©2010 Benchmark Education Company, LLC • FLP047

BENCHMARK EDUCATION COMPANY

Name _____ Date _____

Fluency Self-Assessment Master Checklist

	Yes	No
Speed/Pacing		
Did my speed and pacing match the kind of text I was reading?		
Did my speed and pacing match what the character was saying?		
Did I read with a natural talking voice?		
Did I slow my reading down when appropriate?		
Did I pay attention to punctuation?		
Pausing		
Did I pause to keep from running all my words together?		
Did I pause in the correct locations?		
Did I pause for the appropriate length of time?		
Did I pause to help my reading make sense?		
Did I use punctuation to help me figure out when to pause?		
Inflection/Intonation		
Did I make my voice rise at a question mark?		
Did I make my voice fall at a period?		
Did I think about what the author was saying so I would know when to read louder or softer?		
Did I think about what the author was saying so I would know when to stress or emphasize words?		
Phrasing		
Did I notice the phrases?		
Did I read all the words in each phrase together?		
Did I think about what the words in the phrase mean when they are together?		
Expression		
Did I look for clues so I could anticipate the mood of the passage?		
Did I use my tone of voice, facial expressions, and body language to express what the author or characters were thinking or feeling?		
Did I change my reading when something new was about to happen?		
Integration		
Did I read the words right? (accuracy)		
Did I read the words at the right speed? (rate)		
Did I read with expression? (prosody)		
Did my reading sound like talking?		
Did I understand what I read?		

Name _____   Date _____

Gran: Even before then. And without the Underground Railroad, we might not be here today.

Tanya: What do you mean?

Gran: My great-grandpa John was a slave.

3

READER'S THEATER

Tanya: Gran, I need help. I have to give a speech in class about trains.

Gran: I don't know anything about trains.

Tanya: This one is called the Underground Railroad. I never heard of it.

Gran: Tanya, honey, I don't know anything about trains. But I do know about the Underground Railroad! It has nothing to do with trains that run on tracks.

Tanya: Then what kind of railroad is it?

Gran: The Underground Railroad was a secret way for slaves to get free. It went from the South to the North.

Tanya: People in the South had slaves during the Civil War. Back in the 1860s.

2

Benchmark Literacy • Grade 3 • Unit 1/Week 3

©2011 Benchmark Education Company, LLC

Name _____   Date _____

Adjectives That Describe People

Directions: Write words that describe how people look, act, and feel.

People look . . .	People act . . .	People feel . . .

Name _____   Date _____

READER'S THEATER

John: Mack, hear that song Harriet is singing? "When the sun comes back ..." That means when winter ends and spring begins. That's when we leave.

Mack: I get it. And "the drinking gourd" is the Big Dipper, the stars we see in the night sky. The ladle points to the North Star.

John: We follow that star to go north, to freedom.

Gran: John and Mack went north. Harriet Tubman led the way.

Harriet: Along the way, there are safe houses. People help with food and shelter.

Mack: At every stop?

Harriet: No, Mack. Sometimes, we hide ourselves. I know good places.

John: I've never walked so far or so fast. My shoes are in tatters.

Harriet: In two nights' time, we will stop at the shoe shop of Tom Garrett. He is a good man, a friend.

John: Mack and I are a little scared. Are you sure we won't be found?

10

11

Name _____   Date _____

Reader's Theater Self-Assessment

Directions: Complete the rubric below. Tell how you plan to improve your reading fluency in the areas where you answered no.

Skill	Behavior	Yes	No
Fluency and Phrasing	I read in longer, meaningful phrases.		
	I paid attention to the author's language patterns.		
	I made the reading sound like dialogue.		
	I stressed certain words to emphasize their importance.		
Intonation	I used my voice to make the reading reflect feeling, anticipation, tension, mood, and the personality of my character.		
	I paid attention to punctuation.		
	I raised or lowered my voice to interpret the punctuation of sentences.		
Pacing	I used an appropriate speed of reading.		
	I read the lines with the same speed and flow that I use when I talk.		
	I read with very few hesitations or unnecessary pauses and repetitions.		
Accuracy	I recognized words quickly and read them correctly.		
	I really thought about the meaning of the story and known words and word parts to help me figure out unknown words.		
	I corrected myself when I made an error.		
	I made the words sound meaningful.		
Character Analysis	I made inferences about my character.		
	I used my voice (tone) to sound like the character.		
	I used my voice to express a particular feeling of the character.		
	I used body language (gestures) to better express the feelings of the character.		
	I used appropriate facial expressions to represent my character.		

Plan of Action: Describe how you will improve your reading fluency during the repeated readings of your character's lines.

_____

_____

Visualize/Analyze Character

Unit 2/Week 1 at a Glance

Day	Mini-Lessons
ONE	• Introduce the Comprehension Strategy: *Analyze Character* • Think Aloud and Use the Metacognitive Strategy: *Visualize* • Analyze Characters in a Picture • Connect Thinking, Speaking, and Writing • Reflect and Discuss
TWO	• Review the Metacognitive Strategy: *Visualize* • Use the Comprehension Strategy: *Analyze Character* • Connect Thinking, Speaking, and Writing • Reflect and Discuss
THREE	• Extend the Comprehension Strategy: *Analyze Character* • Observe and Prompt for Strategy Understanding • Reflect and Discuss
FOUR	• Read and Summarize • Answer Text-Dependent Comprehension Questions: *Analyze Character (Level 3: Prove It!)* • Reflect and Discuss
FIVE	• Metacognitive Self-Assessment • Constructed Written Response • Ongoing Comprehension Strategy Assessment

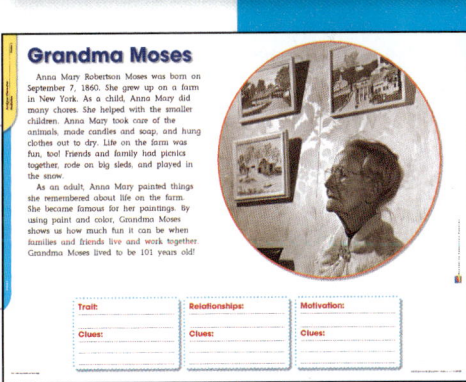

Day One

Can We Keep It?

Comprehension Anchor Poster 1

Lesson Objectives

Students will:

- Analyze characters' traits, feelings, and relationships based on a picture.
- Identify details that support the analysis.
- Visualize characters' actions and feelings based on a picture.
- Use academic sentence frames to discuss strategies.

Related Resources

- Home/School Connections (BLM 1)
- BenchmarkUniverse.com

About the Strategy

- Analyzing a character means figuring out the character's traits, feelings, and relationships.
- Characters' words and actions show their traits, feelings, and relationships.
- Analyzing characters helps readers understand a text.

⏱ Read-Aloud (10 MINUTES)

Select a favorite fiction read-aloud from your classroom or school library with which to model the metacognitive strategy "Visualize." Use the sample read-aloud lessons and suggested titles in the Getting Started Guide.

⏱ Mini-Lessons (20 MINUTES)

Introduce the Comprehension Strategy: Analyze Character

Say: *Fictional stories are about animal or people characters. Biographies and autobiographies are about people. When I read about both fictional characters and real people, I think about the character traits and feelings they show. Thinking about the characters in this way helps me understand what I am reading.*

Ask: *What are some ways you can figure out the traits and feelings of fictional and real characters?*

Turn and talk. Ask students to turn to their partner and share at least three ways they can figure out the traits and feelings of real and fictional characters. Ask a few students to share with the whole group.

Explain: *We can figure out real people's traits and feelings by what the people say and do. We can also figure out people's traits and feelings by the relationships they have with others. We can figure out the traits and feelings of characters in stories in the same way. Good readers analyze what characters do and say to figure out their traits and feelings. We're going to practice analyzing characters this week.*

Think Aloud and Use the Metacognitive Strategy: Visualize

Display Poster 1.

Draw students' attention to the boys and girls and the cat. (Whiteboard users can use the highlighter tool.)

Explain: *When I look at this picture, the first thing I need to do is figure out what it's trying to show me about the boys and girls. One way I can do that is by visualizing. I imagine what the characters are thinking and feeling by visualizing what they say and do. Let me show you how I do it.*

Think aloud: *The picture shows boys and girls with a cat. I can visualize the children finding the cat and liking it and then asking their parents if they can keep it. Visualizing what the children have done and will do next helps me understand more about the characters of the boys and girls.*

Write your visualization on chart paper. Ask students to generate other visualizations they could make about what the children have done and will do, and add these to your list. Explore the visualizations together.

Post these visualizations on the wall as a Visualize anchor chart, or invite students to write them in their reading journals or notebooks to use in the future.

Analyze Characters in a Picture

Ask students what traits and feelings the characters in the poster have. Point out that the title of the poster, "Can We Keep It?" tells them something about what the characters are like.

Ask students to tell which details in the illustration helped them visualize the characters' traits and feelings. Remind them that details tell what the characters are saying and doing.

Provide the following academic sentence frames to support ELLs and struggling students:

> The characters' feelings are _____.
> The characters' traits are _____.
> Clues that help me identify the characters' feelings and traits are _____.

Connect Thinking, Speaking, and Writing

Write down the character traits and feelings students identify and reread them as a group. Then write the details they found that support the analysis. Give students the opportunity to expand on their shared writing.

Reflect and Discuss

Ask and discuss the following questions:
- *Why is it important to analyze characters? How does this help you?*
- *How did visualizing help you understand the picture?*
- *How does recognizing their feelings and traits help you analyze the characters?*

Connect and transfer. Say: *Remember, you can analyze characters in a text, too. Tomorrow, we will practice analyzing characters in a text.*

Make Content Comprehensible for ELLs

Use the following strategies to help ELLs understand the poster content and acquire academic language.

Beginning
Read the title of the poster. Demonstrate the concept of having a pet by role-playing taking care of a pet. For example, **say:**

Dogs and cats are pets. We can feel their soft fur. (Role-play stroking a cat.)

We must care for pets. We feed them and play with them. (Role-play caring for a cat or dog.)

Point to and name people and animals in the picture: boys, girls, cat.

Beginning and Intermediate
Draw and label, or ask ELLs to draw, other pets they have seen.

All Levels
Model the use of academic sentence frames to support ELLs' academic vocabulary and language development. (See suggested sentence frames provided.)

Comprehension Quick-Check

Observe whether students are able to articulate analyzing character in the poster. If they have difficulty, use the following additional explicit instruction.

Draw the analyze character graphic organizer on chart paper.

Under Trait, write *caring*.

Say: *I think the boys and girls in the poster are caring people.*

Under Clues, write *They like the cat and are being kind to it.*

Say: *I looked at the picture, and I identified a character trait of the people in the picture.*

Say: *Now you identify another trait of the people in the picture.*

Support Special Needs Learners

Support visual learners and students with attention issues by projecting the whiteboard version of the posters. Allow students to come to the whiteboard and circle, underline, or highlight the characters in the illustration. Invite them to discuss actions or traits of the characters.

Access the graphic organizer provided on the whiteboard. Record character traits with students.

Provide opportunities for active involvement. For example, assign students the roles of each person pictured in the poster and let them describe the characters' thoughts and feelings.

Access the image bank for enlarged images that students can use to practice visualizing, analyzing character, and describing traits and feelings.

Home/School Connections

On Day 1, distribute copies of Home/School Connections (BLM 1). Each day during the week, assign one of the six home/school connection activities for the students to complete. Ask them to bring their completed assignments to class the following day. Make time at the beginning of each day for students to share their ideas.

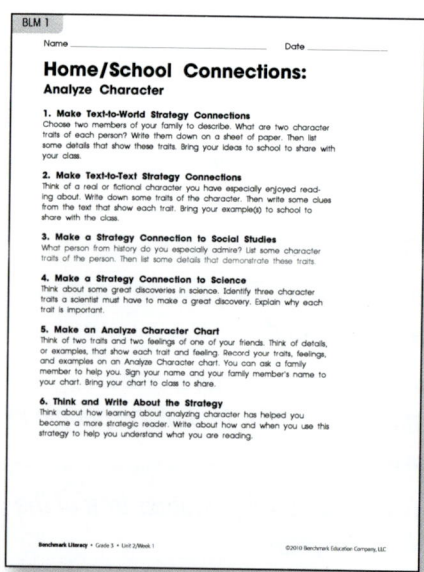

Home/School Connections (BLM 1)

Small-Group Reading Instruction (60 MINUTES)

Based on students' instructional reading levels, select titles that provide opportunities for students to practice analyzing characters. See the Leveled Text Titles chart provided at the back of this Teacher's Resource System.

Use the before-, during-, and after-reading instruction provided in the Teacher's Guide for each text.

Individual Student Conferences (10 MINUTES)

Confer with individual students on their text selections and applications of strategies. Use the Individual Reading Conference Form on page 32 of Informal Assessments for Reading Development to help guide your conferences.

Word Study Workshop (20 MINUTES)

Use the Day 1 instruction provided in Word Study Unit 4.

Read-Aloud (10 MINUTES)

Select a favorite fiction read-aloud from your classroom or school library with which to model the metacognitive strategy "Visualize." Use the sample read-aloud lessons and suggested titles in the Getting Started Guide.

 ## Mini-Lessons (20 MINUTES)

Review the Metacognitive Strategy: Visualize

Display Poster 2 with annotations hidden and/or distribute BLM 2 and read aloud the title.

Read aloud the text with students.

Explain: *Yesterday when I looked at the "Can We Keep It?" poster, I visualized the characters' actions to help me understand their traits and feelings. When I visualize, I imagine what a character is like, and I also think about what I would do and how I would feel if I were the character. I'll show you how I do this.*

Reread the first two sentences of the first paragraph. **Think aloud:** *In these sentences, I find out that Roy lives on a farm and likes helping his parents with chores. I visualize Roy as a strong, healthy boy because he works hard and spends a lot of time outdoors. I also imagine that he is a good son because he helps his parents.*

Reread the first sentence of the third paragraph. **Think aloud:** *In this sentence, Roy says he does not have ten dollars to sign up for the football team. I can imagine how I would feel if this happened to me. I would want to get ten dollars. I would think about how I could do that. I visualize Roy having these feelings.*

Build academic oral language. Reread the last paragraph. Encourage students to visualize the feelings of the two characters and to tell about the details that support their analysis. Invite students to describe how visualizing helped them identify the characters' traits, feelings, and relationships. Reinforce the idea that good readers visualize to understand text better. Support ELLs and struggling readers with the following sentence frames:

Roy's traits are _____.
Roy's parents' traits are _____.
Visualizing helped me _____.

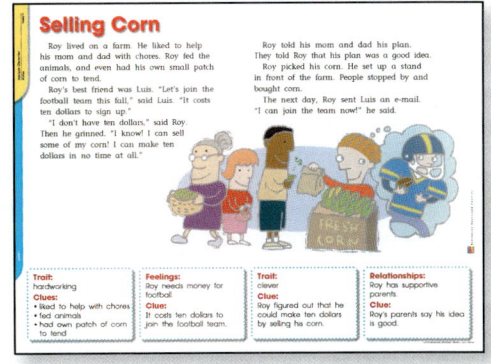

Comprehension Anchor Poster 2 (BLM 2)

Lesson Objectives

Students will:

- Identify the traits, feelings, and relationships of a main character in a fictional passage.
- Identify clues that show the character's traits, feelings, and relationships.
- Visualize to understand a text.
- Use academic sentence frames to discuss strategies.

Related Resources

- Home/School Connections (BLM 1)
- Comprehension Anchor Poster 2 (BLM 2)
- BenchmarkUniverse.com

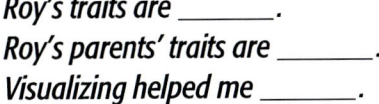

Trait: hardworking

Clues:
• liked to help with chores
• fed animals
• had own patch of corn to tend

Feelings:
Roy needs money for football.

Clue:
It costs ten dollars to join the football team.

Trait: clever

Clue:
Roy figured out that he could make ten dollars by selling his corn.

Relationships:
Roy has supportive parents.

Clue:
Roy's parents say his idea is good.

Comprehension Anchor Poster 2
Sample Annotations

Make Content Comprehensible for ELLs

Use the following strategies to help ELLs understand the poster content and acquire academic language.

Beginning
Read aloud the poster title and passage. Point to what each person is doing as you state the action (selling corn, buying corn, playing football).

Beginning and Intermediate
Ask students to find objects in the classroom that they can pretend to buy and sell and to role-play buying and selling them, using words for each item.

If you have students whose first language is Spanish, share these English/Spanish cognates: **animals/los animales, plan/el plan.**

All Levels
Pair ELLs with fluent English speakers during partner discussions and activities.

Use the Comprehension Strategy: Analyze Character

Reread the poster text with students, annotations still hidden.

Say: *Now think about Roy's character traits. What trait is shown in the first paragraph?*

If necessary, explain that the passage shows that Roy is hardworking. The author provides specific clues, or details, that show this part of his character.

Say: *Let's look closely to find the clues that tell what Roy's character is like. What clues show that he is hardworking?*

Write the details that students identify. Then reveal the first Trait annotation. **Ask:** *Did we find the clues? Let's compare them.*

Build academic oral language. Say: *Authors give clues about a character's feelings as well. Let's think about clues in this passage that show Roy's feelings. What clue in the first part of the story shows how Roy feels?* (It costs ten dollars to join the football team.) *How do you think this makes Roy feel?* (unhappy not to have ten dollars; anxious to find a way to get ten dollars) *How does knowing Roy's traits and feelings help you better understand the story?* (It helps you predict how Roy will solve his problem.)

Connect Thinking, Speaking, and Writing

Prompt students to identify other clues that show Roy's traits, feelings, and relationships. Students should understand that these aspects of Roy's character affect what happens in the story.

Record students' clues on chart paper. Then reveal the second Trait and the Relationships annotations.

Say: *Let's compare our clues list to the list on the poster.* Allow time for discussion.

Reflect and Discuss

Ask and discuss the following questions:
- *How does visualizing characters in the text help you as a reader?*
- *How does analyzing characters help you understand what you are reading?*
- *How do clues help you analyze characters?*

Connect and transfer: *How will you use what we have practiced today when you read on your own?*

Small-Group Reading Instruction (60 MINUTES)

Based on students' instructional reading levels, select titles that provide opportunities for students to practice analyzing characters. See the Leveled Text Titles chart provided at the back of this Teacher's Resource System.

Use the before-, during-, and after-reading instruction provided in the Teacher's Guide for each text.

Individual Student Conferences (10 MINUTES)

Confer with individual students on their text selections and applications of strategies. Use the Individual Reading Conference Form on page 32 of Informal Assessments for Reading Development to help guide your conferences.

Word Study Workshop (20 MINUTES)

Use the Day 2 instruction provided in Word Study Unit 4.

Comprehension Quick-Check

Take note of which students can or cannot contribute to the discussion of the Poster 2 character traits, feelings, and relationships, and their clues. Use the following activity to provide additional explicit instruction for these students.

Use an additional real world example to help students understand character traits and how to identify them. For example: The woman climbed mountains. She went diving deep in the ocean. She parachuted from an airplane. The woman was adventurous. Record the character trait and clues on a graphic organizer. Then write them as a paragraph. Ask students to underline each clue and circle the character trait.

Oral Language Extension

During independent workstation time, pair students to describe the traits of real and fictional characters they have read about in class. Partner A names a character and provides at least two details that reflect the character's traits and/or feelings. Partner B identifies the traits and/or feelings shown by the details. Then partners switch roles. Tell students to be ready to report on their character traits and clues during individual conference time.

Home/School Connections

At the beginning of the day, make time for students to share their ideas based on the activity they completed the previous night.

At the end of the day, ask students to complete another home/school connection activity from BLM 1 and bring their assignment to class the following day.

Day Three

Comprehension Anchor Poster 3 (BLM 3)

Lesson Objectives

Students will:

- Identify the traits, relationships, and motivation of a person in a nonfiction text.

- Identify clues that show the person's traits, relationships, and motivation.

- Visualize to understand a text.

- Use academic sentence frames to discuss strategies.

Related Resources

- Home/School Connections (BLM 1)

- Comprehension Anchor Poster 3 (BLM 3)

- BenchmarkUniverse.com

Comprehension Quick-Check

The responsive prompts on pages 8–9 are designed to help you meet the needs of individual students. Based on your observations, identify students who may need additional explicit reinforcement of the strategy during small-group instruction or intervention time. Use similar responsive prompts during small-group instruction to scaffold students toward independent use of the strategy.

Read-Aloud (10 MINUTES)

Select a favorite nonfiction read-aloud from your classroom or school library with which to model the metacognitive strategy "Visualize." Use the sample read-aloud lessons and suggested titles in the Getting Started Guide.

Mini-Lessons (20 MINUTES)

Extend the Comprehension Strategy: Analyze Character

Display Poster 3 and/or distribute BLM 3 and read aloud the title.

Say: *Today you're going to practice reading and analyzing characters in a text. Remember to use what you've learned. You can visualize details in the text to help you understand.*

Based on students' needs and abilities, ask them to read the passage independently or with a partner. Tell them to locate and write a trait and clues in the Trait box, relationships and clues in the Relationships box, and motivation and clues in the Motivation box. Students should feel free to underline, circle, or flag key information as they read.

Invite individual students or partners to share the traits, relationships, motivations, and clues they identified. Record students' findings on the poster or on chart paper. See the sample annotations.

Observe and Prompt for Strategy Understanding

While using the poster, note students who demonstrate understanding of the concepts and those who seem to struggle. Use appropriate responsive prompting to help students who need modeling or additional guidance, or to validate students who demonstrate mastery.

Goal Oriented
- *I am going to read slowly and reread if necessary to find clues.*
- *I am going to use clues in the text and what I know to identify character traits.*
- *The clue word(s) _____ show that the character is _____.*

Directive and Corrective Feedback
- *What other sentences contain clues to the person's character?*
- *Which details are clues to the person's character? How can you tell?*
- *What do the clues tell you about the character?*

Self-Monitoring and Reflection
- *What could you do to figure out a character's motivation?*
- *What visualizations would help you understand the character better?*
- *How does reading about what a character does show what the character is like?*

Validating and Confirming
- *Great job identifying the character's traits and motivation!*
- *You found all the clues that show the character's traits and motivation.*
- *I like the way you visualized to clarify your understanding of the character.*

Reflect and Discuss

Ask and discuss the following questions:
- *What kinds of texts have you read that include clues to characters' traits?*
- *Do fictional stories have clues about characters' traits? Explain.*
- *What kinds of nonfiction texts have clues about characters' traits?*

Connect and transfer. Say: *Remember that both fiction stories and nonfiction texts that tell about real people have clues about the characters' traits and motivation. Look for the clues to the characters' traits and motivation today when you read in small groups. Visualize to help you analyze what the characters are like.*

Small-Group Reading Instruction (60 MINUTES)

Based on students' instructional reading levels, select titles that provide opportunities for students to practice analyzing characters. See the Leveled Text Titles chart provided at the back of this Teacher's Resource System.

Use the before-, during-, and after-reading instruction provided in the Teacher's Guide for each text.

Individual Student Conferences (10 MINUTES)

Confer with individual students on their text selections and applications of strategies. Use the Individual Reading Conference Form on page 32 of Informal Assessments for Reading Development to help guide your conferences.

Word Study Workshop (20 MINUTES)

Use the Day 3 instruction provided in Word Study Unit 4.

Trait: fun-loving
Clues:
- had picnics
- rode on sleds
- played in the snow

Relationships:
Grandma Moses had a close family.
Clues:
Family members enjoyed living and working together.
Motivation:
Grandma Moses wanted to recall and illustrate her childhood.
Clues:
As an adult, she painted things she remembered about life on the farm.

Comprehension Anchor Poster 3 Sample Annotations

Make Content Comprehensible for ELLs

Use the following strategies to help ELLs understand the poster content and acquire academic language.

Beginning
Point to the poster and provide language for what you see. Invite ELLs to point to and name people and objects with you.

Intermediate
Describe the poster content in simple language. For example, "This woman was an artist. She painted pictures." Encourage students to offer their own descriptions.

Beginning and Intermediate
If you have students whose first language is Spanish, share these English/Spanish cognates: **September/septiembre, animals/los animales, family/la familia, picnic/el picnic, adult/el adulto.**

Home/School Connections

Ask students to complete another activity from BLM 1 and bring it to class the next day.

Day Four

Comprehension Anchor Poster 4 (BLM 4)

Lesson Objectives

Students will:

- Learn strategies for analyzing questions and finding answers, clues, and evidence.

- Analyze characters in a text.

- Answer text-dependent questions about characters in a text.

- Use academic vocabulary to discuss strategies.

Related Resources

- Home/School Connections (BLM 1)

- Comprehension Anchor Poster 4 (BLM 4)

- Comprehension Questions (BLM 5)

- BenchmarkUniverse.com

Read-Aloud (10 MINUTES)

Select a favorite nonfiction read-aloud from your classroom or school library with which to model the metacognitive strategy "Visualize." Use the sample read-aloud lessons and suggested titles in the Getting Started Guide.

Mini-Lessons (20 MINUTES)

Read and Summarize

Display Poster 4 and/or distribute BLM 4.

Based on the needs and abilities of your students, ask them to read the passage independently or with a partner. Remind students to visualize to help them understand what they read.

Build academic oral language. When students have finished, ask individuals or pairs to tell about the traits and motivation of the main character. Encourage ELLs or struggling readers to use the following academic sentence frames:

> *The character is _____. His motivation is _____.*

Answer Text-Dependent Comprehension Questions: Analyze Character (Level 3: Prove It!)

Say: *Sometimes you need to answer questions about a passage you've read. Some questions require you to analyze a character. Today we're going to read and answer questions. Some of the questions will ask you to analyze a character.*

Distribute BLM 5 and read Question 2 together. ("Which clues show that B.A. Kidd is intelligent?")

Ask: *What is the question asking us to do?* If students can't tell you, **ask:** *Is it asking us to compare? Is it asking us to summarize? What strategy will we need?* (analyze character) *How do you know?* (The question asks how a character shows a particular character trait.)

Say: *To prove that the character has this trait, I will have to look for clues in the text. The clues can include things the character says and does and things other characters say about him.*

Say: *Now we're ready to reread the passage to find the information we need. We know we need to find clues that show the character, B.A., is intelligent. I read what the TV reporter says about him, "B.A. Kidd is the first ten-year-old ever elected to Congress." I think that shows he must be smart. In the same paragraph, B.A. says he wants to make laws that are tough on polluters. Then he says he wants to make laws to encourage world peace. I think he is smart to understand that these laws are needed. I have found three clues that show B.A. is smart or intelligent. The clues were in the text, but I had to find them and put them together to get the answer. Answer A includes two of these clues. So I'll choose A.*

Ask students to work independently or with a partner to answer additional text-dependent questions on BLM 5.

Review students' answers and use the poster as needed to model analyzing questions and rereading to find clues and evidence in the text to prove the answers.

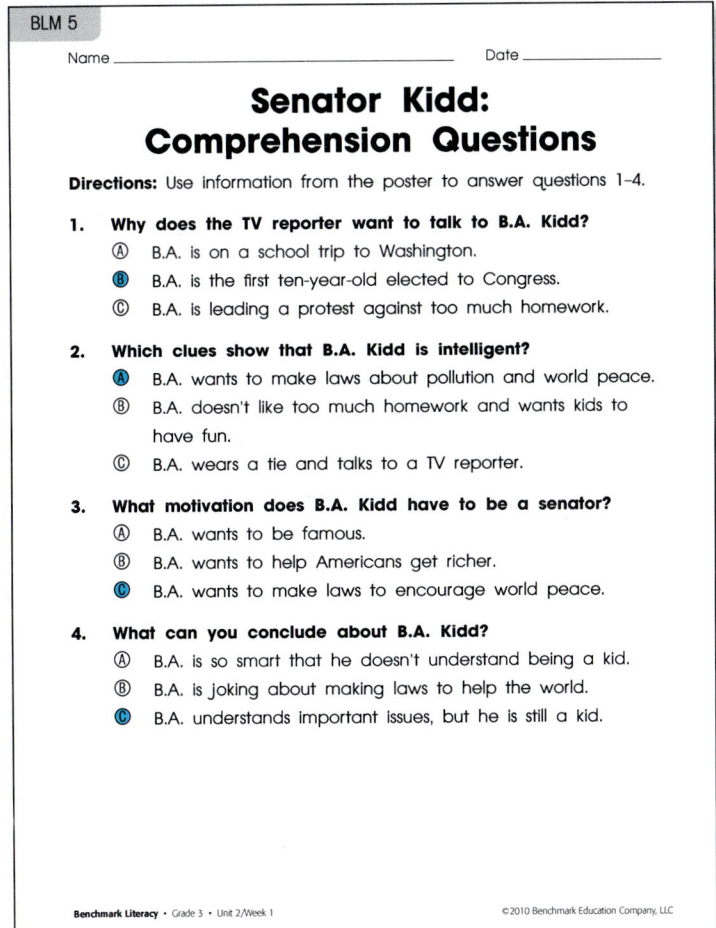

Comprehension Questions (BLM 5)

Trait:
ambitious

Clues:
- first ten year old elected to Congress
- wants to introduce many new laws

Motivation:
to improve the world

Clues:
- wants to make laws that are tough on polluters
- wants to make laws to encourage world peace

Comprehension Anchor Poster 4
Sample Annotations

Make Content Comprehensible for ELLs

Use the following strategies to help ELLs understand the poster content and acquire academic language.

Beginning
Support the concept of a senator by pointing to the photograph of the Capitol and explaining that people vote for senators, who make laws for the country.

Beginning and Intermediate
Point to the poster photo and illustration and **say:** *A senator makes laws in Washington, D.C.*

Use photographs of officials such as the President, senators, and representatives in Washington to show the meaning of *senator*. Encourage students to use the following sentence frame:

A senator works to _____ to talk about these photos.

If you have students whose first language is Spanish, share these academic English/Spanish cognates: **reporter/la reportera, camera/la cámara, laws/las leyes, peace/la paz, investigate/investigar, injustice/la injusticia.**

Comprehension Quick-Check

Note whether students are able to analyze each Level 3 text-dependent comprehension question and return to the text to find the information they need to answer the question correctly. If students have difficulty, use small-group reading time for additional practice answering these kinds of questions, which appear on standardized reading assessments. The Comprehension Question Card for each leveled text provides practice questions at four levels of comprehension. The Comprehension Through Deductive Reasoning Flip Chart helps you model the strategies students need to master.

Oral Language Extension

Display Comprehension Anchor Poster 4 during independent workstation time. Invite pairs of students to read and talk about the poster together. Encourage students to generate a list of other elected officials and to discuss the character traits and motivations of people who run for office. Remind students to be prepared to share their lists and character analyses during independent conference time.

Home/School Connections

At the beginning of the day, make time for students to share their ideas based on the activity they completed the previous night.

At the end of the day, ask students to complete another home/school connection activity from BLM 1 and bring their assignment to class the following day.

Reflect and Discuss the Comprehension Strategy

Ask and discuss the following:
- *What strategy did we use to answer questions about the text?*
- *Notice how we analyzed characters' traits to understand and answer questions.*

Connect and transfer. Say: *Practice analyzing characters. This strategy can help you better understand both fiction and nonfiction texts. It can also help you when you take tests.*

Small-Group Reading Instruction (60 MINUTES)

Based on students' instructional reading levels, select titles that provide opportunities for students to practice analyzing characters. See the Leveled Text Titles chart provided at the back of this Teacher's Resource System.

Use the before-, during-, and after-reading instruction provided in the Teacher's Guide for each text.

Use the Comprehension Question Card for each title and the Comprehension Through Deductive Reasoning Flip Chart to practice answering Level 3 text-dependent comprehension questions.

Individual Student Conferences (10 MINUTES)

Confer with individual students on their text selections and applications of strategies. Use the Individual Reading Conference Form on page 32 of Informal Assessments for Reading Development to help guide your conferences.

Word Study Workshop (20 MINUTES)

Use the Day 4 instruction provided in Word Study Unit 4.

Read-Aloud (10 MINUTES)

Revisit the week's read-alouds to make text-to-text connections and provide opportunities for reader response. Use the suggested activities in the Getting Started Guide, or implement ideas of your own.

Assessment (20 MINUTES)

Metacognitive Self-Assessment

Ask students to reflect on their use of metacognitive and comprehension strategies this week. What did they learn? How will they use the strategies in the future? What do they still need to practice, and how can they do this?

Invite students to share their reflections in one of the following ways: conduct a whole-class discussion; ask students to turn and talk to a partner and then share their ideas with the class; or ask students to record their thoughts in their journals or notebooks.

Constructed Written Response

Distribute copies of Constructed Written Response (BLM 6) and ask students to think about a friend or family member. In the Trait column, have them identify at least two character traits of the person. In the Clues column, students can note actions that illustrate each trait.

Work with students individually. Ask them to write a character analysis of their friend or family member, using notes from the graphic organizer. If students need extra help, prompt them with their notes as they write their paragraphs.

Read aloud the checklist at the bottom of BLM 6 to help students evaluate their work.

Challenge activity. Students who are able to may also write a fictional story about the person that includes events that show the person's traits, using notes from the graphic organizer.

Support activity. If students cannot identify a person's character traits and character trait clues, encourage them to tell you about the person. They can use the sentence frame: _____ *is special because* _____. Reinforce the fact that these details are clues to character traits.

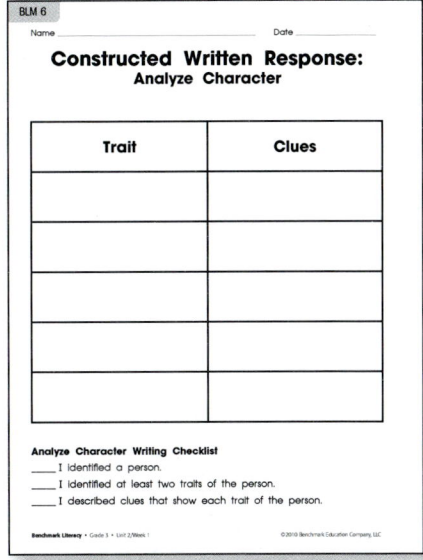

Constructed Written Response (BLM 6)

Lesson Objectives

Students will:

• Reflect orally on their strategy use.

• Create an analyze character graphic organizer and write a paragraph based on it.

• Answer multiple-choice and short-answer questions.

Related Resources

• Home/School Connections (BLM 1)

• Constructed Written Response (BLM 6)

• Comprehension Strategy Assessments, Grade 3

• BenchmarkUniverse.com

Make Assessments Accessible for ELLs

Use the following strategies to help ELLs demonstrate their understanding of the strategies.

Beginning
Use Constructed Written Response (BLM 6) with ELLs at the beginning proficiency level.

Beginning and Intermediate
Use the Comprehension Strategy Assessment as a listening comprehension assessment and scaffold students' understanding of the text. As an alternative, allow students to tell you about the characters' traits and motivations in one of the Comprehension Anchor Posters you have used during the week.

Intermediate and Advanced
Support ELLs with academic sentence frames during the metacognitive self-assessment. Possible sentence frames to use are:

We visualize characters so that _____.

I will think about characters' traits and motivations when I _____.

Pair ELLs with fluent English speakers during partner discussions and activities.

Home/School Connections

At the beginning of the day, make time for students to share their ideas based on the activity they completed the previous night.

Ongoing Comprehension Strategy Assessment

Distribute one of the Analyze Character Comprehension Strategy Assessments from the Grade 3 Comprehension Strategy Assessment book ("First on the Courts," pages 38–39, or "The Contest," pages 40–41). Ask students to read the passage and use the information to answer the questions.

Use the results of this assessment to determine students who need additional work with the strategy.

Record students' assessment scores on the Strategy Assessment Record (page 133) so that you can monitor their progress following additional instruction or intervention.

Provide additional modeling and guided practice during small-group reading instruction using the recommended titles in this Teacher's Guide.

 ## Small-Group Reading Instruction (60 MINUTES)

Based on students' instructional reading levels, select titles that provide opportunities for students to practice analyzing characters. See the Leveled Text Titles chart provided at the back of this Teacher's Resource System.

Use the before-, during-, and after-reading instruction provided in the Teacher's Guide for each text.

 ## Individual Student Conferences (10 MINUTES)

Confer with individual students on their text selections and applications of strategies. Use the Individual Reading Conference Form on page 32 of Informal Assessments for Reading Development to help guide your conferences.

Word Study Workshop (20 MINUTES)

Use the Day 5 instruction provided in Word Study Unit 4.

Name _____ Date _____

Home/School Connections:
Analyze Character

1. Make Text-to-World Strategy Connections
Choose two members of your family to describe. What are two character traits of each person? Write them down on a sheet of paper. Then list some details that show these traits. Bring your ideas to school to share with your class.

2. Make Text-to-Text Strategy Connections
Think of a real or fictional character you have especially enjoyed reading about. Write down some traits of the character. Then write some clues from the text that show each trait. Bring your example(s) to school to share with the class.

3. Make a Strategy Connection to Social Studies
What person from history do you especially admire? List some character traits of the person. Then list some details that demonstrate these traits.

4. Make a Strategy Connection to Science
Think about some great discoveries in science. Identify three character traits a scientist must have to make a great discovery. Explain why each trait is important.

5. Make an Analyze Character Chart
Think of two traits and two feelings of one of your friends. Think of details, or examples, that show each trait and feeling. Record your traits, feelings, and examples on an Analyze Character chart. You can ask a family member to help you. Sign your name and your family member's name to your chart. Bring your chart to class to share.

6. Think and Write About the Strategy
Think about how learning about analyzing character has helped you become a more strategic reader. Write about how and when you use this strategy to help you understand what you are reading.

Name _____ Date _____

Selling Corn

Roy lived on a farm. He liked to help his mom and dad with chores. Roy fed the animals, and even had his own small patch of corn to tend.

Roy's best friend was Luis. "Let's join the football team this fall," said Luis. "It costs ten dollars to sign up."

"I don't have ten dollars," said Roy. Then he grinned. "I know! I can sell some of my corn! I can make ten dollars in no time at all."

Roy told his mom and dad his plan. They told Roy that his plan was a good idea. Roy picked his corn. He set up a stand in front of the farm. People stopped by and bought corn.

The next day, Roy sent Luis an e-mail. "I can join the team now!" he said.

FRESH CORN

Trait:

Clues:

Feelings:

Clue:

Trait:

Clue:

Relationships:

Clue:

Analyze Character
Fiction
Poster 2

Grade 3

BENCHMARK EDUCATION COMPANY

©2011 Benchmark Education Company, LLC

©2010 Benchmark Education Company, LLC • CAP068

Name _____   Date _____

Grandma Moses

Anna Mary Robertson Moses was born on September 7, 1860. She grew up on a farm in New York. As a child, Anna Mary did many chores. She helped with the smaller children. Anna Mary took care of the animals, made candles and soap, and hung clothes out to dry. Life on the farm was fun, too! Friends and family had picnics together, rode on big sleds, and played in the snow.

As an adult, Anna Mary painted things she remembered about life on the farm. She became famous for her paintings. By using paint and color, Grandma Moses shows us how much fun it can be when families and friends live and work together. Grandma Moses lived to be 101 years old!

Motivation:
_____
_____
_____

Clues:
_____
_____

Relationships:
_____
_____
_____

Clues:
_____
_____

Trait:
_____
_____
_____

Clues:
_____
_____

Analyze Character
Nonfiction
Poster 3

Grade 3

BENCHMARK EDUCATION COMPANY

Name _____ Date _____

Senator Kidd

The TV reporter smiled into the camera. "I'm standing on the steps of the Capitol Building with Senator B.A. Kidd. Senator Kidd is the first ten year old ever elected to Congress. What new bills do you hope to introduce, Senator Kidd?"

Senator Kidd adjusted his tie. "I want to make sure we still have a country when I grow up," he said. "I want to make laws that are tough on polluters. I want to make laws that encourage world peace."

"Admirable!" said the reporter. "What else do you hope to accomplish?"

"I plan to form a committee to investigate a big injustice in our country," replied Senator Kidd. "The amount of homework some teachers give is a crime! Teachers used to be kids. They should know we need more time for fun!"

BENCHMARK EDUCATION COMPANY

©2010 Benchmark Education Company, LLC • CAP069

Analyze Character
Fiction
Poster 4

Grade 3

Name _____ Date _____

Senator Kidd:
Comprehension Questions

Directions: Use information from the poster to answer questions 1–4.

1. **Why does the TV reporter want to talk to B.A. Kidd?**

   Ⓐ B.A. is on a school trip to Washington.

   Ⓑ B.A. is the first ten-year-old elected to Congress.

   Ⓒ B.A. is leading a protest against too much homework.

2. **Which clues show that B.A. Kidd is intelligent?**

   Ⓐ B.A. wants to make laws about pollution and world peace.

   Ⓑ B.A. doesn't like too much homework and wants kids to have fun.

   Ⓒ B.A. wears a tie and talks to a TV reporter.

3. **What motivation does B.A. Kidd have to be a senator?**

   Ⓐ B.A. wants to be famous.

   Ⓑ B.A. wants to help Americans get richer.

   Ⓒ B.A. wants to make laws to encourage world peace.

4. **What can you conclude about B.A. Kidd?**

   Ⓐ B.A. is so smart that he doesn't understand being a kid.

   Ⓑ B.A. is joking about making laws to help the world.

   Ⓒ B.A. understands important issues, but he is still a kid.

Name _____   Date _____

Constructed Written Response:
Analyze Character

Trait	Clues

Analyze Character Writing Checklist

_____ I identified a person.

_____ I identified at least two traits of the person.

_____ I described clues that show each trait of the person.

Teacher's Guide | Grade 3 • Unit 2

Week 2

Visualize/Analyze Character

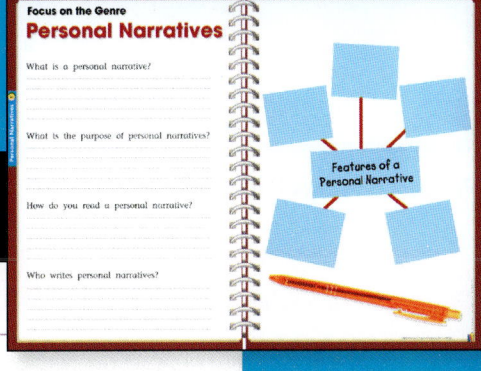

Unit 2/Week 2 at a Glance

Day	Mini-Lessons
ONE	• Build Genre Background • Introduce the Genre: *Personal Narrative* • Focus on Genre Features: *Personal Narrative*
TWO	• Model Metacognitive Strategies: *Visualize* • Introduce Analyze Character • Focus on Genre Features: *Personal Narrative*
THREE	• Visualize to Analyze Character
FOUR	• Build Comprehension: *Make Inferences (About Character)* • Build Tier Two Vocabulary: *Emotion Words*
FIVE	• Synthesize and Assess Genre Understanding • Make Connections Across Texts

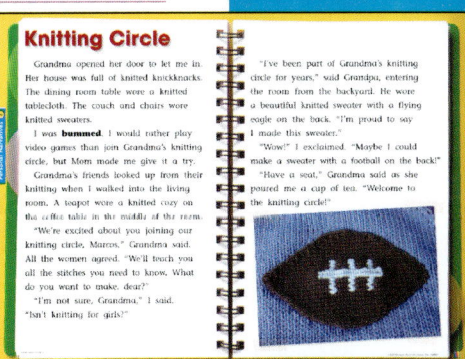

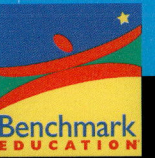

Day One

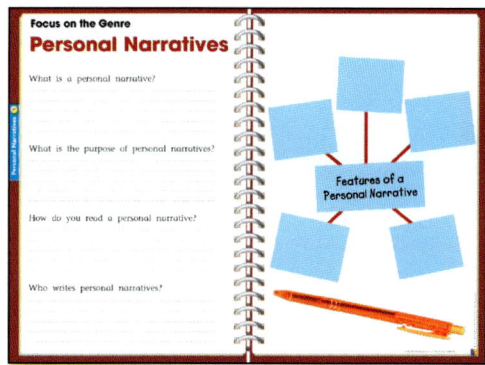

Personal Narrative Poster 1

Read-Aloud (10 MINUTES)

Select a favorite fiction read-aloud from your classroom or school library with which to model the metacognitive strategy "Visualize." Use the sample read-aloud lessons and suggested titles in the Getting Started Guide.

Mini-Lessons (20 MINUTES)

Build Genre Background

Write the word **genre** on chart paper. **Ask:** *Who remembers and can tell me what the word **genre** means?* Allow responses.

Review: *The word **genre** means "a kind of something." Things are grouped in genres because they are all alike in some ways. For example, some people like to play video games that are races. Other people like to play games in which they solve puzzles. Racing games and puzzle games are genres of video games. All racing games share some of the same features. All puzzle games share some of the same features.*

Say: *As readers and writers, we use our knowledge of genres to help us understand text. When we recognize the genre, we can predict what features the text will have. We can predict how it will be presented. As writers, we use our knowledge of genre to help us choose a way to present our ideas.*

Ask: *What are some literary genres you have studied and read in the past? Let's make a chart of genres and their features. What features do you remember about each genre?* Allow responses. Post the list on the classroom wall as an anchor chart.

Introduce the Genre: Personal Narrative

Display Genre Workshop Poster 1 and distribute BLM 1.

Say: *This week we are going to focus on the personal narrative genre. You will read personal narratives in our small reading groups, and you can select other titles from this genre to read independently, too. Let's spend some time thinking about this genre and create our own Personal Narrative anchor chart to record what we already know about personal narratives. Later in the week, we can come back to our chart and reflect on how our understanding of the genre has changed and expanded.*

Display Poster 1 on an easel or use the interactive whiteboard version. You may also make a transparency from BLM 1. Show students several personal narratives from your classroom or school library and ask students to share any personal narratives they have read previously.

Read each question on Poster 1 and encourage volunteers to share ideas they have related to the question. Based on students' prior knowledge, provide additional genre background information as needed to fill in the answers to each question. This poster can serve as an anchor chart that you and students can refer to throughout the week as you read and analyze personal narratives.

Support the academic language development of ELLs and struggling readers by providing the following sentence frames to use as they discuss the genre:
    A personal narrative tells about _____.
    The purpose of a personal narrative is _____.
    A personal narrative usually includes _____.
    People who write personal narratives are _____.

Make Content Comprehensible for ELLs

Beginning and Intermediate
Show various personal narratives from your classroom or school library. Flip through the stories with students. Use simple language to explain that a personal narrative is one person's story about something that happened. For example, **say:** *In a personal narrative, one person writes about something that happened to him or her. Look at this personal narrative. This personal narrative tells about _____.*

All Levels
Model the academic sentence frames provided in this guide to help ELLs contribute their ideas to the discussion of personal narratives.

Support Special Needs Learners

Throughout the week, use these strategies to help students who have learning disabilities access the content and focus on genre studies and comprehension strategies.

Support students by projecting the posters on a whiteboard. Allow students to come to the whiteboard and circle, underline, or highlight features of the genre. Invite them to label what they see on the posters.

Provide opportunities for active involvement. For example, to understand how personal narratives reveal character, allow students to take the role of the subject in a personal narrative and use details from the text to role-play their characters.

Provide repeated opportunities for students to analyze the features of personal narratives. Find features of personal narratives in text examples from read-alouds, small-group, and independent reading. Chart the features on graphic organizers and post them in your classroom as examples.

Find high-interest personal narratives that students can relate to. Use the recommended read-aloud titles provided in the Teacher's Guide, as well as other examples from your school library.

Focus on Genre Features: Personal Narrative

Point to the "Features of a Personal Narrative" web on the right side of the poster.

Say: *As we've discussed, every genre has certain consistent features. Considering our discussions so far, and your own experiences with this genre, what do you think are the consistent features of all, or most, personal narratives? Let's work together to identify them.*

Invite volunteers to name features of personal narratives. As students generate suggested features, encourage other students to think about them and decide whether to add them to the web on Poster 1. As necessary, prompt students with the following questions:

- *What is the focus of a personal narrative? Does it tell about one event or several?*
- *How do you learn about the person telling the narrative?*
- *Whose thoughts and feelings do you read about?*

Connect and transfer. Say: *This week we will read some personal narratives. Pay attention to the features of this genre. Understanding these features will help you read with better comprehension.*

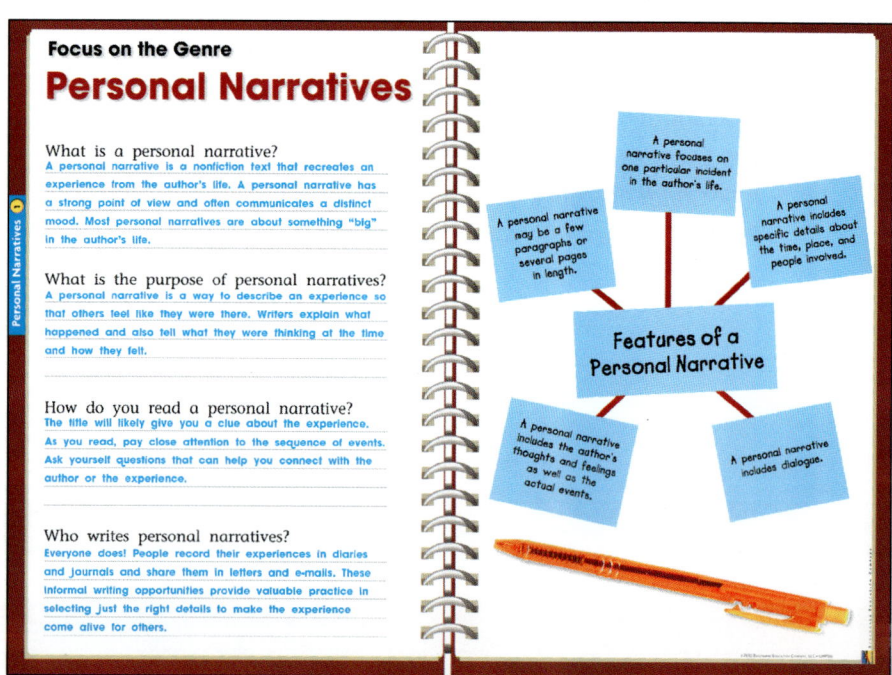

Personal Narrative Poster 1, sample annotations

Small-Group Reading Instruction (60 MINUTES)

Based on students' instructional reading levels, select titles that provide opportunities for students to focus on personal narratives or to practice analyzing characters. See the Leveled Text Titles chart provided at the back of this Teacher's Resource System.

Use the instruction provided in the Teacher's Guide for each title to introduce the text.

Individual Student Conferences (10 MINUTES)

Confer with individual students to discuss their understanding of the genre. Use the Individual Reading Conference Form on page 32 of Informal Assessments for Reading Development to help guide your conferences.

Word Study Workshop (20 MINUTES)

Use the Day 1 instruction provided in Grade 3 Word Study Unit 5.

Comprehension Quick-Check

Note which students do or don't actively participate in the discussion of genre. Ask some questions at the end of the lesson to confirm students' understanding, for example:

- *Can you tell me in your own words what a genre is?*
- *What do you already know about the personal narrative genre?*

Home/School Connection

Ask students to think about an experience or event they would like to write about as a personal narrative. Ask them to make a chart telling what the event or experience was, who else was involved, and why it would make a good personal narrative.

Day Two

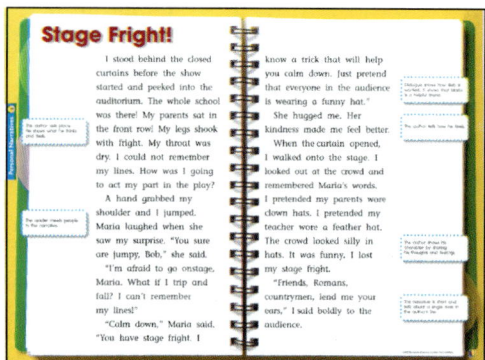

Personal Narrative Poster 2

Lesson Objectives

Students will:

- Visualize details of a personal narrative text.

- Analyze character using a graphic organizer.

- Use academic sentence frames to discuss strategies and features of a personal narrative.

Related Resources

- Personal Narrative Poster 2 (BLM 2)

- BenchmarkUniverse.com

 Read-Aloud (10 MINUTES)

Select a favorite fiction read-aloud from your classroom or school library with which to model the metacognitive strategy "Visualize." Use the sample read-aloud lessons and suggested titles in the Getting Started Guide.

 Mini-Lessons (20 MINUTES)

Model Metacognitive Strategies: Visualize

Display Genre Workshop Poster 2 with the genre annotations concealed. Also distribute copies of BLM 2.

Read aloud the poster passage with students.

Explain: *Good readers visualize to help them understand what they read. Visualizing helps us identify and understand characters' traits, feelings, and actions. Let me show you how I visualize characters and events in this personal narrative.*

Think aloud: *The first paragraph tells me where the author is and what is happening. I can visualize Bob standing behind the curtain and peeking out. I imagine his legs shaking. I understand how he feels because I know what it feels like to be nervous. Visualizing Bob helps me understand how scared and worried he is about going on stage.*

Ask students to visualize other details based on the text and to tell how the visualization helps them identify and understand the characters' traits, feelings, and actions. Write their observations on chart paper and reread them together. Encourage ELLs to use this sentence frame: *I imagine _____.*

Introduce Analyze Character

Explain: *Every personal narrative tells the thoughts and feelings of the author, who is the main character in the narrative. The narrative includes details about the author and the other characters. Visualizing can help you analyze the characters in a personal narrative.*

Reread "Stage Fright!" Ask students to use clues from the narrative to analyze and tell about the characters. Provide the following academic sentence frames to support ELLs and struggling students:

> *The character's name is _____.*
> *Two clues that tell about the character are _____ and _____.*
> *The character's traits are _____.*

Record students' clues and character traits on a graphic organizer like the one shown below.

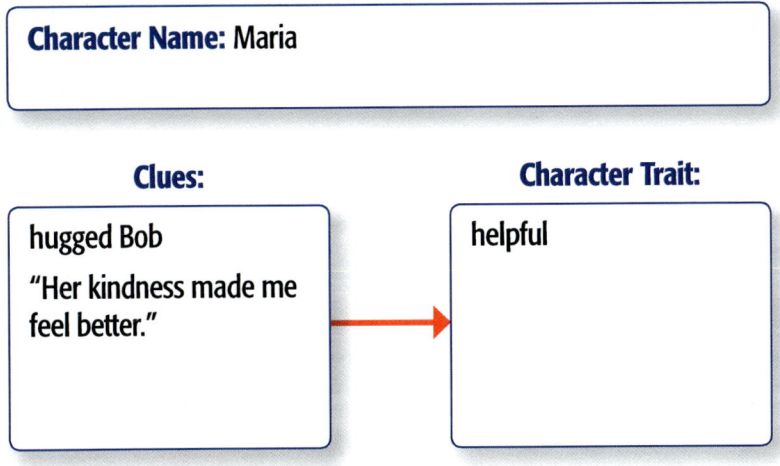

Character Name: Maria

Clues:

hugged Bob

"Her kindness made me feel better."

Character Trait:

helpful

Sample Analyze Character Annotations
(Note: Your class graphic organizer may differ.)

Make Content Comprehensible for ELLs

Beginning
Point to the illustrations as you pantomime stage fright.

Intermediate and Advanced
Model the academic sentence frames provided in this guide to help ELLs contribute their ideas to the discussion of personal narratives.

Have students show what people do when they are scared or nervous and then when they are being brave.

All Levels
Review character traits: **funny**, **nice**, **smart**, **shy**, **helpful**, **brave**, and so forth.

If you have students whose first language is Spanish, explain that the English/Spanish cognate **to pretend/pretender** is a false cognate. A false cognate is a pair of words that look and sound similar but mean different things. **To pretend** means to make believe. **Pretender** means to try to do something.

Comprehension Quick-Check

Note which students are or are not able to generate details to use in analyzing character. Use the following strategies to provide additional explicit instruction.

Use an Analyze Character graphic organizer like the one shown on page 7.

Say: *Let's look for details that help us understand Bob. Bob is the narrator. What is Bob doing? What is he thinking? What details help you know that?*

Help students use the details to analyze Bob's character.

Say: *The clues in the narrative help us know how Bob is feeling and what Bob is like. How is Bob feeling? What words would you use to tell about Bob?*

Oral Language Extension

Display Poster 1 (your class Personal Narrative anchor chart) during independent workstation time. Have pairs of students work together using their homework from the night before as a starting point. Partner A tells Partner B about an event in his or her life using features of a personal narrative on the class anchor chart. Then the partners switch roles. Tell students to listen carefully to their partners so that they can share details from their partner's narrative during independent conference time. Encourage them to take notes as they listen.

Home/School Connection

Have students take home BLM 2, reread the text, and highlight and label the features of a personal narrative present in the passage.

Focus on Genre Features: Personal Narrative

Ask students to name some of the features of a personal narrative that you discussed yesterday.

Say: *Now let's reexamine "Stage Fright!" and look for features of a personal narrative. What do you notice?*

Work with students to identify the following genre features embedded in this passage:
- a focus on one particular event
- details about the time, place, and people involved
- the author's thoughts and feelings
- dialogue

Reveal the poster annotations so that students can confirm or revise their ideas. Reread them as a group.

Connect and transfer. Say: *As you read personal narratives, look for these features. The features of the personal narrative help you understand the event and analyze the characters involved. As you read, remember to visualize to better understand the text.*

Small-Group Reading Instruction (60 MINUTES)

Continue small-group reading instruction from the previous day. Use the instruction provided in the Teacher's Guide for each text.

Individual Student Conferences (10 MINUTES)

Confer with individual students to discuss their understanding of genre and comprehension strategies. Use the Individual Reading Conference Form on page 32 of Informal Assessments for Reading Development to help guide your conferences.

Word Study Workshop (20 MINUTES)

Use the Day 2 instruction provided in Grade 3 Word Study Unit 5.

Read-Aloud (10 MINUTES)

Select a favorite nonfiction read-aloud from your classroom or school library with which to model the metacognitive strategy "Visualize." Use the sample read-aloud lessons and suggested titles in the Getting Started Guide.

Mini-Lessons (20 MINUTES)

Visualize to Analyze Character

Display Genre Workshop Poster 3 and distribute BLM 3.

Read aloud the excerpt with students. **Say:** *We are going to analyze the characters in this passage together. To do that, we're going to visualize. I will use clues and details in the passage to picture what is happening and to help me understand a character's feelings. I know that Marcos would rather be playing video games instead of joining his grandma's knitting circle. I picture him in the room. I imagine how he feels. I think he is probably a little embarrassed.*

Say: *Now you tell me what you visualize and how visualizing helps you understand Marcos or another character.* Allow responses. If students are unable to visualize, prompt them to think about the following:
- *What does Marcos think about Grandpa's sweater? How do you imagine Marcos looks when he sees it?*
- *What do you imagine Grandma looks like? How does she treat Marcos? What does that tell you about Grandma?*

Say: *Visualizing these details helps us analyze and understand the characters. Let's write the clues and details about Marcos and Grandma on a graphic organizer. Then we will use these details to analyze their characters and tell what they are like.*

Work with students to identify and visualize details about Marcos and Grandma from the passage. Reinforce how the details in a personal narrative are related to the specific features of the genre. Record the details on a graphic organizer like the one shown on page 10.

Work with students to analyze characters based on the details on your graphic organizer. Make sure that all of the details relate to character analysis and determining character traits. If a detail does not support the character analysis, remove it from your graphic organizer or reassess your analysis.

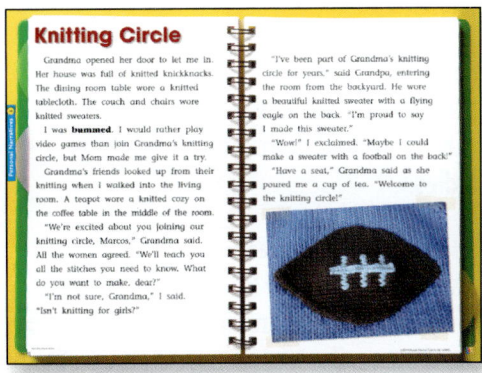
Personal Narrative Poster 3

Lesson Objectives

Students will:
- Review features of the personal narrative genre.
- Visualize characters or events in a text.
- Use their understanding of genre features to analyze character.
- Build oral language and vocabulary through whole-group and partner discussion.

Related Resources
- Personal Narrative Poster 3 (BLM 3)
- Analyze Character (BLM 4)
- BenchmarkUniverse.com

Make Content Comprehensible for ELLs

Beginning
Point to and name the characters. Point out the knitted items and the knitting ladies.

Intermediate and Advanced
Ask students if they know anyone who knits. Pantomime knitting and use the text illustrations if necessary. Discuss whether knitting is something only women and girls can do.

All Levels
Group students with fluent English speakers during all whole-group and partner discussions.

Comprehension Quick-Check

Note whether students can generate details that lead to character analysis based on the passage. If they need additional support, review the features of a personal narrative using Poster 1. Then highlight or underline specific details about the characters on Poster 3 using a write-on/wipe-off marker. Say: *In a personal narrative, the details help you understand what the characters are thinking and feeling and what they are like.* Have students underline or highlight additional details on the poster with you.

Home/School Connection

Have students take home the Analyze Character graphic organizer (BLM 4). Have them read a familiar story with a family member. Then have them choose two characters from the story and write clues or details about each character, and explain what these clues tell them about each character.

Remind students that clues about characters can come from dialogue, as well as from text descriptions. Students may also have to infer certain character traits from clues in the text—not all of the clues are related directly to the characters' words and actions.

Connect and transfer. Say: *The next time you read a personal narrative, visualize to help you understand and analyze the characters.*

	Clues/Details	What That Tells You
Marcos	would rather be playing video games "Isn't knitting for girls?" excited about Grandpa's sweater	doesn't want to be there likes to do "boy" things willing to change his mind
Grandma	has many friends "We're excited about your joining our knitting circle, Marcos." ready to teach Marcos to knit pours tea for Marcos	friendly welcoming kind loving

Sample Analyze Character Annotations

Small-Group Reading Instruction (60 MINUTES)

Continue small-group reading instruction from the previous day. Use the instruction provided in the Teacher's Guide for each text.

Individual Student Conferences (10 MINUTES)

Confer with individual students to discuss their developing understanding of genre and comprehension strategies. Use the Individual Reading Conference Form on page 32 of Informal Assessments for Reading Development to help guide your conferences.

Word Study Workshop (20 MINUTES)

Use the Day 3 instruction provided in Grade 3 Word Study Unit 5.

Read-Aloud (10 MINUTES)

Select a favorite nonfiction read-aloud from your classroom or school library with which to model the metacognitive strategy "Visualize." Use the sample read-aloud lessons and suggested titles in the Getting Started Guide.

Mini-Lessons (20 MINUTES)

Build Comprehension: Make Inferences (About Character)

Say: *When you read a personal narrative, you learn about an experience in the writer's life. The author includes details about the time, place, and people involved. You can use these written details to understand the writing and analyze the characters. But sometimes the writer does not directly state all the information. You can still use clues in the writing combined with things you already know to infer, or figure out, something about a character.*

Reread Poster 3 with students.

Say: *We are going to make an inference chart. We will put on our chart clues from the passage that help us make inferences and tell about the characters. What kinds of information will you look for to understand the characters?* Allow responses.

Engage students in a discussion to ensure they understand that they can use text and illustrations to make inferences. They can combine clues with what they know to infer additional information about a character.

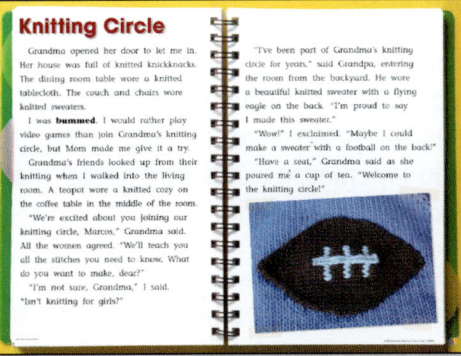

Personal Narrative Poster 3

Lesson Objectives

Students will:

- Make inferences about characters.
- Extend Tier Two Vocabulary by focusing on emotion words.
- Build oral language and vocabulary through whole-group and partner discussion.

Related Resources

- Personal Narrative Poster 3 (BLM 3)
- BenchmarkUniverse.com

Make Content Comprehensible for ELLs

Beginning
Explain that emotions are feelings. Have students pantomime emotions with you as you say emotion words: **sad**, **happy**, **mad**, **excited**, and so forth.

Intermediate and Advanced
Ask students to say other emotion words they know. Record responses on chart paper.

All Levels
Pair beginning ELLs with advanced students who speak the same home language to say and pantomime emotion words, including **bummed**.

Comprehension Quick-Check

Take note of students who may need more support to make inferences about the characters in a personal narrative. Provide additional modeling during small-group reading, and have them practice during independent workstation time by making inferences based on another personal narrative excerpt that you assign.

On chart paper, draw a two-column chart like the one shown below.

Think/Pair/Write/Share. Tell students they will complete this chart. **Say:** *Work with a partner to write clues about two characters from the passage. Make a chart like the one I just drew, and fill in your ideas. Put one or two clues in each clue box, then write an inference about each character that the clues helped you make. We will share the charts as a group.*

Connect and transfer. Say: *Remember, when you read a personal narrative, you can use clues in the narrative to make inferences about the characters. You can figure out what the characters are like.*

CLUES	INFERENCE
• dining room table and couch have knitted covers • teapot has a knitted cozy	Grandma loves to knit and spends a lot of time knitting. Knitting is important to her.
• Marcos exclaims, "Wow!" when he sees Grandpa's sweater. • Marcos wants to make a sweater with Spider-Man on it.	Marcos decides knitting is a good idea because Grandpa does it and because he wants a cool sweater.

Build Tier Two Vocabulary: Emotion Words

On chart paper, write the word **bummed**.

Say: *Marcus was bummed when he went to Grandma's for the knitting circle. He wanted to play video games, not learn to knit.* **Bummed** *is an emotion word. What do you think the word* **bummed** *means?*

Turn and talk. Ask students to turn and talk with their neighbor for a moment to come up with a definition.

Ask students to share their definitions and record them on chart paper. Students should understand that **bummed** means "upset, disappointed, or annoyed." Discuss why **bummed** is a good choice to tell how Marcos feels. Would it be a good word to use for Grandma or Grandpa?

Say: *Turn back to talk again with your neighbor. Work together to list other emotion words you have read. Try to think of words that are more descriptive than* **happy** *or* **sad***.* Allow students to talk and write for one minute. Then have them share their words with the group.

Small-Group Reading Instruction (60 MINUTES)

Continue small-group reading instruction from the previous day. Use the instruction provided in the Teacher's Guide for each text.

Individual Student Conferences (10 MINUTES)

Confer with individual students to discuss their developing understanding of genre and word-solving strategies. Use the Individual Reading Conference Form on page 32 of Informal Assessments for Reading Development to help guide your conferences.

Word Study Workshop (20 MINUTES)

Use the Day 4 instruction provided in Grade 3 Word Study Unit 5.

Oral Language Extension

During independent workstation time, ask pairs of students to tell their partners about an event or experience in their own lives using the features of a personal narrative and at least three emotion words.

Home/School Connection

Have students take home BLM 3 and read it with a family member to practice fluent reading. Tell students to have their family members sign the page to indicate they have participated in the reading.

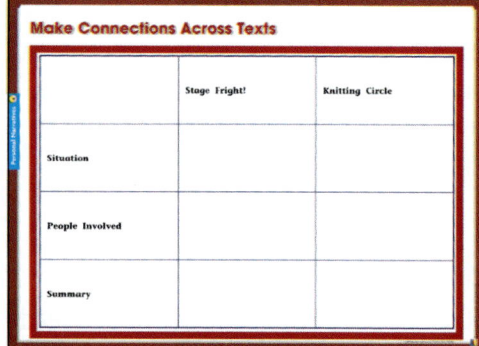

Personal Narrative Poster 4

Lesson Objectives

Students will:

• Identify elements of and summarize personal narratives.

• Review features of the personal narrative genre.

• Make text-to-text connections.

• Build academic oral language and vocabulary through small-group and whole-group discussions.

Related Resources

• Personal Narrative Poster 4 (BLM 5)

• BenchmarkUniverse.com

Read-Aloud (10 MINUTES)

Revisit the week's read-alouds to make text-to-text connections and provide opportunities for reader response. Use the suggested activities in the Getting Started Guide or implement ideas of your own.

Mini-Lessons (20 MINUTES)

Synthesize and Assess Genre Understanding

Synthesize genre understanding. Ask students to work in teams to summarize what they now know about the personal narrative genre. Tell students that each group member should contribute an idea to the discussion. Each group should appoint one member to be the group's recorder. Another student should be the group's spokesperson.

Give students five to seven minutes to discuss and record their ideas.

Have each group's spokesperson share his or her group's ideas.

Record key concepts from each group on chart paper.

Self-assessment. Display the class Personal Narrative anchor chart from Day 1. Ask each group to compare their group's ideas to the information they recorded on the anchor chart on Day 1.

Ask: *How has your understanding of the personal narrative genre developed? What do you know now that you didn't know before?* Encourage individual students to share their personal insights.

Connect and transfer. Ask: *How can you use your new understandings of this genre as a reader the next time you read a personal narrative? How do you think you can use your genre knowledge as a writer?*

Make Connections Across Texts

Display Personal Narrative Poster 4.

Say: *You have read personal narratives this week. Sometimes in school and on tests, you will be asked to make connections between different fiction and nonfiction texts. Today we are going to practice making connections between personal narratives.*

Tell students they will compare the two personal narratives from the posters—"Stage Fright!" and "Knitting Circle." Ask them to complete the graphic organizer about the two selections on BLM 5.

Give students about five minutes to record their ideas. Then bring the groups together and have them share their ideas.

Challenge students to express their own opinions on these subjects:
- *Which personal narrative did you like more? Why?*
- *Which character did you feel a connection to? Why?*

Connect and transfer. Say: *When you analyze two personal narratives, think about how each one reflects the features of the genre. What one particular incident in his or her life did the writer focus on? What did you learn about the writer's thoughts and feelings?*

Small-Group Reading Instruction (60 MINUTES)

Continue small-group reading instruction from the previous day. Use the instruction provided in the Teacher's Guide for each text.

Individual Student Conferences (10 MINUTES)

Ask students to reflect on what they have learned about the personal narrative genre. Use the Individual Reading Conference Form on page 32 of Informal Assessments for Reading Development to help guide your conferences.

Word Study Workshop (20 MINUTES)

Use the Day 5 instruction provided in Grade 3 Word Study Unit 5.

Make Content Comprehensible for ELLs

Beginning
Allow beginning ELLs to participate as active listeners in their groups.

Intermediate and Advanced
Provide sentence frames to help ELLs contribute to their groups' discussions, for example:

This personal narrative made me feel _____.

The personal narratives are different because _____.

The personal narratives are alike because _____.

All Levels
Pair ELLs with fluent English speakers during all partner and group activities.

Encourage ELLs to revisit the personal narratives they are comparing and to find specific information in the text to help them communicate their ideas.

Name _____   Date _____

Focus on the Genre

Personal Narratives

Personal Narratives ①

What is a personal narrative?

What is the purpose of personal narratives?

How do you read a personal narrative?

Who writes personal narratives?

Name _____   Date _____

Stage Fright!

I stood behind the closed curtains before the show started and peeked into the auditorium. The whole school was there! My parents sat in the front row! My legs shook with fright. My throat was dry. I could not remember my lines. How was I going to act my part in the play?

A hand grabbed my shoulder and I jumped. Maria laughed when she saw my surprise. "You sure are jumpy, Bob," she said.

"I'm afraid to go onstage, Maria. What if I trip and fall? I can't remember my lines!"

"Calm down," Maria said. "You have stage fright. I know a trick that will help you calm down. Just pretend that everyone in the audience is wearing a funny hat."

She hugged me. Her kindness made me feel better.

When the curtain opened, I walked onto the stage. I looked out at the crowd and remembered Maria's words. I pretended my parents wore clown hats. I pretended my teacher wore a feather hat. The crowd looked silly in hats. It was funny. I lost my stage fright.

"Friends, Romans, countrymen, lend me your ears," I said boldly to the audience.

The author sets place. He shows what he thinks and feels.

The reader meets people in the narrative.

Dialogue shows how Bob is worried. It shows that Maria is a helpful friend.

The author tells how he feels.

The author shows his character by sharing his thoughts and feelings.

The narrative is short and tells about a single time in the author's life.

Personal Narratives 2

Name _____ Date _____

Knitting Circle

Grandma opened her door to let me in. Her house was full of knitted knickknacks. The dining room table wore a knitted tablecloth. The couch and chairs wore knitted sweaters.

I was **bummed**. I would rather play video games than join Grandma's knitting circle, but Mom made me give it a try. Grandma's friends looked up from their knitting when I walked into the living room. A teapot wore a knitted cozy on the coffee table in the middle of the room.

"We're excited about you joining our knitting circle, Marcos," Grandma said. All the women agreed. "We'll teach you all the stitches you need to know. What do you want to make, dear?"

"I'm not sure, Grandma," I said.

"Isn't knitting for girls?"

"I've been part of Grandma's knitting circle for years," said Grandpa, entering the room from the backyard. He wore a beautiful knitted sweater with a flying eagle on the back. "I'm proud to say I made this sweater."

"Wow!" I exclaimed. "Maybe I could make a sweater with a football on the back!"

"Have a seat," Grandma said as she poured me a cup of tea. "Welcome to the knitting circle!"

Name _____   Date _____

Analyze Character

Directions: Choose two characters from a story that you read with a family member. Write at least two clues or details about each character. Then write what these clues tell you about the character.

	Clues/Details	What That Tells You
Character:		
Character:		

Name _____ Date _____

Make Connections Across Texts

	Situation	People Involved	Summary
Stage Fright!			
Knitting Circle			

Personal Narratives 4

Visualize/Analyze Character

Reader's Theater

Our New Home

by Suzy Wall • illustrated by Karen Leon

Unit 2/Week 3 at a Glance

Day	Mini-Lessons
ONE	• Introduce Fluency Skills: *Pausing—Short Pause* • Model the Skill
TWO	• Practice and Self-Assess Fluency Skills: *Pausing—Short Pause* • Connect Fluency and Comprehension: *Analyze Author's Purpose*
THREE	• Apply Fluency Skills to Reader's Theater • Build Comprehension: *Analyze Author's Purpose*
FOUR	• Build Tier Two Vocabulary: *Antonyms*
FIVE	• Prepare for and Manage Student Performances: *Audience and Performer Expectations* • Show Time! • Assess and Reflect

Cutting Down on Trash

You eat a banana . . . you throw away the peel. You empty your backpack . . . you throw away your old math papers. You pour a glass of milk . . . you throw away the carton. Sadly, most of our garbage ends up in a trash bin—and then in a landfill.

Many people have found a different way to handle trash: reuse items in a new way. They put things like grass clippings and eggshells in a pile outdoors to make compost, a rich soil for the garden. They use the backs of junk mail letters—in place of new paper—in their computer printer. They use an empty green bean can, washed and wrapped in leftover yarn, to hold markers on a desk. The list goes on and on . . .

So what about your trash—the banana peel, old math papers, and milk carton? The banana peel can go in your new compost pile; the family can write grocery lists on the backs of your old math papers; you can make a bird feeder from the milk carton. You've done it—you've reused instead of throwing away!

Day One

Fluency Poster

Cutting Down on Trash

You eat a banana . . . you throw away the peel. You empty your backpack . . . you throw away your old math papers. You pour a glass of milk . . . you throw away the carton. Sadly, most of our garbage ends up in a trash bin—and then in a landfill.

Many people have found a different way to handle trash: reuse items in a new way. They put things like grass clippings and eggshells in a pile outdoors to make compost, a rich soil for the garden. They use the backs of junk mail letters—in place of new paper—in their computer printer. They use an empty

green bean can, washed and wrapped in leftover yarn, to hold markers on a desk. The list goes on and on . . .

So what about your trash—the banana peel, old math papers, and milk carton? The banana peel can go in your new compost pile; the family can write grocery lists on the backs of your old math papers; you can make a bird feeder from the milk carton. You've done it—you've reused instead of throwing away!

Fluency Poster

Lesson Objectives

Students will:

- Utilize punctuation to signal short pauses while reading.
- Demonstrate understanding of the text through purposeful pausing.
- Use effective pausing to make their reading sound like talking.

Related Resources

- BenchmarkUniverse.com

🕐 Read-Aloud (10 MINUTES)

Select a favorite fiction read-aloud from your classroom or school library with which to model the metacognitive strategy "Visualize." Use the sample read-aloud lessons and suggested titles provided in the Getting Started Guide.

🕐 Mini-Lessons (20 MINUTES)

Introduce Fluency Skills: Pausing–Short Pause

Explain: *When we talk, we do not run all our words together. Instead, we pause, or rest between some words. The pause may be very short or it may be longer. Why do you think it is important to pause when we talk?* Allow responses.

Reinforce the idea that pausing helps listeners understand what we are saying. In reading, punctuation helps us figure out when to pause.

Ask:
- *What punctuation marks signal that you should take a short pause?*
    (a comma, dash, semicolon, colon, ellipsis)
- *At which one should you pause longer, a comma or a dash?*
    (a dash)
- *Do you make a full stop when you see a semicolon?*
    (No, you take a short pause and then continue reading.)

Say: *Pausing helps us divide sentences into meaningful parts when we speak and when we read.*

Model the Skill

Display the fluency poster "Cutting Down on Trash" and read aloud the title.

Say: *This passage is about reusing items rather than putting them in the trash. The author uses commas, dashes, semicolons, colons, and ellipses to show us when to pause. A short pause at each of these punctuation marks helps the sentences sound right and make sense.*

Ask students to listen and follow along as you read the passage aloud, pausing briefly at each comma, dash, semicolon, colon, and ellipsis.

Say: *I will read the first paragraph three times. First, I will read it the way I did before, pausing at the punctuation marks within each sentence. Next, I will read it without pausing. Finally, I will ignore the punctuation and pause in different places.*

Read the first paragraph as written, in a word-by-word manner, and with awkward pauses.

Turn and talk. Have students turn to a neighbor and compare and evaluate your readings. Ask them to think about how each reading affected them as listeners. Then have pairs of students share their ideas with the whole class. Reinforce the idea that pausing correctly at punctuation helps the sentences sound right and make sense.

Shared Writing. Invite students to help you create a class anchor chart to remind them how good readers use pausing. (See the example below.) When you are finished, ask students to echo-read the entire chart. Display the chart in the classroom for future reference.

Pausing

- We do not run all our words together.
- We pause, or rest, between some words.
- Pausing divides sentences into meaningful parts.
- Pausing makes our reading easier to understand.
- Punctuation helps us figure out when to pause.
- Punctuation helps us figure out how long to pause.

Sample Anchor Chart

Make Content Comprehensible for ELLs

Beginning

Orally demonstrate making a short pause as opposed to a full stop. Invite students to repeat oral sentences with short pauses.

Demonstrate the meaning of **throw away**.

Intermediate and Advanced

Engage ELLs in a discussion about reusing (or recycling) items. Ask them to tell what they recycle or reuse at home or at school using the sentence frame: *I reuse _____.* Record their sentences and reread them together.

All Levels

Before reading to model fluency, read to support comprehension of unfamiliar Tier Two words through explanation, gestures, and role-play, or by using props. Difficult words may include: **landfill, reuse, junk mail, soil, leftover**.

Support Special Needs Learners

Throughout the week, use the following strategies to help students who have learning disabilities access the content and focus on skills and strategies.

During partner reading practice, pair special needs students with more fluent readers who can model fluency and support their development.

Group students heterogeneously for small-group reading of the script so that struggling students benefit from working with more fluent readers.

Assign multiple students to specific reader's theater roles so that they can support each other.

Fluency and Comprehension Quick-Check

Throughout the week, refer to the Fluency Rubric provided in the Benchmark Literacy Assessments to help you informally assess where students are in their development of key areas of fluency.

The end goal of all fluency practice is increased comprehension. Use the following questions to check students' comprehension of the passage they have read:

- *What was this passage mostly about? What does the word **reuse** mean?*

- *Why is it a good idea to reuse items? What is something in your desk you could reuse?*

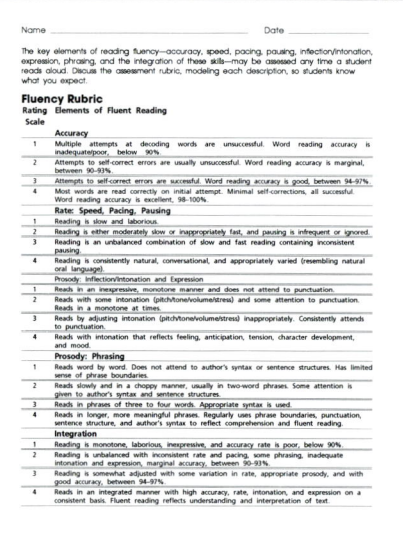

Fluency Rubric

Connect and transfer. Say: *Today during small-group reading, we will read a reader's theater script. As we read the script, one skill we will practice is pausing at punctuation marks to make our reading easier to understand.*

Small-Group Reading Instruction (60 MINUTES)

Introduce and read *Our New Home*. Use the before- and during-reading instruction in the Teacher's Guide for the script.

Individual Student Conferences (10 MINUTES)

Confer with individual students to discuss their understanding of the script. Use the Individual Reading Conference Form on page 32 of Informal Assessments for Reading Development to help guide your conferences.

Word Study Workshop (20 MINUTES)

Use the Day 1 instruction provided in Grade 3 Word Study Unit 6.

Read-Aloud (10 MINUTES)

Select a favorite fiction read-aloud from your classroom or school library with which to model the metacognitive strategy "Visualize." Use the sample read-aloud lessons and suggested titles provided in the Getting Started Guide.

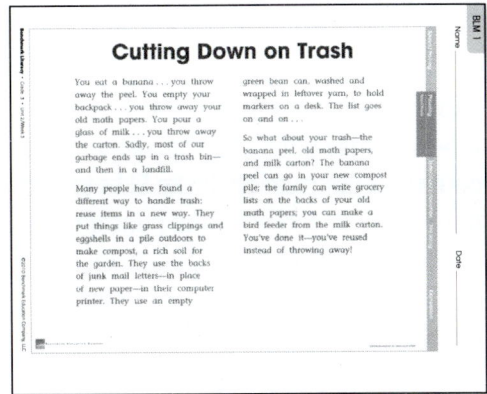

Cutting Down on Trash (BLM 1)

Mini-Lessons (20 MINUTES)

Practice and Self-Assess Fluency Skills:
Pausing—Short Pause

Distribute copies of Cutting Down on Trash (BLM 1).

Ask students to echo-read each sentence, and then have them choral-read the passage with you.

Next, allow the group to choral-read the passage without your assistance.

Distribute the Fluency Self-Assessment Master Checklist (BLM 2) and review the assessment criteria for pausing and integration. Ask students to give a thumbs-up or thumbs-down on each question based on the group's choral-reading. Discuss their responses.

Partner reading. Pair students and ask them to read "Cutting Down on Trash" together one or more times, alternating sentences.

Monitor students' partner rereading practice and provide responsive feedback using the prompts provided on page 6.

Ask students to rate themselves on specific fluency skills covered in this lesson using their Fluency Self-Assessment Master Checklist (BLM 2).

Connect and transfer. Ask students to reflect on their fluency practice, using the following prompts:
- *When did you take quick pauses? When did you take slightly longer pauses? When did you make a full stop?*
- *How did pausing help you read and understand?*
- *Remember, you will need this skill as we practice and perform a reader's theater script this week.*

Lesson Objectives

Students will:

- Utilize punctuation to signal short pauses while reading.
- Demonstrate understanding of the text through purposeful pausing.
- Use effective pausing to make their reading sound like talking.

Related Resources
- Cutting Down on Trash (BLM 1)
- Fluency Self-Assessment Master Checklist (BLM 2)
- BenchmarkUniverse.com

Make Content Comprehensible for ELLs

Beginning

Allow ELLs to participate through active listening while other students demonstrate pausing at punctuation. Invite ELLs to track print with you and point out punctuation. As students point to each punctuation mark, say its name and have students repeat.

Intermediate and Advanced

Read the Fluency Self-Assessment Master Checklist (BLM 2) with students to ensure understanding. Demonstrate **running all my words together**.

All Levels

Pair ELLs with fluent English speakers during partner discussions and activities.

BLM 2
Name _____ Date _____
Fluency Self-Assessment Master Checklist

Fluency Self-Assessment Master Checklist (BLM 2)

Responsive Prompts for Pausing

As students work together, observe those who demonstrate understanding and those who struggle. Use appropriate responsive prompting to provide additional support or to validate students who demonstrate mastery.

Goal Oriented

- Listen to me read this. Can you hear me take a little breath at the comma (semicolon, dash, colon, ellipsis)?
- The period (question mark, exclamation point) means your voice makes a full stop.
- When I make a short pause, I don't stop completely and break the flow.
- When I finish a sentence, I make a full stop before continuing.
- Notice what I do when I see a(n) comma (semicolon, dash, colon, ellipsis). My reading pauses briefly and then continues.
- Notice what I do when I see a period (question mark, exclamation point). My reading pauses with a full stop.

Directive and Corrective Feedback

- Make a full stop at the period (question mark, exclamation point).
- Take a little breath at a(n) comma (semicolon, dash, colon, ellipsis).
- Read the punctuation.
- Read it like this with a short pause between the words.
- Read it like this with a full stop after the word.
- Make your pause longer.
- Make your pause shorter.

Self-Monitoring and Reflection

- How did you know to make a short pause here?
- How did you know to make a full stop here?
- Did you know where to make a short pause or full stop as you read?
- Was your pausing too short, too long, or just right?
- Where did you make short pauses as you read?
- Where did you make full stops as you read?

Validating and Confirming

- Good—you took a little breath.
- Good—you made a full stop.
- I liked the way you made a short pause/full stop here.
- I like the way you used the _____ punctuation mark to help you make a short pause/full stop here.
- Good—you used punctuation marks to help you know when to pause and for how long!

Connect Fluency and Comprehension:
Analyze Author's Purpose

Say: *Pausing in the correct places helps you make sense of the words and sentences you read, but you also need to understand what the author is trying to tell you. When you understand why an author wrote a piece, you can use your voice to help your audience understand as well. What are some reasons, or purposes, authors may have for writing?* Allow responses.

Say: *Now think about "Cutting Down on Trash." Why do you think the author wrote this passage?* Allow responses.

Discuss whether the author is successful at persuading the reader to try reusing items when possible. Ask students what makes the passage persuasive instead of merely informative.

Ask: *How does understanding the author's purpose of "Cutting Down on Trash" change how you sound when you read it aloud?*

Connect and transfer. Say: *Today during small-group reading, focus on understanding the purpose of the passage. This will help you read with the right expression.*

Small-Group Reading Instruction (60 MINUTES)

Reread *Our New Home* to build comprehension and critical thinking using the After Reading Interpret the Script questions. Assign roles to individual students.

Individual Student Conferences (10 MINUTES)

Confer with individual students to discuss their script roles and how they plan to rehearse and read their part. Use the Individual Reading Conference Form on page 32 of Informal Assessments for Reading Development to help guide your conferences.

Word Study Workshop (20 MINUTES)

Use the Day 2 instruction provided in Grade 3 Word Study Unit 6.

Oral Language Extension

Have pairs of students practice the fluency passage during independent workstation time.

Home/School Connection

Have students practice reading Cutting Down on Trash (BLM 1) again with a family member. Ask students to focus on reading smoothly and with appropriate pauses.

Ask students to have their family member sign the page to indicate they have participated in the reading.

Day Three

Our New Home, pages 2–3 (BLM 3)

Lesson Objectives

Students will:

- Utilize punctuation to signal short pauses while reading a script.

- Demonstrate understanding of the text through purposeful pausing.

- Use effective pausing to make their reading sound like talking.

- Use metacognitive strategies to help them analyze the author's purpose.

- Build oral language and vocabulary through whole-group and partner discussion.

Related Resources

- *Our New Home*, pages 2–3 (BLM 3)
- BenchmarkUniverse.com

Read-Aloud (10 MINUTES)

Select a favorite nonfiction read-aloud from your classroom or school library with which to model the metacognitive strategy "Visualize." Use the sample read-aloud lessons and suggested titles provided in the Getting Started Guide.

Mini-Lessons (20 MINUTES)

Apply Fluency Skills to Reader's Theater

Distribute the first two pages of *Our New Home* (BLM 3), which students have completed during small-group reading time.

Say: *Yesterday you practiced making short pauses as you read a passage. Now I want you to apply what you learned to the script we will perform this week. Listen as I read these two pages to you.*

Read pages 2–3 of the script to model how you use short pauses to make the dialogue sound natural. Use the suggestions below or interpret the text in your own way:

- Mom: addresses Daniela directly, taking a slightly longer pause at comma, then speeding up when looking at pictures
- Daniela: a little distracted by the boxes, speaks faster than Mom

Ask students to comment on how your reading affected them as listeners. How did you use pauses to vary the characters' voices?

Partner reading. Have pairs of students practice reading these pages together. Monitor their practice and provide responsive prompting as needed to validate their efforts, give corrective feedback, or encourage them to self-monitor. Use the responsive prompts provided on page 6.

Build Comprehension: Analyze Author's Purpose

Say: *Yesterday we discussed why the author of "Cutting Down on Trash" wrote that passage. Today let's think about why the author of* Our New Home *wrote about these events and characters. Understanding the author's purpose will help you interpret the script more effectively.*

Activate metacognitive strategies. Ask: *What strategies can we use to help ourselves understand the author's purpose?* Allow responses. If necessary, prompt students to use the following strategies:

Make connections. Ask: *What connections can you make between your own experiences and Daniela's? What connections can you make between Janina and Stefan's experience and your own or someone else's that you've read about?*

Make inferences. Say: *How does Daniela feel about finding the diary? How do you know? Is Daniela interested in her great-grandmother's life? How do you know?*

Support ELLs' and struggling readers' participation in the discussion by providing the following sentence frames:

I was like Daniela when _____.
Janina and Stefan are like _____.
I think Daniela feels _____ because _____.

Shared Writing. Make a list of students' ideas about the author's purpose. Post this on the wall.

Connect and transfer. Say: *Today, as you practice the script, think about what the author wants people to experience through the script. Use what you have learned about pausing to help you express her purpose.*

Small-Group Reading Instruction (60 MINUTES)

Have students rehearse their roles in *Our New Home* together as a group. Offer suggestions for voice, expression, and pausing.

Individual Student Conferences (10 MINUTES)

Confer with individual students to discuss their script roles and their rehearsal progress. Use the Individual Reading Conference Form on page 32 of Informal Assessments for Reading Development to help guide your conferences.

Word Study Workshop (20 MINUTES)

Use the Day 3 instruction provided in Grade 3 Word Study Unit 6.

Make Content Comprehensible for ELLs

Beginning
Allow ELLs to participate through active listening while other students demonstrate pausing. Invite them to indicate when they hear a short pause. Reinforce the connection between the pause and the written punctuation mark.

Intermediate and Advanced
Allow ELLs to read parts of the script chorally with you or other students as they demonstrate their use of pauses.

All Levels
Pair ELLs with fluent English speakers during partner reading practice.

Model the use of academic sentence frames to support ELLs' academic vocabulary and language development. (See suggested sentence frames provided.)

Home/School Connection

Have students take home *Our New Home*, pages 2–3 (BLM 3) and read it with a family member to practice fluent reading. Ask students to have their family member sign the script page to indicate that they have participated in the reading.

Fluency Quick-Check

As students practice oral reading with a partner, note students who would benefit from additional repeated oral reading practice during independent workstation time.

Day Four

Our New Home, pages 14–15 (BLM 5)

Lesson Objectives

Students will:

- Extend Tier Two Vocabulary by analyzing antonyms.
- Partner-read to build fluency.
- Build oral language and vocabulary through whole-group and partner discussion.

Related Resources

- Antonyms (BLM 4)
- *Our New Home*, pages 14–15 (BLM 5)
- BenchmarkUniverse.com

Read-Aloud (10 MINUTES)

Select a favorite nonfiction read-aloud from your classroom or school library with which to model the metacognitive strategy "Visualize." Use the sample read-aloud lessons and suggested titles provided in the Getting Started Guide.

Mini-Lessons (20 MINUTES)

Build Tier Two Vocabulary: Antonyms

On chart paper, draw a graphic organizer like the one below (BLM 4). Remind students that antonyms are words that have opposite meanings. Today they will discuss words that are antonyms.

Think/Pair/Write/Share. Distribute the graphic organizer Antonyms (BLM 4). Ask students to work with a partner to list two pairs of words that are antonyms and write a brief definition for each word. Let students use dictionaries if necessary. Give students approximately three minutes, and then bring them back together to share their answers. If students are unable to come up with antonyms, prompt them with the following:

- *Think of a word that tells about how something feels. Write the word. Now think of a word that means the opposite.*
- *Think of a word that tells the size of something. What word means the opposite?*

Record students' responses on the chart. Ask students to use their antonyms in sentences.

Distribute *Our New Home*, pages 14–15 (BLM 5).

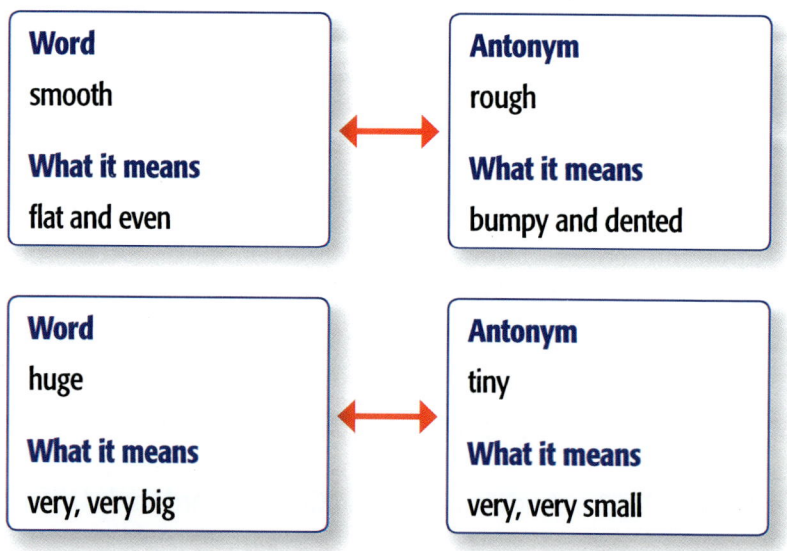

Sample Antonyms Annotations (BLM 4)

Say: *Writers use antonyms to give readers context clues about word meaning and to be descriptive. Read the text with a partner. Find two words that are antonyms.*

Have pairs read the script excerpt on BLM 5 and find a pair of words that are antonyms (**same**, **different**). Ask students to raise their hands when they have found the antonyms. When a majority of hands are raised, point out the answer. Discuss why the words **same** and **different** are important in the passage.

Discuss fix-up monitoring strategies. Ask students how knowing about antonyms can help them determine the meaning of an unfamiliar word. Generate discussion of the strategies that help good readers. For example, students can reread and look for clues in nearby sentences. Some of the clue words might be familiar antonyms.

Connect and transfer. Say: *Sometimes thinking about a word's opposite can help you get a clearer picture of what is happening to your character in the script. As you read, pay attention to words that tell about what happens to your character or how your character feels. Think about what you know about the word's meaning, including the opposite.*

Small-Group Reading Instruction (60 MINUTES)

Have students continue to rehearse their roles in *Our New Home* together as a group. Discuss and plan how students will stage their script performance tomorrow.

Individual Student Conferences (10 MINUTES)

Confer with individual students on sections of the script you would like them to work on before the performance. Use the Individual Reading Conference Form on page 32 of Informal Assessments for Reading Development to help guide your conferences.

Word Study Workshop (20 MINUTES)

Use the Day 4 instruction provided in Grade 3 Word Study Unit 6.

Make Content Comprehensible for ELLs

Beginning
Help ELLs understand antonyms by using props and drawings as you state simple sentences: *The desk is big. The block is little.* **Big** and **little** are antonyms.

Intermediate
Work with students to list familiar pairs of antonyms. Point to classroom objects or pictures and provide sentence frames: *The desk is _____. The opposite of _____ is _____.*

All Levels
Pair ELLs with fluent English speakers during partner discussions and activities.

Oral Language Extension

Write several glossary words from the reader's theater script on chart paper and display the list during independent workstation time. Challenge pairs of students to use each word in meaningful oral sentences. Ask students to write down at least five sentences to show you during independent student conference time.

Home/School Connection

Have students take home *Our New Home*, pages 14–15 (BLM 5) and read it with a family member to practice fluency skills. Ask students to have their family member sign the script page to indicate that they have participated in the reading.

Day Five

Reader's Theater Script

Lesson Objectives

Students will:

- Demonstrate their level of fluency development through an oral reading interpretation of the script.
- Demonstrate active listening skills.
- Reflect on and assess their own fluency development.

Related Resources

- Reader's Theater Self-Assessment (BLM 6)
- BenchmarkUniverse.com

Read-Aloud (10 MINUTES)

Revisit the week's read-alouds to make text-to-text connections and to provide opportunities for reader response. Use the suggested activities in the Getting Started Guide, or implement ideas of your own.

Mini-Lessons (20 MINUTES)

Prepare for and Manage Student Performances: Audience and Performer Expectations

Prepare students for their reader's theater performances by sharing your expectations of audience members and performers.

Audience expectations. Say: *While you are listening to the other groups perform, I expect you to do the following:*
- Give your classmates your full attention.
- Do not speak to your neighbors or make any noise.
- Enjoy their performance and show your appreciation by clapping when they are finished.
- Be prepared to give your feedback on the script, and always remember to make your feedback constructive, or helpful.

Performer expectations. Say: *While you and your group are performing the script, remember to do these things:*
- Read in a loud, clear voice and act out your role.
- Use expression and fluency to help everyone listening to understand your character.
- Remember to use punctuation clues to take pauses.
- When it is not your turn to read, follow along in the script so you know when to come in.
- If one of your group members gets lost or forgets to come in, prompt him or her quietly.
- Accept both suggestions and praise from your audience.

Show Time!

Invite students to perform the script for an audience such as members of the class, students from other classes, school staff members, or parents.

Continue your performances during small-group reading time, giving each group the opportunity to perform.

Assess and Reflect

After all groups have completed their performance, use the following self-assessment activity to help students reflect on their performance, identify how they have improved as readers and performers, and determine what they will focus on as they participate in future reader's theater experiences throughout the year.

Draw a three-column reflection chart on chart paper. Include a column for **Reflection Questions** and columns to answer **Yes** or **No** in response. Use the following questions to guide the group's assessment of their performance, or use the Reader's Theater Self-Assessment (BLM 6). Place a check mark in the appropriate column, noting their responses.

- Did we make our reading sound smooth like talking?
- Did we make our characters sound and feel like real people (or animals/objects) with feelings?
- Did we act out our parts with our voices and body language?
- Were our parts at "just right" reading levels?
- Did we practice our reading many times before performing?
- Did we pause in the correct places to help our audience understand the characters and message of the script?

Connect and transfer. Discuss ways to improve future performances based on the self-assessment and reflections.

Small-Group Reading Instruction (60 MINUTES)

Use the small-group reading time to continue students' performances of *Our New Home*.

After all groups have performed, use the Assess and Reflect activity above.

Individual Student Conferences (10 MINUTES)

Have students use their self-reflection to show how they would read differently next time. Discuss how students plan to apply what they learned to future performances and independent reading.

Word Study Workshop (20 MINUTES)

Use the Day 5 instruction provided in Grade 3 Word Study Unit 6.

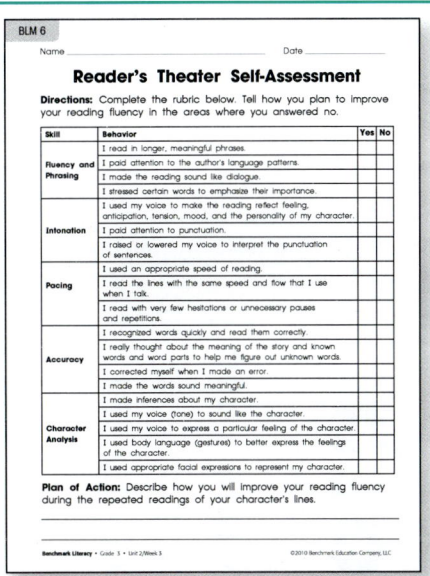

Reader's Theater Self-Assessment (BLM 6)

Make Content Comprehensible for ELLs

Beginning
Allow beginning ELLs to participate as active listeners. Track print with students, emphasizing the relationship between the bold names in the script and the changes in speaker in the performance.

Intermediate and Advanced
Pair ELLs with more fluent readers to chorally read their parts in the script. Encourage students to highlight their lines.

Assessment Tip

During student performances, record anecdotal notes that focus on how students are developing fluency skills and how they are meeting performer and audience member expectations.

Name _____ Date _____

Speed/Pacing	Pausing	Inflection/Intonation	Phrasing	Expression
	Short Pause			

Cutting Down on Trash

You eat a banana...you throw away the peel. You empty your backpack...you throw away your old math papers. You pour a glass of milk...you throw away the carton. Sadly, most of our garbage ends up in a trash bin—and then in a landfill.

Many people have found a different way to handle trash: reuse items in a new way. They put things like grass clippings and eggshells in a pile outdoors to make compost, a rich soil for the garden. They use the backs of junk mail letters—in place of new paper—in their computer printer. They use an empty green bean can, washed and wrapped in leftover yarn, to hold markers on a desk. The list goes on and on . . .

So what about your trash—the banana peel, old math papers, and milk carton? The banana peel can go in your new compost pile; the family can write grocery lists on the backs of your old math papers; you can make a bird feeder from the milk carton. You've done it—you've reused instead of throwing away!

Name _____ Date _____

Fluency Self-Assessment Master Checklist

	Yes	No
Speed/Pacing		
Did my speed and pacing match the kind of text I was reading?		
Did my speed and pacing match what the character was saying?		
Did I read with a natural talking voice?		
Did I slow my reading down when appropriate?		
Did I pay attention to punctuation?		
Pausing		
Did I pause to keep from running all my words together?		
Did I pause in the correct locations?		
Did I pause for the appropriate length of time?		
Did I pause to help my reading make sense?		
Did I use punctuation to help me figure out when to pause?		
Inflection/Intonation		
Did I make my voice rise at a question mark?		
Did I make my voice fall at a period?		
Did I think about what the author was saying so I would know when to read louder or softer?		
Did I think about what the author was saying so I would know when to stress or emphasize words?		
Phrasing		
Did I notice the phrases?		
Did I read all the words in each phrase together?		
Did I think about what the words in the phrase mean when they are together?		
Expression		
Did I look for clues so I could anticipate the mood of the passage?		
Did I use my tone of voice, facial expressions, and body language to express what the author or characters were thinking or feeling?		
Did I change my reading when something new was about to happen?		
Integration		
Did I read the words right? (accuracy)		
Did I read the words at the right speed? (rate)		
Did I read with expression? (prosody)		
Did my reading sound like talking?		
Did I understand what I read?		

Name _____   Date _____

Mom: Let me see. Oh, these are my grandparents, Janina and Stefan. They came from Poland to live in the United States.

Daniela: There's a lot of cool stuff in these boxes. Hey, look what I found! An old diary! Was this Janina's?

Mom: Yes, it looks like it was.

Dad: What are you two up to in this dusty attic?

Daniela: We were just talking about Mom's grandparents from Poland. Why would they leave everything to go to a new country?

Mom: Thanks for helping me clean out the attic today, Daniela.

Daniela: It's no problem, Mom.

Mom: These boxes are very old. I haven't opened them since we moved them from my grandparents' house.

Daniela: Mom, look! There are old pictures in this box. Who are the people in this picture by the Statue of Liberty?

Name _____   Date _____

Antonyms

Directions: Write a word and its antonym. Then write what each word means.

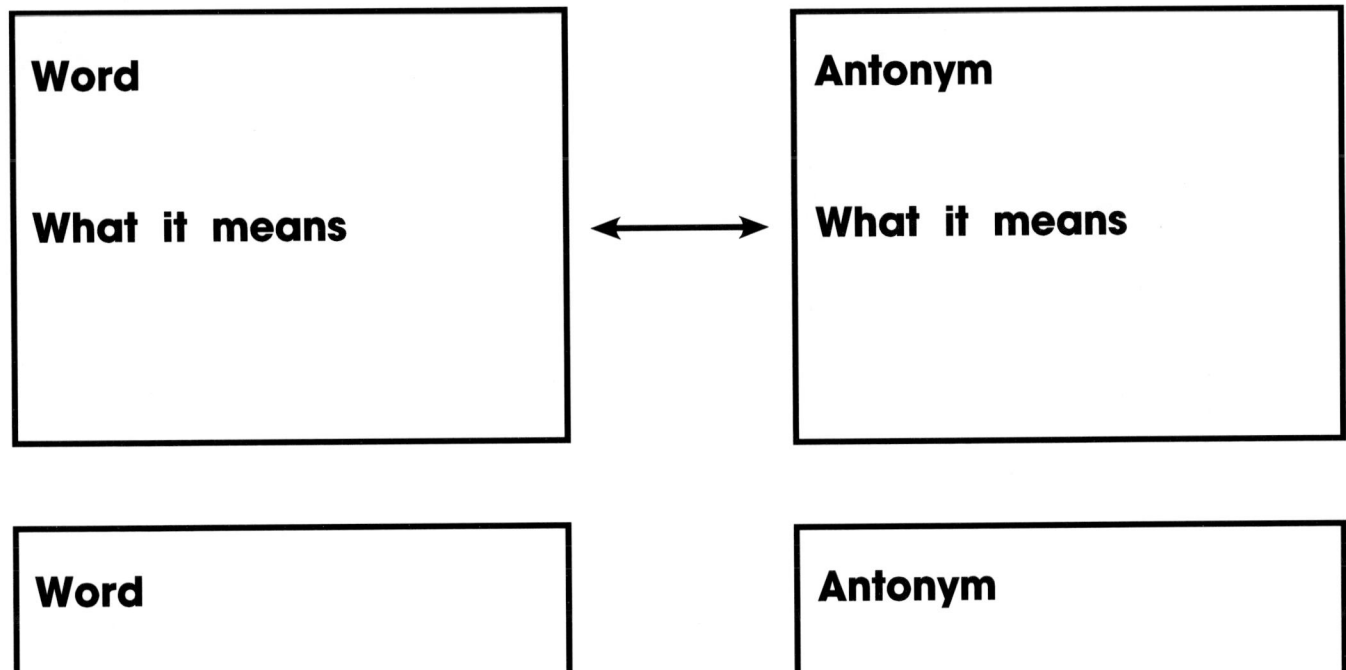

Name _____ Date _____

Daniela: I remember them talking about "the neighborhood." Did they stay there?

Mom: Yes. My father took over the newspaper when Eric got older. And my mother was a teacher. They still love that neighborhood. And they live in the very same house that Janina and Stefan lived in.

Dad: My parents lived down the block. That's how Mom and I met, in the neighborhood. It's different now, but it's still home to our parents.

Daniela: I'm happy that Mom's grandparents were brave enough to move to America. If they hadn't, I wouldn't be here!

Mom: They were happy, too, Daniela. Listen to Janina's last diary entry.

15

14

Name _____   Date _____

Reader's Theater Self-Assessment

Directions: Complete the rubric below. Tell how you plan to improve your reading fluency in the areas where you answered no.

Skill	Behavior	Yes	No
Fluency and Phrasing	I read in longer, meaningful phrases.		
	I paid attention to the author's language patterns.		
	I made the reading sound like dialogue.		
	I stressed certain words to emphasize their importance.		
Intonation	I used my voice to make the reading reflect feeling, anticipation, tension, mood, and the personality of my character.		
	I paid attention to punctuation.		
	I raised or lowered my voice to interpret the punctuation of sentences.		
Pacing	I used an appropriate speed of reading.		
	I read the lines with the same speed and flow that I use when I talk.		
	I read with very few hesitations or unnecessary pauses and repetitions.		
Accuracy	I recognized words quickly and read them correctly.		
	I really thought about the meaning of the story and known words and word parts to help me figure out unknown words.		
	I corrected myself when I made an error.		
	I made the words sound meaningful.		
Character Analysis	I made inferences about my character.		
	I used my voice (tone) to sound like the character.		
	I used my voice to express a particular feeling of the character.		
	I used body language (gestures) to better express the feelings of the character.		
	I used appropriate facial expressions to represent my character.		

Plan of Action: Describe how you will improve your reading fluency during the repeated readings of your character's lines.

_____

_____

BENCHMARK LITERACY

Make Connections/Make Inferences

Celebration

Unit 5/Week 1 at a Glance

Day	Mini-Lessons
ONE	• Introduce the Comprehension Strategy: *Make Inferences* • Think Aloud and Use the Metacognitive Strategy: *Make Connections* • Make an Inference About a Picture • Connect Thinking, Speaking, and Writing • Reflect and Discuss
TWO	• Review the Metacognitive Strategy: *Make Connections* • Use the Comprehension Strategy: *Make Inferences* • Connect Thinking, Speaking, and Writing • Reflect and Discuss
THREE	• Extend the Comprehension Strategy: *Make Inferences* • Observe and Prompt for Strategy Understanding • Reflect and Discuss
FOUR	• Read and Summarize • Answer Text-Dependent Comprehension Questions: *Make Inferences (Level 3: Prove It!)* • Reflect and Discuss
FIVE	• Metacognitive Self-Assessment • Constructed Written Response • Ongoing Comprehension Strategy Assessment

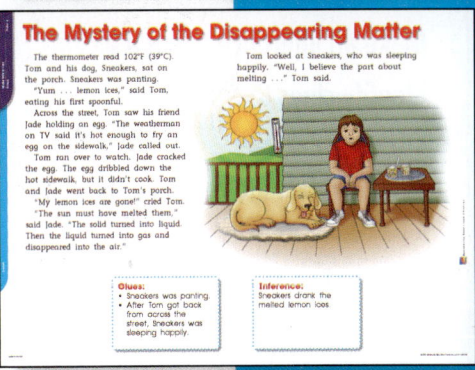

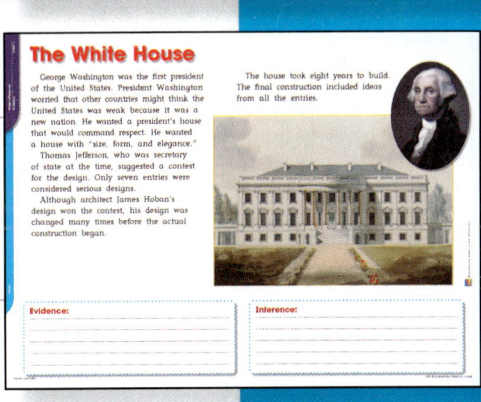

BENCHMARK EDUCATION COMPANY

Day One

Celebration

Comprehension Anchor Poster 1

Lesson Objectives

Students will:

- Make an inference about a picture.
- Identify clues that support the inference.
- Make connections to the topic of a picture.
- Use academic sentence frames to discuss strategies.

Related Resources

- Home/School Connections (BLM 1)
- BenchmarkUniverse.com

About the Strategy

- Making an inference means to figure out something that is not stated directly in a text.
- An inference is based on one or two clues in the text.
- Authors do not always tell readers everything, but they include clues that readers can put together for themselves.
- Making inferences helps readers better understand the ideas in a text.

Read-Aloud (10 MINUTES)

Select a favorite fiction read-aloud from your classroom or school library with which to model the metacognitive strategy "Make Connections." Use the sample read-aloud lessons and suggested titles in the Getting Started Guide.

Mini-Lessons (20 MINUTES)

Introduce the Comprehension Strategy: Make Inferences

Say: *A boy named Eric asked his friend Matt to go swimming with him. Matt said he could not go because he did not know how to swim. Eric did not see Matt for several weeks because Matt went to summer camp. When Matt returned, he invited Eric to go swimming, and they swam together.*

Ask: *What could you infer, or figure out, about how Matt changed while he was away?*

Turn and talk. Ask students to turn to a partner and share their inferences. Ask a few students to share with the whole group.

Explain: *I would infer that Matt had learned how to swim while he was at summer camp. When you make an inference, you use one or two clues or pieces of evidence to state a fact. Matt could not swim. After he went to summer camp, he knew how to swim. These clues or pieces of evidence lead to the inference that Matt learned how to swim at summer camp. Good readers know how to make inferences in fiction and nonfiction texts. We're going to practice making inferences this week.*

Think Aloud and Use the Metacognitive Strategy: Make Connections

Display Poster 1.

Draw students' attention to the fireworks. (Whiteboard users can use the highlighter tool.)

Explain: *When I look at this picture, the first thing I need to do is figure out what it is trying to show me. One way I can do that is by making connections. I can make connections to my own experiences. Let me show you how I do it.*

Think aloud: *The picture shows fireworks going off. It reminds me of times when I have seen fireworks. I have often seen fireworks on the Fourth of July. I can infer that the fireworks are going off for the Fourth of July. Making connections helped me make an inference about the picture.*

Write your connection on chart paper. Ask students to generate other connections they could make about the picture, and add these to your list. Explore possible answers together.

Post these connections on the wall as a Make Connections anchor chart, or invite students to write them in their reading journals or notebooks to use in the future.

Make an Inference About a Picture

Ask students to make an inference about the reason for the fireworks in the picture. Point out that the title of the poster, "Celebration," can help them make an inference.

Ask students to tell which details in the photo and what connections they made helped them make an inference about the reason for the fireworks.

Provide the following academic sentence frames to support ELLs and struggling students:

The reason for the fireworks in the picture is _____.
Information in the picture that supports this inference is _____.
Connections I can make that support this inference are _____.

Connect Thinking, Speaking, and Writing

Write down the inferences students make and reread them as a group. Then write the information and connections they used to make the inference. Give students the opportunity to expand on their shared writing.

Reflect and Discuss

Ask and discuss the following questions:
- *What does it mean to make an inference?*
- *How many clues do you need to make an inference?*
- *How can making connections help you make an inference?*

Connect and transfer. Say: *Remember, you can make inferences based on clues in a text, too. Tomorrow, we will practice making inferences based on clues in a text.*

Make Content Comprehensible for ELLs

Use the following strategies to help ELLs understand the poster content and acquire academic language.

Beginning
Read the title of the poster. Discuss the concept of fireworks and celebrations. For example, **say:** *We celebrate special days. We celebrate birthdays. We celebrate the Fourth of the July. When we celebrate, we have fun with our friends and family.*

Point to and name the fireworks in the photograph. Explain how fireworks work. Note that fireworks are a special way to celebrate.

Beginning and Intermediate
Draw and label, or ask ELLs to draw, other objects related to celebrations, such as cakes and piñatas.

All Levels
Pair ELLs with fluent English speakers during partner discussions and activities.

Comprehension Quick-Check

Observe whether students are able to articulate inferences about the poster. If they have difficulty, use the following additional explicit instruction.

Draw the make inferences graphic organizer on chart paper.

In the Clues column, write *fireworks*.

Say: *The picture shows fireworks going off, and the title says "Celebration." I know that fireworks are often used in Fourth of July celebrations.*

In the Inference column, write *People are celebrating the Fourth of July*.

Say: *I looked at clues in the picture, and I made connections to experiences I have had. I combined these two clues to make an inference about the picture.*

Say: *Now think of another inference we could make about the photo.*

Support Special Needs Learners

Support visual learners and students with attention issues by projecting the whiteboard version of the posters. Allow students to come to the whiteboard and circle, underline, or highlight sentences and illustrations. Invite them to discuss and then make inferences about what they see.

Access the graphic organizer provided on the whiteboard. Record clues and inferences with students.

Provide opportunities for active involvement. For example, ask students to make connections to content on the posters. Or point out clues on the poster, and ask students to make an inference based on the clues.

Access the image bank for enlarged images that students can use to practice making connections, finding clues, and making inferences.

Home/School Connections

On Day 1, distribute copies of Home/ School Connections (BLM 1). Each day during the week, assign one of the six home/school connection activities for the students to complete. Ask them to bring their completed assignments to class the next day. Make time at the beginning of each day for students to share their ideas.

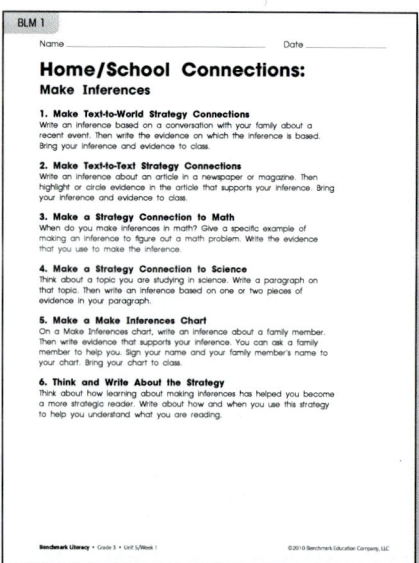

Home/School Connections (BLM 1)

Small-Group Reading Instruction (60 MINUTES)

Based on students' instructional reading levels, select titles that provide opportunities for students to practice making inferences. See the Leveled Te Titles chart provided at the back of this Teacher's Resource System.

Use the before-, during-, and after-reading instruction provided in the Teacher's Guide for each text.

Individual Student Conferences (10 MINUTES)

Confer with individual students on their text selections and applications of strategies. Use the Individual Reading Conference Form on page 32 of Inform Assessments for Reading Development to help guide your conferences.

Word Study Workshop (20 MINUTES)

Use the Day 1 instruction provided in Word Study Unit 13.

Read-Aloud (10 MINUTES)

Select a favorite fiction read-aloud from your classroom or school library with which to model the metacognitive strategy "Make Connections." Use the sample read-aloud lessons and suggested titles in the Getting Started Guide.

Mini-Lessons (20 MINUTES)

Review the Metacognitive Strategy: Make Connections

Display Poster 2 with annotations hidden and/or distribute BLM 2 and read aloud the title.

Read aloud the text with students.

Explain: *Yesterday when I looked at the "Celebration" poster, I made a connection to my own life to help me understand. When I make connections, I can also make a connection between the text and the world. I'll show you how I do this.*

Reread the first paragraph. **Think aloud:** *In the first paragraph, I learn that the temperature is 102 degrees, and that the dog is panting. I can make connections to what I know about hot days and about dogs. I know that 102 degrees is extremely hot, and that dogs pant to keep cool when it is hot.*

Write your connections on chart paper.

Reread the rest of the passage. **Think aloud:** *I can make more text-to-world connections as I read the rest of the story. For example, I know that when ice, a solid, melts, it turns to water, a liquid.* Write the connection on the chart paper.

Ask students to generate other text-to-world connections. Add their connections to the list on the chart paper. Ask students to write the connections in their reading journals to use in the future.

Build academic oral language. Encourage students to ask themselves what kinds of text-to-world connections they can make. Invite students to describe how making connections helps them solve the mystery in the story. Reinforce the idea that good readers make connections to understand text better. Support ELLs and struggling readers with the following sentence frames:

The mystery in the story is _____.
One text-to-world connection I can make about the story is _____.
An inference I can make about the story is _____.

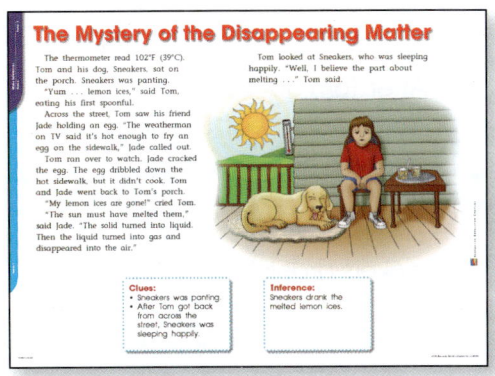

Comprehension Anchor Poster 2 (BLM 2)

Lesson Objectives

Students will:
- Identify clues that help readers make inferences about a text.
- Make inferences based on clues in a text.
- Make connections to understand a text.
- Use academic sentence frames to discuss strategies.

Related Resources
- Home/School Connections (BLM 1)
- Comprehension Anchor Poster 2 (BLM 2)
- BenchmarkUniverse.com

Comprehension Anchor Poster 2 Sample Annotations

Make Content Comprehensible for ELLs

Use the following strategies to help ELLs understand the poster content and acquire academic language.

Beginning

Read aloud the poster title and passage. Point to each person, animal, or thing in the picture and say the word (boy, dog, sun, chair, table, ices).

Beginning and Intermediate

Ask students to make up a sentence using each word.

If you have students whose first language is Spanish, share these English/Spanish cognates: **thermometer/el termómetro, lemon/el limón, fry/freír, solid/el sólido, liquid/el líquido, gas/el gas, disappeared/desaparecer, air/el aire**.

All Levels

Pair ELLs with fluent English speakers during partner discussions and activities.

Model the use of academic sentence frames to support ELLs' academic vocabulary and language development. (See suggested sentence frames provided.)

Use the Comprehension Strategy: Make Inferences

Reread the poster text with students, annotations still hidden.

Say: *Now think about the content of this passage. What inference can I ma to solve the mystery?*

If necessary, explain that the passage's mystery is what happened to Tom's lemon ices. The author provides clues that help solve the mystery.

Say: *Let's look closely to find clues that help solve the mystery. What is the first clue?*

Write the sentence that students identify. Then reveal the first Clues annotation. **Ask:** *Did we find the first clue? Let's compare sentences.*

Build academic oral language. Say: *Clues help us make inferences. Let's look for another clue in the passage that helps us solve the mystery. What i the next clue about what happened to the lemon ices?* (Sneakers was sleepi happily.) *What inference can we make based on these two clues?* (The lemo ices melted, and Sneakers drank the liquid.)

Connect Thinking, Speaking, and Writing

Prompt students to make an inference based on the clues they have recorded. Students should understand that an inference is usually based on one or two pieces of evidence plus connections readers make to themselves, the world, or other texts.

Record students' inferences on chart paper. Then reveal the Inference annotation.

Say: *Let's compare our inference sentence to the sentence on the poster.* Allow time for discussion.

Reflect and Discuss

Ask and discuss the following questions:
- *How does making text-to-world connections help you as a reader?*
- *Why is it important to look for clues as you read?*
- *How does making inferences help you understand what you are reading?*

Connect and transfer. Say: *How will you use what we have practiced today when you read on your own?*

Small-Group Reading Instruction (60 MINUTES)

Based on students' instructional reading levels, select titles that provide opportunities for students to practice making inferences. See the Leveled Text Titles chart provided at the back of this Teacher's Resource System.

Use the before-, during-, and after-reading instruction provided in the Teacher's Guide for each text.

Individual Student Conferences (10 MINUTES)

Confer with individual students on their text selections and applications of strategies. Use the Individual Reading Conference Form on page 32 of Informal Assessments for Reading Development to help guide your conferences.

Word Study Workshop (20 MINUTES)

Use the Day 2 instruction provided in Word Study Unit 13.

Comprehension Quick-Check

Take note of which students can or cannot contribute to the discussion of the Poster 2 inferences. Use the following activity to provide additional explicit instruction for these students.

Use an additional real-world example to help students understand how to make inferences. For example: Jill and Sara have similar backpacks. One day, Jill is the last person to leave the classroom. The only backpack left is Sara's. Ask students to state the clues and make an inference. Record the clues and inference on a graphic organizer. Then write them as a paragraph. Ask students to underline the inference and circle each clue.

Oral Language Extension

During independent workstation time, pair students to discuss hobbies and extracurricular activities they enjoy. Ask one partner to describe an activity. Then ask the second partner to make an inference about the information and to identify the clues on which the inference is based. The partner can state whether the inference is or is not correct. For example, Partner A says she takes ballet lessons once a week and tap lessons once a week. Partner B infers that Partner A enjoys dancing. Then partners switch roles. Tell students to be ready to report on their inferences and clues during individual conference time.

Home/School Connections

At the beginning of the day, make time for students to share their ideas based on the activity they completed the previous night.

At the end of the day, ask students to complete another home/school connection activity from BLM 1 and bring their assignment to class tomorrow.

Day Three

Comprehension Anchor Poster 3 (BLM 3)

Lesson Objectives

Students will:

- Make an inference about unstated information in a passage.

- Identify clues that support the inference.

- Make connections to information in a text to help make inferences.

- Use academic sentence frames to discuss strategies.

Related Resources

- Home/School Connections (BLM 1)

- Comprehension Anchor Poster 3 (BLM 3)

- BenchmarkUniverse.com

Evidence: Washington's government held a contest to design the White House. The final White House included ideas from the seven contest finalists.

Inference: President Washington and his government wanted to have ordinary Americans participate in building the White House.

Comprehension Anchor Poster 3 Sample Annotations

Read-Aloud (10 MINUTES)

Select a favorite nonfiction read-aloud from your classroom or school librar with which to model the metacognitive strategy "Make Connections." Use th sample read-aloud lessons and suggested titles in the Getting Started Guide

Mini-Lessons (20 MINUTES)

Extend the Comprehension Strategy: Make Inferences

Display Poster 3 and/or distribute BLM 3 and read aloud the title.

Say: *Today you're going to practice reading and making inferences about a text. You can make connections to the text to help you understand.*

Based on students' needs and abilities, ask them to read the passage independently or with a partner. Tell them to locate and write in the Evidenc box clues to information the author does not provide. Encourage students to make an inference based on the clues in the Inference box. Tell students to underline, circle, or flag key information as they read.

Invite individual students or pairs to share the clues they identified and the inferences they made. Record students' findings on the poster or on chart paper. See the sample annotations.

Observe and Prompt for Strategy Understanding

While using the poster, note students who demonstrate understanding of the concepts and those who seem to struggle. Use appropriate responsive prompting to help students who need modeling or additional guidance, or to validate students who demonstrate mastery.

Goal Oriented
- *I am going to read slowly and reread if necessary to locate clues.*
- *I am going to use clues in the text and what I know to make inferences.*
- *The clue word(s) _____ help(s) me figure out, or infer, that _____ .*

Directive and Corrective Feedback
- *Does that word provide a clue to what the author does not state?*
- *What clues help you understand what the author means?*
- *What inference can you make? What helped you make the inference?*

Self-Monitoring and Reflection
- *What could you do to help yourself make an inference?*
- *What connections could you make?*

Validating and Confirming
- *You really understand what the author did not state directly.*
- *You really picked up on the clues and used what you knew to make an inference. Good job!*

Build academic oral language. Ask students to share the connections they made to help them make an inference.

Reflect and Discuss

Ask and discuss the following questions:
- *What kinds of texts have you read for which you had to make inferences?*
- *What kinds of inferences might you need to make in a fictional story?*
- *Why is it important to make inferences?*

Connect and transfer. Say: *Remember that authors do not always state facts directly. Look for clues that you can use to make inferences today when you read in small groups. Make connections to your life, other texts, and the world to help you make inferences.*

Small-Group Reading Instruction (60 MINUTES)

Based on students' instructional reading levels, select titles that provide opportunities for students to practice making inferences. See the Leveled Text Titles chart provided at the back of this Teacher's Resource System.

Use the before-, during-, and after-reading instruction provided in the Teacher's Guide for each text.

Individual Student Conferences (10 MINUTES)

Confer with individual students on their text selections and applications of strategies. Use the Individual Reading Conference Form on page 32 of Informal Assessments for Reading Development to help guide your conferences.

Word Study Workshop (20 MINUTES)

Use the Day 3 instruction provided in Word Study Unit 13.

Make Content Comprehensible for ELLs

Use the following strategies to help ELLs understand the poster content and acquire academic language.

Beginning
Point to the poster illustrations and provide the language for what you see. For example: White House, President George Washington. Invite ELLs to point to and name people and objects with you.

Beginning and Intermediate
If you have students whose first language is Spanish, share these English/Spanish cognates: **president/el presidente, nation/la nación, respect/el respeto, form/la forma, elegance/la elegancia, secretary/el secretario, suggest/sugerir**.

Intermediate
Describe the poster content in your own words. For example, **say:** *George Washington was our first President. He wanted a great president's house. He wanted the house to show what a great country the United States is.* Encourage students to add their own comments about the poster.

Comprehension Quick-Check

The responsive prompts on pages 8–9 are designed to help you meet the needs of individual students. Based on your observations, identify students who may need additional explicit reinforcement of the strategy during small-group instruction or intervention time. Use similar responsive prompts during small-group instruction to scaffold students toward independent use of the strategy.

Home/School Connections

At the end of the day, ask students to complete another home/school connection activity from BLM 1 and bring their assignment to class tomorrow.

Plants, Animals, and Humans

Why do plants, animals, and humans live where they do? Part of the answer is climate. Climate is the typical weather for an area over a long period of time. Many things affect an area's climate. Places on or near the equator are much warmer than those far away. The climate is drier and colder high above sea level. Oceans tend to make a climate milder.

Within climate zones are different biomes. A biome is an area with a climate that suits a certain set of plants and animals. Humans have found ways to live in most biomes, but many plants and animals are not as flexible. Now, humans are taking up more and more of Earth's land and water.

Comprehension Anchor Poster 4 (BLM 4)

Lesson Objectives

Students will:

- Learn strategies for analyzing questions and finding answers, clues, and evidence.

- Identify clues to answer questions that are not directly answered in a text.

- Answer text-dependent make inferences questions.

- Use academic vocabulary to discuss strategies.

Related Resources

- Home/School Connections (BLM 1)

- Comprehension Anchor Poster 4 (BLM 4)

- Comprehension Questions (BLM 5)

- BenchmarkUniverse.com

Read-Aloud (10 MINUTES)

Select a favorite nonfiction read-aloud from your classroom or school librar with which to model the metacognitive strategy "Make Connections." Use t sample read-aloud lessons and suggested titles in the Getting Started Guide

Mini-Lessons (20 MINUTES)

Read and Summarize

Display Poster 4 and/or distribute BLM 4.

Based on students' needs and abilities, ask them to read the passage independently or with a partner. Remind students to make connections to h them understand what they read.

Build academic oral language. When students have finished, ask individua or pairs to tell inferences they made about the passage. Encourage ELLs or struggling readers to use these academic sentence frames:

> One clue is _____.
> Another clue is _____.
> My inference is _____.

Answer Text-Dependent Comprehension Questions: Make Inferences (Level 3: Prove It!)

Say: *Sometimes you need to answer questions about a passage you've rea Some questions require you to make inferences. Today we're going to read and answer questions. Some of the questions will ask you to make inference*

Distribute BLM 5 and read Question 2 together. ("How would a scientist figu out a biome's climate?")

Ask: *What is the question asking us to do?* If students can't tell you, **say:** *The question is asking us for an answer that is not stated directly in the passage. What strategy will we need?* (make inferences) *How do you know?* (An inference is not stated in the text but is based on clues in the text.)

Say: *The text doesn't say how a scientist figures out a biome's climate. So I will look for details about scientists, biomes, and climate in the text and the put them together to answer the question. I'm going to read this question again carefully to be sure I understand the information I need to look for.*

Say: *Now we're ready to reread the passage to find the information we need. We know we need to find clues about figuring out a biome's climate. The third sentence says climate is the typical weather for an area over a long period of time. So I know that scientists must study a biome's weather over a long period to know what the biome's climate is. Answers B and C both describe long periods of time. However, I know that weather includes not just temperature but temperature and rainfall. So I know that answer B is not correct. I'll choose answer C. The clues were in the text, but I had to put them together, along with what I already knew about weather, to get the answer. I made an inference to answer the question.*

Ask students to work independently or with a partner to answer additional text-dependent questions on BLM 5.

Review students' answers and use the poster as needed to model analyzing questions and rereading to make inferences that answer the questions.

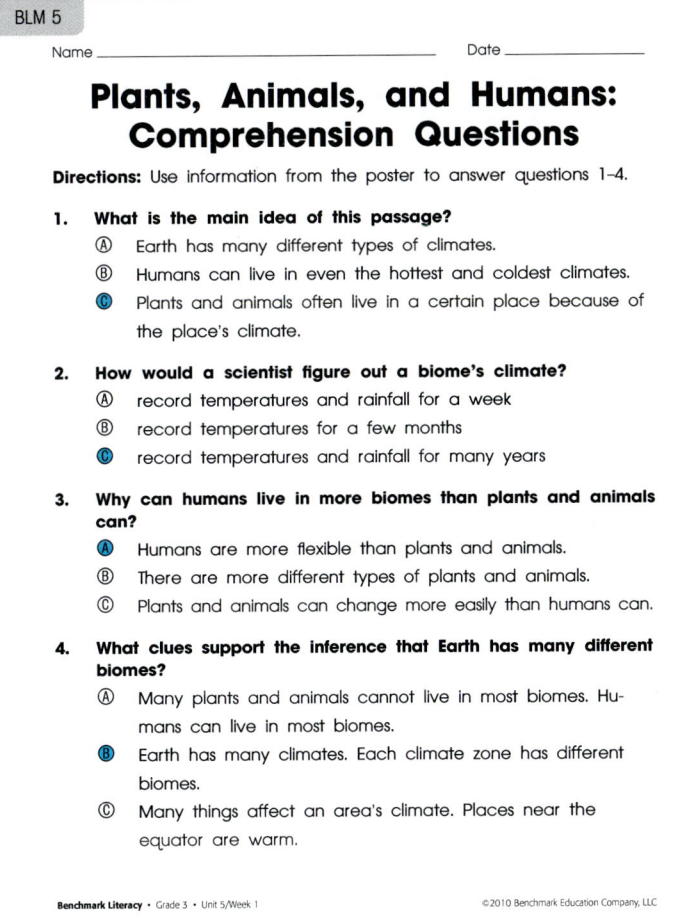

Comprehension Questions (BLM 5)

Make Content Comprehensible for ELLs

Use the following strategies to help ELLs understand the poster content and acquire academic language.

Beginning
Support the concepts of weather and climate by pointing to the weather outside and **saying** *The weather today is _____* and statements such as *We have cool winters and warm summers, so we have a mild climate.*

Beginning and Intermediate
Point to the poster illustration and **say:** *The weather in the picture is warm and dry.* Ask students to explain how you can tell.

Use photos of different types of weather and places with a variety of climates to illustrate the concepts of weather and climate. Encourage students to use the sentence frame:

In [name of season] the weather is

_____.

If you have students whose first language is Spanish, share these academic English/ Spanish cognates: **plants/las plantas, animals/los animales, humans/los humanos, climate/el clima, typical/ típico, area/el área, period/el periodo, equator/el ecuador, zones/las zonas, flexible/flexible.**

Evidence:
• Each biome has a climate that suits a certain set of plants and animals.
• Plants and animals are not able to live in most biomes as humans are.

Inference:
• Some biomes have fewer types of plants and animals than others.

Comprehension Anchor Poster 4
Sample Annotations

Comprehension Quick-Check

Note whether students are able to analyze each Level 3 text-dependent comprehension question and return to the text to find the information they need to answer the question correctly. If students have difficulty, use small-group reading time for additional practice answering these kinds of questions, which appear on standardized reading assessments. The Comprehension Question Card for each leveled text provides practice questions at four levels of comprehension. The Comprehension Through Deductive Reasoning Flip Chart helps you model the strategies students need to master.

Oral Language Extension

Display Comprehension Anchor Poster 4 during independent workstation time. Invite pairs of students to read and talk about the poster together. Encourage them to list and describe some specific climates and the types of weather that characterize each. Ask students to make one or two inferences about the weather and climates they discuss. Remind them to be prepared to share their lists and inferences during independent conference time.

Home/School Connections

At the beginning of the day, make time for students to share their ideas based on the activity they completed the previous night.

At the end of the day, ask students to complete another home/school connection activity from BLM 1 and bring their assignment to class tomorrow.

Reflect and Discuss the Comprehension Strategy

Ask and discuss the following:
- *What strategy did we use to answer questions about the text?*
- *Notice how we looked for clues and made inferences to answer questions.*

Connect and transfer. Say: *Practice making inferences. This strategy can h you better understand and remember the ideas in what you read. It can als help you when you take tests.*

Small-Group Reading Instruction (60 MINUTES)

Based on students' instructional reading levels, select titles that provide opportunities for students to practice making inferences. See the Leveled Te Titles chart provided at the back of this Teacher's Resource System.

Use the before-, during-, and after-reading instruction provided in the Teacher's Guide for each text.

Use the Comprehension Question Card for each title and the Comprehensio Through Deductive Reasoning Flip Chart to practice answering Level 3 text-dependent comprehension questions.

Individual Student Conferences (10 MINUTES)

Confer with individual students on their text selections and applications of strategies. Use the Individual Reading Conference Form on page 32 of Inforn Assessments for Reading Development to help guide your conferences.

Word Study Workshop (20 MINUTES)

Use the Day 4 instruction provided in Word Study Unit 13.

Read-Aloud (10 MINUTES)

Revisit the week's read-alouds to make text-to-text connections and provide opportunities for reader response. Use the suggested activities in the Getting Started Guide, or implement ideas of your own.

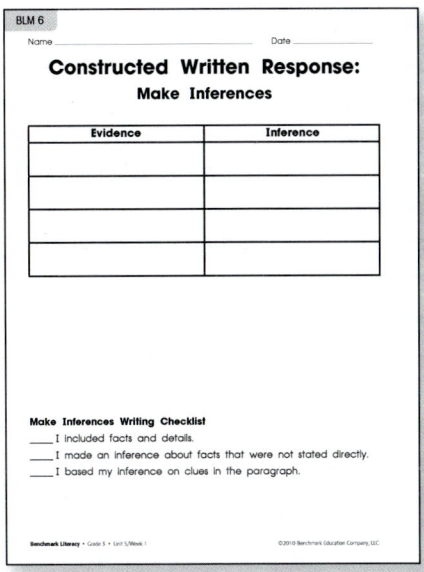

Constructed Written Response (BLM 6)

Assessment (20 MINUTES)

Metacognitive Self-Assessment

Ask students to reflect on their use of metacognitive and comprehension strategies this week. What did they learn? How will they use the strategies in the future? What do they still need to practice, and how can they do this?

Invite students to share their reflections in one of the following ways: conduct a whole-class discussion; ask students to turn and talk to a partner and then share their ideas with the class; or ask students to record their thoughts in their journals or notebooks.

Constructed Written Response

Distribute copies of Constructed Written Response (BLM 6) and ask students to think about a specific biome (such as ocean, desert, or mountain) and to list plants and animals that live in that biome. In the Inference column, students should make an inference about the biome, the plants, and/or the animals. In the Evidence column, students can note the clues that support the inference.

Work with students individually. Ask them to write a paragraph describing the biome and its plants and animals, using notes from the graphic organizer. If students need extra help, encourage them to use reference books about biomes in the classroom.

Read aloud the checklist at the bottom of BLM 6 to help students evaluate their work.

Challenge activity. Students who are able to may also find out more about their biome in a library book and add information to their paragraphs.

Support activity. If students cannot make inferences about biomes, plants, and animals, review clues in their paragraphs with them. They can use the sentence frames: *I can make the inference that _____. The clues to this inference are _____ and _____.* Reinforce the fact that inferences are made about facts that are not directly stated.

Lesson Objectives

Students will:

- Reflect orally on their strategy use.
- Create a make inferences graphic organizer and write a paragraph based on it.
- Answer multiple-choice and short-answer questions.

Related Resources

- Home/School Connections (BLM 1)
- Constructed Written Response (BLM 6)
- Comprehension Strategy Assessments, Grade 3
- BenchmarkUniverse.com

Make Assessments Accessible for ELLs

Use the following strategies to help ELLs demonstrate their understanding of the strategies.

Beginning
Use Constructed Written Response (BLM 6) with ELLs at the beginning proficiency level.

Beginning and Intermediate
Use the Comprehension Strategy Assessment as a listening comprehension assessment and scaffold students' understanding of the text. As an alternative, allow students to tell you about making inferences in one of the Comprehension Anchor Posters you have used during the week.

Intermediate and Advanced
Support ELLs with academic sentence frames during the metacognitive self-assessment. Possible sentence frames to use are:

We make connections so that _____.

I will make connections when I _____.

All Levels
Pair ELLs with fluent English speakers during partner discussions and activities.

Home/School Connections

At the beginning of the day, make time for students to share their ideas based on the activity they completed the previous night.

Ongoing Comprehension Strategy Assessment

Distribute one of the Make Inferences Comprehension Strategy Assessment from the Grade 3 Comprehension Strategy Assessment book ("Just Not Herself," pages 82–83, or "Harriet the Tortoise," pages 84–85). Ask students read the passage and use the information to answer the questions.

Use the results of this assessment to determine students who need addition work with the strategy.

Record students' assessment scores on the Strategy Assessment Record (page 133) so that you can monitor their progress following additional instruction or intervention.

Provide additional modeling and guided practice during small-group readin instruction using the recommended titles in this Teacher's Guide.

Small-Group Reading Instruction (60 MINUTES)

Based on students' instructional reading levels, select titles that provide opportunities for students to practice making inferences. See the Leveled Tex Titles chart provided at the back of this Teacher's Resource System.

Use the before-, during-, and after-reading instruction provided in the Teacher's Guide for each text.

Individual Student Conferences (10 MINUTES)

Confer with individual students on their text selections and applications of strategies. Use the Individual Reading Conference Form on page 32 of Inform Assessments for Reading Development to help guide your conferences.

Word Study Workshop (20 MINUTES)

Use the Day 5 instruction provided in Word Study Unit 13.

Name _____ Date _____

Home/School Connections:
Make Inferences

Make Text-to-World Strategy Connections

Write an inference based on a conversation with your family about a recent event. Then write the evidence on which the inference is based. Bring your inference and evidence to class.

Make Text-to-Text Strategy Connections

Write an inference about an article in a newspaper or magazine. Then highlight or circle evidence in the article that supports your inference. Bring your inference and evidence to class.

Make a Strategy Connection to Math

When do you make inferences in math? Give a specific example of making an inference to figure out a math problem. Write the evidence that you use to make the inference.

Make a Strategy Connection to Science

Think about a topic you are studying in science. Write a paragraph on that topic. Then write an inference based on one or two pieces of evidence in your paragraph.

Make a Make Inferences Chart

On a Make Inferences chart, write an inference about a family member. Then write evidence that supports your inference. You can ask a family member to help you. Sign your name and your family member's name to your chart. Bring your chart to class.

Think and Write About the Strategy

Think about how learning about making inferences has helped you become a more strategic reader. Write about how and when you use this strategy to help you understand what you are reading.

Name _____   Date _____

The Mystery of the Disappearing Matter

The thermometer read 102°F (39°C). Tom and his dog, Sneakers, sat on the porch. Sneakers was panting.

"Yum . . . lemon ices," said Tom, eating his first spoonful.

Across the street, Tom saw his friend Jade holding an egg. "The weatherman on TV said it's hot enough to fry an egg on the sidewalk," Jade called out. Tom ran over to watch. Jade cracked the egg. The egg dribbled down the hot sidewalk, but it didn't cook. Tom and Jade went back to Tom's porch.

"My lemon ices are gone!" cried Tom. "The sun must have melted them," said Jade. "The solid turned into liquid. Then the liquid turned into gas and disappeared into the air."

Tom looked at Sneakers, who was sleeping happily. "Well, I believe the part about melting . . ." Tom said.

Inference:

Clues:

Make Inferences
Fiction
Poster 2

Grade 3

Name _____ Date _____

The White House

George Washington was the first president of the United States. President Washington worried that other countries might think the United States was weak because it was a new nation. He wanted a president's house that would command respect. He wanted a house with "size, form, and elegance."

Thomas Jefferson, who was secretary of state at the time, suggested a contest for the design. Only seven entries were considered serious designs.

Although architect James Hoban's design won the contest, his design was changed many times before the actual construction began.

BENCHMARK EDUCATION COMPANY

The house took eight years to build. The final construction included ideas from all the entries.

Inference:

Evidence:

©2010 Benchmark Education Company, LLC • CAP089

Make Inferences
Nonfiction
Poster 3

Grade 3

Name _____ Date _____

Plants, Animals, and Humans

Why do plants, animals, and humans live where they do? Part of the answer is climate. Climate is the typical weather for an area over a long period of time. Many things affect an area's climate. Places on or near the equator are much warmer than those far away. The climate is drier and colder high above sea level. Oceans tend to make a climate milder.

Within climate zones are different biomes. A biome is an area with a climate that suits a certain set of plants and animals. Humans have found ways to live in most biomes, but many plants and animals are not as flexible. Now, humans are taking up more and more of Earth's land and water.

Make Inferences
Nonfiction
Poster 4

Grade 3

ame _____   Date _____

Plants, Animals, and Humans: Comprehension Questions

irections: Use information from the poster to answer questions 1–4.

What is the main idea of this passage?

Ⓐ   Earth has many different types of climates.

Ⓑ   Humans can live in even the hottest and coldest climates.

Ⓒ   Plants and animals often live in a certain place because of the place's climate.

How would a scientist figure out a biome's climate?

Ⓐ   record temperatures and rainfall for a week

Ⓑ   record temperatures for a few months

Ⓒ   record temperatures and rainfall for many years

Why can humans live in more biomes than plants and animals can?

Ⓐ   Humans are more flexible than plants and animals.

Ⓑ   There are more different types of plants and animals.

Ⓒ   Plants and animals can change more easily than humans can.

What clues support the inference that Earth has many different biomes?

Ⓐ   Many plants and animals cannot live in most biomes. Humans can live in most biomes.

Ⓑ   Earth has many climates. Each climate zone has different biomes.

Ⓒ   Many things affect an area's climate. Places near the equator are warm.

Name _____   Date _____

Constructed Written Response:
Make Inferences

Evidence	Inference

Make Inferences Writing Checklist

_____ I included facts and details.

_____ I made an inference about facts that were not stated directly.

_____ I based my inference on clues in the paragraph.

Teacher's Guide | Grade 3 • Unit 5

Week 2

Make Connections/Make Inferences

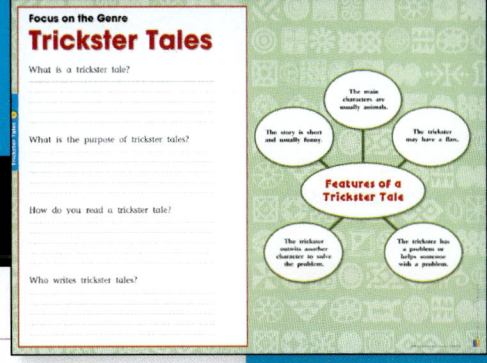

Unit 5/Week 2 at a Glance

Day	Mini-Lessons
ONE	• Activate Prior Knowledge About Genres • Introduce the Genre: *Trickster Tale* • Focus on Genre Features: *Trickster Tale*
TWO	• Model Metacognitive Strategies: *Make Connections* • Introduce Make Inferences • Focus on Genre Features: *Trickster Tale*
THREE	• Make Inferences and Connections
FOUR	• Build Comprehension: *Analyze Story Elements* • Build Tier Two Vocabulary: *Antonyms*
FIVE	• Synthesize and Assess Genre Understanding • Make Connections Across Texts

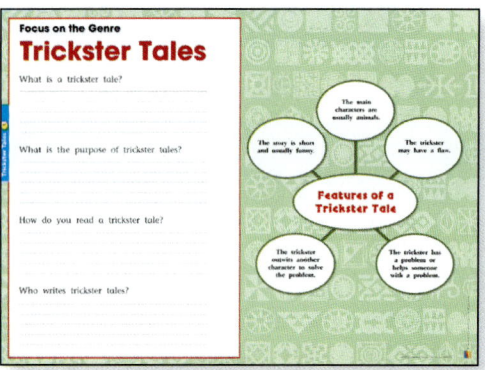

Trickster Tale Poster 1

Lesson Objectives

Students will:

- Review the concept of genre and previously studied genres.

- Create a Trickster Tale anchor chart to demonstrate prior knowledge.

- Build academic oral language and vocabulary as they engage in partner and whole-group discussion.

Related Resources

- Trickster Tale Poster 1 (BLM 1)

- BenchmarkUniverse.com

Read-Aloud (10 MINUTES)

Select a favorite fiction read-aloud from your classroom or school library with which to model the metacognitive strategy "Make Connections." Use the sample read-aloud lessons and suggested titles in the Getting Started Guide.

Mini-Lessons (20 MINUTES)

Activate Prior Knowledge About Genres

Write the word **genre** on chart paper. **Ask:** *Who can tell me what the word* **genre** *means?* Allow responses.

Review: *The word* **genre** *means "a kind of something." Items grouped together in the same genre are similar in certain ways. They share some of the same features. Suppose you read a story about a family who lived in Texas in the 1860s. You want to read more about people in that time. What genres could you look in? Why?* Allow responses.

Say: *Knowing the features of a literature genre helps us predict what the text will include and what to look for as we read. We know what the important elements will be. We can look for important information and make connections between stories. When we write in a certain genre, we know how to structure our writing.*

Ask: *What are some literary genres you have studied and read? Let's make a list of genres.* (Allow responses). *What is one important feature you remember about each genre? Let's list them.*

Introduce the Genre: Trickster Tale

Display Trickster Tale Poster 1 and distribute BLM 1.

Say: *This week we are going to focus on the trickster tale genre. You will read trickster tales in our small reading groups, and you can select other titles from this genre to read independently, too. Let's spend some time thinking about this genre and create our own Trickster Tale anchor chart to record what we already know about trickster tales. Later in the week, we can come back to our chart and reflect on how our understanding of the genre has changed and expanded.*

Display Poster 1 on an easel or use the interactive whiteboard version. You may also make a transparency from Trickster Tale Poster 1 (BLM 1). Show students several trickster tales from your classroom or school library and ask students to share any trickster tales they have read previously.

Read each question on Poster 1 and encourage volunteers to share ideas they have related to the question. Based on students' prior knowledge, provide additional genre background information as needed to fill in the answers to each question. This poster can serve as an anchor chart that you and students can refer to throughout the week as you read and analyze trickster tales.

Support the academic language development of ELLs and struggling readers by providing the following sentence frames to use as they discuss the genre:

> *A trickster tale is _____.*
> *The purpose of a trickster tale is to _____.*
> *When you read a trickster tale, pay attention to _____.*
> *People who write trickster tales are _____.*

Make Content Comprehensible for ELLs

Beginning and Intermediate

Show various examples of trickster tales from your classroom or school library. Read the titles and point to and name the tricksters. Use simple language to explain that trickster tales are usually about animal characters that trick others. For example, **say:** *A trickster tale tells a story about an animal character who tricks somebody. When you trick someone, you make him or her believe something that is not true or real. Look at this trickster tale. This trickster tale is about _____.*

All Levels

Define **trick**, **trickster**, and **tricky**. For example, **say:** *When you trick someone or play a trick on someone, you fool that person. You make her or him believe something that is not true. A trickster is a person who likes to play tricks. Something or someone who is tricky is very clever or sneaky.* Write the words and underline the root in **trickster** and **tricky**.

Model the academic sentence frames provided in this guide to help ELLs contribute their ideas to the discussion of trickster tales.

Support Special Needs Learners

Throughout the week, use these strategies to help students who have learning disabilities access the content and focus on genre studies and comprehension strategies.

Support students by projecting the posters on a whiteboard. Allow students to come to the whiteboard and circle, underline, or highlight features of the genre. Invite them to label what they see on the posters.

Provide opportunities for active involvement. For example, to help students understand the character of the trickster, have students pantomime how the trickster might look when he comes up with his trick and how he might look when he is or is not successful.

Provide repeated opportunities for students to analyze the features of trickster tales. Find features of trickster tales in text examples from read-alouds, small-group, and independent reading. Chart the features on graphic organizers and post them in your classroom as examples.

Find high-interest trickster tales that students can relate to. Use the recommended read-aloud titles provided in the Teacher's Guide, as well as other examples from your school library.

Focus on Genre Features: Trickster Tale

Point to the "Features of a Trickster Tale" web on the right side of the poster.

Say: *As we've discussed, every genre has certain consistent features. Considering our discussions so far, and your own experiences with this genre, what do you think are the consistent features of all, or most, trickster tales? Let's work together to identify them.*

Allow students enough time to generate their own ideas, and record the features they identify on the web. Reread the features together. As necessary, prompt students with the following questions and statements:
- *What does a trickster do?*
- *What is a trickster usually like?*
- *Why does a trickster play a trick?*

Connect and transfer. Say: *This week we will read some trickster tales. Understanding the genre features will help you read with better comprehension.*

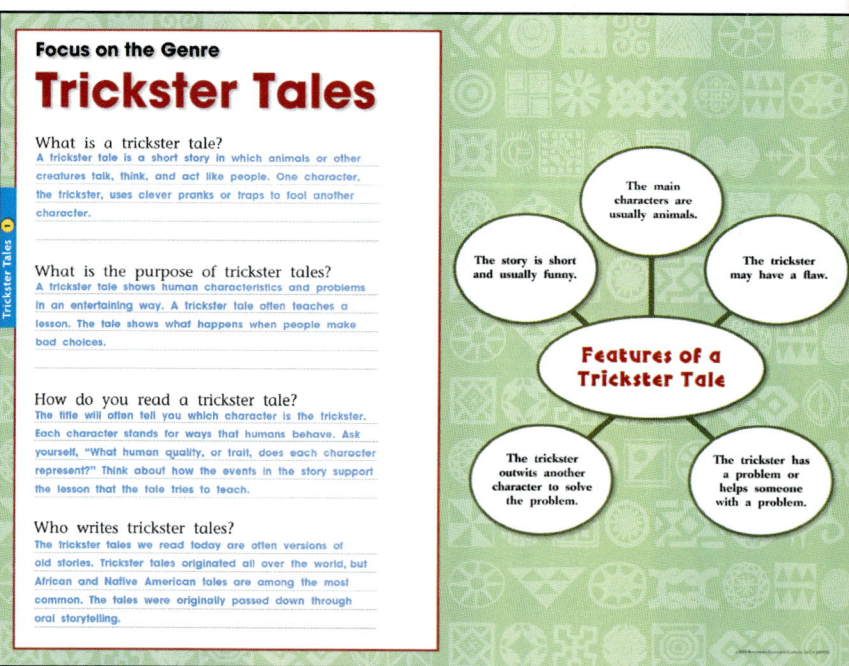

Trickster Tale Poster 1, sample annotations

Small-Group Reading Instruction (60 MINUTES)

Based on students' instructional reading levels, select titles that provide opportunities for students to focus on the trickster tale genre or to practice making inferences. See the Leveled Text Titles chart provided at the back of this Teacher's Resource System.

Use the instruction provided in the Teacher's Guide for each title to introduce the text.

Individual Student Conferences (10 MINUTES)

Confer with individual students to discuss their understanding of the genre. Use the Individual Reading Conference Form on page 32 of Informal Assessments for Reading Development to help guide your conferences.

Word Study Workshop (20 MINUTES)

Use the Day 1 instruction provided in Grade 3 Word Study Unit 14.

Comprehension Quick-Check

Note which students do or don't actively participate in the discussion of genre. Ask some questions at the end of the lesson to confirm students' understanding. For example:

- *What is a trickster tale about?*
- *Tell me what else you know about trickster tales.*

Home/School Connection

Have students list three animals that they think would make good characters for trickster tales. Ask students to write a sentence telling why each animal would be a good trickster.

Day Two

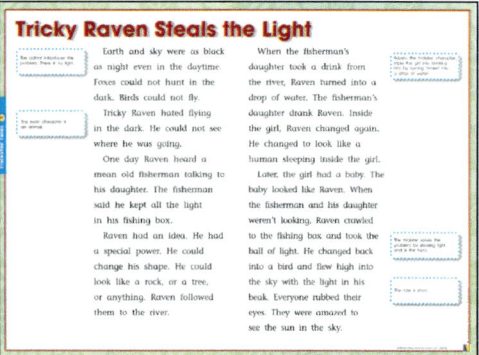

Trickster Tale Poster 2

Lesson Objectives

Students will:

- Make connections with trickster tales.
- Make inferences using a graphic organizer.
- Use academic sentence frames to discuss strategies and features of trickster tales.

Related Resources

- Trickster Tale Poster 2 (BLM 2)
- BenchmarkUniverse.com

Read-Aloud (10 MINUTES)

Select a favorite fiction read-aloud from your classroom or school library with which to model the metacognitive strategy "Make Connections." Use t[he] sample read-aloud lessons and suggested titles in the Getting Started Guide

Mini-Lessons (20 MINUTES)

Model Metacognitive Strategies: Make Connections

Display Trickster Tale Poster 2 with the genre annotations concealed. Also distribute copies of BLM 2.

Read aloud the poster story with students.

Explain: *One way to help you understand what you read is to make connections between the story and your own life. You can also make connections between the story and the world or the story and other stories you have read.*

Think aloud: *I will think about connections I can make between "Tricky Rav[en] Steals the Light" and other things I already know about. I read in the story that the earth and sky are dark as night because the fisherman keeps all th[e] light in his fishing box. I think about what the sky is like at night, especially when I go camping. There is no extra light and it is hard to see. I can understand why Raven doesn't like flying at night!*

Ask students to tell about connections they can make to the story. Ask them [to] share text-to-self, text-to-world, or text-to-text connections. Prompt students [to] think about how this story is like other stories they have read. Have students explain how the connection helps them understand a specific feature of the story. Encourage ELLs to use the sentence frame: *I can make a connection t[o] this part of the story because _____.*

Introduce Make Inferences

Explain: *A writer does not always tell the reader everything. Sometimes the reader must use clues to figure out what the writer wants him or her to understand. When you use clues from the story and your own knowledge to state a fact, you are making an inference. You can use connections between what you know and what you read to help you make inferences.*

Reread "Tricky Raven Steals the Light." Ask students to use clues from the story to make an inference about Raven by answering the question: *Is Raven good or bad at being a trickster?* Provide the following academic sentence frames to support ELLs and struggling students:

> *The author describes Raven as _____.*
> *Raven's power is to _____.*
> *Raven tricks the fisherman's daughter by _____.*
> *I can infer that Raven is _____ at being a trickster.*

Record students' responses on a graphic organizer like the one shown below.

Story Title: Tricky Raven Steals the Light	
Clues	**Inference**
Raven is tricky.	Raven is good at being a trickster.
Raven's tricky power lets him change shape.	
Raven changes into a water drop to trick the fisherman's daughter.	
Raven steals the light.	

Sample Make Inferences Annotations
(Note: Your class graphic organizer may differ.)

Make Content Comprehensible for ELLs

Beginning
Point to and name the characters and items shown on the poster. Have students repeat the words.

Ask students to tell where the light in the sky comes from during the day. Explain that in the story, the sun is in the sky because Raven put it there a long time ago.

Intermediate
Model the academic sentence frames provided in this guide to help ELLs contribute their ideas to the discussion of the trickster.

Advanced
Ask students to retell the story in their own words.

All Levels
Explain that a **raven** is a big, black bird. It is also the trickster's name.

Comprehension Quick-Check

Note which students are or are not able to make inferences. Use the following strategies to provide additional explicit instruction.

Use a Make Inferences graphic organizer like the one shown on page 7.

Say: *I'll tell you a story. A girl stands on the sidewalk. She looks very worried. She is holding a leash with a broken collar at the end of it. What inference can you make about what just happened?*

Ask students to listen for clues as you tell the story again. Then have them list two clues and an inference in the graphic organizer.

Say: *What do you think happened? What clues in the story help you make that inference?*

Oral Language Extension

Display Poster 1 (your class Trickster Tale anchor chart) during independent workstation time. Have pairs of students work together to plan a trickster tale using the features listed on the poster. Have them tell who the trickster is, who will be tricked, and what the problem is that the trickster needs to solve. Encourage students to make a chart showing their plan.

Home/School Connection

Have students take home BLM 2, reread the text, and highlight and label the features of trickster tales present in the passage.

Focus on Genre Features: Trickster Tale

Ask students to name some of the features of a trickster that you discussed yesterday.

Say: *Now let's reexamine "Tricky Raven Steals the Light" and look for feature of trickster tales. What do you notice?*

Work with students to identify the following genre features embedded in the story:
- The main character, the trickster, is an animal.
- The trickster's problem is that there is no light.
- Raven tricks the girl by turning into a drop of water and then a baby.
- The problem is solved when Raven steals the light.

Reveal the poster annotations so that students can confirm or revise their ideas. Reread them as a group.

Connect and transfer. Say: *As you read trickster tales, look for these featur and use clues in the tales to make inferences. Then check your understandi of the story by making connections to your own life, the world, or other thir you have read.*

Small-Group Reading Instruction (60 MINUTES)

Continue small-group reading instruction from the previous day. Use the instruction provided in the Teacher's Guide for each text.

Individual Student Conferences (10 MINUTES)

Confer with individual students to discuss their understanding of genre and comprehension strategies. Use the Individual Reading Conference Form on page 32 of Informal Assessments for Reading Development to help guide yo conferences.

Word Study Workshop (20 MINUTES)

Use the Day 2 instruction provided in Grade 3 Word Study Unit 14.

Read-Aloud (10 MINUTES)

Select a favorite nonfiction read-aloud from your classroom or school library with which to model the metacognitive strategy "Make Connections." Use the sample read-aloud lessons and suggested titles in the Getting Started Guide.

Mini-Lessons (20 MINUTES)

Make Inferences and Connections

Display Genre Workshop Poster 3 and distribute Trickster Tale Poster 3 (BLM 3).

Read aloud the poster story with students. **Say:** *We are going to use clues in the story to make inferences. Remember, you can also use your own experiences to help you make an inference. You can make a connection between your life and what you read to help you figure out things the author does not tell you directly. I'll start by looking for clues in the story. I read that Guinea Pig has stolen the farmer's food for many nights. I think that might be important to know about Guinea Pig, so I'll underline it.*

Say: *Now you tell me other clues in the story about Guinea Pig. Look for things that help you understand the character.* Allow responses. If students are unable to find specific clues, ask the following:
- *What does Guinea Pig do when he sees the tar guard?*
- *What happens when the tar guard does not answer?*
- *How does Guinea Pig trick Fox?*

Say: *When we use clues to make an inference, we are figuring out a fact that the author does not tell us directly. Part of making an inference is connecting your own experiences or knowledge to the story. Let's write a clue that we know from our own lives about Guinea Pig. Is a guinea pig big or small? What else do you know about guinea pigs?*

Work with students to list additional clues from the story and connections from their own lives in order to make an inference. As you work, relate the story to specific features of the trickster tale genre, pointing out how the information/ inference about Guinea Pig helps the readers understand that he is a trickster and that he has a flaw: greed. Record the details on a graphic organizer like the one on page 10.

Work with students to determine which clues and connections are important enough to include on the chart. Then have students use the clues to make an inference about Guinea Pig.

Trickster Tale Poster 3

Lesson Objectives

Students will:
- Review features of the trickster tale genre.
- Make connections.
- Use their understanding of genre features to make inferences.
- Build oral language and vocabulary through whole-group and partner discussion.

Related Resources
- Trickster Tale Poster 3 (BLM 3)
- Make Inferences (BLM 4)
- BenchmarkUniverse.com

Make Content Comprehensible for ELLs

Beginning

Point to and name the characters and items in the illustration and ask students to repeat. Show pictures or classroom materials (glue, tape) to demonstrate **sticky**.

Intermediate and Advanced

Ask questions to help students retell the story:

- *What does Guinea Pig do that makes the farmer mad?*
- *What does the farmer do?*
- *What happens next?*
- *How does Guinea Pig trick Fox?*
- *What happens to Guinea Pig?*
- *What happens to Fox?*

All Levels

Explain that **tar** is a thick, black, sticky material used to patch roads or roofs.

If you have students whose first language is Spanish, share these English/Spanish cognates: **magic/mágico; giant/el gigante; to escape/escapar(se)**.

Comprehension Quick-Check

Note whether students can identify clues and make inferences. If necessary, reread Poster 3 and use a write-on/wipe-off marker to underline story clues. **Say:** *To make an inference, look for clues in the story. An inference is information that the author does not tell you.* Have students underline two clues and then make an inference about the character: *He is quick. He can get tricked.*

Home/School Connection

Have students take home the Make Inferences graphic organizer (BLM 4). Ask students to fill in the chart with clues and an inference about a story they read at home.

Write the inference (or inferences) on the chart and discuss with students h the inference helps them understand the character and the story. Repeat th process to make an inference about Fox.

Connect and transfer. Say: *The next time you read a trickster tale, make inferences and connections to help you understand what you read.*

Story Title: Fox and Guinea Pig	
Clues	**Inference**
Guinea Pig has stolen food for many nights.	Guinea Pig is quick and clever, but h can be tricked, too.
Guinea Pig thinks the tar guard is a thief.	
Guinea Pig tricks Fox by telling him the tar is magic.	

Sample Make Inferences Annotations

Small-Group Reading Instruction (60 MINUTES)

Continue small-group reading instruction from the previous day. Use the instruction provided in the Teacher's Guide for each text.

Individual Student Conferences (10 MINUTES)

Confer with individual students to discuss their developing understanding of genre and comprehension strategies. Use the Individual Reading Conference Form on page 32 of Informal Assessments for Reading Development to help guide your conferences.

Word Study Workshop (20 MINUTES)

Use the Day 3 instruction provided in Grade 3 Word Study Unit 14.

Read-Aloud (10 MINUTES)

Select a favorite nonfiction read-aloud from your classroom or school library with which to model the metacognitive strategy "Make Connections." Use the sample read-aloud lessons and suggested titles in the Getting Started Guide.

Mini-Lessons (20 MINUTES)

Build Comprehension: Analyze Story Elements

Say: *Trickster tales, just like other fiction stories, have story elements: characters, a setting, and a plot that includes a problem and a solution. We can use what we know about story elements to understand and remember a trickster tale.*

Reread Trickster Tale Poster 3 with students.

Say: *We are going to make a chart to help us analyze the story elements in "Fox and Guinea Pig."* Draw a chart like the one shown on page 12. *Let's start with the characters. Who are the characters in the story? Name the main character first and tell me about him.* Allow responses.

Work with students to list the characters and a brief description of each. Ask students to use genre features in their descriptions. For example: *Guinea Pig is the trickster. Fox is the character who gets outwitted.*

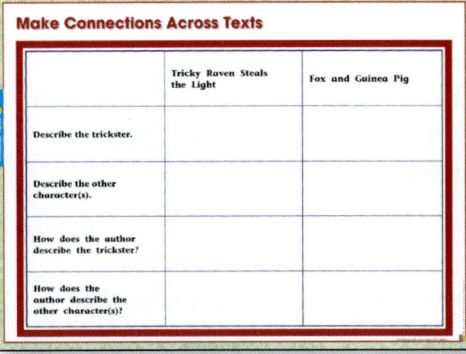

Trickster Tale Poster 4

Lesson Objectives

Students will:

- Analyze story elements.
- Extend Tier Two Vocabulary by focusing on antonyms.
- Build oral language and vocabulary through whole-group and partner discussion.

Related Resources

- Trickster Tale Poster 3 (BLM 3)
- BenchmarkUniverse.com

Make Content Comprehensible for ELLs

Beginning

Briefly review story elements: **character**, **setting**, **plot**, **problem**, **solution**. Ask questions:

- *Who is the trickster?*
- *Who else is in the story?*
- *Where does the story take place?*

Intermediate

Provide sentence frames to help students analyze story elements. For example:

The main character is _____.

The other characters are _____.

The trickster's problem is _____.

The trickster solves the problem by _____.

Advanced

Ask students to tell the story in their own words. Write their retelling in the **Plot Summary** section of the chart.

All Levels

Group ELLs with pairs of fluent English speakers to complete the chart.

Comprehension Quick-Check

Take note of students who may need more support to analyze story elements. Provide additional modeling during small-group reading, and have students practice during independent workstation time by analyzing story elements of familiar stories.

Think/Pair/Write/Share. Tell students they will complete the chart. **Say:** *Work with a partner to analyze the story elements in "Fox and Guinea Pig." Make a chart like the one I just drew, and fill in your ideas. We will share th charts as a group.*

Connect and transfer. Say: *Remember, when you read, you can use what you know about the genre to help you analyze the story elements. In a trickster tale, the trickster is usually an animal who has a problem. Looking that information helps you answer questions about the story elements.*

Characters	Guinea Pig, the trickster and thief; the farmer; Fox
Setting	the farmer's field
Problem/Solution	Guinea Pig is stuck in the tar. He tricks Fox into helping him get free.
Plot Summary	To stop Guinea Pig from stealing his food, the farmer makes a tar guard. Guinea Pig gets stuck in the tar. Fox comes. Guinea Pig tells Fox the tar is magic and will make him taller and help him marry the farmer's daughter. Greedy Fox believes the story. When he help Guinea Pig get out, Fox gets stuck.

Build Tier Two Vocabulary: Antonyms

On chart paper, write the words **loose** and **stuck**.

Say: *In the story, Fox helped Guinea Pig get loose. Then Fox got stuck. What can you tell about the words **loose** and **stuck**? How are they related to each other?*

Turn and talk. Ask students to turn and talk with their neighbor for a moment to come up with an idea.

Ask students to share their ideas about how the words are related. (They are opposites.) Explain that words that mean the opposite are called **antonyms**. Writers sometimes define vocabulary words by including the word's opposite in a nearby sentence.

Say: *Turn back to your neighbor and work together to list pairs of antonyms. Write your words.*

Invite students to share their antonyms with the group. Record several examples on chart paper. Then work with students to write sentences using one or two pairs of words in a way that shows they are antonyms: *The <u>cold</u> winter soon gave way to <u>warm</u> spring. The <u>giant</u> tree towered over the <u>tiny</u> flowers. The <u>hot</u> sun warmed the <u>icy</u> ground.*

Small-Group Reading Instruction (60 MINUTES)

Continue small-group reading instruction from the previous day. Use the instruction provided in the Teacher's Guide for each text.

Individual Student Conferences (10 MINUTES)

Confer with individual students to discuss their developing understanding of genre and word-solving strategies. Use the Individual Reading Conference Form on page 32 of Informal Assessments for Reading Development to help guide your conferences.

Word Study Workshop (20 MINUTES)

Use the Day 4 instruction provided in Grade 3 Word Study Unit 14.

Oral Language Extension

During independent workstation time, ask pairs of students to discuss whether tricksters are characters that readers are supposed to like. Ask them to consider these ideas:

- *Are tricksters nice?*
- *What do readers learn from tricksters?*
- *Are readers supposed to like tricksters?*

Home/School Connection

Have students take home Trickster Tale Poster 3 (BLM 3) and read it with a family member to practice fluent reading. Tell students to have their family member sign the page to indicate they have participated in the reading.

Day Five

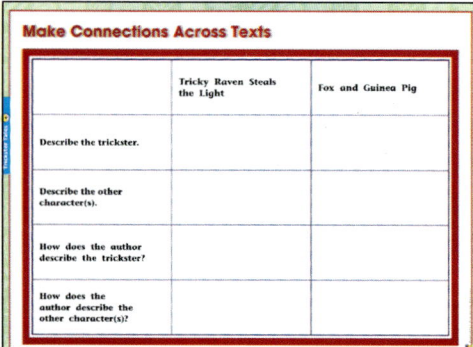

Make Connections Across Texts

	Tricky Raven Steals the Light	Fox and Guinea Pig
Describe the trickster.		
Describe the other character(s).		
How does the author describe the trickster?		
How does the author describe the other character(s)?		

Trickster Tale Poster 4

Lesson Objectives

Students will:

- Identify elements of and summarize trickster tales.
- Review features of the trickster tale genre.
- Make text-to-text connections.
- Build academic oral language and vocabulary through small-group and whole-group discussions.

Related Resources

- Trickster Tale Poster 4 (BLM 5)
- BenchmarkUniverse.com

Read-Aloud (10 MINUTES)

Revisit the week's read-alouds to make text-to-text connections and provide opportunities for reader response. Use the suggested activities in the Gettir Started Guide, or implement ideas of your own.

Mini-Lessons (20 MINUTES)

Synthesize and Assess Genre Understanding

Synthesize genre understanding. Ask students to work in teams to summarize what they now know about the trickster tale genre. Tell student that each group member should contribute an idea to the discussion. Each group should appoint one member to be the group's recorder. Another student should be the group's spokesperson.

Give students five to seven minutes to discuss and record their ideas.

Have each group's spokesperson share his or her group's ideas.

Record key concepts from each group on chart paper.

Self-assessment. Display the class Trickster Tale anchor chart from Day 1. A each group to compare their group's ideas to the information they recorded on the anchor chart on Day 1.

Ask: *How has your understanding of the trickster tale genre developed? Wh do you know now that you didn't know before?* Encourage individual stude to share their personal insights.

Connect and transfer. Ask: *How will your understanding of this genre help you as a reader the next time you read a trickster tale? How can you use yo understanding of the genre to write your own trickster tale?*

Make Connections Across Texts

Display Trickster Tale Poster 4.

Say: *You have read trickster tales this week. Sometimes in school and on tests, you will be asked to make connections between different fiction and nonfiction texts. Today we are going to practice making connections betwee trickster tales.*

Ask each group to use Trickster Tale Poster 4 (BLM 5) to analyze the features of the two trickster tales: "Tricky Raven Steals the Light" and "Fox and Guinea Pig." Ask them to work together to answer each of the questions on the chart.

Give students about five minutes to record their ideas. Then bring the groups together and have them share their ideas.

Challenge students to express their own opinions on these stories:
- *Do you think stories should teach lessons? Why or why not?*
- *Which trickster do you think is trickier? Why?*

Connect and transfer. Say: *When you analyze two trickster tales, think about how each one reflects the features of the genre. Who is the trickster? What problem does the trickster have? How does the trickster outwit another character?*

Small-Group Reading Instruction (60 MINUTES)

Continue small-group reading instruction from the previous day. Use the instruction provided in the Teacher's Guide for each text.

Individual Student Conferences (10 MINUTES)

Ask students to reflect on what they have learned about the trickster tale genre. Use the Individual Reading Conference Form on page 32 of *Informal Assessments for Reading Development* to help guide your conferences.

Word Study Workshop (20 MINUTES)

Use the Day 5 instruction provided in Grade 3 Word Study Unit 14.

Make Content Comprehensible for ELLs

Beginning
Ask students to name the trickster in each story. Ask questions to help students compare the tricksters. For example, **ask:** *How did Raven trick the girl? How did Guinea Pig trick Fox?*

Intermediate and Advanced
Provide sentence frames to help ELLs contribute to their groups' discussions. For example:

The tricksters are alike because _____.

The tricksters are different because _____.

The story endings are alike/different because _____.

All Levels
Pair ELLs with fluent English speakers during all partner and group activities.

Encourage ELLs to point to illustrations and read aloud specific examples in the text to help them share their ideas with the group.

Name _____   Date _____

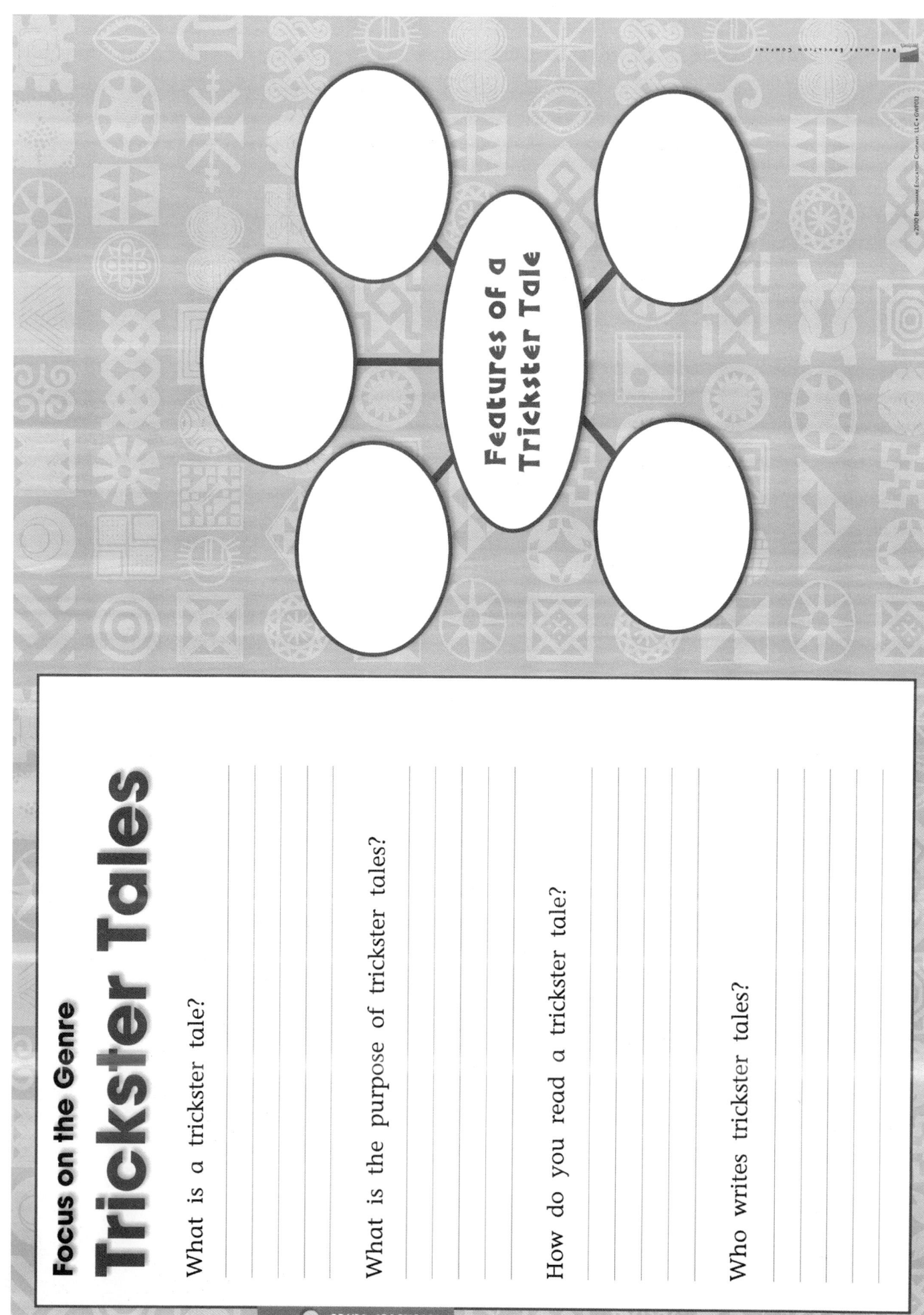

Features of a Trickster Tale

Focus on the Genre
Trickster Tales

What is a trickster tale?

_____
_____

What is the purpose of trickster tales?

_____
_____

How do you read a trickster tale?

_____
_____

Who writes trickster tales?

_____
_____

Trickster Tales 1

Name _____   Date _____

Tricky Raven Steals the Light

The author introduces the problem. There is no light.

Earth and sky were as black as night even in the daytime. Foxes could not hunt in the dark. Birds could not fly.

The main character is an animal.

Tricky Raven hated flying in the dark. He could not see where he was going.

One day Raven heard a mean old fisherman talking to his daughter. The fisherman said he kept all the light in his fishing box.

Raven had an idea. He had a special power. He could change his shape. He could look like a rock, or a tree, or anything. Raven followed them to the river.

Raven, the trickster character, tricks the girl into drinking him by turning himself into a drop of water.

When the fisherman's daughter took a drink from the river, Raven turned into a drop of water. The fisherman's daughter drank Raven. Inside the girl, Raven changed again. He changed to look like a human sleeping inside the girl.

Later, the girl had a baby. The baby looked like Raven. When the fisherman and his daughter weren't looking, Raven crawled to the fishing box and took the ball of light. He changed back into a bird and flew high into the sky with the light in his beak. Everyone rubbed their eyes. They were amazed to see the sun in the sky.

The trickster solves the problem by stealing light and is the hero.

The tale is short.

©2010 Benchmark Education Company, LLC • GW902

Trickster Tales 2

Name _____ Date _____

Fox and Guinea Pig

Night after night, Guinea Pig stole food from a farm. To stop the thief, the farmer made a guard out of sticky tar.

When Guinea Pig spotted the tar guard, he thought it was another thief. "Go away," Guinea Pig ordered. "This is my food."

The guard did not answer.

"Can you hear?" Guinea Pig asked. "Go away!"

The guard remained still and silent.

Guinea Pig tried to push the guard out of the yard, but his paws **stuck** in the goo! Just then, Fox came along. "What are you doing?" he asked.

Guinea Pig saw a chance and said, "The farmer said I could marry his daughter if I were taller. This magic tar will make me grow. But I'm tired of waiting to become a giant. Help pull my paws out of the magic tar and I'll let you put your paws in. By morning, the farmer will see how tall you are and will ask *you* to marry his gorgeous daughter."

"I'll be rich!" Fox exclaimed. "All the chickens will be mine to eat!"

Fox helped Guinea Pig get **loose** and then put his paws into the gooey tar. Now Fox was stuck!

"Thanks for helping me escape," Guinea Pig said. Then he swiftly ran away, laughing.

ame _____   Date _____

Make Inferences

irections: Reread a favorite story. Write at least two clues and an
ference about the story.

Story Title:	
Clues	**Inference**

Name _____   Date _____

Make Connections Across Texts

	Tricky Raven Steals the Light	Fox and Guinea Pig
Describe the trickster.		
Describe the other character(s).		
How does the author describe the trickster?		
How does the author describe the other character(s)?		

Determine Text Importance/ Identify Sequence of Events

Unit 3/Week 1 at a Glance

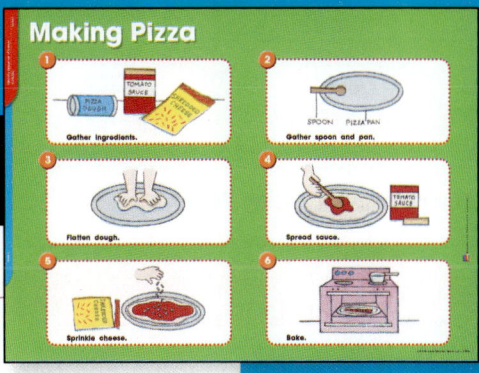

Day	Mini-Lessons
ONE	• Introduce the Comprehension Strategy: *Identify Sequence of Events*
	• Think Aloud and Use the Metacognitive Strategy: *Determine Text Importance*
	• Find the Sequence of Events in a Picture
	• Connect Thinking, Speaking, and Writing
	• Reflect and Discuss
TWO	• Review the Metacognitive Strategy: *Determine Text Importance*
	• Use the Comprehension Strategy: *Identify Sequence of Events*
	• Connect Thinking, Speaking, and Writing
	• Reflect and Discuss
THREE	• Extend the Comprehension Strategy: *Identify Sequence of Events*
	• Observe and Prompt for Strategy Understanding
	• Reflect and Discuss
FOUR	• Read and Summarize
	• Answer Text-Dependent Comprehension Questions: *Identify Sequence of Events (Level 2: Look Closer!)*
	• Reflect and Discuss
FIVE	• Metacognitive Self-Assessment
	• Constructed Written Response
	• Ongoing Comprehension Strategy Assessment

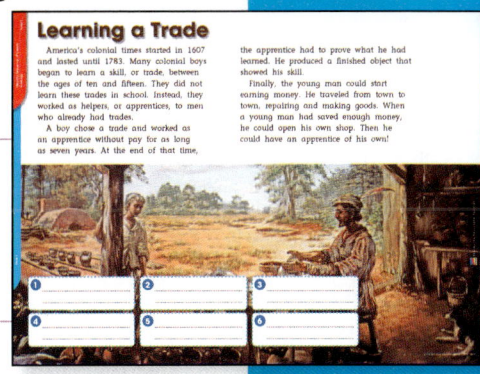

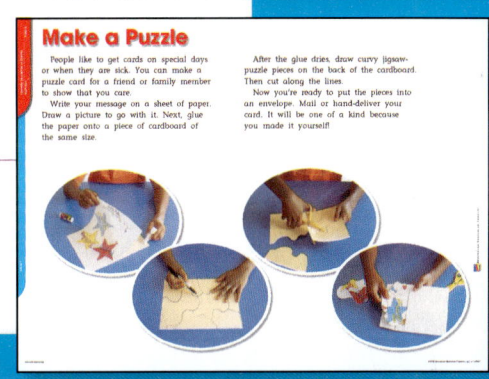

Day One

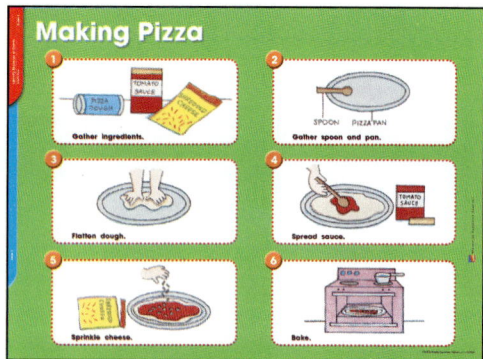

Making Pizza

Comprehension Anchor Poster 1

Lesson Objectives

Students will:

- Identify the sequence of events in pictures and text.
- Identify and use the signal language for sequence of events.
- Determine important information in text.
- Use academic sentence frames to discuss strategies.

Related Resources

- Home/School Connections (BLM 1)
- BenchmarkUniverse.com

About the Strategy

- The order in which events happen is called a sequence of events.
- Signal language, such as **first**, **next**, **then**, **after**, and **finally**, can help readers recognize and understand sequence.
- Recognizing sequence helps readers follow directions, learn steps in a new process, or understand how events unfold over time.

Read-Aloud (10 MINUTES)

Select a favorite fiction read-aloud from your classroom or school library with which to model the metacognitive strategy "Determine Text Importance." Use the sample read-aloud lessons and suggested titles in the Getting Started Guide.

Mini-Lessons (20 MINUTES)

Introduce the Comprehension Strategy:
Identify Sequence of Events

Say: *Every morning before I come to school, I follow the same routine. First I get up. Next I brush my teeth. Then I get dressed and make my breakfast. The last thing I do before I leave my house is say goodbye to my dog.*

Ask: *What things do you do every day before you come to school? In what order do you do these things?*

Turn and talk. Ask students to turn to a partner and share at least three things they do every morning and the order in which they do them. Ask a few students to share with the whole group.

Explain: *You have described a sequence of events to your partner. When you talk to people, you often describe things that happened in a certain order. Writers do this, too. Good readers know how to recognize a sequence of events in fiction and nonfiction texts. We're going to practice recognizing sequence of events this week.*

Think Aloud and Use the Metacognitive Strategy:
Determine Text Importance

Display Poster 1.

Draw students' attention to the six steps in making pizza. (Whiteboard users can use the highlighter tool.)

Explain: *When I look at these pictures, the first thing I need to do is figure out what they are showing me. One way I can help myself is to think about what the important information is. One way I can do that is by paying attention to specific details, such as the numbers and the order of the pictures. Figuring out what information is important makes things clearer in my mind. Let me show you how I do it.*

Think aloud: *I see that each picture has a number. I think this means I should look at the pictures in a certain order, beginning with picture 1 and ending with picture 6. If the numbers are steps, and I should look at the steps in order, then I know the numbers are important to understanding these pictures. Determining important information helps me identify the sequence, or order, of the steps.*

Write what you have determined is important information on chart paper. Ask students to share other information about the poster that they think is important. Add their ideas to your list.

Post the ideas on the wall as a Determining Text Importance anchor chart, or invite students to write them in their reading journals or notebooks to use in the future.

Find the Sequence of Events in a Picture

Ask students to use the pictures to articulate the sequence of events involved in making pizza.

Point out the signal language students naturally use as they verbally describe each step. Prompt them with signal words, such as *first, next, then,* and *last,* if they don't use any.

Provide the following academic sentence frames to support ELLs and struggling students:
> *The first step is _____.*
> *The second step is _____.*
> *The last step is _____.*
> *Clues that help me identify the sequence of events are _____.*

Connect Thinking, Speaking, and Writing

Write down the steps students describe and reread them as a group. Underline the signal language. Give students the opportunity to expand on their shared writing of the sequence of events.

Reflect and Discuss

Ask and discuss the following questions:
- *Why is it important to recognize a sequence of events? How does this help you as a reader?*
- *How did determining important information help you understand the pictures?*
- *What are some signal words for sequence of events that we used today?*

Make Content Comprehensible for ELLs

Use the following strategies to help ELLs understand the poster content and acquire academic language.

Beginning
Read the title of the poster. Demonstrate the process of making a pizza by acting out each step and reading the text with a signal word. For example, say:

> *This is the first step. First, we gather the ingredients.*

Point to and name objects in the photograph: pizza dough, tomato sauce, shredded cheese, spoon, pizza pan, stove. Use hand gestures to indicate whether each object is eaten or used.

Beginning and Intermediate
Draw and label, or ask ELLs draw, the steps in making another familiar food, such as a peanut butter and jelly sandwich.

Comprehension Quick-Check

Observe whether students are able to articulate the sequence of events in the poster. If they have difficulty, use the following additional explicit instruction.

Draw the sequence of events flowchart graphic organizer on chart paper.

Above the flowchart, write the title "How to Make a Pizza."

In the first box, write *First, we gather pizza dough, tomato sauce, and shredded cheese.*

Say: *This is the first step in making a pizza. We gather the ingredients we need to make the pizza. These are the ingredients for our pizza.*

Say: *I looked at the first picture, and I wrote about the first step. I used the picture and text to understand the first event in a sequence of events.*

Say: *Now you tell about the second step in making a pizza.*

Support Special Needs Learners

Support visual learners and students with attention issues by projecting the whiteboard version of the posters. Allow students to come to the whiteboard and circle, underline, or highlight the events in each sequence of events in the text. Invite them to label the events with numbers.

Access the graphic organizer provided on the whiteboard. Record sequences of events with students.

Provide opportunities for active involvement. For example, assign students the roles of Event 1, Event 2, Event 3, and so on, and let them retell the sequence of events in each poster.

Access the image bank for enlarged images that students can use to practice determining important information, identifying sequence of events, and retelling facts.

Home/School Connections

On Day 1, distribute copies of Home/School Connections (BLM 1). Each day during the week, assign one of the six home/school connections activities for the students to complete. Ask them to bring their completed assignments to class the following day. Make time at the beginning of each day for students to share their ideas.

Home/School Connections (BLM 1)

Connect and transfer. Say: *Remember, you can look for sequence of events in a text, too. Tomorrow, we will practice looking for sequence of events in a text.*

Small-Group Reading Instruction (60 MINUTES)

Based on students' instructional reading levels, select titles that provide opportunities for students to practice identifying sequence of events. See the Leveled Text Titles chart provided at the back of this Teacher's Resource System.

Use the before-, during-, and after-reading instruction provided in the Teacher's Guide for each text.

Individual Student Conferences (10 MINUTES)

Confer with individual students on their text selections and applications of strategies. Use the Individual Reading Conference Form on page 32 of Informal Assessments for Reading Development to help guide your conferences.

Word Study Workshop (20 MINUTES)

Use the Day 1 instruction provided in Word Study Unit 7.

Read-Aloud (10 MINUTES)

Select a favorite fiction read-aloud from your classroom or school library with which to model the metacognitive strategy "Determine Text Importance." Use the sample read-aloud lessons and suggested titles in the Getting Started Guide.

Mini-Lessons (20 MINUTES)

Review the Metacognitive Strategy:
Determine Text Importance

Display Poster 2 with annotations hidden and/or distribute BLM 2 and read aloud the title.

Read aloud the text with students.

Explain: *Yesterday when I looked at the "Making Pizza" poster, I determined the most important information in the picture to help me understand. To determine text importance, I pay attention to specific words. Some words help know which details are most important. I'll show you how I pay attention to certain words.*

Reread paragraphs 1 and 2. **Think aloud:** *These paragraphs focus on glaciers and how they form. I pay attention to the word **first** in paragraph 2. This word lets me know that I'm about to read the first step in how glaciers form. The phrase **by summer** lets me know that the author is going to give me new information about what happens to glaciers. The process of how glaciers form is the most important information in these paragraphs, and I used specific words to help me determine this important information.*

Reread paragraph 3. **Think aloud:** *The phrases **the next winter** and **over time** also help me focus on how glaciers form. The author wants me to understand the glaciers form over a very long period of time.*

Build academic oral language. Reread paragraphs 4 and 5. Ask students to think about words and phrases that help them determine the most important information. Invite them to describe how determining text importance helped them identify the sequence of events in these paragraphs. Reinforce the idea that good readers determine text importance because figuring out what information is most important can help them better understand what they are reading. Support ELLs and struggling readers with the following sentence frames:

> *The fist step is _____.*
> *The second step is _____.*
> *The last step is _____.*
> *Clues that help me identify the sequence of events are _____.*

Comprehension Anchor Poster 2 (BLM 2)

Lesson Objectives

Students will:

- Identify the sequence of events in a passage.
- Identify and use the signal language for sequence of events.
- Determine important information in a text.
- Use academic sentence frames to discuss strategies.

Related Resources

- Home/School Connections (BLM 1)
- Comprehension Anchor Poster 2 (BLM 2)
- BenchmarkUniverse.com

1 **First,** winter brings snow.

2 **By summer,** some snow has melted.

3 **The next winter,** new snow falls.

4 New snow packs down old snow.

5 **Over time,** layers become thick ice.

6 **After hundreds or thousands of years,** the glacier becomes heavy.

7 **Then** the glacier moves.

8 The glacier slowly makes changes to Earth's surface.

Comprehension Anchor Poster 2
Sample Annotations

Make Content Comprehensible for ELLs

Use the following strategies to help ELLs understand the poster content and acquire academic language.

Beginning

Read aloud the poster title and passage. Point to and emphasize the signal words as you read the sentences in which they appear.

Assign pairs or small groups one or two pictures to draw and label for the steps in how a glacier forms. Then help students arrange the pictures to show the sequence of events.

Beginning and Intermediate

If you have students whose first language is Spanish, share these English/Spanish cognates: **glacier/el glaciar**, **form/formar**, **mountain/la montaña**, **move/mover**.

All Levels

Pair ELLs with fluent English speakers during partner discussions and activities.

Model the use of academic sentence frames to support ELLs' academic vocabulary and language development. (See suggested sentence frames provided.)

Use the Comprehension Strategy:
Identify Sequence of Events

Reread the poster text with students, annotations still hidden.

Say: *Now think about why the author wrote this passage. What information was he or she trying to communicate?*

If necessary, point out that the author wanted readers to understand the long, slow process of how glaciers form and change Earth. To explain this process, the author described a sequence of events.

Say: *Let's look more closely at the text and find the first event in the sequence of events in how glaciers form. What is the first event you can find?*

Write the event that students identify. Then reveal the first Sequence of Events annotation. **Ask:** *Did we find the first event in the sequence? Let's compare our event to the event on the poster.*

Build academic oral language. Say: *A sequence of events has multiple events. Signal words can help us identify the individual events and their order in the sequence. Now let's look for signal words in the first step of the formation of a glacier. What is the first step?* (Winter brings snow.) *What signal word lets us know this?* (first)

Connect Thinking, Speaking, and Writing

Prompt students to identify each subsequent event in the sequence and any signal language that helped them identify it. Students should understand that sometimes events in a sequence are not identified by signal words.

Record students' ideas on chart paper. Then reveal the remaining Sequence of Events annotations.

Say: *Let's compare our sequence of events to the sequence of events on the poster.* Allow time for discussion.

Reflect and Discuss

Ask and discuss the following questions:
- *What does it mean to determine text importance, and how does this help you as a reader?*
- *How does identifying a sequence of events help you understand what you are reading?*
- *How do signal words help you recognize the events in a sequence?*

Connect and transfer. Ask: *How will you use what we have practiced today when you read on your own?*

Small-Group Reading Instruction (60 MINUTES)

Based on students' instructional reading levels, select titles that provide opportunities for students to practice identifying sequence of events. See the Leveled Text Titles chart provided at the back of this Teacher's Resource System.

Use the before-, during-, and after-reading instruction provided in the Teacher's Guide for each text.

Individual Student Conferences (10 MINUTES)

Confer with individual students on their text selections and applications of strategies. Use the Individual Reading Conference Form on page 32 of Informal Assessments for Reading Development to help guide your conferences.

Word Study Workshop (20 MINUTES)

Use the Day 2 instruction provided in Word Study Unit 7.

Comprehension Quick-Check

Take note of which students can or cannot contribute to the discussion of the Poster 2 sequence of events. Use the following activity to provide additional explicit instruction for these students.

Use an additional real-world example to help students recognize a sequence of events. For example: Tara kicked the ball. Claire blocked the kick. She threw the ball out to Sue. Sue tried to get past Jan. Jan knocked the ball away from Sue. The ball rolled out of bounds.

Record the events on a graphic organizer. Then write them as a paragraph. Ask students to first number the events on the graphic organizer and then add signal words to the sentences in the paragraph.

Oral Language Extension

During independent workstation time, pair students to construct a sequence of events related to any topic they have studied in class. Partner A states the first event. Partner B states the second event. The partners continue until they decide the sequence of events is complete. Tell students to be ready to report on their sequence of events during individual conference time.

Home/School Connections

At the beginning of the day, make time for students to share their ideas based on the activity they completed the previous night.

At the end of the day, ask students to complete another home/school connections activity from BLM 1 and bring their assignment to class the following day.

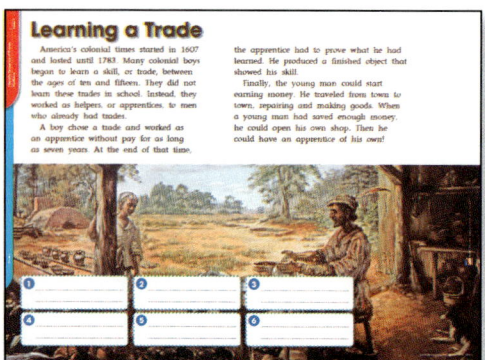

Comprehension Anchor Poster 3 (BLM 3)

Lesson Objectives

Students will:

- Identify the sequence of events in a passage.
- Identify and use the signal language for sequence of events.
- Determine important information in a text.
- Use academic sentence frames to discuss strategies.

Related Resources

- Home/School Connections (BLM 1)
- Comprehension Anchor Poster 3 (BLM 3)
- BenchmarkUniverse.com

1 A boy chose a trade.
2 The boy worked as an apprentice without pay for years.
3 At the end of that time, the apprentice had to show what he had learned.
4 Finally, the young man could start earning money.
5 When he had saved enough money, he could open his own shop.
6 Then he could have an apprentice of his own.

Comprehension Anchor Poster 3
Sample Annotations

Read-Aloud (10 MINUTES)

Select a favorite nonfiction read-aloud from your classroom or school library with which to model the metacognitive strategy "Determine Text Importance." Use the sample read-aloud lessons and suggested titles in the Getting Started Guide.

Mini-Lessons (20 MINUTES)

Extend the Comprehension Strategy:
Identify Sequence of Events

Display Poster 3 and/or distribute BLM 3 and read aloud the title.

Say: *Today you're going to practice reading and identifying sequence of events in a text. Remember to use what you've learned. You can focus on the most important ideas in the text to help you understand. You can also use signal words to help you identify events in the sequence.*

Based on students' needs and abilities, ask them to read the passage independently or with a partner. Tell them to locate and write the events in the numbered sequence of events boxes. Remind students to underline, circle, or flag key information as they read, including signal language for sequence of events.

Invite individual students or pairs to share the events and signal words they identified. Record students' findings on the poster or on chart paper. See the sample annotations.

Observe and Prompt for Strategy Understanding

While using the poster, note students who demonstrate understanding of the concepts and those who seem to struggle. Use appropriate responsive prompting to help students who need modeling or additional guidance, or to validate students who demonstrate mastery.

Goal Oriented
- *I am going to read slowly to notice any signal language for sequence of events.*
- *The words _____ let me know when these events happened.*

Directive and Corrective Feedback
- *Does that word (phrase) tell about time order?*
- *What event happened first? How do you know?*

©2011 Benchmark Education Company, LLC

Self-Monitoring and Reflection

- *What could you do to help yourself understand sequence of events better?*
- *What questions could you ask yourself?*
- *Did you try to identify the most important information?*

Validating and Confirming

- *You really understand what steps the author was describing.*
- *You really picked up on the signal language for sequence of events. Great job!*
- *I like the way you identified the sequence of events even when there were no signal words to help you.*

Reflect and Discuss

Ask and discuss the following questions:

- *What kinds of texts have you read that include a sequence of events?*
- *Would a biography have a sequence of events? Why or why not?*
- *Why is it important to understand sequence of events?*

Connect and transfer. Say: *Remember that many nonfiction texts require readers to identify sequence of events. Look for sequence of events today when you read in small groups. Focus on the most important information to help you figure out the sequence of events.*

Small-Group Reading Instruction (60 MINUTES)

Based on students' instructional reading levels, select titles that provide opportunities for students to practice identifying sequence of events. See the Leveled Text Titles chart provided at the back of this Teacher's Resource System.

Use the before-, during-, and after-reading instruction provided in the Teacher's Guide for each text.

Individual Student Conferences (10 MINUTES)

Confer with individual students on their text selections and applications of strategies. Use the Individual Reading Conference Form on page 32 of Informal Assessments for Reading Development to help guide your conferences.

Word Study Workshop (20 MINUTES)

Use the Day 3 instruction provided in Word Study Unit 7.

Make Content Comprehensible for ELLs

Use the following strategies to help ELLs understand the poster content and acquire academic language.

Beginning
Point to the poster illustration and provide the language for what you see. For example: boy, apprentice, man, master, potter, clay, pots, oven. Invite ELLs to point to and name people and objects with you.

Intermediate
Describe what is happening in the poster illustration in simple language. For example, **say:** *This man is a master potter. He is making a pot out of clay. This boy is an apprentice. He is watching the potter. He is learning how to make pots.* Encourage students to describe the poster illustration in their own words.

All Levels
If you have students whose first language is Spanish, share these English/Spanish cognates: **colonial/colonial, apprentice/el aprendiz, object/el objeto**.

Comprehension Quick-Check

The responsive prompts on page 8–9 are designed to help you meet the needs of individual students. Based on your observations, identify students who may need additional explicit reinforcement of the strategy during small-group instruction or intervention time. Use similar responsive prompts during small-group instruction to scaffold students toward independent use of the strategy.

Home/School Connections

At the end of the day, ask students to complete another home/school connections activity from Home/School Connections (BLM 1) and bring their assignment to class the following day.

Day Four

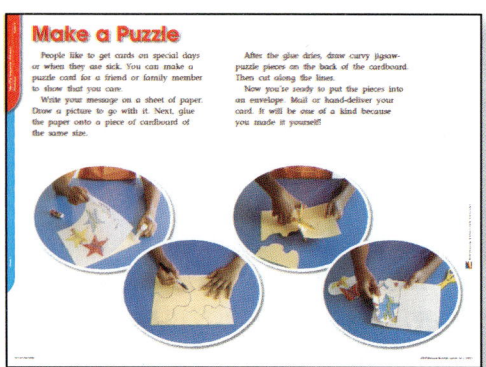

Comprehension Anchor Poster 4 (BLM 4)

Lesson Objectives

Students will:

- Learn strategies for analyzing questions and finding answers, clues, and evidence.

- Identify the sequence of events in a text.

- Answer text-dependent sequence of events questions.

- Use academic vocabulary to discuss strategies.

Related Resources

- Home/School Connections (BLM 1)

- Comprehension Anchor Poster 4 (BLM 4)

- Comprehension Questions (BLM 5)

- BenchmarkUniverse.com

1 Write your message on paper.
2 Draw a picture to go with your message.
3 **Next,** glue the paper onto cardboard.
4 **After** the glue dries, draw curvy puzzle pieces on the back.
5 **Then,** cut along the lines.
6 **Now,** put the pieces in an envelope.
7 Mail or hand-deliver your card.

**Comprehension Anchor Poster 4
Sample Annotations**

 ## Read-Aloud (10 MINUTES)

Select a favorite nonfiction read-aloud from your classroom or school library with which to model the metacognitive strategy "Determine Text Importance." Use the sample read-aloud lessons and suggested titles in the Getting Started Guide.

 ## Mini-Lessons (20 MINUTES)

Read and Summarize

Display Poster 4 and/or distribute BLM 4.

Based on students' needs and abilities, ask them to read the passage independently or with a partner. Remind students to determine the most important information in the text to help them understand what they read.

Build academic oral language. When students have finished, ask individuals or pairs to tell the sequence of events. Encourage ELLs or struggling readers to use the academic sentence frames:
The first (second, third, fourth, fifth, sixth, seventh) step is _____.

Answer Text-Dependent Comprehension Questions: Identify Sequence of Events (Level 2: Look Closer!)

Say: *Sometimes you need to answer questions about a passage you've read. Some questions require you to identify a sequence of events. Today we're going to read and answer questions about sequence of events.*

Distribute BLM 5 and read Question 1 together. ("What should you do after the glue dries?")

Ask: *What is the question asking us to do?* If students can't tell you, **ask:** *Is the question asking us to make a prediction? Is it asking us to identify a cause and an effect? What strategy will we need?* (identify sequence of events) *How do you know?* (The question is asking what event, or step, happens after another event, or step.)

Say: *Now think about what words in the question can help us find the answer in the passage. Let's look at the question more closely. What words will help us?* (after the glue dries)

Say: *Now we're ready to reread the passage to find the information we need. We know we need to find out what happens after the glue dries. I'll skim the first two paragraphs to see if glue is mentioned. It's not, so the answer isn't in that part of the passage. But as I continue skimming, I see that the author does mention glue in paragraph 3. The author says, "After the glue dries, draw curvy jigsaw-puzzle pieces . . ." That is the information I'm looking for. So that must be the answer. The answer was right in the text, and I found it by searching for the clue words from the question. The answer makes sense. So I'll choose A.*

Have students work independently or with a partner to answer additional text-dependent questions on BLM 5.

Review students' answers and use the poster as needed to model analyzing questions and rereading to find answers in the text.

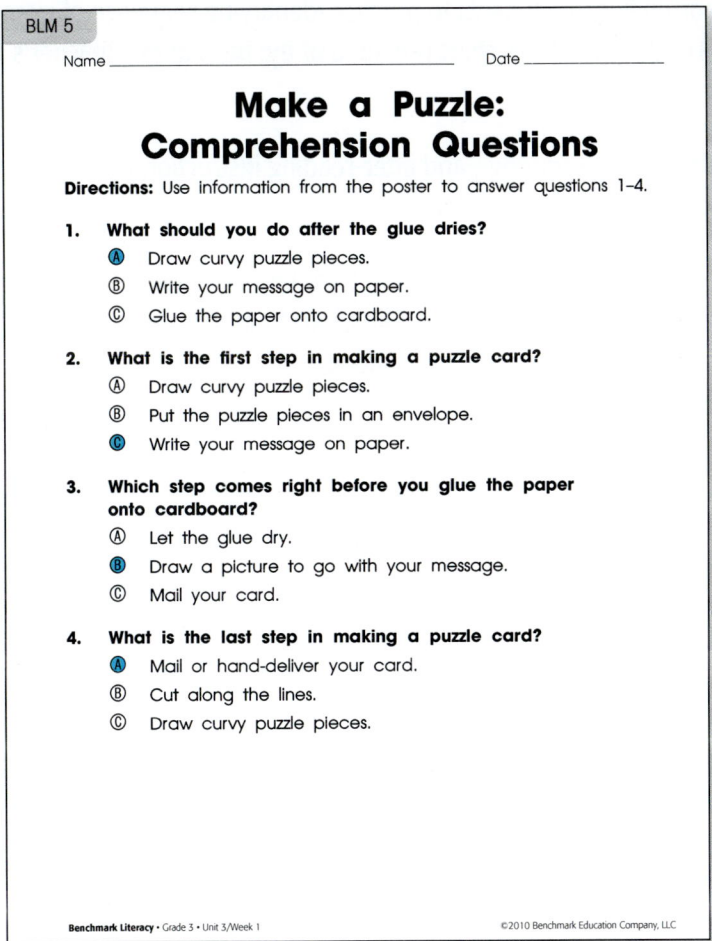

Comprehension Questions (BLM 5)

Make Content Comprehensible for ELLs

Use the following strategies to help ELLs understand the poster content and acquire academic language.

Beginning
Support the concept of steps in a process by demonstrating how you write on the chalkboard and explaining each step as you do it.

Beginning and Intermediate
Point to the first poster photo and **say:** *The child glues the paper to cardboard.* Continue with the other three photos.

Use realia such as construction paper and colored markers to demonstrate how to make a birthday card. Encourage students to use the sentence frames:

> *The first (second, third, and so on) step is _____ to describe what you are doing.*

Intermediate and Advanced
Model the use of academic sentence frames to support ELLs' academic vocabulary and language development. (See suggested sentence frames provided.)

All Levels
If you have students whose first language is Spanish, share these academic English/Spanish cognates: **special/especial, curvy/con curvas, pieces/las piezas, lines/las líneas.**

Comprehension Quick-Check

Note whether students are able to analyze each Level 2 text-dependent comprehension question and return to the text to find the information they need to answer the question correctly. If students have difficulty, use small-group reading time for additional practice answering these kinds of questions, which appear on standardized reading assessments. The Comprehension Question Card for each leveled text provides practice questions at four levels of comprehension. The Comprehension Through Deductive Reasoning Flip Chart helps you model the strategies students need to master.

Oral Language Extension

Display Comprehension Anchor Poster 4 during independent workstation time. Invite pairs of students to read and talk about the poster together. Encourage students to think of something they know how to make or do and write the steps in the process as a sequence of events. Remind students to be prepared to share their ideas and sequences during independent conference time.

Home/School Connections

At the beginning of the day, make time for students to share their ideas based on the activity they completed the previous night.

At the end of the day, ask students to complete another home/school connections activity from BLM 1 and bring their assignment to class the following day.

Reflect and Discuss the Comprehension Strategy

Ask and discuss the following:
- *What strategy did we use to answer questions about the text?*
- *Notice how we followed a sequence of events to understand and answer questions.*

Connect and transfer. Say: *Practice identifying sequence of events. This strategy can help you understand the information in many kinds of nonfiction texts as well as the plots in fictional stories. It can also help you when you take tests.*

Small-Group Reading Instruction (60 MINUTES)

Based on students' instructional reading levels, select titles that provide opportunities for students to practice identifying sequence of events. See the Leveled Text Titles chart provided at the back of this Teacher's Resource System.

Use the before-, during-, and after-reading instruction provided in the Teacher's Guide for each text.

Use the Comprehension Question Card for each title and Comprehension Through Deductive Reasoning Flip Chart to practice answering Level 2 text-dependent comprehension questions.

Individual Student Conferences (10 MINUTES)

Confer with individual students on their text selections and applications of strategies. Use the Individual Reading Conference Form on page 32 of Informal Assessments for Reading Development to help guide your conferences.

Word Study Workshop (20 MINUTES)

Use the Day 4 instruction provided in Word Study Unit 7.

Read-Aloud (10 MINUTES)

Revisit the week's read-alouds to make text-to-text connections and provide opportunities for reader response. Use the suggested activities in the Getting Started Guide, or implement ideas of your own.

Assessment (20 MINUTES)

Metacognitive Self-Assessment

Ask students to reflect on their use of metacognitive and comprehension strategies this week. What did they learn? How will they use the strategies in the future? What do they still need to practice, and how can they do this?

Invite students to share their reflections in one of the following ways: conduct a whole-class discussion; ask students to turn and talk to a partner and then share their ideas with the class; or ask students to record their thoughts in their journals or notebooks.

Constructed Written Response

Distribute copies of Constructed Written Response (BLM 6) and ask students to think of three to five events from their lives. Students should write the events in the order in which they happened in the boxes on the flowchart.

Work with students individually. Ask students to write a paragraph or two based on the sequence of events on their graphic organizer. Encourage them to use signal language that would help a reader understand and follow the sequence of events.

Read aloud the checklist at the bottom of BLM 6 to help students evaluate their work.

Challenge activity. Students who are able to may also write a passage about a typical school day or their favorite day, telling about events in sequence and using sequence signal words.

Support activity. If students cannot think of events or put them in order, ask them to draw pictures of three major events in their lives and then help them put the pictures in time order. Ask students to tell you about their pictures, using the signal words **first, next,** and **then.** Reinforce the idea that by using time order and these signal words, students have created a sequence of events.

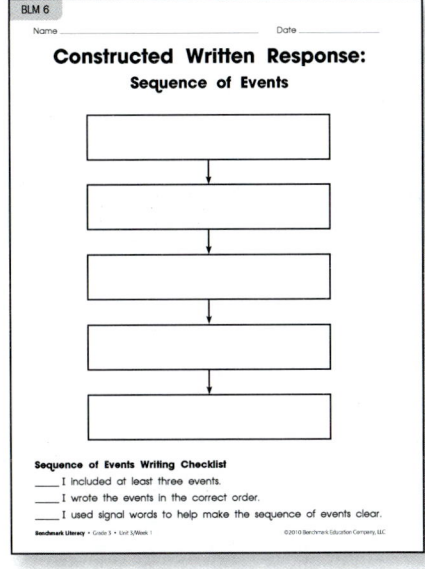

Constructed Written Response (BLM 6)

Lesson Objectives

Students will:

- Reflect orally on their strategy use.
- Create a sequence of events graphic organizer and write a paragraph based on it.
- Answer multiple-choice and short-answer questions.

Related Resources

- Home/School Connections (BLM 1)
- Constructed Written Response (BLM 6)
- Comprehension Strategy Assessments, Grade 3
- BenchmarkUniverse.com

Make Assessments Accessible for ELLs

Use the following strategies to help ELLs demonstrate their understanding of the strategies.

Beginning
Use Constructed Written Response (BLM 6) with ELLs at the beginning proficiency level.

Beginning and Intermediate
Use the Comprehension Strategy Assessment as a listening comprehension assessment and scaffold students' understanding of the text. As an alternative, allow students to tell you about the sequence of events in one of the Comprehension Anchor Posters you have used during the week.

Intermediate and Advanced
Support ELLs with academic sentence frames during the metacognitive self-assessment. Possible sentence frames to use are:

We pay attention to important information because _____.

We look for sequence of events so that _____.

All Levels
Pair ELLs with fluent English speakers during partner discussions and activities.

Home/School Connections

At the beginning of the day, make time for students to share their ideas based on the activity they completed the previous night.

Ongoing Comprehension Strategy Assessment

Distribute one of the Sequence of Events Comprehension Strategy Assessments from the Grade 3 Comprehension Strategy Assessment book ("Making a Budget," pages 78–79, or "All Mixed Up," pages 80–81). Ask students to read the passage and use the information to answer the questions.

Use the results of this assessment to determine students who need additional work with the strategy.

Record students' assessment scores on the Strategy Assessment Record (page 133) so that you can monitor their progress following additional instruction or intervention.

Provide additional modeling and guided practice during small-group reading instruction using the recommended titles in this Teacher's Guide.

 ## Small-Group Reading Instruction (60 MINUTES)

Based on students' instructional reading levels, select titles that provide opportunities for students to practice identifying sequence of events. See the Leveled Text Titles chart provided at the back of this Teacher's Resource System.

Use the before-, during-, and after-reading instruction provided in the Teacher's Guide for each text.

 ## Individual Student Conferences (10 MINUTES)

Confer with individual students on their text selections and applications of strategies. Use the Individual Reading Conference Form on page 32 of Informal Assessments for Reading Development to help guide your conferences.

Word Study Workshop (20 MINUTES)

Use the Day 5 instruction provided in Word Study Unit 7.

Name _____   Date _____

Home/School Connections:
Identify Sequence of Events

1. Make Text-to-World Strategy Connections
How do you and your family use sequence of events at home? Explain to your family members what a sequence of events is. Brainstorm and write down sequences that happen in your home every day. Bring your list of sequences to school to share with the class.

2. Make Text-to-Text Strategy Connections
Find one or more examples of a sequence of events in books, magazines, or newspapers in your home. Write down the title of each text and the passage that tells about a sequence of events. Bring your example(s) to school to share with the class.

3. Make a Strategy Connection to Math
How do you use sequence of events in math? Give a specific example of how understanding a sequence of events, such as the steps in multiplying or dividing, has helped you solve math problems.

4. Make a Strategy Connection to Social Studies
Think about something that has changed over time, such as clothing, transportation, or technology. Draw three pictures that represent the topic at three different historical periods. Number your pictures to show the sequence of events.

5. Make a Sequence of Events Chart
Think about how your family uses sequence of events when getting ready in the morning or having dinner in the evening. Make sequence of events flowchart to show the events in one of these sequences. You can ask a family member to help you. Sign your name and your family member's name on your flowchart. Bring it to class to share.

6. Think and Write About the Strategy
Think about how learning about sequence of events has helped you become a more strategic reader. Write about how and when you use this strategy to help you understand what you are reading.

Name _____   Date _____

Mountain Glaciers

Glaciers cover almost 10 percent of Earth's land. Most of Earth's glaciers are in Greenland and Antarctica.

Some glaciers form in high mountains. First, winter comes, and so does the snow. By summer, some snow has melted, but some stays on the ground.

The next winter, new snow falls on top of the old snow. The weight of the new snow packs down the old snow. Over time, the layers of old snow become solid ice. The ice becomes thicker and thicker.

After hundreds or thousands of years, a mountain glacier becomes very heavy. Then the glacier begins to move. Sometimes the glacier slides down the mountain on water. Other times the glacier slides down on soft dirt.

As the glacier forms and moves, it slowly causes changes to Earth's surface.

Identify Sequence of Events
Nonfiction
Poster 2

Grade 3

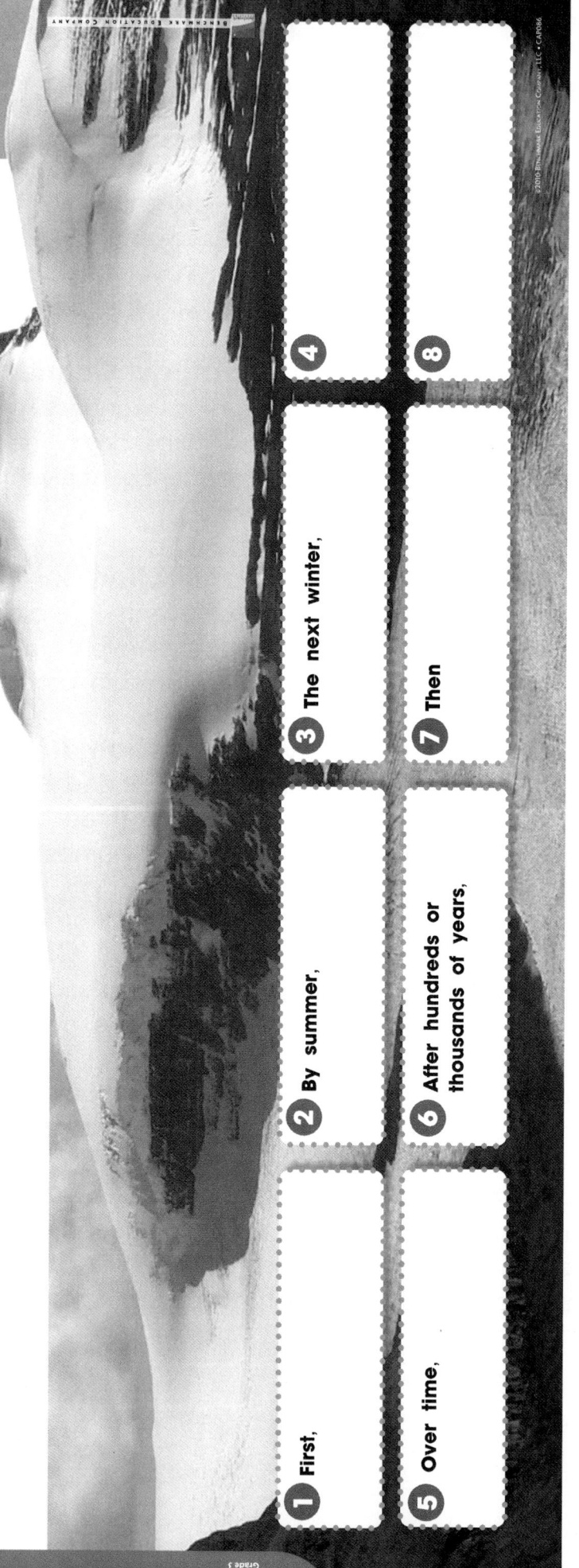

1 First,

2 By summer,

3 The next winter,

4

5 Over time,

6 After hundreds or thousands of years,

7 Then

8

Name _____   Date _____

Learning a Trade

America's colonial times started in 1607 and lasted until 1783. Many colonial boys began to learn a skill, or trade, between the ages of ten and fifteen. They did not learn these trades in school. Instead, they worked as helpers, or apprentices, to men who already had trades.

A boy chose a trade and worked as an apprentice without pay for as long as seven years. At the end of that time, the apprentice had to prove what he had learned. He produced a finished object that showed his skill.

Finally, the young man could start earning money. He traveled from town to town, repairing and making goods. When a young man had saved enough money, he could open his own shop. Then he could have an apprentice of his own!

Name _____ Date _____

Make a Puzzle

People like to get cards on special days or when they are sick. You can make a puzzle card for a friend or family member to show that you care.

Write your message on a sheet of paper. Draw a picture to go with it. Next, glue the paper onto a piece of cardboard of the same size.

After the glue dries, draw curvy jigsaw-puzzle pieces on the back of the cardboard. Then cut along the lines.

Now you're ready to put the pieces into an envelope. Mail or hand-deliver your card. It will be one of a kind because you made it yourself!

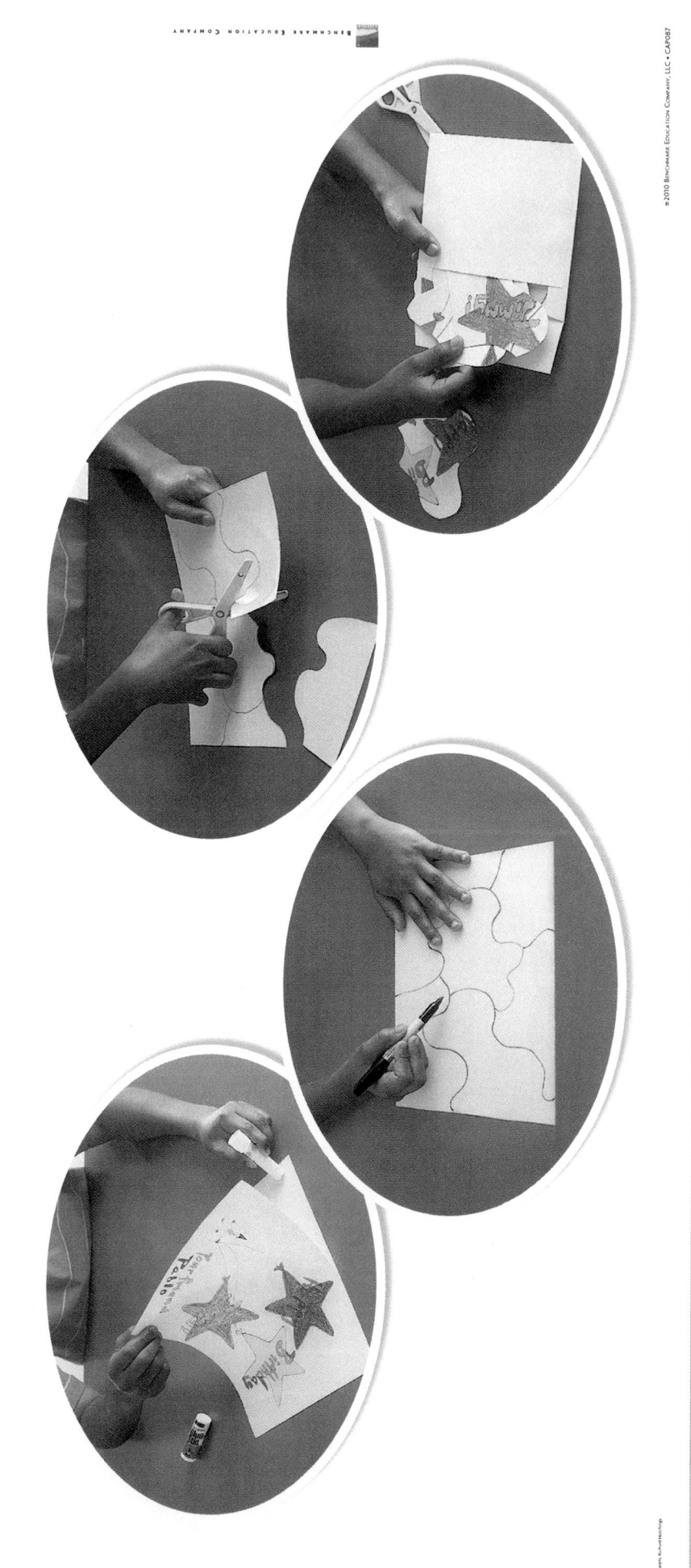

Name _____   Date _____

Make a Puzzle: Comprehension Questions

Directions: Use information from the poster to answer questions 1–4.

1. **What should you do after the glue dries?**

   Ⓐ   Draw curvy puzzle pieces.

   Ⓑ   Write your message on paper.

   Ⓒ   Glue the paper onto cardboard.

2. **What is the first step in making a puzzle card?**

   Ⓐ   Draw curvy puzzle pieces.

   Ⓑ   Put the puzzle pieces in an envelope.

   Ⓒ   Write your message on paper.

3. **Which step comes right before you glue the paper onto cardboard?**

   Ⓐ   Let the glue dry.

   Ⓑ   Draw a picture to go with your message.

   Ⓒ   Mail your card.

4. **What is the last step in making a puzzle card?**

   Ⓐ   Mail or hand-deliver your card.

   Ⓑ   Cut along the lines.

   Ⓒ   Draw curvy puzzle pieces.

Name _____   Date _____

Constructed Written Response:
Sequence of Events

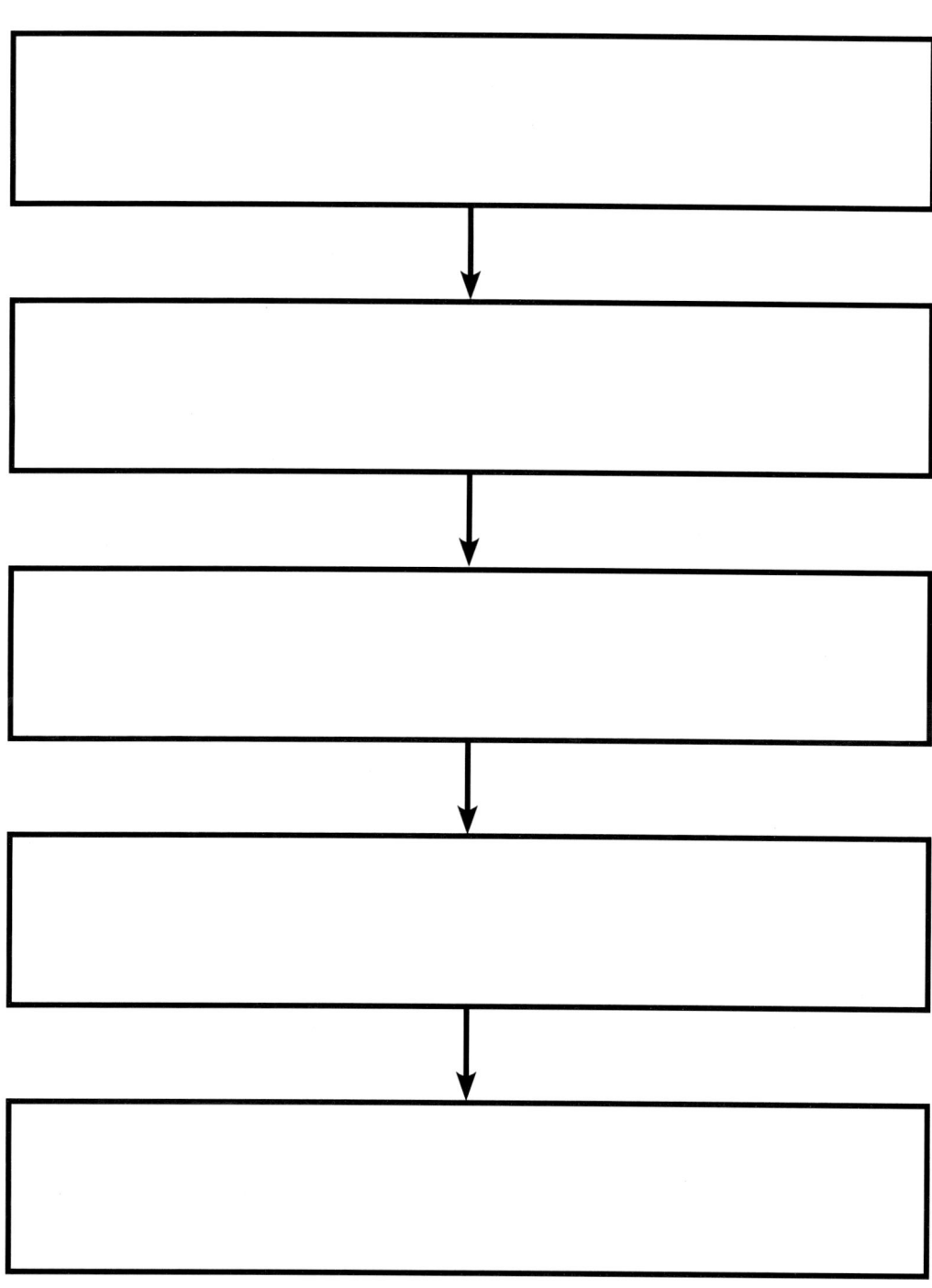

Sequence of Events Writing Checklist

_____ I included at least three events.

_____ I wrote the events in the correct order.

_____ I used signal words to help make the sequence of events clear.

©2011 Benchmark Education Company, LLC

Determine Text Importance/ Identify Sequence of Events

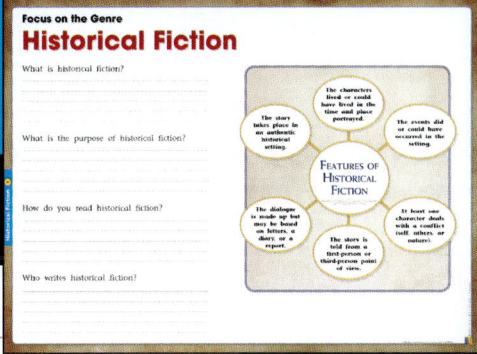

Unit 3/Week 2 at a Glance

Day	Mini-Lessons
ONE	• Build Genre Background • Introduce the Genre: *Historical Fiction* • Focus on Genre Features: *Historical Fiction*
TWO	• Model Metacognitive Strategies: *Determine Text Importance* • Introduce Sequence of Events • Focus on Genre Features: *Historical Fiction*
THREE	• Determine Text Importance and Sequence of Events
FOUR	• Build Comprehension: *Evaluate Author's Purpose* • Build Tier Two Vocabulary: *Using Context Clues*
FIVE	• Synthesize and Assess Genre Understanding • Make Connections Across Texts

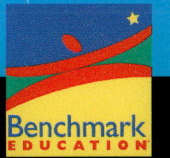

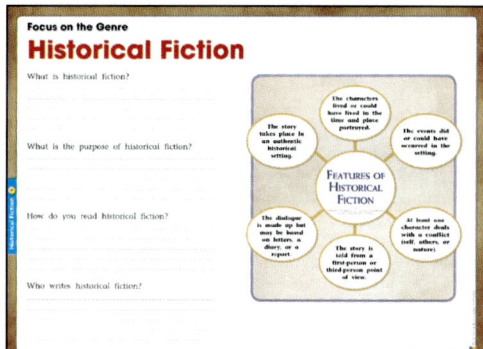

Historical Fiction Poster 1

Lesson Objectives

Students will:

- Review the concept of genre and previously studied genres.

- Create a Historical Fiction anchor chart to demonstrate prior knowledge.

- Build academic oral language and vocabulary as they engage in partner and whole-group discussion.

Related Resources

- Historical Fiction Poster 1 (BLM 1)

- BenchmarkUniverse.com

Read-Aloud (10 MINUTES)

Select a favorite fiction read-aloud from your classroom or school library with which to model the metacognitive strategy "Determine Text Importance." Use the sample read-aloud lessons and suggested titles in the Getting Started Guide.

Mini-Lessons (20 MINUTES)

Build Genre Background

Write the word **genre** on chart paper. **Ask:** *Who remembers and can tell me what the word genre means?* Allow responses.

Review: *The word genre means "a kind of something." Things are grouped in genres because they have certain things in common. We've learned that music, video games, and literature can be grouped into genres. What else can you think of that is grouped into genres?* Allow responses.

Say: *We pay attention to the genre of what we're reading so that we can anticipate and understand what the text will include. We can predict what features the text will have. We can predict how the story will be presented. We can look for important information.*

Ask: *What are some literary genres you have studied and read? Let's make a list of genres. What did you like most about each genre? Which genre do you like to read most?* Allow responses. Tally the votes for each kind of genre mentioned and post the vote. Revote at the end of the week with historical fiction added to the list.

Introduce the Genre: Historical Fiction

Display Genre Workshop Poster 1 and distribute Historical Fiction Poster 1 (BLM 1).

Say: *This week we are going to focus on the historical fiction genre. You will read historical fiction in our small reading groups, and you can select other titles from this genre to read independently, too. Let's spend some time thinking about this genre and create our own Historical Fiction anchor chart to record what we already know about historical fiction. Later in the week, we can come back to our chart and reflect on how our understanding of the genre has changed and expanded.*

Display Poster 1 on an easel or use the interactive whiteboard version. You may also make a transparency from BLM 1. Show students several historical fiction stories from your classroom or school library and ask students to share any historical fiction stories they have read previously.

Read each question on Poster 1 and encourage volunteers to share ideas they have related to the question. Based on students' prior knowledge, provide additional genre background information as needed to fill in the answers to each question. This poster can serve as an anchor chart that you and students can refer to throughout the week as you read and analyze historical fiction stories.

Support the academic language development of ELLs and struggling readers by providing the following sentence frames to use as they discuss the genre:

The purpose of historical fiction is to _____.
The setting of a historical fiction text is _____.
Characters in historical fiction are _____.
When you read historical fiction, pay attention to _____.

Make Content Comprehensible for ELLs

Beginning and Intermediate
Show various examples of historical fiction from your classroom or school library. Flip through the stories with students. Use simple language to explain that historical fiction includes facts and fiction. For example, **say:** *Historical fiction tells a story about people in a real time in history but with made-up details. Look at this historical fiction story. This historical fiction story tells about _____.*

All Levels
Model the academic sentence frames provided in this guide to help ELLs contribute their ideas to the discussion of historical fiction.

Support Special Needs Learners

Throughout the week, use these strategies to help students who have learning disabilities access the content and focus on genre studies and comprehension strategies.

Support students by projecting the posters on a whiteboard. Allow students to come to the whiteboard and circle, underline, or highlight features of the genre. Invite them to label what they see on the posters.

Provide opportunities for active involvement. For example, to understand how historical fiction reveals character, allow students to take the roles of the main characters in historical fiction and use details from the text to role-play their characters.

Provide repeated opportunities for students to analyze the features of historical fiction. Find features of historical fiction in text examples from read-alouds, small-group, and independent reading. Chart the features on graphic organizers and post them in your classroom as examples.

Find high-interest historical fiction stories that students can relate to. Use the recommended read-aloud titles provided in the Teacher's Guide, as well as other examples from your school library.

Focus on Genre Features: Historical Fiction

Point to the "Features of Historical Fiction" web on the right side of the poster.

Say: *As we've discussed, every genre has certain consistent features. Considering our discussions so far, and your own experiences with this genre, what do you think are the consistent features of all, or most, historical fiction stories? Let's work together to identify them.*

Allow students enough time to generate their own ideas, and record the features they identify on the web. Reread the features together. As necessary, prompt students with the following questions and statements:
- *What does historical fiction tell about?*
- *How is historical fiction different from a biography?*
- *Who are the characters in historical fiction?*

Connect and transfer. Say: *This week we will read some historical fiction stories. Pay attention to the features of these stories. Understanding the genre features will help you read with better comprehension.*

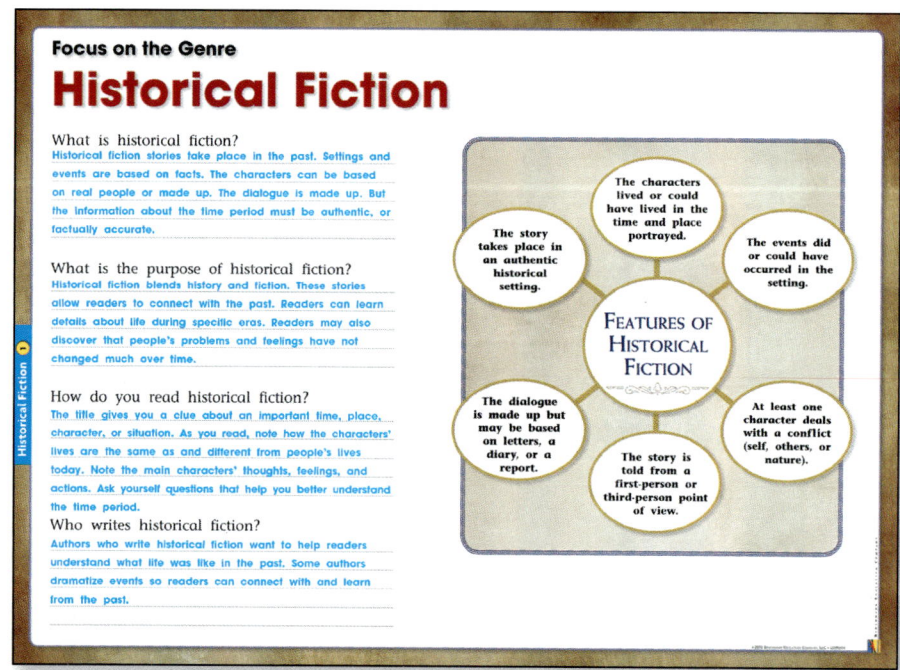

Historical Fiction Poster 1, sample annotations

Small-Group Reading Instruction (60 MINUTES)

Based on students' instructional reading levels, select titles that provide opportunities for students to focus on the historical fiction genre or to practice identifying sequence of events. See the Leveled Text Titles chart provided at the back of this Teacher's Resource System.

Individual Student Conferences (10 MINUTES)

Confer with individual students to discuss their understanding of the genre. Use the Individual Reading Conference Form on page 32 of Informal Assessments for Reading Development to help guide your conferences.

Word Study Workshop (20 MINUTES)

Use the Day 1 instruction provided in Grade 3 Word Study Unit 8.

Comprehension Quick-Check

Note which students do or don't actively participate in the discussion of genre. Ask some questions at the end of the lesson to confirm students' understanding, for example:

- *Can you tell me in your own words what a genre is?*
- *What do you already know about the historical fiction genre?*

Home/School Connection

Ask students to think about a historical event that they think would make a good historical fiction story. Ask them to make a list of what the story would include, answering these questions: *What is the historical event? When and where did the event take place? Who is involved? What made-up details could be included?*

Day Two

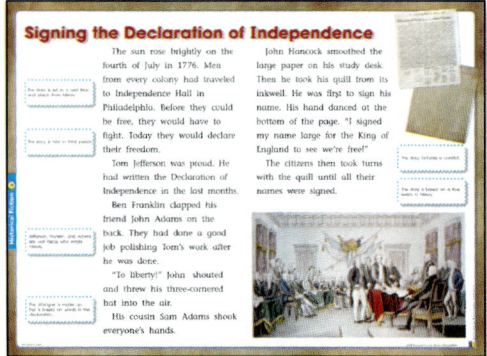

Historical Fiction Poster 2

Lesson Objectives

Students will:

- Determine text importance in a historical fiction story.
- Determine sequence of events using a graphic organizer.
- Use academic sentence frames to discuss strategies and features of historical fiction.

Related Resources

- Historical Fiction Poster 2 (BLM 2)
- BenchmarkUniverse.com

Read-Aloud (10 MINUTES)

Select a favorite fiction read-aloud from your classroom or school library with which to model the metacognitive strategy "Determine Text Importance." Use the sample read-aloud lessons and suggested titles in the Getting Started Guide.

Mini-Lessons (20 MINUTES)

Model Metacognitive Strategies: Determine Text Importance

Display Genre Workshop Poster 2 with the genre annotations concealed. Also distribute copies of Historical Fiction Poster 2 (BLM 2).

Read aloud the poster passage with students.

Explain: *Good readers think about what is important in a text as they read. They look for important facts and details. Determining what is important helps them understand and remember what they have read. Let me show you how I determine what is important in this historical fiction story.*

Think aloud: *I start by reading the title. This tells me what the story is about—the signing of the Declaration of Independence. I know this was an important historic event in the United States. I will read to find out more facts. In the first sentence, I read the date of the event. That is important. I will keep reading to find out exactly what happened on that day. Men traveled to Independence Hall in Philadelphia. That is important information. It tells me where the event happened.*

Ask students to determine the importance of other facts and details from the story. Write their observations on chart paper and reread them together. Encourage ELLs to use the sentence frames:

_____ *is important in this story.*
This information is important because _____.

Introduce Sequence of Events

Explain: *A historical fiction story tells about people and events in a real period of history. The story includes characters, a setting, dialogue, and a sequence of events. Following the sequence of events helps you understand the story and determine the importance of information.*

Reread "The Signing of the Declaration of Independence." Ask students to use details and signal words in the story to determine the sequence of events. Provide the following academic sentence frames to support ELLs and struggling students:

> *The first thing that happens is _____.*
> *The next thing that happens is _____.*
> *The first person to sign is _____.*
> *The last thing to happen is _____.*

Record students' sequence of events on a graphic organizer like the one shown below.

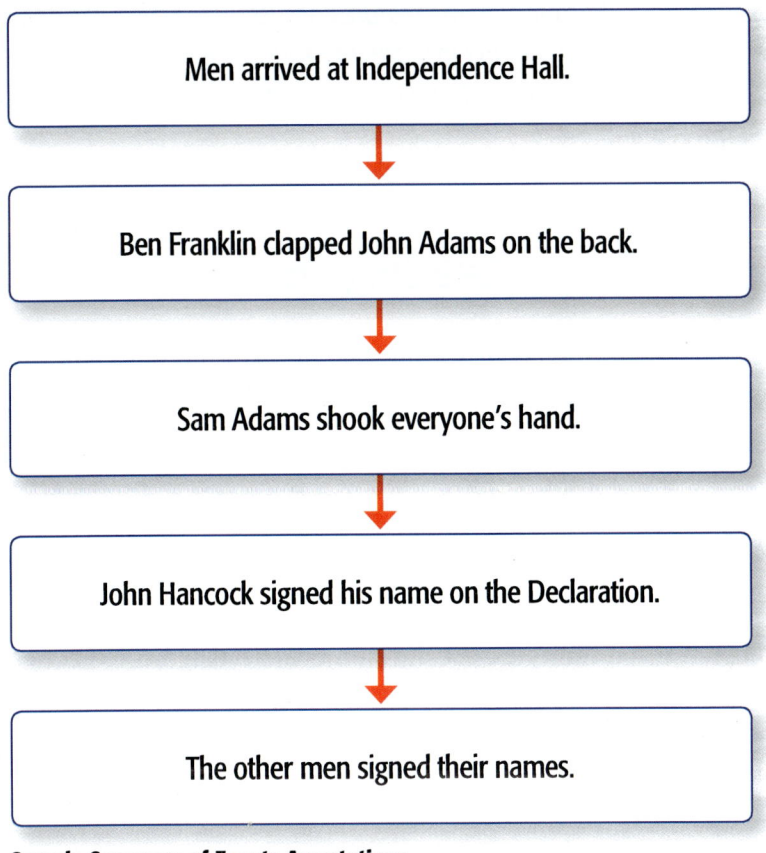

Sample Sequence of Events Annotations
(Note: Your class graphic organizer may differ.)

Make Content Comprehensible for ELLs

Beginning
Point to and name the images on the poster. Ask students to repeat each name after you.

All Levels
Help students understand the concept of independence. Model what it looks like to be trapped behind your desk by someone, then show how it looks to be free. Explain that **independence** means "being free from outside control."

Then help students understand what a declaration is. **Say:** *From now on, we have recess three times a day!* Explain that you just made a declaration, or a formal announcement.

Then explain that the Declaration of Independence was a formal announcement of the colonies' freedom from England's control.

If you have students whose first language is Spanish, share these English/Spanish cognates: **declaration/la declaración; independence/la independencia**.

Comprehension Quick-Check

Note which students are or are not able to recognize the sequence of events. Use the following strategies to provide additional explicit instruction.

Use an Identify Sequence of Events graphic organizer like the one shown on page 7.

Say: *Let's look for details and signal words that help us identify the sequence of events, or the order in which things happen.*

Help students use the story details and signal words to recognize and identify the sequence of events.

Say: *We know the story tells about what happened on July 4, 1776. What happened first on that day? Men arrived at Independence Hall. Who was there? What did they do?*

Oral Language Extension

Display Poster 1 (your class Historical Fiction anchor chart) during independent workstation time. Have pairs of students work together to plan a historical fiction story using the features of historical fiction listed on the poster. Encourage them to use the ideas they recorded in yesterday's homework as a starting point.

Home/School Connection

Have students take home BLM 2, reread the text, and highlight and label the features of historical fiction present in the passage.

Focus on Genre Features: Historical Fiction

Ask students to name some of the features of historical fiction that you discussed yesterday.

Say: *Now let's reexamine "The Signing of the Declaration of Independence" and look for features of historical fiction. What do you notice?*

Work with students to identify the following genre features embedded in this passage:

- The story is set in a real time and place from history.
- The characters are men who lived in that time period.
- The dialogue is made up but based on language from the Declaration.
- The characters are in conflict with the King of England.

Reveal the poster annotations so that students can confirm or revise their ideas. Reread them as a group.

Connect and transfer. Say: *As you read historical fiction stories, look for these features. Recognizing the features of historical fiction will help you determine what parts of the text are important. Identifying the sequence of events will also help you determine what is important and understand what you are reading.*

 # Small-Group Reading Instruction (60 MINUTES)

Continue small-group reading instruction from the previous day. Use the instruction provided in the Teacher's Guide for each text.

 # Individual Student Conferences (10 MINUTES)

Confer with individual students to discuss their understanding of genre and comprehension strategies. Use the Individual Reading Conference Form on page 32 of *Informal Assessments for Reading Development* to help guide your conferences.

 # Word Study Workshop (20 MINUTES)

Use the Day 2 instruction provided in Grade 3 Word Study Unit 8.

Read-Aloud (10 MINUTES)

Select a favorite nonfiction read-aloud from your classroom or school library with which to model the metacognitive strategy "Determine Text Importance." Use the sample read-aloud lessons and suggested titles in the Getting Started Guide.

Mini-Lessons (20 MINUTES)

Determine Text Importance and Sequence of Events

Display Genre Workshop Poster 3 and distribute BLM 3.

Read aloud the excerpt with students. **Say:** *We are going to figure out what information is important to remember about this historical fiction story. We will do that by looking at the sequence of events. I will start by identifying what happens first, and then I want you to tell what happens next.*

Say: *I read the first paragraph. I learn that two astronauts have landed on the moon. The first thing that happens is they open the door of their spaceship.*

Say: *Now you tell me what the next important thing is that happens.* Allow responses. If students are unable to determine sequence, prompt them to think about the following:
- *Does the sentence "Neil was brave" tell us anything about the sequence of events?*
- *What is the next important thing that happens after the astronauts open the door? What does Neil do? What happens next?*

Say: *Identifying the sequence of events helps us determine what parts of the story are important. Let's write the sequence of events of the moon landing on a graphic organizer. Then we will look at the sequence of events of the whole space race.*

Work with students to identify the sequence of events of just the moon landing. As you work, relate the sequence of events to specific features of the historical fiction genre. Record the details on a graphic organizer like the one shown on page 10.

Work with students to determine which events actually belong on the graphic organizer. Make sure that all of the events relate to the moon landing. Then repeat the process, filling in events related to the space race.

Historical Fiction Poster 3

Lesson Objectives

Students will:

- Review features of the historical fiction genre.
- Determine text importance.
- Use their understanding of genre features to identify sequence of events.
- Build oral language and vocabulary through whole-group and partner discussion.

Related Resources

- Historical Fiction Poster 3 (BLM 3)
- Sequence of Events (BLM 4)
- BenchmarkUniverse.com

Make Content Comprehensible for ELLs

Beginning

Show pictures of space, including Earth and the moon. Be sure students understand that the astronauts are on the moon.

Intermediate and Advanced

Help children understand the difference between **man** and **mankind**. Draw one stick figure on the board and label it **man**. Then draw an outline of Earth with stick figures on all the continents. Explain that all the people of the world are **mankind**.

All Levels

Group students with fluent English speakers during all whole-group and partner discussions.

Comprehension Quick-Check

Note whether students can identify sequence of events. For extra support, review the features of historical fiction using Poster 1. Then highlight or underline events and signal words on Poster 3 using a write-on/wipe-off marker. **Say:** *In historical fiction, the writer tells you what happened in a real time and place in history. Understanding the order of events helps you understand the story.* Have students underline or highlight events with you.

Home/School Connection

Have students take home the Sequence of Events graphic organizer (BLM 4) and identify the sequence of events in a favorite story.

Remind students that not every event will be identified with a signal word such as **first**, **second**, **next**, or **last**. Students may have to use dates and other details in the text to determine the order of events.

Connect and transfer. Say: *Today as you continue to read historical fiction in your small groups, identify the sequence of events to help you determine text importance.*

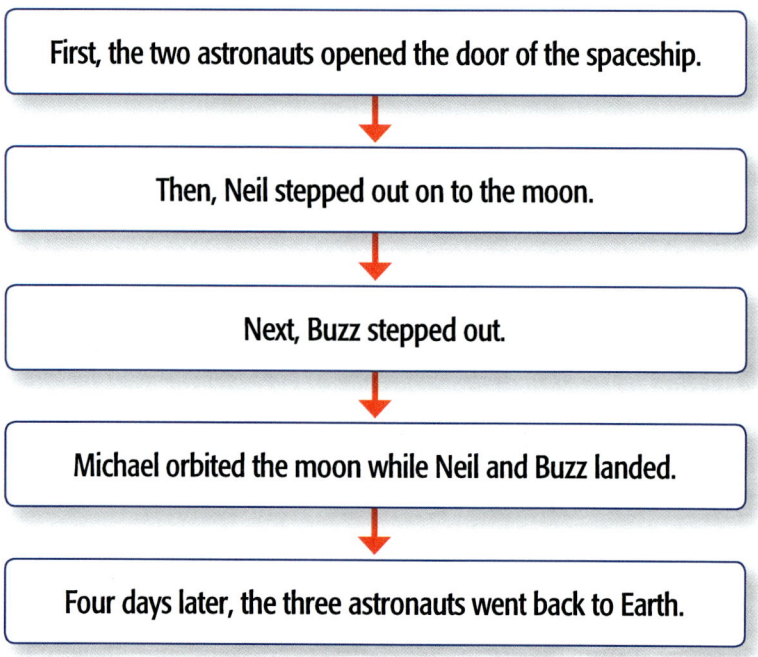

First, the two astronauts opened the door of the spaceship.

Then, Neil stepped out on to the moon.

Next, Buzz stepped out.

Michael orbited the moon while Neil and Buzz landed.

Four days later, the three astronauts went back to Earth.

Sample Sequence of Events Annotations

 ## Small-Group Reading Instruction (60 MINUTES)

Continue small-group reading instruction from the previous day. Use the instruction provided in the Teacher's Guide for each text.

 ## Individual Student Conferences (10 MINUTES)

Confer with individual students to discuss their developing understanding of genre and comprehension strategies. Use the Individual Reading Conference Form on page 32 of Informal Assessments for Reading Development to help guide your conferences.

 ## Word Study Workshop (20 MINUTES)

Use the Day 3 instruction provided in Grade 3 Word Study Unit 8.

Read-Aloud (10 MINUTES)

Select a favorite nonfiction read-aloud from your classroom or school library with which to model the metacognitive strategy "Determine Text Importance." Use the sample read-aloud lessons and suggested titles in the Getting Started Guide.

The First Man on the Moon

The two **astronauts** helped each other open the door of their spaceship. Neil was brave. He was first to step onto the moon. "This is one small step for man, one giant leap for mankind," he said.

Buzz was second to step onto the moon. The spacemen had waited a long time for this moment. Now the world cheered them. America had won the space race!

The race to put people in space started in 1961. That was when Russia was first to have a man orbit Earth. Then, in 1963, Russia was first to put a woman into space. But President Kennedy said America would win the race to the moon. Six years later, Neil and Buzz made that dream come true.

Michael orbited the moon in their spaceship. He waited to pick up Neil and Buzz. Then they came home.

After four days in space, Neil, Buzz, and Michael returned safely to Earth.

Historical Fiction Poster 3

 Mini-Lessons (20 MINUTES)

Build Comprehension: Evaluate Author's Purpose

Say: *An author has a purpose, or reason, for writing. The purpose can be to inform, to entertain, or to persuade the reader. To inform means to share information. To entertain means to tell a funny story. To persuade means to try to get the reader to think a certain way. Thinking about the author's purpose when you read historical fiction can help you understand the story and determine what is important in the story. Let's look again at the story and think about the author's purpose for writing it. As we read, ask yourself, "What is the author trying to do?"*

Reread Poster 3 with students.

Say: *We are going to make a chart to help us evaluate the author's purpose. We will list information from the story that helps us prove what the author's purpose is. What kinds of information will you look for to understand the author's reason for writing?* **Allow responses.**

Engage students in a discussion to ensure they understand they can use genre features to help them determine the author's purpose. Review the features of historical fiction in terms of author's purpose. Ask students to think about what the author is sharing with the reader.

Lesson Objectives

Students will:

- Evaluate author's purpose.

- Extend Tier Two Vocabulary by focusing on direct definitions.

- Build oral language and vocabulary through whole-group and partner discussion.

Related Resources

- Historical Fiction Poster 3 (BLM 3)

- BenchmarkUniverse.com

Make Content Comprehensible for ELLs

Beginning
Read aloud the poster title. Point to the illustration and name what it shows. Ask students to tell if these seem like funny things or things to learn about.

Use additional photos to define **astronauts**.

Intermediate and Advanced
Ask students to tell what the story is about. Then ask them if the story is funny, if it gives information, or if it tries to persuade them to think the same way as the author does about something.

All Levels
Pair ELLs with fluent English speakers to complete the chart. Encourage active listening for beginners.

Comprehension Quick-Check

Take note of students who may need more support to evaluate the author's purpose for writing. Provide additional modeling during small-group reading, and have students practice during independent workstation time by evaluating the author's purpose based on another historical fiction excerpt that you assign.

On chart paper, draw a two-column chart like the one shown below.

Think/Pair/Write/Share. Tell students they will complete this chart. **Say:** *Work with a partner to determine the author's purpose for writing this story. Make a chart like the one I just drew, and fill in your ideas. Put at least three details that show proof of your choice of author's purpose. We will share the charts as a group.*

Connect and transfer. Say: *Remember, when you read, you can use what you know about the genre to determine the author's purpose for writing the story. Historical fiction tells a story that gives information about events and characters in a real time period.*

AUTHOR'S PURPOSE	PROOF FROM THE STORY
to inform the reader about the moon landing and the space race	tells facts about historical event
	setting is a real time and place
	characters are real people who made history
	tells about a real challenge

Build Tier Two Vocabulary: Using Context Clues

On chart paper, write the word **astronauts**.

Say: *The astronauts helped each other open the door of the spaceship. What do you think the word **astronaut** means?*

Turn and talk. Ask students to turn and talk with their neighbor for a moment to come up with a definition.

Ask students to share their definitions and record them on chart paper. Students should understand that **astronauts** means "people who fly into space." Discuss how the author lets the reader know what an astronaut is. Point out the clue words **spaceship** and **moon** in the first sentences. Explain that the author has defined the word in the story.

Say: *Turn back to talk again with your neighbor. Work together to write a sentence using the word **astronauts**. Include two clue words in your sentence that tell what an astronaut is, but do not use the words **spaceship** or **moon**. Allow students to talk and write. Then have them share their sentences with the group.*

Small-Group Reading Instruction (60 MINUTES)

Continue small-group reading instruction from the previous day. Use the instruction provided in the Teacher's Guide for each text.

Individual Student Conferences (10 MINUTES)

Confer with individual students to discuss their developing understanding of genre and word-solving strategies. Use the Individual Reading Conference Form on page 32 of Informal Assessments for Reading Development to help guide your conferences.

Word Study Workshop (20 MINUTES)

Use the Day 4 instruction provided in Grade 3 Word Study Unit 8.

Oral Language Extension

During independent workstation time, ask pairs of students to discuss whether an author's purpose for writing historical fiction would ever be to entertain or to persuade. Refer students to the Historical Fiction anchor chart to aid their discussion.

Home/School Connection

Have students take home BLM 3 and read it with a family member to practice fluent reading. Tell students to have their family members sign the page to indicate they have participated in the reading.

Day Five

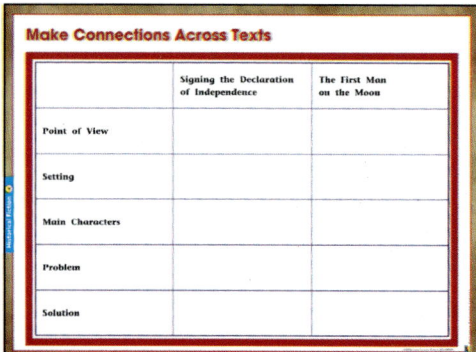

	Signing the Declaration of Independence	The First Man on the Moon
Point of View		
Setting		
Main Characters		
Problem		
Solution		

Historical Fiction Poster 4

Lesson Objectives

Students will:

- Identify elements of and compare historical fiction.
- Review features of the historical fiction genre.
- Make text-to-text connections.
- Build academic oral language and vocabulary through small-group and whole-group discussions.

Related Resources

- Historical Fiction Poster 4 (BLM 5)
- BenchmarkUniverse.com

Read-Aloud (10 MINUTES)

Revisit the week's read-alouds to make text-to-text connections and provide opportunities for reader response. Use the suggested activities in the Getting Started Guide, or implement ideas of your own.

Mini-Lessons (20 MINUTES)

Synthesize and Assess Genre Understanding

Synthesize genre understanding. Review the features of historical fiction on Poster 1 with students. Then pair students and have each pair find one example of each feature from the stories they have read this week. Have them record their examples on a sheet of paper.

Give students five to seven minutes to discuss and record their ideas. Then have each pair share their example of each feature with the class.

Record the examples from each pair on chart paper.

Self-assessment. Display the class Historical Fiction anchor chart from Day 1. Ask students to discuss how the examples they found illustrate the features they listed on the anchor chart.

Ask: *How has your understanding of the historical fiction genre developed? What do you know now that you didn't know before?* Encourage individual students to share their personal insights.

Connect and transfer. Say: *How will your understanding of this genre help you as a reader the next time you read a historical fiction story? How can you use your understanding of the genre to write your own historical fiction?*

Make Connections Across Texts

Display Historical Fiction Poster 4.

Say: *You have read historical fiction stories this week. Sometimes in school and on tests, you will be asked to make connections between different fiction and nonfiction texts. Today we are going to practice making connections between historical fiction stories.*

Ask each group to analyze the poster passages. Ask them to complete the graphic organizer and answer the questions about the two selections on Historical Fiction Poster 4 (BLM 5).

Give students about five minutes to record their ideas. Then bring the groups together and have them share their ideas.

Challenge students to express their own opinions on these stories:
- *Which historical fiction story did you like more? Why?*
- *Which event would you like to learn more about? Why?*

Connect and transfer. Say: *When you analyze two historical fiction stories, think about how each one reflects the features of the genre. What historical time period is the author writing about? Are the characters real people, or are they based on real people? Where did the author get ideas for the dialogue in the story? What is the conflict?*

Small-Group Reading Instruction (60 MINUTES)

Continue small-group reading instruction from the previous day. Use the instruction provided in the Teacher's Guide for each text.

Individual Student Conferences (10 MINUTES)

Ask students to reflect on what they have learned about the historical fiction genre. Use the Individual Reading Conference Form on page 32 of Informal Assessments for Reading Development to help guide your conferences.

Word Study Workshop (20 MINUTES)

Use the Day 5 instruction provided in Grade 3 Word Study Unit 8.

Make Content Comprehensible for ELLs

Beginning
Ask students to point to the story and character they liked most and to any additional illustrations that helped them understand the story.

Intermediate and Advanced
Provide sentence frames to help ELLs contribute to their groups' discussions. For example:

I acted like this character when I _____.

The story endings are different because _____.

Readers could learn _____ from this story.

All Levels
Pair ELLs with fluent English speakers during all partner and group activities.

Encourage ELLs to revisit the books they are analyzing and to find and read specific information in the text to help them communicate their ideas.

Name _____ Date _____

FEATURES OF HISTORICAL FICTION

Focus on the Genre
Historical Fiction

What is historical fiction?

What is the purpose of historical fiction?

How do you read historical fiction?

Who writes historical fiction?

Historical Fiction ❶

Name _____ Date _____

The story includes a conflict.

The story is based on a true event in history.

Signing the Declaration of Independence

The sun rose brightly on the fourth of July in 1776. Men from every colony had traveled to Independence Hall in Philadelphia. Before they could be free, they would have to fight. Today they would declare their freedom.

Tom Jefferson was proud. He had written the Declaration of Independence in the last months. Ben Franklin clapped his friend John Adams on the back. They had done a good job polishing Tom's work after he was done.

"To liberty!" John shouted and threw his three-cornered hat into the air.

His cousin Sam Adams shook everyone's hands.

John Hancock smoothed the large paper on his study desk. Then he took his quill from its inkwell. He was first to sign his name. His hand danced at the bottom of the page. "I signed my name large for the King of England to see we're free!"

The citizens then took turns with the quill until all their names were signed.

The story is set in a real time and place from history.

The story is told in third person.

Jefferson, Franklin, and Adams are real heros who made history.

The dialogue is made up, but is based on words in the declaration.

Name _____   Date _____

The First Man on the Moon

The two **astronauts** helped each other open the door of their spaceship. Neil was brave. He was first to step onto the moon. "This is one small step for man, one giant leap for mankind," he said.

Buzz was second to step onto the moon. The spacemen had waited a long time for this moment. Now the world cheered them. America had won the space race!

The race to put people in space started in 1961. That was when Russia was first to have a man orbit Earth. Then, in 1963, Russia was first to put a woman into space. But President Kennedy said America would win the race to the moon. Six years later, Neil and Buzz made that dream come true.

Michael orbited the moon in their spaceship. He waited to pick up Neil and Buzz. Then they came home.

After four days in space, Neil, Buzz, and Michael returned safely to Earth.

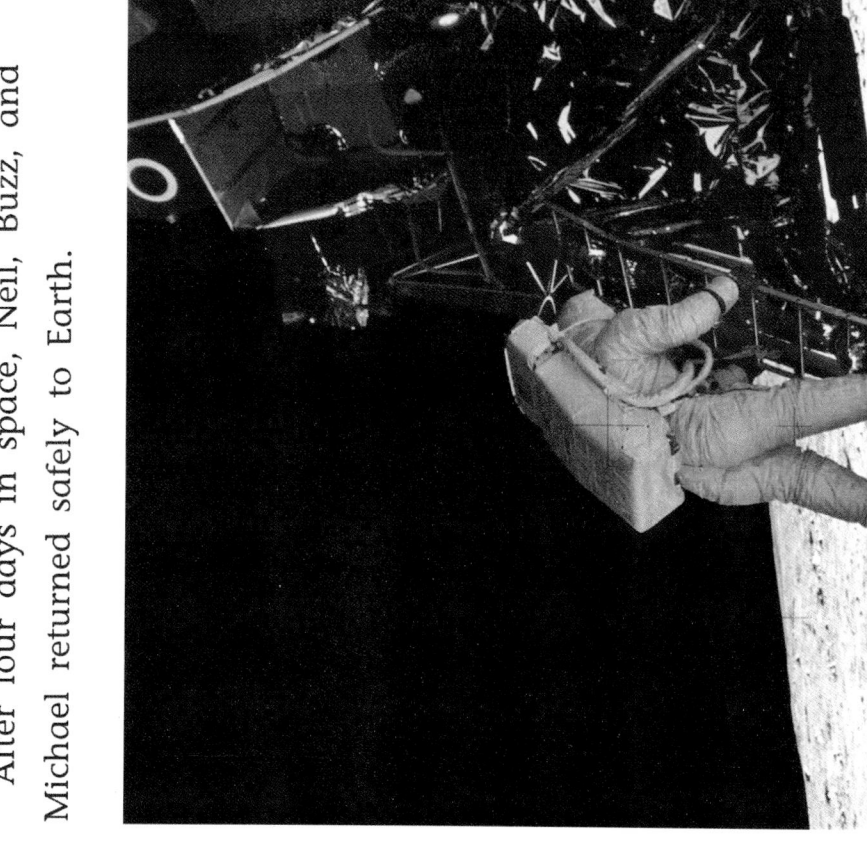

Historical Fiction 3

Name _____ Date _____

Sequence of Events

Directions: Identify the most important events in the story and record them in the chart below. Be sure to record the events in order.

Story Title: _____

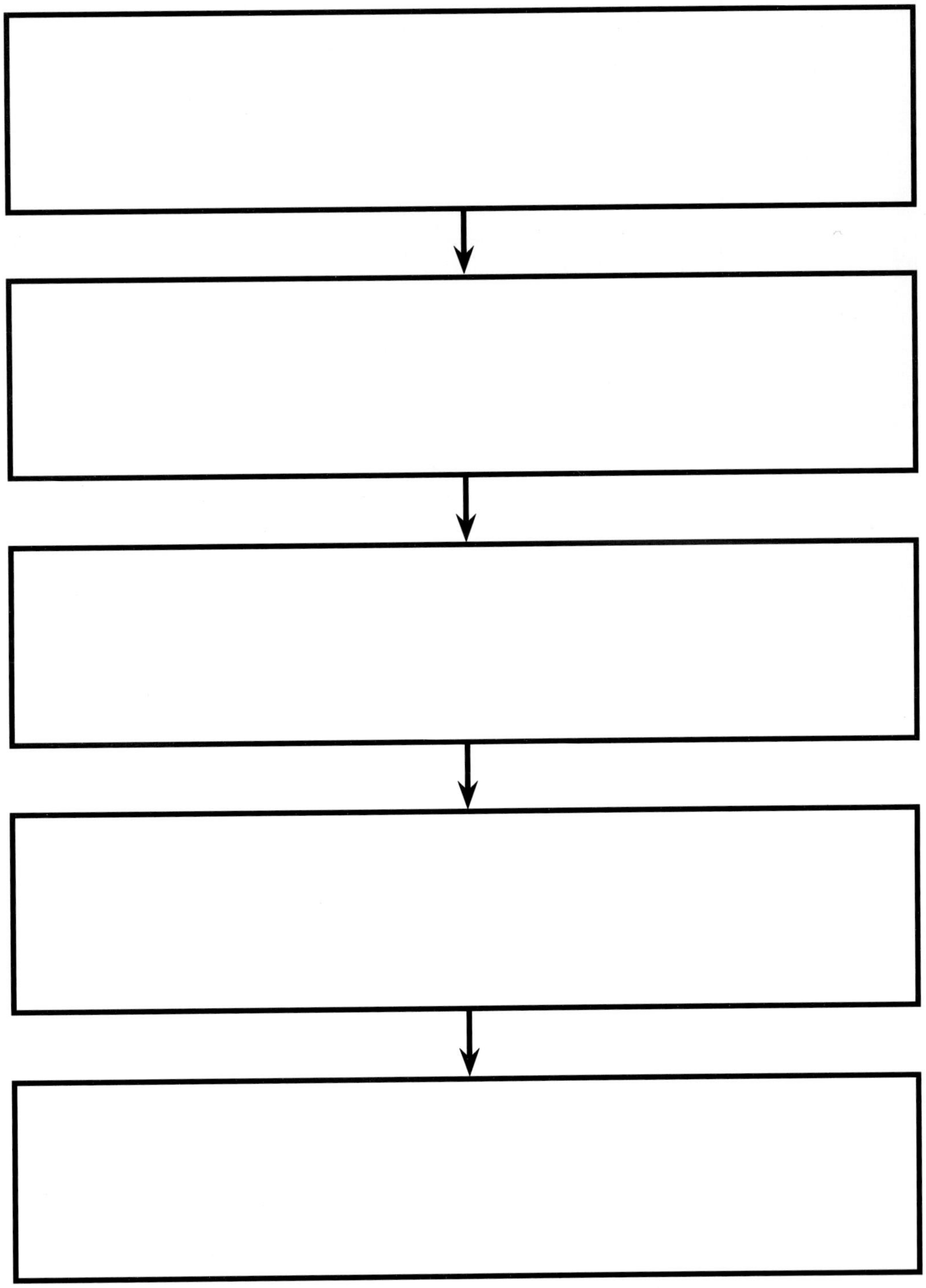

```
┌─────────────────────────────┐
│                             │
│                             │
└─────────────────────────────┘
              ↓
┌─────────────────────────────┐
│                             │
│                             │
└─────────────────────────────┘
              ↓
┌─────────────────────────────┐
│                             │
│                             │
└─────────────────────────────┘
              ↓
┌─────────────────────────────┐
│                             │
│                             │
└─────────────────────────────┘
              ↓
┌─────────────────────────────┐
│                             │
│                             │
└─────────────────────────────┘
```

Name _____   Date _____

Make Connections Across Texts

	Signing the Declaration of Independence	The First Man on the Moon
Point of View		
Setting		
Main Characters		
Problem		
Solution		

Historical Fiction 4

BENCHMARK LITERACY™

Determine Text Importance/ Identify Sequence of Events

Reader's Theater

Cesar Chavez Comes to Visit

by Candice Kramer • illustrated by Karen Leon

Unit 3/Week 3 at a Glance

Day	Mini-Lessons
ONE	• Introduce Fluency Skills: *Pausing–Full Stop* • Model the Skill
TWO	• Practice and Self-Assess Fluency Skills: *Pausing–Full Stop* • Connect Fluency and Comprehension: *Analyze Author's Purpose*
THREE	• Apply Fluency Skills to Reader's Theater • Build Comprehension: *Analyze Author's Purpose*
FOUR	• Build Tier Two Vocabulary: *Adverbs*
FIVE	• Prepare for and Manage Student Performances: *Audience and Performer Expectations* • Show Time! • Assess and Reflect

Baseball Jokes

Reader 1: The stadium was really cold at the baseball game last night.
Reader 2: Why? Was the temperature below zero?
Reader 1: No, but every seat had a fan in it!

Reader 1: It took the baseball player longer to run from second to third base than from first to second base.
Reader 2: Why? Are second and third base farther apart?
Reader 1: No, but there's a shortstop between them!

Reader 1: My dog reminds me of a baseball player.
Reader 2: Why? Does he catch flies?
Reader 1: No, but he runs for home when he sees the catcher!

Reader 1: Cinderella would never have made it as a baseball player.
Reader 2: Why? Because she wore all those fancy clothes?
Reader 1: No, because she had a pumpkin for a coach!

BENCHMARK EDUCATION COMPANY

Baseball Jokes

Reader 1: The stadium was really cold at the baseball game last night.
Reader 2: Why? Was the temperature below zero?
Reader 1: No, but every seat had a fan in it!

Reader 1: It took the baseball player longer to run from second to third base than from first to second base.
Reader 2: Why? Are second and third base farther apart?
Reader 1: No, but there's a shortstop between them!

Reader 1: My dog reminds me of a baseball player.
Reader 2: Why? Does he catch flies?
Reader 1: No, but he runs for home when he sees the catcher!

Reader 1: Cinderella would never have made it as a baseball player.
Reader 2: Why? Because she wore all those fancy clothes?
Reader 1: No, because she had a pumpkin for a coach!

Fluency Poster

Lesson Objectives

Students will:

- Utilize punctuation to signal full stops while reading.
- Demonstrate understanding of the text through purposeful pausing.
- Use effective pausing to make their reading sound like talking.

Related Resources

- BenchmarkUniverse.com

Read-Aloud (10 MINUTES)

Select a favorite fiction read-aloud from your classroom or school library with which to model the metacognitive strategy "Determine Text Importance." Use the sample read-aloud lessons and suggested titles provided in the Getting Started Guide.

Mini-Lessons (20 MINUTES)

Introduce Fluency Skills: Pausing—Full Stop

Explain: *We have learned that we do not run all our words together when reading. Instead, we pause, or rest, between some words. Punctuation helps us figure out when to pause. What kind of punctuation tells us to take short pauses?* Allow responses.

Reinforce the idea that pausing helps listeners understand what we are saying. Punctuation at the end of a sentence signals a longer pause than the punctuation inside the sentence.

Ask:
- *Do you take a bigger breath at the end of a sentence or in the middle of a sentence?*
  (at the end of a sentence)
- *What kinds of punctuation marks do you see at the end of a sentence?*
  (period, question mark, exclamation point)
- *Do you come to a full stop or take a short pause at the end of a sentence?*
  (You come to a full stop.)

Say: *We come to a full stop at the end of a sentence and take a breath before beginning the next sentence.*

Model the Skill

Display the fluency poster "Baseball Jokes" and read aloud the title.

Say: *These are jokes. The author uses periods, question marks, and exclamation points to show us when to come to a full stop. Coming to a full stop helps the jokes sound right and make sense.*

Ask students to listen and follow along as you read the jokes aloud, coming to a full stop at each period, question mark, and exclamation point.

Say: *Now I will read the first joke without pausing. Listen closely.*

Read the entire joke in a word-by-word manner without coming to a full stop at the period, question marks, and exclamation point.

Turn and talk. Have students turn to a neighbor and compare and evaluate your readings. Ask them to think about how each reading affected them as listeners. Then have pairs of students share their ideas with the whole class. Reinforce the idea that pausing correctly at punctuation helps the sentences sound right and make sense.

Shared Writing. Invite students to help you create a class anchor chart (or review the one from the previous lesson on pausing) to remind them how good readers use pausing. (See the example below.) When you are finished, ask students to echo-read the entire chart. Display the chart in the classroom for future reference.

Pausing

- We do not run all our words together.
- We pause, or rest, between some words.
- Pausing divides sentences into meaningful parts.
- Pausing makes our reading easier to understand.
- Punctuation helps us figure out when to pause.
- Punctuation helps us figure out how long to pause.

Sample Anchor Chart

Make Content Comprehensible for ELLs

Beginning
Jokes that depend on wordplay are especially challenging for ELLs. Use props, drawings, role-play, and gestures to define the multiple-meaning words **fan**, **coach**, **flies**, and **catcher** (baseball and dog).

Intermediate and Advanced
Engage ELLs in a discussion about baseball to determine prior knowledge. Ask them to tell what they know about the game. Record a list of baseball-specific terms students generate.

All Levels
Before reading to model fluency, read to support comprehension of unfamiliar Tier Two words through explanation, gestures, and role-play, or by using props. Difficult words may include: **stadium**, **temperature**, **pumpkin**. Draw and label a simple baseball diamond with bases, home, catcher, shortstop.

Support Special Needs Learners

Throughout the week, use the following strategies to help students who have learning disabilities access the content and focus on skills and strategies.

During partner reading practice, pair special needs students with more fluent readers who can model fluency and support their development.

Group students heterogeneously for small-group reading of the script so that struggling students benefit from working with more fluent readers.

Assign multiple students to specific reader's theater roles so that they can support each other.

Fluency and Comprehension Quick-Check

Throughout the week, refer to the Fluency Rubric provided in the Benchmark Literacy Assessments to help you informally assess where students are in their development of key areas of fluency.

The end goal of all fluency practice is increased comprehension. Use the following questions to check students' comprehension of the passage they have read:

- *Which joke did you think was funniest? Why?*

- *What are all of the jokes about?*

Fluency Rubric

Connect and transfer. Say: *Today during small-group reading, we will read a reader's theater script. As we read the script, one skill we will practice is stopping at end punctuation marks to make our reading easier to understand.*

Small-Group Reading Instruction (60 MINUTES)

Introduce and read *Cesar Chavez Comes to Visit*. Use the before- and during-reading instruction in the Teacher's Guide for the script.

Individual Student Conferences (10 MINUTES)

Confer with individual students to discuss their understanding of the script. Use the Individual Reading Conference Form on page 32 of Informal Assessments for Reading Development to help guide your conferences.

Word Study Workshop (20 MINUTES)

Use the Day 1 instruction provided in Grade 3 Word Study Unit 9.

Read-Aloud (10 MINUTES)

Select a favorite fiction read-aloud from your classroom or school library with which to model the metacognitive strategy "Determine Text Importance." Use the sample read-aloud lessons and suggested titles provided in the Getting Started Guide.

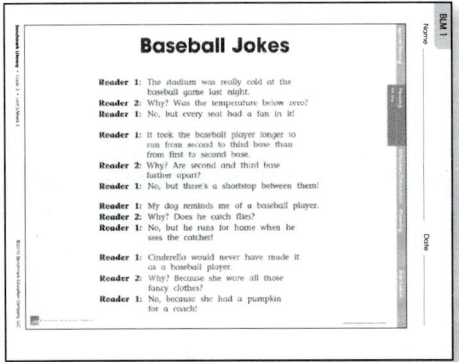

Baseball Jokes (BLM 1)

Mini-Lessons (20 MINUTES)

Practice and Self-Assess Fluency Skills: Pausing—Full Stop

Distribute copies of Baseball Jokes (BLM 1).

Ask students to choral-read the jokes with you one or more times.

Next, allow the group to choral-read the jokes without your assistance.

Distribute the Fluency Self-Assessment Master Checklist (BLM 2) and review the assessment criteria for pausing and integration. Ask students to give a thumbs-up or thumbs-down on each question based on the group's choral-reading. Discuss their responses.

Partner reading. Pair students and ask them to read "Baseball Jokes" together one or more times, alternating lines.

Monitor students' partner rereading practice and provide responsive feedback using the prompts provided on page 6.

Ask students to rate themselves on specific fluency skills covered in this lesson using their Fluency Self-Assessment Master Checklist (BLM 2).

Connect and transfer. Ask students to reflect on their fluency practice, using the following prompts:
- *When did you take quick pauses? When did you come to a full stop?*
- *How did pausing help you read and understand?*
- *Remember, you will need this skill as we practice and perform a reader's theater script this week.*

Lesson Objectives

Students will:
- Utilize punctuation to signal full stops while reading.
- Demonstrate understanding of the text through purposeful pausing.
- Use effective pausing to make their reading sound like talking.

Related Resources
- Baseball Jokes (BLM 1)
- Fluency Self-Assessment Master Checklist (BLM 2)
- BenchmarkUniverse.com

Make Content Comprehensible for ELLs

Beginning
Allow ELLs to participate through active listening while other students demonstrate pausing at punctuation. Invite ELLs to track print with you and give a thumbs-up when they see end punctuation and hear the reader breathe.

Intermediate and Advanced
Monitor students' understanding of the humor in the jokes. Revisit the baseball terminology and use pantomime to act out each joke as necessary.

All Levels
Pair ELLs with fluent English speakers during partner discussions and activities.

Fluency Self-Assessment Master Checklist (BLM 2)

Responsive Prompts for Pausing

As students work together, observe those who demonstrate understanding and those who struggle. Use appropriate responsive prompting to provide additional support or to validate students who demonstrate mastery.

Goal Oriented
- Listen to me read this. Can you hear me take a little breath at the comma?
- The period (question mark, exclamation point) means your voice makes a full stop.
- When I make a short pause, I don't stop completely and break the flow.
- When I finish a sentence, I make a full stop before continuing.
- Notice what I do when I see a comma. My reading pauses briefly and then continues to help make ideas clear as I read.
- Notice what I do when I see a period (question mark, exclamation point). My reading pauses with a full stop to show that I've read a complete sentence or idea.

Directive and Corrective Feedback
- Make a full stop at the period (question mark, exclamation point).
- Take a little breath when you see a comma.
- Read the punctuation.
- Read it like this with a short pause between the words.
- Read it like this with a full stop after the word.
- Make your pause longer.
- Make your pause shorter.

Self-Monitoring and Reflection
- How did you know to make a short pause here?
- How did you know to make a full stop here?
- Did you know where to make a short pause or full stop as you read?
- Was your pausing too short, too long, or just right?
- What did you notice about your reading?
- Where did you make short pauses as you read?
- Where did you make full stops as you read?

Validating and Confirming
- Good—you took a little breath.
- Good—you made a full stop.
- I like the way you made a short pause/full stop here.
- I like the way you used the _____ punctuation mark to help you make a short pause/full stop here.
- Good—you used punctuation marks to help you know when to pause and for how long!

Connect Fluency and Comprehension:
Analyze Author's Purpose

Say: *Taking short pauses and making full stops in the correct places helps you make sense of the words and sentences you read. You also need to understand why the author wrote a particular passage. When you understand why an author wrote something, you can use your voice to help your audience understand as well. What purposes do authors have for writing?* Allow responses.

Say: *Now think about "Baseball Jokes." Why do you think the author wrote these jokes?* Allow responses.

Discuss with students whether jokes are always intended to entertain and how they should be read. Are jokes ever serious? Should students read jokes in a slow, solemn way or in some other way?

Ask: *How does understanding the author's purpose of "Baseball Jokes" change how you sound when you read it aloud?*

Connect and transfer. Say: *Today during small-group reading, focus on understanding the purpose of the passage. This will help you read with the right feeling and expression.*

Small-Group Reading Instruction (60 MINUTES)

Reread *Cesar Chavez Comes to Visit* to build comprehension and critical thinking using the After Reading Interpret the Script questions. Assign roles to individual students.

Individual Student Conferences (10 MINUTES)

Confer with individual students to discuss their script roles and how they plan to rehearse and read their part. Use the Individual Reading Conference Form on page 32 of Informal Assessments for Reading Development to help guide your conferences.

Word Study Workshop (20 MINUTES)

Use the Day 2 instruction provided in Grade 3 Word Study Unit 9.

Oral Language Extension

Have pairs of students practice the fluency passage during independent workstation time.

Home/School Connection

Have students practice reading Baseball Jokes (BLM 1) again with a family member. Ask students to focus on reading smoothly and with appropriate pauses. Have them alternate roles with their family member so that they practice all the lines in the jokes.

Ask students to have their family member sign the page to indicate they have participated in the reading.

Day Three

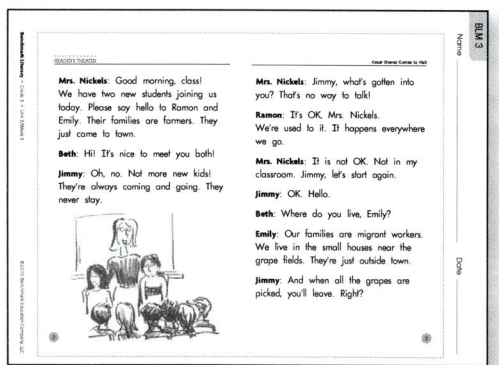

Cesar Chavez Comes to Visit, pages 2–3 (BLM 3)

Lesson Objectives

Students will:

- Utilize punctuation to signal full stops while reading a script.

- Demonstrate understanding of the text through purposeful pausing.

- Use effective pausing to make their reading sound like talking.

- Use metacognitive strategies to help them analyze the author's purpose.

- Build oral language and vocabulary through whole-group and partner discussion.

Related Resources

- *Cesar Chavez Comes to Visit,* pages 2–3 (BLM 3)

- BenchmarkUniverse.com

Read-Aloud (10 MINUTES)

Select a favorite nonfiction read-aloud from your classroom or school library with which to model the metacognitive strategy "Determine Text Importance." Use the sample read-aloud lessons and suggested titles provided in the Getting Started Guide.

Mini-Lessons (20 MINUTES)

Apply Fluency Skills to Reader's Theater

Distribute the first two pages of *Cesar Chavez Comes to Visit* (BLM 3), which students have completed during small-group reading time.

Say: *Yesterday you practiced coming to a full stop as you read some jokes. Now I want you to apply what you learned to the script we will perform this week. Listen as I read these two pages to you.*

Read pages 2–3 of the script to model how you use short pauses and full stops to make the dialogue sound natural. Use the suggestions below or interpret the text in your own way:
- Mrs. Nickels: brightly, with enthusiasm, but speaking clearly and taking longer pauses between sentences
- Beth: excited, speaking quickly
- Jimmy: not happy, speaking in lower tone than Beth, sullen and slow with second greeting
- Ramon: in between Beth and Jimmy, resigned
- Emily: speaks clearly, ready to explain

Ask students to comment on how your reading affected them as listeners. How did you use pauses to vary the characters' voices?

Partner reading. Have pairs of students practice reading these pages together. Monitor their practice and provide responsive prompting as needed to validate their efforts, give corrective feedback, or encourage them to self monitor. Use the responsive prompts provided on page 6.

Build Comprehension: Analyze Author's Purpose

Say: *Yesterday we discussed why the author of "Baseball Jokes" wrote that passage. Today let's think about why the author of* Cesar Chavez Comes to Visit *wrote about these events and characters. Understanding the author's purpose will help you interpret the script more effectively.*

Activate metacognitive strategies. Ask: *What strategies can we use to help ourselves understand the author's purpose?* Allow responses. If necessary, prompt students to use the following strategies:

Ask questions. Ask: *What questions can you ask yourself as you read to make sure you understand what's happening in the script? What does the author want you to learn about? What do you think her purpose is? How do you know?*

Visualize. Ask: *If you imagine the characters in your mind, what do you see? What expression do you see on Jimmy's face? On Ramon's? How does visualizing help you understand what the script is about?*

Support ELLs' and struggling readers' participation in the discussion by providing the following sentence frames:

> *I think the author wants me to learn about _____.*
> *I think the author's purpose is to _____.*
> *I imagine Jimmy/Ramon looks _____.*

Shared Writing. Make a list of students' ideas about the author's purpose. Post this on the wall.

Connect and transfer. Say: *Today, as you practice the script, think about what the author wants people to experience through the script. Use what you have learned about pausing to help you express her purpose.*

Small-Group Reading Instruction (60 MINUTES)

Have students rehearse their roles in *Cesar Chavez Comes to Visit* together as a group. Offer suggestions for voice, expression, and pausing.

Individual Student Conferences (10 MINUTES)

Confer with individual students to discuss their script roles and their rehearsal progress. Use the Individual Reading Conference Form on page 32 of *Informal Assessments for Reading Development* to help guide your conferences.

Word Study Workshop (20 MINUTES)

Use the Day 3 instruction provided in Grade 3 Word Study Unit 9.

Make Content Comprehensible for ELLs

Beginning
Allow ELLs to participate through active listening while other students demonstrate pausing. Invite them to indicate when they hear a full stop. Reinforce the connection between the stop and the written punctuation mark.

Intermediate and Advanced
Allow ELLs to read parts of the script chorally with you or other students as they demonstrate their use of pauses.

All Levels
Pair ELLs with fluent English speakers during partner reading practice.

Model the use of academic sentence frames to support ELLs' academic vocabulary and language development. (See suggested sentence frames provided.)

Home/School Connection

Have students take home *Cesar Chavez Comes to Visit*, pages 2–3 (BLM 3) and read it with a family member to practice fluent reading. Ask students to have their family member sign the script page to indicate that they have participated in the reading.

Fluency Quick-Check

As students practice oral reading with a partner, note students who would benefit from additional repeated oral reading practice during independent workstation time.

Day Four

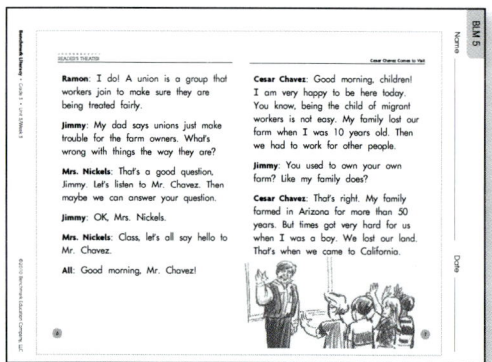

Cesar Chavez Comes to Visit, pages 6–7 (BLM 5)

Lesson Objectives

Students will:

• Extend Tier Two Vocabulary by analyzing adverbs.

• Partner-read to build fluency.

• Build oral language and vocabulary through whole-group and partner discussion.

Related Resources

• Adverbs (BLM 4)

• *Cesar Chavez Comes to Visit,* pages 6–7 (BLM 5)

• BenchmarkUniverse.com

Read-Aloud (10 MINUTES)

Select a favorite nonfiction read-aloud from your classroom or school library with which to model the metacognitive strategy "Determine Text Importance." Use the sample read-aloud lessons and suggested titles provided in the Getting Started Guide.

Mini-Lessons (20 MINUTES)

Build Tier Two Vocabulary: Adverbs

On chart paper, draw a graphic organizer like the one below (BLM 4). Remind students that adverbs are words that tell how, when, where, and how much. Today they will discuss adverbs.

Think/Pair/Write/Share. Distribute the Adverbs graphic organizer (BLM 4). Ask students to work with a partner to list adverbs that tell how, when, where, and how much. Give students approximately three minutes, and then bring them back together to share their answers. If students are unable to come up with adverbs, prompt them with the following:

- *How do we talk in the library?*
- *When will you eat breakfast again?*
- *Where is the playground?*
- *If you can't figure out a math problem, what would you say about how hard it is?*

Record students' responses on the chart. Ask students to use their adverbs in sentences.

Distribute *Cesar Chavez Comes to Visit,* pages 6–7 (BLM 5).

How	When	Where	How Much
quietly	tomorrow	outside	too
slowly	now	here	almost

Sample Adverbs Annotations (BLM 4)

Say: *Writers use adverbs to give readers information about other words. Adverbs usually tell about verbs, but they can also tell more about adjectives or other adverbs. Read the text with a partner. Find two words that are adverbs.*

Have pairs read the script excerpt on BLM 5 and find two adverbs. (fairly, then, here, when, more (than), not, very) Have them record the adverbs on BLM 4 and share the information with the class.

Discuss fix-up monitoring strategies. Ask students what they can do when they read an adverb and are not sure what it means. Generate discussion of the strategies that help good readers. For example, students can use context clues to determine meaning. They can also break longer adverbs into smaller chunks to see if the base word is familiar.

Connect and transfer. Say: *Adverbs tell when, where, how, and how much. Paying attention to adverbs can help you understand the action and the characters in the script.*

Small-Group Reading Instruction (60 MINUTES)

Have students continue to rehearse their roles in *Cesar Chavez Comes to Visit* together as a group. Discuss and plan how students will stage their script performance tomorrow.

Individual Student Conferences (10 MINUTES)

Confer with individual students on sections of the script you would like them to work on before the performance. Use the Individual Reading Conference Form on page 32 of Informal Assessments for Reading Development to help guide your conferences.

Word Study Workshop (20 MINUTES)

Use the Day 4 instruction provided in Grade 3 Word Study Unit 9.

Make Content Comprehensible for ELLs

Beginning
Help ELLs understand adverbs such as **quietly**, **slowly**, **later**, and **very** by using role-playing and realia. For example, walk slowly across the room. **Say:** *I am walking slowly.* (Walk slower.) *Now I am walking very slowly.*

Intermediate
Provide sentence frames such as the following and have students fill in adverbs:

We will go to the library _____.
We play _____.

All Levels
Pair ELLs with fluent English speakers during partner discussions and activities.

Oral Language Extension

Write several glossary words from the reader's theater script on chart paper and display the list during independent workstation time. Challenge pairs of students to use each word in meaningful oral sentences. Ask students to write down at least five sentences to show you during independent student conference time.

Home/School Connection

Have students take home *Cesar Chavez Comes to Visit*, pages 6–7 (BLM 5) and read it with a family member to practice fluency skills. Ask students to have their family member sign the script page to indicate that they have participated in the reading.

Day Five

Reader's Theater Script

Lesson Objectives

Students will:

- Demonstrate their level of fluency development through an oral reading interpretation of the script.

- Demonstrate active listening skills.

- Reflect on and assess their own fluency development.

Related Resources

- Reader's Theater Self-Assessment (BLM 6)

- BenchmarkUniverse.com

Read-Aloud (10 MINUTES)

Revisit the week's read-alouds to make text-to-text connections and to provide opportunities for reader response. Use the suggested activities in the Getting Started Guide, or implement ideas of your own.

Mini-Lessons (20 MINUTES)

Prepare for and Manage Student Performances:
Audience and Performer Expectations

Prepare students for their reader's theater performances by sharing your expectations of audience members and performers.

Audience expectations. Say: *While you are listening to the other groups perform, I expect you to do the following:*
- Give your classmates your full attention.
- Do not speak to your neighbors or make any noise.
- Enjoy their performance and show your appreciation by clapping when they are finished.
- Be prepared to give your feedback on the script, and always remember to make your feedback constructive, or helpful.

Performer expectations. Say: *While you and your group are performing the script, remember to do these things:*
- Read in a loud, clear voice and act out your role.
- Use expression and fluency to help everyone listening to understand your character.
- Remember to use punctuation clues to take pauses.
- When it is not your turn to read, follow along in the script so you know when to come in.
- If one of your group members gets lost or forgets to come in, prompt him or her quietly.
- Accept both suggestions and praise from your audience.

Show Time!

Invite students to perform the script for an audience such as members of the class, students from other classes, school staff members, or parents.

Continue your performances during small-group reading time, giving each group the opportunity to perform.

Assess and Reflect

After all groups have completed their performance, use the following self-assessment activity to help students reflect on their performance, identify how they have improved as readers and performers, and determine what they will focus on as they participate in future reader's theater experiences throughout the year.

Draw a three-column reflection chart on chart paper. Include a column for **Reflection Questions** and columns to answer **Yes** or **No** in response. Use the following questions to guide the group's assessment of their performance, or use the Reader's Theater Self-Assessment (BLM 6). Place a check mark in the appropriate column, noting their responses.

- Did we make our reading sound smooth like talking?
- Did we make our characters sound and feel like real people (or animals/objects) with feelings?
- Did we act out our parts with our voices and body language?
- Were our parts at "just right" reading levels?
- Did we practice our reading many times before performing?
- Did we pause in the correct places to help our audience understand the characters and message of the script?

Connect and transfer. Discuss ways to improve future performances based on the self-assessment and reflections.

Small-Group Reading Instruction (60 MINUTES)

Use the small-group reading time to continue students' performances of *Cesar Chavez Comes to Visit*.

After all groups have performed, use the Assess and Reflect activity above.

Individual Student Conferences (10 MINUTES)

Have students use their self-reflection to show how they would read differently next time. Discuss how students plan to apply what they learned to future performances and independent reading.

Word Study Workshop (20 MINUTES)

Use the Day 5 instruction provided in Grade 3 Word Study Unit 9.

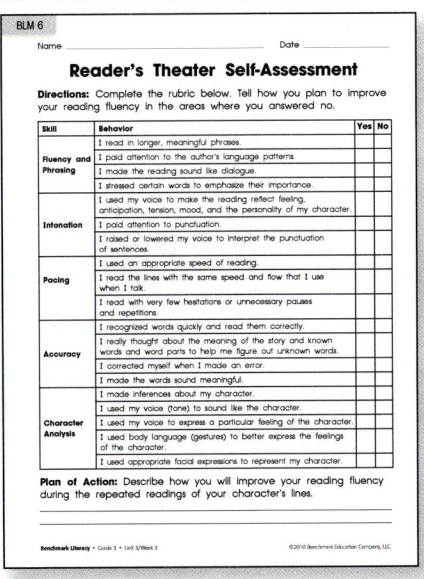

Reader's Theater Self-Assessment (BLM 6)

Make Content Comprehensible for ELLs

Beginning
Allow beginning ELLs to participate as active listeners. Encourage students to listen for pauses between sentences and pauses between speakers.

Intermediate and Advanced
Pair ELLs with more fluent readers to chorally read their parts in the script. Encourage students to highlight their lines, using a different color to highlight where they should pause to take a breath between sentences.

Assessment Tip

During student performances, record anecdotal notes that focus on how students are developing fluency skills and how they are meeting performer and audience-member expectations.

Name _____ Date _____

Speed/Pacing	Pausing	Inflection/Intonation	Phrasing	Expression
	Full Stop			

Baseball Jokes

Reader 1: The stadium was really cold at the baseball game last night.

Reader 2: Why? Was the temperature below zero?

Reader 1: No, but every seat had a fan in it!

Reader 1: It took the baseball player longer to run from second to third base than from first to second base.

Reader 2: Why? Are second and third base farther apart?

Reader 1: No, but there's a shortstop between them!

Reader 1: My dog reminds me of a baseball player.

Reader 2: Why? Does he catch flies?

Reader 1: No, but he runs for home when he sees the catcher!

Reader 1: Cinderella would never have made it as a baseball player.

Reader 2: Why? Because she wore all those fancy clothes?

Reader 1: No, because she had a pumpkin for a coach!

Name _____ Date _____

Fluency Self-Assessment Master Checklist

	Yes	No
Speed/Pacing		
Did my speed and pacing match the kind of text I was reading?		
Did my speed and pacing match what the character was saying?		
Did I read with a natural talking voice?		
Did I slow my reading down when appropriate?		
Did I pay attention to punctuation?		
Pausing		
Did I pause to keep from running all my words together?		
Did I pause in the correct locations?		
Did I pause for the appropriate length of time?		
Did I pause to help my reading make sense?		
Did I use punctuation to help me figure out when to pause?		
Inflection/Intonation		
Did I make my voice rise at a question mark?		
Did I make my voice fall at a period?		
Did I think about what the author was saying so I would know when to read louder or softer?		
Did I think about what the author was saying so I would know when to stress or emphasize words?		
Phrasing		
Did I notice the phrases?		
Did I read all the words in each phrase together?		
Did I think about what the words in the phrase mean when they are together?		
Expression		
Did I look for clues so I could anticipate the mood of the passage?		
Did I use my tone of voice, facial expressions, and body language to express what the author or characters were thinking or feeling?		
Did I change my reading when something new was about to happen?		
Integration		
Did I read the words right? (accuracy)		
Did I read the words at the right speed? (rate)		
Did I read with expression? (prosody)		
Did my reading sound like talking?		
Did I understand what I read?		

Name _____   Date _____

3

Mrs. Nickels: Jimmy, what's gotten into you? That's no way to talk!

Ramon: It's OK, Mrs. Nickels. We're used to it. It happens everywhere we go.

Mrs. Nickels: It is not OK. Not in my classroom. Jimmy, let's start again.

Jimmy: OK. Hello.

Beth: Where do you live, Emily?

Emily: Our families are migrant workers. We live in the small houses near the grape fields. They're just outside town.

Jimmy: And when all the grapes are picked, you'll leave. Right?

READER'S THEATER

Mrs. Nickels: Good morning, class! We have two new students joining us today. Please say hello to Ramon and Emily. Their families are farmers. They just came to town.

Beth: Hi! It's nice to meet you both!

Jimmy: Oh, no. Not more new kids! They're always coming and going. They never stay.

2

Name _____   Date _____

Adverbs

Directions: List adverbs that tell *how, when, where,* and *how much*.

How	When	Where	How Much

Name _____   Date _____

Cesar Chavez: Good morning, children! I am very happy to be here today. You know, being the child of migrant workers is not easy. My family lost our farm when I was 10 years old. Then we had to work for other people.

Jimmy: You used to own your own farm? Like my family does?

Cesar Chavez: That's right. My family farmed in Arizona for more than 50 years. But times got very hard for us when I was a boy. We lost our land. That's when we came to California.

7

Ramon: I do! A union is a group that workers join to make sure they are being treated fairly.

Jimmy: My dad says unions just make trouble for the farm owners. What's wrong with things the way they are?

Mrs. Nickels: That's a good question, Jimmy. Let's listen to Mr. Chavez. Then maybe we can answer your question.

Jimmy: OK, Mrs. Nickels.

Mrs. Nickels: Class, let's all say hello to Mr. Chavez.

All: Good morning, Mr. Chavez!

6

Name _____ Date _____

Reader's Theater Self-Assessment

Directions: Complete the rubric below. Tell how you plan to improve your reading fluency in the areas where you answered no.

Skill	Behavior	Yes	No
Fluency and Phrasing	I read in longer, meaningful phrases.		
	I paid attention to the author's language patterns.		
	I made the reading sound like dialogue.		
	I stressed certain words to emphasize their importance.		
Intonation	I used my voice to make the reading reflect feeling, anticipation, tension, mood, and the personality of my character.		
	I paid attention to punctuation.		
	I raised or lowered my voice to interpret the punctuation of sentences.		
Pacing	I used an appropriate speed of reading.		
	I read the lines with the same speed and flow that I use when I talk.		
	I read with very few hesitations or unnecessary pauses and repetitions.		
Accuracy	I recognized words quickly and read them correctly.		
	I really thought about the meaning of the story and known words and word parts to help me figure out unknown words.		
	I corrected myself when I made an error.		
	I made the words sound meaningful.		
Character Analysis	I made inferences about my character.		
	I used my voice (tone) to sound like the character.		
	I used my voice to express a particular feeling of the character.		
	I used body language (gestures) to better express the feelings of the character.		
	I used appropriate facial expressions to represent my character.		

Plan of Action: Describe how you will improve your reading fluency during the repeated readings of your character's lines.

_____

_____

Summarize & Synthesize/Analyze Story Elements

Unit 4/Week 1 at a Glance

Day	Mini-Lessons
ONE	• Introduce the Comprehension Strategy: *Analyze Story Elements* • Think Aloud and Use the Metacognitive Strategy: *Summarize and Synthesize* • Find Story Elements in a Picture • Connect Thinking, Speaking, and Writing • Reflect and Discuss
TWO	• Review the Metacognitive Strategy: *Summarize and Synthesize* • Use the Comprehension Strategy: *Analyze Story Elements* • Connect Thinking, Speaking, and Writing • Reflect and Discuss
THREE	• Extend the Comprehension Strategy: *Analyze Story Elements* • Observe and Prompt for Strategy Understanding • Reflect and Discuss
FOUR	• Read and Summarize • Answer Text-Dependent Comprehension Questions: *Analyze Story Elements (Level 3: Prove It!)* • Reflect and Discuss
FIVE	• Metacognitive Self-Assessment • Constructed Written Response • Ongoing Comprehension Strategy Assessment

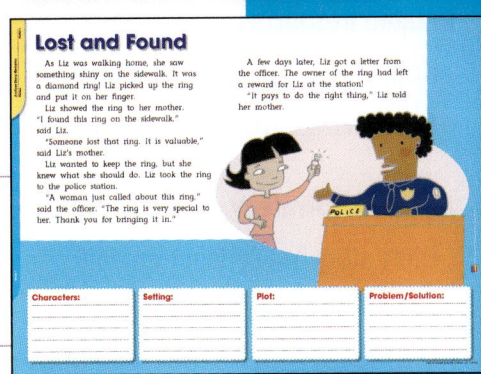

BENCHMARK EDUCATION COMPANY

Day One

Comprehension Anchor Poster 1

Read-Aloud (10 MINUTES)

Select a favorite fiction read-aloud from your classroom or school library with which to model the metacognitive strategy "Summarize and Synthesize." Use the sample read-aloud lessons and suggested titles in the Getting Started Guide.

Mini-Lessons (20 MINUTES)

Introduce the Comprehension Strategy: Analyze Story Elements

Say: *I read a story about a girl on a basketball team. She and her team members practiced hard every day at school. When game day came, her team won the game. The girl and her team members are the story's characters, their school is the setting, and their practicing every day, playing a game, and winning are the events in the plot.*

Ask: *Who are the characters, and what are the setting and plot in a story you have read?*

Turn and talk. Ask students to turn to a partner and tell about the characters, setting, and plot in a story they have read. Ask a few students to share with the whole group.

Explain: *Every story has characters, setting, and plot. These are called story elements. The people or animals in a story are the characters. The time and place of the story is the setting. The events that happen are the plot. The plot usually includes a problem that the story characters must solve. Good readers know how to identify and analyze story elements in fiction texts. We're going to practice analyzing story elements this week.*

Think Aloud and Use the Metacognitive Strategy: Summarize and Synthesize

Display Poster 1.

Draw students' attention to the people on the magic carpet. (Whiteboard users can use the highlighter tool.)

Explain: *When I look at this picture, the first thing I need to do is figure out what it's trying to show me. One way I can do this is to find the most important information and summarize, or put in my own words, what the poster shows. I also put together, or synthesize, what I see in the poster and my own experiences to understand what the poster means. Let me show you how I do it.*

Think aloud: *The title of the poster is "Magic Carpet Ride." The picture shows three people on a magic carpet flying above a house. They like what they are seeing. To summarize, I can say "Three people had great fun going on a magic carpet ride." I know magic carpets exist in fairy tales, but they are make-believe. These people look ordinary, not like fairy tale characters. Some people use the phrase "magic carpet ride" to describe the excitement of imagining something far away. Maybe the poster is suggesting that these people had a fun, exciting time using their imaginations instead of watching television. Summarizing and synthesizing what I know about the poster helps me understand it.*

Write your summary and synthesis of the poster's meaning on chart paper. Ask students to generate a summary and synthesize their own meaning for the picture. Add their summaries and syntheses to the chart.

Post these summaries and syntheses on the wall as a Summarize and Synthesize anchor chart, or invite students to write the summary and synthesis in their reading journals or notebooks to use in the future.

Find Story Elements in a Picture

Ask students to identify the story elements in the picture. Have them talk about the characters, setting, and a possible plot.

Ask students to look at the picture and tell what problem and solution it suggests. Have them pretend to be on a magic carpet and identify a problem that could arise and how they would solve the problem.

Provide the following academic sentence frames to support ELLs and struggling students:

> The characters are _____.
> The setting is _____.
> The plot is _____.
> A problem and a solution are _____.

Connect Thinking, Speaking, and Writing

Write down the story elements students identify and reread them as a group. Write the words *character, plot, setting, problem,* and *solution* by each idea. Give students the opportunity to expand on their shared writing.

Make Content Comprehensible for ELLs

Use the following strategies to help ELLs understand the poster content and acquire academic language.

Beginning

Read the title of the poster. Explain the concept of a magic carpet. For example, **say:** *These people are flying through the sky on a rug that is called a magic carpet. We know this is make-believe, as people cannot ride on a rug in the sky.* Place a large rug on the floor and have three children pretend to be the people on the magic carpet.

Point to and name people and objects in the picture: carpet, birds, boy, girl, woman, television. Have ELLs repeat the words as they point to the people and objects.

Beginning and Intermediate

Draw and label, or ask ELLs to draw, other things that could be seen in the sky below the magic carpet.

Comprehension Quick-Check

Observe whether students are able to articulate the story elements in the poster. If they have difficulty, use the following additional explicit instruction.

Draw a four-box story elements chart on chart paper.

In the Characters box, write *woman, girl,* and *boy.*

Say: *These are the characters.*

In the Setting box, write *during the day on a magic carpet flying in the sky.*

Say: *This is the setting. The time is during the day. The place is on a magic carpet flying in the sky. The time and the place are the setting.*

Say: *Now let's think of a plot and a possible problem and solution to write in the other two boxes.*

Support Special Needs Learners

Support visual learners and students with attention issues by projecting the whiteboard versions of the posters. Allow students to point to story elements on the whiteboard. Invite them to label the story elements.

Access the graphic organizer provided on the whiteboard. Record the story elements with students.

Provide opportunities for active involvement. For example, assign pairs a story element from a poster or let them choose their own. Ask them to tell about the words *characters, setting, plot, problem,* and *solution*.

Access the image bank for enlarged images that students can use to practice summarizing and synthesizing important ideas and identifying story elements in pictures.

Home/School Connections

On Day 1, distribute copies of Home/School Connections (BLM 1). Each day during the week, assign one of the six home/school connections activities for the students to complete. Ask them to bring their completed assignments to class the following day. Make time at the beginning of each day for students to share their ideas.

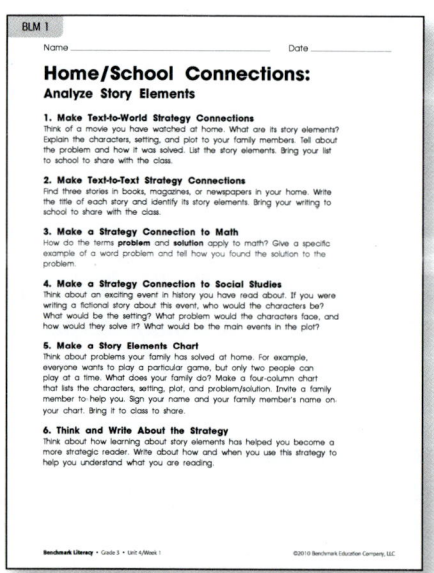

Home/School Connections (BLM 1)

Reflect and Discuss

Ask and discuss the following questions:
- *Why is it important to recognize the characters, setting, and plot of a story? How does this help you as a reader?*
- *How did summarizing and synthesizing help you understand the poster?*
- *What are the story elements that we identified today?*

Connect and transfer. Say: *Remember, you can look for story elements in a text, too. Tomorrow, we will practice looking for story elements in a text.*

Small-Group Reading Instruction (60 MINUTES)

Based on students' instructional reading levels, select titles that provide opportunities for students to practice analyzing story elements. See the Leveled Text Titles chart provided at the back of this Teacher's Resource System.

Use the before-, during-, and after-reading instruction provided in the Teacher's Guide for each text.

Individual Student Conferences (10 MINUTES)

Confer with individual students on their text selections and applications of strategies. Use the Individual Reading Conference Form on page 32 of Informal Assessments for Reading Development to help guide your conferences.

Word Study Workshop (20 MINUTES)

Use the Day 1 instruction provided in Word Study Unit 10.

Read-Aloud (10 MINUTES)

Select a favorite fiction read-aloud from your classroom or school library with which to model the metacognitive strategy "Summarize and Synthesize." Use the sample read-aloud lessons and suggested titles in the Getting Started Guide.

Mini-Lessons (20 MINUTES)

Review the Metacognitive Strategy: Summarize and Synthesize

Display Poster 2 with annotations hidden and/or distribute BLM 2 and read aloud the title.

Read aloud the text with students.

Explain: *Yesterday when I looked at the "Magic Carpet Ride" poster, I summarized, or stated the general idea, about its important parts. I synthesized, or put together, what I saw and what I know to help me see the poster's meaning. Now I will summarize and synthesize the story we just read. I'll show you how I do this.*

Reread paragraphs 1 and 2. **Think aloud:** *Ali went to breakfast. It was her birthday. On my birthday, I expect my family to celebrate with me. Ali expected her family to wish her a happy birthday, but they said nothing about it. Neither did her friends. On a birthday, a person expects some attention. Everyone ignored Ali's birthday. I understand why Ali was sad. This part of the story means that Ali was sad because none of her family or friends remembered her birthday.*

Reread the other paragraphs. **Think aloud:** *When Ali got home, she heard people saying, "Happy Birthday!" Ali saw cake and presents. I know that a gathering with a cake and presents is a party. Ali found out her family and friends wanted to surprise her. A party that the guest of honor doesn't know about is a surprise party. Ali is happy about the surprise. In this part of the story, I learned that Ali was happy when her friends and family had a surprise party for her.*

Ask students to tell briefly in their own words what happens in the story and what it means to them.

Comprehension Anchor Poster 2 (BLM 2)

Lesson Objectives

Students will:

- Identify the story elements of characters, setting, plot, problem, and solution in a story.
- Identify and use the academic language for story elements.
- Summarize and synthesize to gain fuller meaning from a story.
- Use academic sentence frames to discuss strategies.

Related Resources

- Home/School Connections (BLM 1)
- Comprehension Anchor Poster 2 (BLM 2)
- BenchmarkUniverse.com

Characters:

- Ali
- her mom
- her dad
- her brother
- her friends

Setting:

Ali's house and school

Plot:

It was Ali's birthday, but no one said anything about it. Her family made a surprise party for her.

Problem/Solution:

Problem:

Ali thought no one remembered her birthday.

Solution:

She was happy when her family and friends surprised her with a party.

Comprehension Anchor Poster 2
Sample Annotations

Make Content Comprehensible for ELLs

Use the following strategies to help ELLs understand the poster content and acquire academic language.

Beginning

Read aloud the poster title and story. Ask students questions about the characters and plot of the story.

Beginning and Intermediate

Ask students to name objects they have with them that they received as presents and show how they eat a piece of birthday cake.

If you have students whose first language is Spanish, share these English/Spanish cognates: **family/la familia, secret/el secreto, present/el presente, surprise/la sorpresa.**

Build academic oral language. Reread paragraphs 3 and 7. Ask students to use what they read and what they know to summarize and synthesize Ali's problem and the solution. Invite students to tell how summarizing and synthesizing helped them identify and analyze story elements. Reinforce the idea that good readers summarize and synthesize to gain a deeper understanding of a story. Support ELLs and struggling readers with the following sentence frames:

Ali's problem is _____.
The solution to the problem is _____.
Summarizing and synthesizing helped me _____.

Use the Comprehension Strategy: Analyze Story Elements

Reread the poster text with students, annotations still hidden.

Say: *Now think about the characters in this story. Whom is the story about and what other people are in the story?*

If necessary, explain that the characters are Ali, her mom, her dad, her brother, and her friends.

Say: *Now think about the setting in this story. When and where does the story take place?*

If necessary, explain that the setting is Ali's home and school.

Write the characters and setting students identify on the board. Then reveal the Characters and Setting annotations. **Ask:** *Did we correctly identify the characters and setting? Let's compare lists.*

Build academic oral language. Say: *The plot of a story is the series of events that happen. The plot in this story centers around a problem that is making Ali sad. What is the problem?* (Ali is unhappy because she thinks no one has remembered her birthday.) *What is the solution to Ali's problem?* (Ali's family and friends have a surprise party for her that makes her happy.)

Connect Thinking, Speaking, and Writing

Prompt students to summarize what happens in the story. Encourage students to use the academic language for story elements.

Record students' responses on chart paper. Then reveal the Plot and Problem/Solution annotations.

Say: *Let's compare our lists to the lists on the poster.* Allow time for discussion.

Reflect and Discuss

Ask and discuss the following questions:
- *How does summarizing and synthesizing help you understand the story?*
- *Why do you need to identify the story elements when you are reading?*
- *How does identifying the problem and solution in a story help you?*

Connect and transfer. Ask: *How will you use what we have practiced today when you read on your own?*

Small-Group Reading Instruction (60 MINUTES)

Based on students' instructional reading levels, select titles that provide opportunities for students to practice analyzing story elements. See the Leveled Text Titles chart provided at the back of this Teacher's Resource System.

Use the before-, during-, and after-reading instruction provided in the Teacher's Guide for each text.

Individual Student Conferences (10 MINUTES)

Confer with individual students on their text selections and applications of strategies. Use the Individual Reading Conference Form on page 32 of Informal Assessments for Reading Development to help guide your conferences.

Word Study Workshop (20 MINUTES)

Use the Day 2 instruction provided in Word Study Unit 10.

Comprehension Quick-Check

Take note of which students can or cannot contribute to the discussion of the Poster 2 story elements. Use the following activity to provide additional explicit instruction for these students.

Use an additional example to help students understand story elements. Page through and review a familiar story with students. Ask students to identify the characters, setting, problem, solution, and plot events in order. Record these story elements on a graphic organizer. Write a paragraph about the story that describes the elements on the graphic organizer. Ask students to point to each story element in the paragraph as you name it.

Oral Language Extension

During independent workstation time, pair students to construct oral story elements for a story they have read. Partner A identifies the characters and setting. Partner B tells the plot and identifies the problem and solution. If necessary, Partner A assists. Then partners pick a second story and reverse roles. Tell students to be ready to report on their story elements during individual conference time.

Home/School Connections

At the beginning of the day, make time for students to share their ideas based on the activity they completed the previous night.

At the end of the day, ask students to complete another home/school connections activity from BLM 1 and bring their assignment to class the following day.

Day Three

Comprehension Anchor Poster 3 (BLM 3)

Lesson Objectives

Students will:

- Identify and analyze story elements in a story.
- Identify and use the academic language for story elements.
- Summarize and synthesize to show understanding of a story.
- Use academic sentence frames to discuss strategies.

Related Resources

- Home/School Connections (BLM 1)
- Comprehension Anchor Poster 3 (BLM 3)
- BenchmarkUniverse.com

 Read-Aloud (10 MINUTES)

Select a favorite nonfiction read-aloud from your classroom or school library with which to model the metacognitive strategy "Summarize and Synthesize." Use the sample read-aloud lessons and suggested titles in the Getting Started Guide.

 Mini-Lessons (20 MINUTES)

Extend the Comprehension Strategy: Analyze Story Elements

Display Poster 3 and/or distribute BLM 3 and read aloud the title.

Say: *Today you're going to practice reading and analyzing story elements in a text. Remember to use what you've learned. You can summarize and synthesize as you read to help you understand.*

Based on students' needs and abilities, ask them to read the passage independently or with a partner. Tell them to locate and write each story element in the appropriate box. Tell students to underline, circle, or flag key information as they read.

Invite individual students or pairs to share the story elements they listed. Record students' findings on the poster or on chart paper. See the sample annotations.

Observe and Prompt for Strategy Understanding

While using the poster, note students who demonstrate understanding of the concepts and those who seem to struggle. Use appropriate responsive prompting to help students who need modeling or additional guidance, or to validate students who demonstrate mastery.

Goal Oriented
- *I am going to read slowly to identify characters, setting, and plot.*
- *I am going to summarize as I read to help me analyze story elements.*
- *The plot is made up of these events: _____.*

Directive and Corrective Feedback
- *How can you tell how the characters feel?*
- *What is the setting? Why is it important?*
- *How can you tell what the problem is?*

Self-Monitoring and Reflection
• *What could you do to help yourself understand the plot and characters?*
• *What details tell where and when the story takes place?*
• *How did you summarize the story?*

Validating and Confirming
• *You really understand the story elements in this passage.*
• *You did a great job of identifying the problem and the solution in the plot.*
• *I like the way you summarized the plot events and synthesized them with your own experiences.*

Reflect and Discuss

Ask and discuss the following questions:
• *What have you read that has characters, plot, and setting?*
• *Do you think you would find story elements in a nonfiction article?*
• *Does a play have story elements? How about a fairy tale?*

Connect and transfer. Say: *Remember that fiction texts have these story elements: characters, setting, plot, problem, and solution. Look for story elements today when you read in small groups. Summarize and synthesize to help you better understand the story elements.*

Small-Group Reading Instruction (60 MINUTES)

Based on students' instructional reading levels, select titles that provide opportunities for students to practice analyzing story elements. See the Leveled Text Titles chart provided at the back of this Teacher's Resource System.

Use the before-, during-, and after-reading instruction provided in the Teacher's Guide for each text.

Individual Student Conferences (10 MINUTES)

Confer with individual students on their text selections and applications of strategies. Use the Individual Reading Conference Form on page 32 of Informal Assessments for Reading Development to help guide your conferences.

Word Study Workshop (20 MINUTES)

Use the Day 3 instruction provided in Word Study Unit 10.

Make Content Comprehensible for ELLs

Use the following strategies to help ELLs understand the poster content and acquire academic language.

Beginning
Point to the poster picture and provide the language for what you see. For example: girl, ring, police officer, badge, sign. Invite ELLs to point to and name people and objects with you.

Beginning and Intermediate
If you have students whose first language is Spanish, share these English/Spanish cognates: **diamond/el diamante, police/ la policía, station/la estación, special/ especial**.

Comprehension Quick-Check

The responsive prompts on pages 8–9 are designed to help you meet the needs of individual students. Based on your observations, identify students who may need additional explicit reinforcement of the strategy during small-group instruction or intervention time.

Day Four

Comprehension Anchor Poster 4 (BLM 4)

Lesson Objectives

Students will:

• Learn strategies for analyzing questions and finding answers, clues, and evidence.

• Identify and analyze story elements in a text.

• Answer text-dependent analyze story elements questions.

• Use academic vocabulary to discuss strategies.

Related Resources

• Home/School Connections (BLM 1)

• Comprehension Anchor Poster 4 (BLM 4)

• Comprehension Questions (BLM 5)

• BenchmarkUniverse.com

 Read-Aloud (10 MINUTES)

Select a favorite nonfiction read-aloud from your classroom or school library with which to model the metacognitive strategy "Summarize and Synthesize." Use the sample read-aloud lessons and suggested titles in the Getting Started Guide.

 Mini-Lessons (20 MINUTES)

Read and Summarize

Display Poster 4 and/or distribute BLM 4.

Based on students' needs and abilities, ask them to read the passage independently or with a partner. Remind students to summarize and synthesize to help them understand what they read.

Build academic oral language. When students have finished, ask individuals or pairs to tell about the story elements. Encourage ELLs or struggling readers to use the academic sentence frames:

> *The characters are _____. The setting (plot, problem, solution) is _____.*

Answer Text-Dependent Comprehension Questions: Analyze Story Elements (Level 3: Prove It!)

Say: *Sometimes you need to answer questions about a passage you've read. Some questions require you to analyze story elements. Today we're going to read and answer questions about story elements.*

Distribute BLM 5 and read Question 1 together. ("Who is the main character in the story?")

Ask: *What is the question asking us to do?* If students can't tell you, **ask:** *Is the question asking us to draw conclusions? Is it asking us to compare? What strategy will we need?* (analyze story elements) *How do you know?* (It is asking about the story's main character, and a character is a story element.)

Say: *To find the main character of the story, I will have to identify the people or animals that the story is about and then think about which person or animal is the most important in the story.*

Say: *Now we're ready to reread the passage to find the information we need. We know we need to find who the main characters are. I notice that the story title mentions Charlie. When I skim the passage, I see that Charlie is the one who has a problem to solve. So, I think Charlie is the main character. I used what I know about story elements and searched for clues in the text to figure out the answer. The answer makes sense. So, I'll choose B.*

Ask students to work independently or with a partner to answer additional text-dependent questions on BLM 5.

Review students' answers and use the poster as needed to model analyzing questions, rereading to find answers in the text, or figuring out answers on one's own.

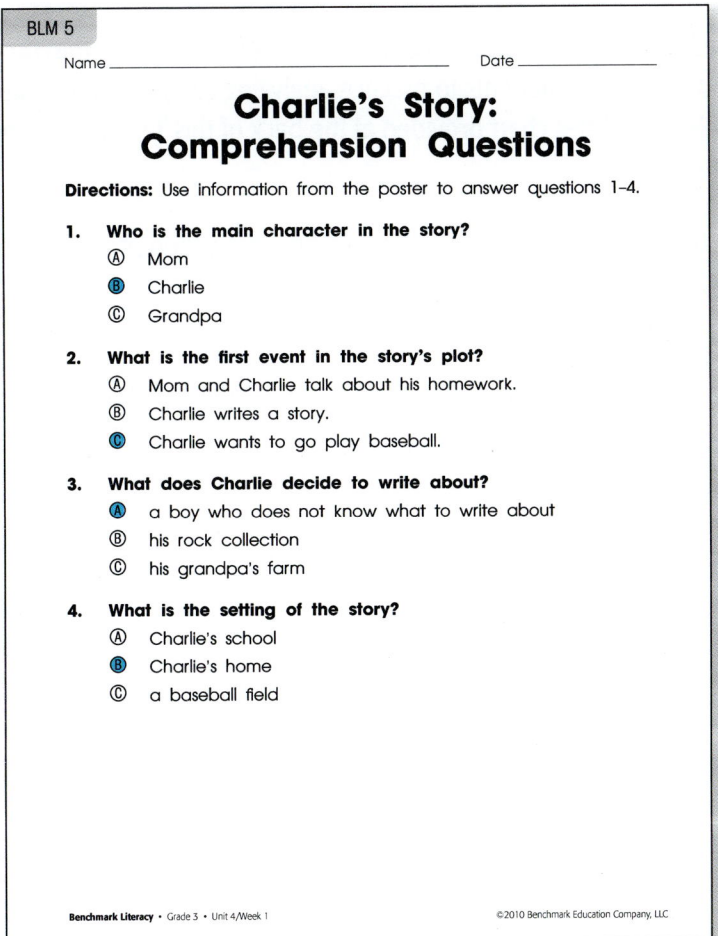

Comprehension Questions (BLM 5)

Characters:
• Charlie
• Mom

Setting:
Charlie's house

Plot:
Charlie wants to play baseball, but Mom tells him he must do his homework first. Charlie is supposed to write a story, but can't think of anything to write about. He writes a story about his problem, and Mom lets him go play baseball.

Problem/Solution:

Problem:
Charlie does not know what to write his story about.

Solution:
Charlie writes about a boy who does not know what to write about.

Comprehension Anchor Poster 4 Sample Annotations

Make Content Comprehensible for ELLs

Use the following strategies to help ELLs understand the poster content and acquire academic language.

Beginning
Support the concept of homework by showing various homework assignments. Explain that schoolwork done at home is called homework.

Beginning and Intermediate
Point to the poster picture and **ask:** *What are Charlie and his mom doing? Why do they clap their hands together like that?*

If you have students whose first language is Spanish, share these academic English/Spanish cognates: **baseball/el béisbol, collection/la colección, idea/la idea.**

Comprehension Quick-Check

Note whether students are able to analyze each Level 3 text-dependent comprehension question and return to the text to find the information they need to answer the question correctly. If students have difficulty, use small-group reading time for additional practice answering these kinds of questions, which appear on standardized reading assessments. The Comprehension Question Card for each leveled text provides practice questions at four levels of comprehension. The Comprehension Through Deductive Reasoning Flip Chart helps you model the strategies students need to master.

Home/School Connections

At the end of the day, ask students to complete another home/school connections activity from BLM 1 and bring their assignment to class the following day.

Reflect and Discuss the Comprehension Strategy

Ask and discuss the following:
- *What strategy did we use to answer questions about the text?*
- *Notice how we looked for story elements to understand and answer questions.*

Connect and transfer. Say: *Practice analyzing story elements. This strategy can help you answer questions you may have about stories you read. It can also help you when you take tests.*

 ## Small-Group Reading Instruction (60 MINUTES)

Based on students' instructional reading levels, select titles that provide opportunities for students to practice analyzing story elements. See the Leveled Text Titles chart provided at the back of this Teacher's Resource System.

Use the before-, during-, and after-reading instruction provided in the Teacher's Guide for each text.

Use the Comprehension Question Card for each title and the Comprehension Through Deductive Reasoning Flip Chart to practice answering Level 3 text-dependent comprehension questions.

 ## Individual Student Conferences (10 MINUTES)

Confer with individual students on their text selections and applications of strategies. Use the Individual Reading Conference Form on page 32 of Informal Assessments for Reading Development to help guide your conferences.

 ## Word Study Workshop (20 MINUTES)

Use the Day 4 instruction provided in Word Study Unit 10.

Read-Aloud (10 MINUTES)

Revisit the week's read-alouds to make text-to-text connections and provide opportunities for reader response. Use the suggested activities in the Getting Started Guide, or implement ideas of your own.

Assessment (20 MINUTES)

Metacognitive Self-Assessment

Ask students to reflect on their use of metacognitive and comprehension strategies this week. What did they learn? How will they use the strategies in the future? What do they still need to practice, and how can they do this?

Invite students to share their reflections in one of the following ways: conduct a whole-class discussion; ask students to turn and talk to a partner and then share their ideas with the class; or ask students to record their thoughts in their journals or notebooks.

Constructed Written Response

Distribute copies of Constructed Written Response (BLM 6) and ask students to think of a story they would like to write and write the story elements for it on the chart.

Ask students to write a summary of this story, using the characters, setting, plot, and problem/solution ideas they wrote on the chart. Remind students that they will not include details or dialogue in their summaries.

Read aloud the checklist at the bottom of BLM 6 to help students evaluate their work.

Challenge activity. Students who are able to may also write one or more text-dependent comprehension questions for a partner to answer based on their story summary. These questions should focus on story elements.

Support activity. If students cannot think of a problem/solution, encourage them to use the following sentence frames to generate ideas:
My problem is _____. My solution is _____.

Reinforce their efforts by suggesting that they think of the problem as a question and the solution as the answer. For example, Question: How can I make a friend? Answer: I can smile and be friendly to others.

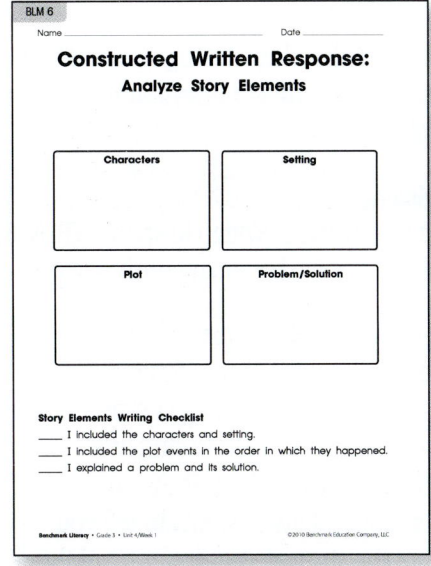

Constructed Written Response (BLM 6)

Lesson Objectives

Students will:

- Reflect orally on their strategy use.
- Create a story elements chart and write a story based on it.
- Answer multiple-choice and short-answer questions.

Related Resources

- Home/School Connections (BLM 1)
- Constructed Written Response (BLM 6)
- Comprehension Strategy Assessments, Grade 3
- BenchmarkUniverse.com

Make Assessments Accessible for ELLs

Use the following strategies to help ELLs demonstrate their understanding of the strategies.

Beginning
Use Constructed Written Response (BLM 6) with ELLs at the beginning proficiency level.

Beginning and Intermediate
Use the Comprehension Strategy Assessment as a listening comprehension assessment and scaffold students' understanding of the text. As an alternative, allow students to tell you about the story elements in one of the Comprehension Anchor Posters you have used during the week.

Intermediate and Advanced
Support ELLs with academic sentence frames during the metacognitive self-assessment. Possible sentence frames to use are:

When I summarize, I _____.

Synthesizing story events with what I know helps me _____.

All Levels
Pair ELLs with fluent English speakers during partner discussions and activities.

Home/School Connections

At the beginning of the day, make time for students to share their ideas based on the activity they completed the previous night.

Ongoing Comprehension Strategy Assessment

Distribute one of the Analyze Story Elements Comprehension Strategy Assessments from the Grade 3 Comprehension Strategy Assessment book ("Buried Alive," pages 42–43, or "A Long Week," pages 44–45). Ask students to read the passage and use the information to answer the questions.

Use the results of this assessment to determine students who need additional work with the strategy.

Record students' assessment scores on the Strategy Assessment Record (page 133) so that you can monitor their progress following additional instruction or intervention.

Provide additional modeling and guided practice during small-group reading instruction using the recommended titles in this Teacher's Guide.

Small-Group Reading Instruction (60 MINUTES)

Based on students' instructional reading levels, select titles that provide opportunities for students to practice analyzing story elements. See the Leveled Text Titles chart provided at the back of this Teacher's Resource System.

Use the before-, during-, and after-reading instruction provided in the Teacher's Guide for each text.

Individual Student Conferences (10 MINUTES)

Confer with individual students on their text selections and applications of strategies. Use the Individual Reading Conference Form on page 32 of Informal Assessments for Reading Development to help guide your conferences.

Word Study Workshop (20 MINUTES)

Use the Day 5 instruction provided in Word Study Unit 10.

Name _____ Date _____

Home/School Connections:
Analyze Story Elements

1. Make Text-to-World Strategy Connections
Think of a movie you have watched at home. What are its story elements? Explain the characters, setting, and plot to your family members. Tell about the problem and how it was solved. List the story elements. Bring your list to school to share with the class.

2. Make Text-to-Text Strategy Connections
Find three stories in books, magazines, or newspapers in your home. Write the title of each story and identify its story elements. Bring your writing to school to share with the class.

3. Make a Strategy Connection to Math
How do the terms **problem** and **solution** apply to math? Give a specific example of a word problem and tell how you found the solution to the problem.

4. Make a Strategy Connection to Social Studies
Think about an exciting event in history you have read about. If you were writing a fictional story about this event, who would the characters be? What would be the setting? What problem would the characters face, and how would they solve it? What would be the main events in the plot?

5. Make a Story Elements Chart
Think about problems your family has solved at home. For example, everyone wants to play a particular game, but only two people can play at a time. What does your family do? Make a four-column chart that lists the characters, setting, plot, and problem/solution. Invite a family member to help you. Sign your name and your family member's name on your chart. Bring it to class to share.

6. Think and Write About the Strategy
Think about how learning about story elements has helped you become a more strategic reader. Write about how and when you use this strategy to help you understand what you are reading.

Name _____ Date _____

Ali's Surprise

Today is Ali's birthday. When Ali went to breakfast, her mom didn't say anything about her birthday. Her dad didn't say anything. Her brother didn't say anything. Ali walked to school alone. She felt sad.

At school, Ali's friends didn't say anything about her birthday, either. "This is *not* a good day," Ali thought as she walked home alone.

Ali was feeling sad as she opened the door to her house.

Then suddenly she heard, "Happy birthday!" Everyone was there: her mom, dad, brother, and friends. There were even a big cake and piles of presents.

"I thought you forgot my birthday," said Ali.

"We wanted to keep the party a secret," said her mom.

"It's a good day after all," Ali replied with a smile.

Problem/Solution:

Plot:

Setting:

Characters:

Name _____   Date _____

Lost and Found

As Liz was walking home, she saw something shiny on the sidewalk. It was a diamond ring! Liz picked up the ring and put it on her finger.

Liz showed the ring to her mother.

"I found this ring on the sidewalk," said Liz.

"Someone lost that ring. It is valuable," said Liz's mother.

Liz wanted to keep the ring, but she knew what she should do. Liz took the ring to the police station.

"A woman just called about this ring," said the officer. "The ring is very special to her. Thank you for bringing it in."

A few days later, Liz got a letter from the officer. The owner of the ring had left a reward for Liz at the station!

"It pays to do the right thing," Liz told her mother.

POLICE

Problem/Solution:

Plot:

Setting:

Characters:

Analyze Story Elements
Fiction
Poster 1

Grade 3

Charlie's Story

"Bye, Mom! I'm going to play baseball with the guys!" called Charlie.

"Whoa!" said Mom. "Don't you have to write a story for school tomorrow?"

"Yes," Charlie said slowly. "But I can't think of anything to write about. Maybe I'll get an idea while I'm playing baseball."

"Sorry, but homework comes first," Mom said firmly. "You could write about our trip to Grandpa's farm."

"I already tried that," said Charlie.

"You could write about your rock collection," Mom suggested.

"I tried that, too," said Charlie. "I know! I'll write a story about a boy who couldn't think of anything to write about!"

Charlie wrote his story. Then he read it to Mom. "Great work!" she said. "Now you can go play baseball!!"

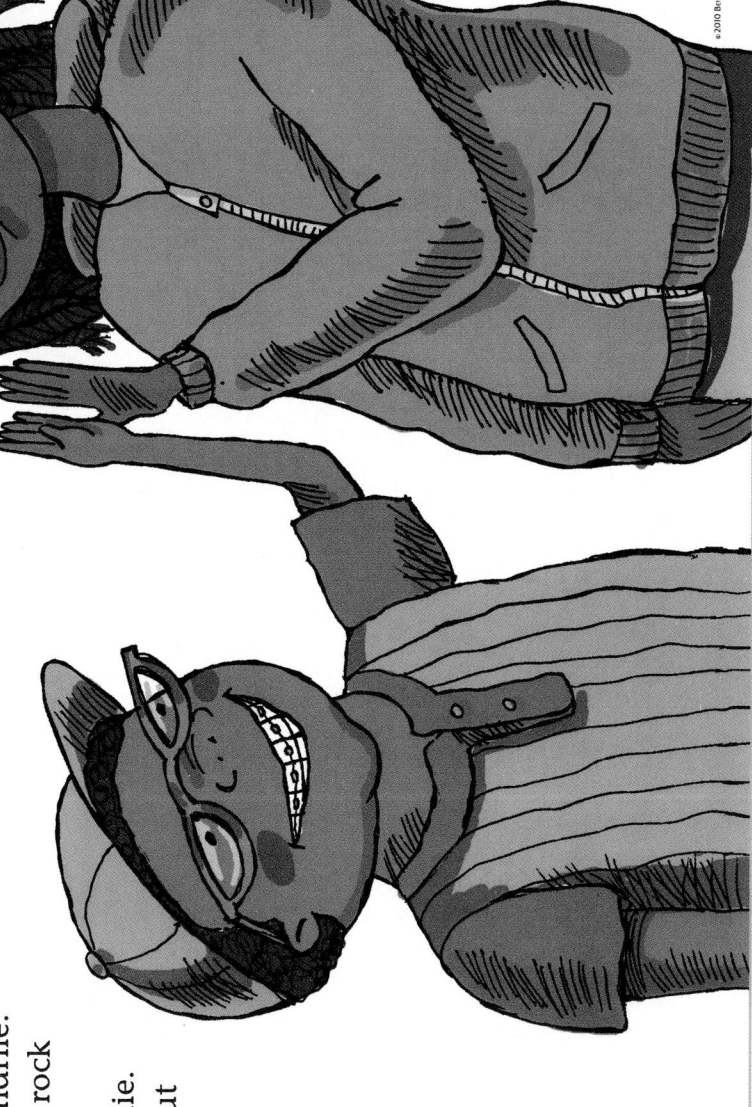

Name _____   Date _____

Charlie's Story: Comprehension Questions

Directions: Use information from the poster to answer questions 1–4.

1. **Who is the main character in the story?**

   Ⓐ Mom

   Ⓑ Charlie

   Ⓒ Grandpa

2. **What is the first event in the story's plot?**

   Ⓐ Mom and Charlie talk about his homework.

   Ⓑ Charlie writes a story.

   Ⓒ Charlie wants to go play baseball.

3. **What does Charlie decide to write about?**

   Ⓐ a boy who does not know what to write about

   Ⓑ his rock collection

   Ⓒ his grandpa's farm

4. **What is the setting of the story?**

   Ⓐ Charlie's school

   Ⓑ Charlie's home

   Ⓒ a baseball field

Name _____   Date _____

Constructed Written Response:
Analyze Story Elements

Characters	Setting

Plot	Problem/Solution

Story Elements Writing Checklist

_____ I included the characters and setting.

_____ I included the plot events in the order in which they happened.

_____ I explained a problem and its solution.

Summarize and Synthesize/Analyze Story Elements

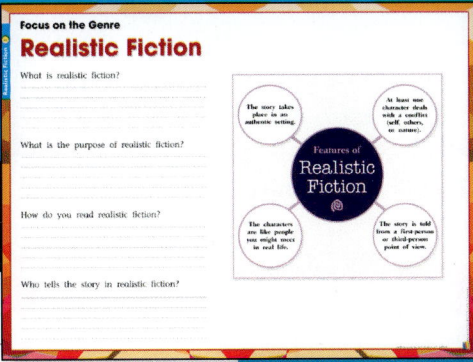

Unit 4/Week 2 at a Glance

Day	Mini-Lessons
ONE	• Build Genre Background • Introduce the Genre: *Realistic Fiction* • Focus on Genre Features: *Realistic Fiction*
TWO	• Model Metacognitive Strategies: *Summarize and Synthesize* • Introduce Analyze Story Elements • Focus on Genre Features: *Realistic Fiction*
THREE	• Analyze Story Elements to Summarize and Synthesize
FOUR	• Build Comprehension: *Draw Conclusions* • Build Tier Two Vocabulary: *Synonyms*
FIVE	• Synthesize and Assess Genre Understanding • Make Connections Across Texts

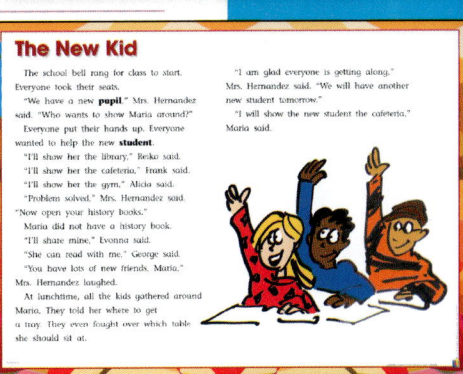

Day One

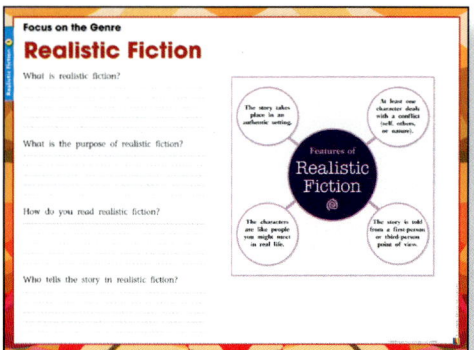

Realistic Fiction Poster 1

Read-Aloud (10 MINUTES)

Select a favorite fiction read-aloud from your classroom or school library with which to model the metacognitive strategy "Summarize and Synthesize." Use the sample read-aloud lessons and suggested titles in the Getting Started Guide.

Mini-Lessons (20 MINUTES)

Build Genre Background

Write the word **genre** on chart paper. **Ask:** *Who remembers and can tell me what the word genre means?* **Allow responses.**

Review: *The word genre means "a kind of something." Items grouped together in the same genre have elements in common. Suppose you read a book about a famous athlete. You want to read more about other athletes. What genre would you look in? Why?* **Allow responses.**

Say: *Knowing the features of a literature genre helps us predict what the text will include and what to look for as we read. We know what the important elements will be. We can look for important information. When we write in a certain genre, we know what to include.*

Ask: *What are some literary genres you have studied and read? Let's make a list of genres.* **(Allow responses.)** *Which of these are fiction genres? Which ones are nonfiction? What's the most important difference between fiction and nonfiction?*

Introduce the Genre: Realistic Fiction

Display Genre Workshop Poster 1 and distribute BLM 1.

Say: *This week we are going to focus on the realistic fiction genre. You will read realistic fiction in our small reading groups, and you can select other titles from this genre to read independently, too. Let's spend some time thinking about this genre and create our own Realistic Fiction anchor chart to record what we already know about realistic fiction. Later in the week, we can come back to our chart and reflect on how our understanding of the genre has changed and expanded.*

Display Poster 1 on an easel or use the interactive whiteboard version. You may also make a transparency from BLM 1. Show students several realistic fiction stories from your classroom or school library and ask students to share any realistic fiction stories they have read previously.

Read each question on Poster 1 and encourage volunteers to share ideas they have related to the question. Based on students' prior knowledge, provide additional genre background information as needed to fill in the answers to each question. This poster can serve as an anchor chart that you and students can refer to throughout the week as you read and analyze realistic fiction stories.

Support the academic language development of ELLs and struggling readers by providing the following sentence frames to use as they discuss the genre:
Realistic fiction is _____ .
The purpose of realistic fiction is to _____ .
When you read realistic fiction, pay attention to _____ .
People who write realistic fiction are _____ .

Make Content Comprehensible for ELLs

Beginning and Intermediate
Show various examples of realistic fiction from your classroom or school library. Flip through the stories with students. Use simple language to explain that realistic fiction stories are made up but include characters and events that could really happen. For example, **say:** *Realistic fiction tells a made-up story. But the characters are like real people and the setting is a real place. Look at this realistic fiction story. This realistic fiction story is about _____ .*

All Levels
If you have students whose first language is Spanish, share the English/Spanish cognate **real/real**.

Model the academic sentence frames provided in this guide to help ELLs contribute their ideas to the discussion of realistic fiction.

Support Special Needs Learners

Throughout the week, use these strategies to help students who have learning disabilities access the content and focus on genre studies and comprehension strategies.

Support students by projecting the posters on a whiteboard. Allow students to come to the whiteboard and circle, underline, or highlight features of the genre. Invite them to label what they see on the posters.

Provide opportunities for active involvement. For example, to understand how realistic fiction includes characters and places that could be real, have students compare what they see and know from real life to what they see and read in the stories.

Provide repeated opportunities for students to analyze the features of realistic fiction. Find features of realistic fiction in text examples from read-alouds, small-group, and independent reading. Chart the features on graphic organizers and post them in your classroom as examples.

Find high-interest realistic fiction stories that students can relate to. Use the recommended read-aloud titles provided in the Teacher's Guide, as well as other examples from your school library.

Focus on Genre Features: Realistic Fiction

Point to the "Features of Realistic Fiction" web on the right side of the poster.

Say: *As we've discussed, every genre has certain consistent features. Based on our discussions so far, what do you think are the consistent features of all, or most, realistic fiction stories? Let's work together to identify them.*

Allow students enough time to generate their own ideas, and record the features they identify on the web. Reread the features together. As necessary, prompt students with the following questions and statements:
- *What does realistic fiction tell about?*
- *Who are the characters in realistic fiction?*
- *What is the setting for a realistic fiction story?*

Connect and transfer. Say: *This week we will read some realistic fiction stories. We will look for these features in the stories we read.*

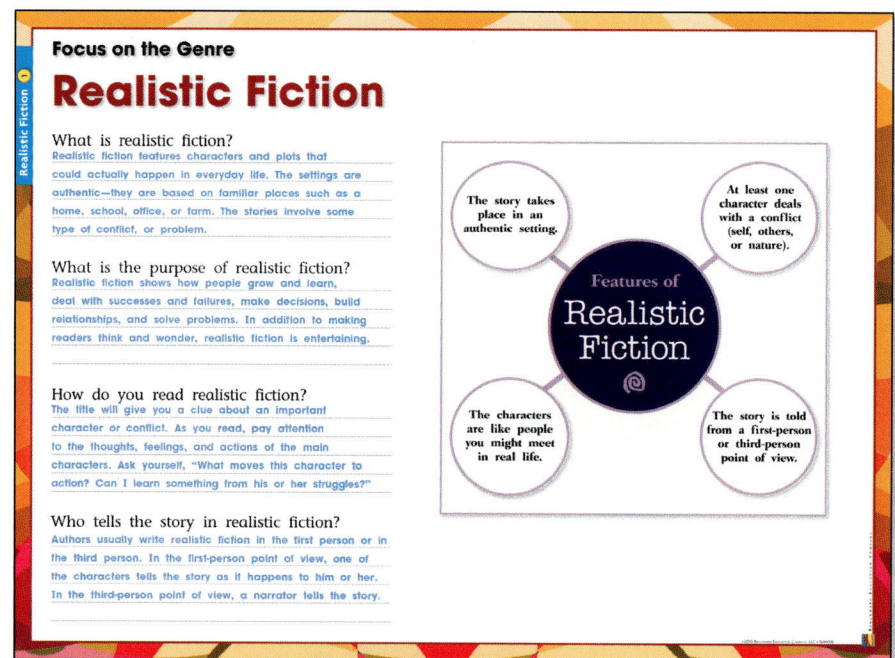

Realistic Fiction Poster 1, sample annotations

Small-Group Reading Instruction (60 MINUTES)

Based on students' instructional reading levels, select titles that provide opportunities for students to focus on realistic fiction stories or to practice analyzing story elements. See the Leveled Text Titles chart provided at the back of this Teacher's Resource System.

Use the instruction provided in the Teacher's Guide for each title to introduce the text.

Individual Student Conferences (10 MINUTES)

Confer with individual students to discuss their understanding of the genre. Use the Individual Reading Conference Form on page 32 of Informal Assessments for Reading Development to help guide your conferences.

Word Study Workshop (20 MINUTES)

Use the Day 1 instruction provided in Grade 3 Word Study Unit 11.

Comprehension Quick-Check

Note which students do or don't actively participate in the discussion of genre. Ask some questions at the end of the lesson to confirm students' understanding. For example:

- *Can you tell me in your own words what a genre is?*
- *What do you already know about the realistic fiction genre?*

Home/School Connection

Ask students to tell a family member about a favorite realistic fiction story. Have students complete these sentence frames on notebook paper and have the family member sign the paper:

I told about the story _____.

I know it is realistic fiction because it has

_____.

Day Two

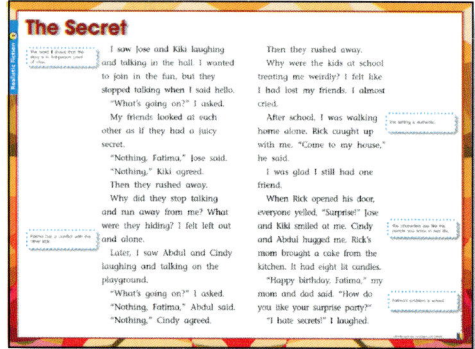

Realistic Fiction Poster 2

Lesson Objectives

Students will:

- Summarize and synthesize a realistic fiction story.
- Analyze story elements using a graphic organizer.
- Use academic sentence frames to discuss strategies and features of realistic fiction.

Related Resources

- Realistic Fiction Poster 2 (BLM 2)
- BenchmarkUniverse.com

Read-Aloud (10 MINUTES)

Select a favorite fiction read-aloud from your classroom or school library with which to model the metacognitive strategy "Summarize and Synthesize." Use the sample read-aloud lessons and suggested titles in the Getting Started Guide.

Mini-Lessons (20 MINUTES)

Model Metacognitive Strategies: Summarize and Synthesize

Display Genre Workshop Poster 2 with the genre annotations concealed. Also distribute copies of Realistic Fiction Poster 2 (BLM 2).

Read aloud the poster passage with students.

Explain: *When you summarize a story, you retell the main parts of a story in your own words. When you synthesize, you make connections between the story and what you already know to understand what you read. Good readers summarize and synthesize to get a full understanding of the story.*

Think aloud: *I just read the story "The Secret." I can summarize the story by telling what it's mostly about. The story is about a girl named Fatima who thinks her friends don't like her anymore. Her friends stop talking when she comes near. They look like they have a secret. Fatima finds out that the secret is a surprise birthday party for her. I can synthesize the story and my own experiences to figure out what Fatima probably feels in each part of the story and better understand her character.*

Ask students to share their own experiences with friends, feeling left out, having secrets, and surprises. Write their observations on chart paper and reread them together. Discuss how synthesizing and applying their own knowledge helps them understand the story. Encourage ELLs to use this sentence frame: *I know how Fatima feels because _____.*

Introduce Analyze Story Elements

Explain: *A realistic fiction story includes characters who are like real people, a setting that could be a real place, and a conflict, or problem, that involves the main character. The problem is solved during the events of the story, or the plot. These three things—character, setting, and plot—are called story elements. Summarizing and analyzing the story elements helps us better understand the story.*

Reread "The Secret." Ask students to identify the story elements. Provide the following academic sentence frames to support ELLs and struggling students:

The characters are _____.
The setting is _____.
The plot is _____.
The problem is _____.
The solution is _____.

Record students' responses on a graphic organizer like the one shown below.

Story Title: The Secret	
Characters	Fatima, an 8-year-old girl; Jose, Kiki, Abdul, Cindy, Rick, Rick's mom; Fatima's mom and dad
Setting	Fatima's school; Rick's house
Plot Summary	Fatima's friends stop talking and laughing whenever she comes near. They act like they have a secret. Fatima thinks she is losing her friends. She is sad. Her friend Rick asks her to come to his house. At his house, Fatima finds all her friends and her parents waiting. It is a surprise birthday party for her.
Problem/ Solution	Fatima thinks her friends don't like her. She learns she is wrong when she walks into her own surprise party.

Sample Analyze Story Elements Annotations
(Note: Your class graphic organizer may differ.)

Make Content Comprehensible for ELLs

Beginning
Use body language and facial expressions to demonstrate the meaning of the word **surprise**.

Then point to and name the characters shown on the poster. Help students summarize the story by asking simple questions. For example, **ask:** *Who is this character? Is Fatima happy or sad? Why is she sad? What happens at the end of the story?*

Intermediate and Advanced

Have students share their own experiences with birthday parties or surprise parties.

All Levels
Explain that a "juicy" secret is a big or exciting secret.

If you have students whose first language is Spanish, share these English/Spanish cognates: **secret/el secreto; surprise/la sorpresa**.

Comprehension Quick-Check

Note which students are or are not able to analyze story elements. Use the following strategies to provide additional explicit instruction.

Use an Analyze Story Elements graphic organizer like the one shown on page 7.

Say: *Let's look for each story element in "The Secret." We'll start with the characters, the people the story is about. Who is the story about? Let's find their names.*

Continue with each story element, encouraging students to point to story details as you add them to the graphic organizer.

Ask: *What is the setting of the story— where does it happen? What is the plot of the story? What happens, in order? What is the problem and solution?*

Oral Language Extension

Display Poster 1 (your class Realistic Fiction anchor chart) during independent workstation time. Have pairs of students work together to plan a realistic fiction story using the features of realistic fiction listed on the poster and the story elements they have discussed. Encourage them to make a chart showing their plan.

Home/School Connection

Have students take home BLM 2, reread the text, and highlight and label the features of realistic fiction present in the passage.

Focus on Genre Features: Realistic Fiction

Ask students to name some of the features of realistic fiction that you discussed yesterday.

Say: *Now let's reexamine "The Secret" and look for features of realistic fiction. What do you notice?*

Work with students to identify the following genre features embedded in this passage:
- The story is told in first person.
- Fatima has a conflict with the other kids.
- The setting is authentic, or realistic.
- The characters are familiar, or like people we know.

Reveal the poster annotations so that students can confirm or revise their ideas. Reread them as a group.

Connect and transfer. Say: *As you read realistic fiction stories, look for these features and notice the story elements. Then check your understanding of the story by summarizing and synthesizing.*

 # Small-Group Reading Instruction (60 MINUTES)

Continue small-group reading instruction from the previous day. Use the instruction provided in the Teacher's Guide for each text.

 # Individual Student Conferences (10 MINUTES)

Confer with individual students to discuss their understanding of genre and comprehension strategies. Use the Individual Reading Conference Form on page 32 of Informal Assessments for Reading Development to help guide your conferences.

Word Study Workshop (20 MINUTES)

Use the Day 2 instruction provided in Grade 3 Word Study Unit 11.

Read-Aloud (10 MINUTES)

Select a favorite nonfiction read-aloud from your classroom or school library with which to model the metacognitive strategy "Summarize and Synthesize." Use the sample read-aloud lessons and suggested titles in the Getting Started Guide.

Realistic Fiction Poster 3

Mini-Lessons (20 MINUTES)

Analyze Story Elements to Summarize and Synthesize

Display Genre Workshop Poster 3 and distribute BLM 3.

Read aloud the excerpt with students. **Say:** *We are going to use our understanding of story elements to summarize and synthesize the story. The story elements are character, setting, and plot. Those are all important things to include in our summary of the story, and understanding the story elements will help us synthesize our own experiences with what we read. I'll start the summary. This story is called "The New Kid." It is about a new student.*

Say: *Now you tell me about the first setting of the story and some characters in the story.* Allow responses. If students are unable to analyze story elements, prompt them to think about the following:
  • *Where does the story happen? What clues in the story help you?*
  • *Who is the new student? What are the other characters' names?*

Say: *Analyzing the story elements helps us summarize the story. When we use what we know from our lives, we synthesize our experiences with the experiences of the characters. Let's summarize the plot of the story now and tell what problem is solved as the story unfolds.*

Work with students to use story elements to summarize and synthesize. As you work, relate the story to specific features of the realistic fiction genre. Record the details on a graphic organizer like the one shown on page 10.

Work with students to determine which story details are important enough to include on the chart. When the graphic organizer is complete, work with students to use the chart information to write a brief summary of the story on chart paper.

Lesson Objectives

Students will:

• Review features of the realistic fiction genre.

• Summarize and synthesize text.

• Use their understanding of genre features to analyze story elements.

• Build oral language and vocabulary through whole-group and partner discussion.

Related Resources

• Realistic Fiction Poster 3 (BLM 3)

• Analyze Story Elements (BLM 4)

• BenchmarkUniverse.com

Make Content Comprehensible for ELLs

Beginning
Point to and name the characters and items in the illustration and ask students to repeat. Point out specific clues about the setting and ask students to tell where the story is happening.

Intermediate and Advanced
Use riddles to review school locations. Have students provide the answers. For example, say: *This place has lots of books. We eat lunch in this place. We have PE in this place.*

Have students find and read each place name in the story.

All Levels
Explain that the word **kid** means "child."

If you have students whose first language is Spanish, share these English/Spanish cognates: **student/el, la estudiante; history/la historia.**

Comprehension Quick-Check

Note whether students can identify and analyze story elements. If they need additional support, review the features of realistic fiction using Poster 1. Then highlight or underline story elements on Poster 3 using a write-on/wipe-off marker. **Say:** *In realistic fiction, the writer tells a story about familiar characters in a realistic place.* Have students underline or highlight character names, setting clues, and plot events with you.

Home/School Connection

Have students take home the Analyze Story Elements graphic organizer (BLM 4). Ask students to fill in the chart with the story elements from a favorite or familiar realistic fiction story.

Begin the summary with the sentences you started with: *This story is called "The New Kid." It is about a new student.* Ask students to continue the summary, including information about characters and their reactions to plot events. Remind students to synthesize their own experiences with the story characters and events to gain a better understanding.

Connect and transfer. Say: *Today as you continue to read realistic fiction in your small groups, analyze story elements to help you summarize and synthesize.*

Story Title: The New Kid	
Characters	Mrs. Hernandez, the teacher; Maria, the new student; Reiko, Frank, Alicia, Evonna, George, other students in the class
Setting	a school classroom and cafeteria
Plot	Mrs. Hernandez introduces Maria. Reiko, Frank, and Alicia offer to show Maria around. Evonna and George help Maria in class. All the students help Maria in the cafeteria. Maria offers to help tomorrow's new student.
Problem/ Solution	Maria is the new kid in school. She does not know where to go. She does not have a book. The other students help her.

Sample Analyze Story Elements Annotations

Small-Group Reading Instruction (60 MINUTES)

Continue small-group reading instruction from the previous day. Use the instruction provided in the Teacher's Guide for each text.

Individual Student Conferences (10 MINUTES)

Confer with individual students to discuss their developing understanding of genre and comprehension strategies. Use the Individual Reading Conference Form on page 32 of Informal Assessments for Reading Development to help guide your conferences.

Word Study Workshop (20 MINUTES)

Use the Day 3 instruction provided in Grade 3 Word Study Unit 11.

Read-Aloud (10 MINUTES)

Select a favorite nonfiction read-aloud from your classroom or school library with which to model the metacognitive strategy "Summarize and Synthesize." Use the sample read-aloud lessons and suggested titles in the Getting Started Guide.

Realistic Fiction Poster 3

 ## Mini-Lessons (20 MINUTES)

Build Comprehension: Draw Conclusions

Say: *Writers do not always tell readers everything. Sometimes readers have to use clues from the writer to figure things out, or draw a conclusion. Good readers know how to find three or more clues to draw a conclusion, or make a good guess, about a character or an event in a story. A good conclusion makes sense and is supported by evidence from the story and from the reader's own experiences.*

Reread Poster 3 with students.

Say: *We are going to make a chart to help us draw a conclusion about Maria. We will list clues from the story that help us draw a conclusion about what kind of first day Maria had. What kinds of clues will you look for? How will you use your own experiences to help draw a conclusion?* **Allow responses.**

Discuss with students how drawing conclusions about realistic fiction might be easier than drawing conclusions about other genres. Review features of the genre and point out that because the story includes familiar characters and settings, readers might have an easier time recognizing clues and relating their own experiences to the story.

Lesson Objectives

Students will:

- Draw conclusions.
- Extend Tier Two Vocabulary by focusing on synonyms.
- Build oral language and vocabulary through whole-group and partner discussion.

Related Resources

- Realistic Fiction Poster 3 (BLM 3)
- BenchmarkUniverse.com

Make Content Comprehensible for ELLs

Beginning

Briefly summarize the story using simple language. **Say:** *Maria is new at school. The other students are nice to her. They help her. She makes new friends. Maria will help the next new student.* Then **ask:** *Did Maria have a good day at school?*

Intermediate

Provide sentence frames to help students draw conclusions. For example:

The other students are _____.

They help Maria by _____.

At the end, Maria says _____.

I have a good day when _____.

I think Maria's first day was _____.

Advanced

Invite students to share their own first-day experiences.

All Levels

Pair ELLs with fluent English speakers to complete the chart.

Comprehension Quick-Check

Take note of students who may need more support to draw conclusions. Provide additional modeling during small-group reading, and have students practice during independent workstation time by drawing conclusions about another realistic fiction excerpt that you assign.

On chart paper, draw a three-column chart like the one shown below.

Think/Pair/Write/Share. Tell students they will complete this chart. **Say:** *Work with a partner to draw a conclusion about Maria's first day at school. Make a chart like the one I just drew, and fill in your ideas. Write three clues from the story, one thing you already know, and your conclusion. We will share the charts as a group.*

Connect and transfer. Say: *Remember, when you read, you can use what you know about the genre to help you draw conclusions. Realistic fiction is about people and places we recognize.*

CLUES FROM THE STORY	WHAT I ALREADY KNOW	CONCLUSION
Kids helped Maria in class and showed her around. Maria made lots of new friends. Maria wants to show the next new kid the cafeteria.	I have a good day when people are nice to me.	Maria had a very good first day at school.

Build Tier Two Vocabulary: Synonyms

On chart paper, write the word **pupil**.

Say: *I'm going to read the first part of the story again. Listen for the word* **pupil***.* Read from the beginning of the story through "Everyone wanted to help the new student." **Ask:** *What is a pupil?*

Turn and talk. Ask students to turn and talk with their neighbor for a moment to come up with a definition.

Ask students to share their definitions and to tell what clue in the story helped them figure out the meaning of the word. Explain that **pupil** and **student** are synonyms. They are words that mean the same thing.

Say: *As writers, we can use synonyms to replace words that we use too often. Write this list of words:* **nice, good, fun***. Use a thesaurus to find a synonym for each word, and then use each new word in a sentence.*

Invite students to share their words and sentences with the group.

Small-Group Reading Instruction (60 MINUTES)

Continue small-group reading instruction from the previous day. Use the instruction provided in the Teacher's Guide for each text.

Individual Student Conferences (10 MINUTES)

Confer with individual students to discuss their developing understanding of genre and word-solving strategies. Use the Individual Reading Conference Form on page 32 of Informal Assessments for Reading Development to help guide your conferences.

Word Study Workshop (20 MINUTES)

Use the Day 4 instruction provided in Grade 3 Word Study Unit 11.

Oral Language Extension

During independent workstation time, ask pairs of students to discuss why they like or dislike realistic fiction. If they dislike the genre, have them discuss what genres they prefer and why. Refer students to the Realistic Fiction anchor poster to aid their discussion.

Home/School Connection

Have students take home BLM 3 and read it with a family member to practice fluent reading. Tell students to have their family member sign the page to indicate they have participated in the reading.

Day Five

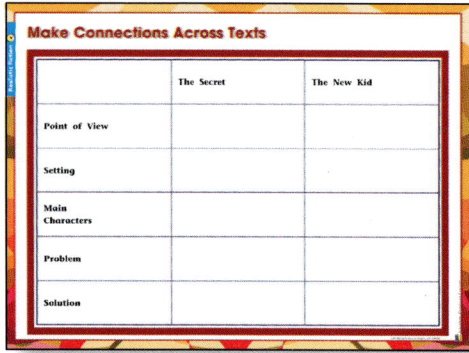

Realistic Fiction Poster 4

Lesson Objectives

Students will:

- Identify elements of and summarize realistic fiction.
- Review features of the realistic fiction genre.
- Make text-to-text connections.
- Build academic oral language and vocabulary through small-group and whole-group discussions.

Related Resources

- Realistic Fiction Poster 4 (BLM 5)
- BenchmarkUniverse.com

Read-Aloud (10 MINUTES)

Revisit the week's read-alouds to make text-to-text connections and provide opportunities for reader response. Use the suggested activities in the Getting Started Guide, or implement ideas of your own.

Mini-Lessons (20 MINUTES)

Synthesize and Assess Genre Understanding

Synthesize genre understanding. Ask students to work in teams to summarize what they now know about the realistic fiction genre. Tell students that each group should come up with a sentence that tells what realistic fiction includes. Each group should appoint one member to be the group's recorder and write the sentence on chart paper.

Give students five to seven minutes to discuss and record their ideas.

Have each read their sentence chorally.

Post the sentences together and discuss similarities.

Self-assessment. Display the class Realistic Fiction anchor chart from Day 1. Ask each group to compare their group's ideas to the information they recorded on the anchor chart on Day 1.

Ask: *How has your understanding of the realistic fiction genre developed? What do you know now that you didn't know before?* Encourage individual students to share their personal insights.

Connect and transfer. Ask: *How will your understanding of this genre help you as a reader the next time you read a realistic fiction story? How can you use your understanding of the genre to write your own realistic fiction?*

Make Connections Across Texts

Display Realistic Fiction Poster 4.

Say: *You have listened to realistic fiction stories this week and you have read them, too. Sometimes in school and on tests, you will be asked to make connections between different fiction and nonfiction texts. Today we are going to practice making connections between realistic fiction stories.*

Ask each group to analyze the poster passages. Ask them to complete the graphic organizer on Realistic Fiction Poster 4 (BLM 5).

Give students about five minutes to record their ideas. Then bring the groups together and have them share their ideas.

Challenge students to express their own opinions on these stories:
- *Do you think it's easier to write realistic fiction or historical fiction? Why?*
- *What did you like most about these stories? What did you dislike about these stories?*

Connect and transfer. Say: *When you analyze two realistic fiction stories, think about how each one reflects the features of the genre. How are the characters like people you know? How is the conflict like something you've experienced? Do you recognize the setting?*

Small-Group Reading Instruction (60 MINUTES)

Continue small-group reading instruction from the previous day. Use the instruction provided in the Teacher's Guide for each text.

Individual Student Conferences (10 MINUTES)

Ask students to reflect on what they have learned about the realistic fiction genre. Use the Individual Reading Conference Form on page 32 of Informal Assessments for Reading Development to help guide your conferences.

Word Study Workshop (20 MINUTES)

Use the Day 5 instruction provided in Grade 3 Word Study Unit 11.

Make Content Comprehensible for ELLs

Beginning
Ask students to point to the story and/or character they liked most. Ask simple questions about the stories to determine students' opinions. For example, **ask:** *Which person did you like? Is [character] a nice person? How did [character] feel at the end?*

Intermediate and Advanced
Provide sentence frames to help ELLs contribute to their groups' discussions. For example:

The setting makes me think of _____.

The characters are alike because _____.

I like this character because _____.

All Levels
Pair ELLs with fluent English speakers during all partner and group activities.

Encourage ELLs to point to illustrations and read aloud specific examples in the text to help them share their ideas with the group.

Name _____   Date _____

Focus on the Genre
Realistic Fiction

What is realistic fiction?

_____

_____

What is the purpose of realistic fiction?

_____

_____

How do you read realistic fiction?

_____

_____

Who tells the story in realistic fiction?

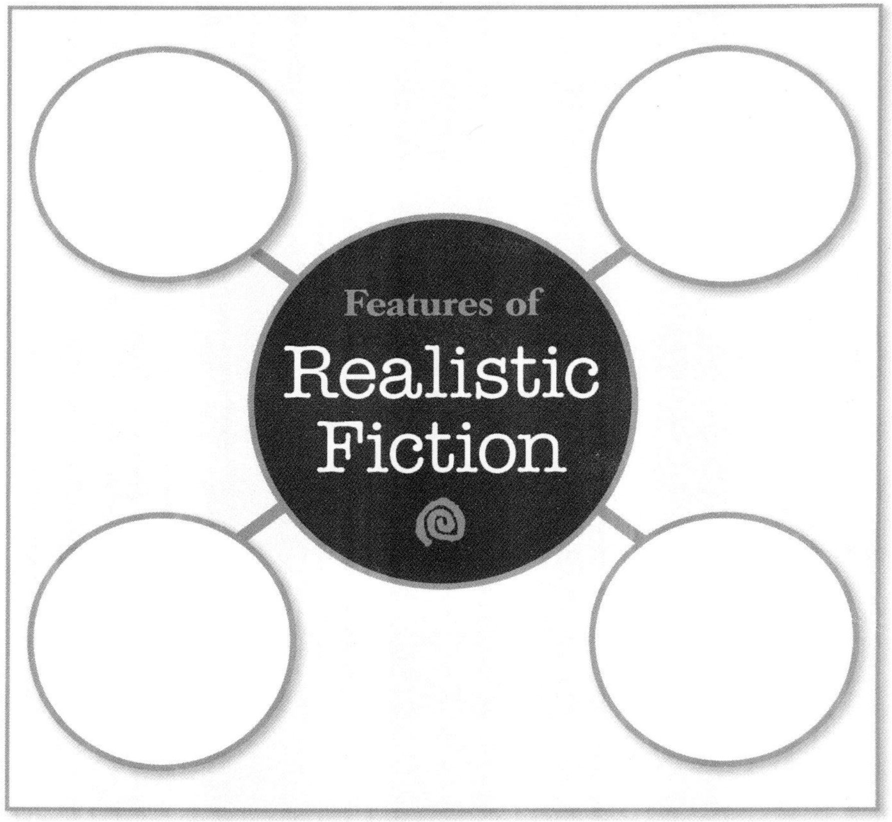

_____

_____

Features of Realistic Fiction

Realistic Fiction ❶

Name _____   Date _____

The Secret

The word **I** shows that the story is in first-person point of view.

I saw Jose and Kiki laughing and talking in the hall. I wanted to join in the fun, but they stopped talking when I said hello.

"What's going on?" I asked.

My friends looked at each other as if they had a juicy secret.

"Nothing, Fatima," Jose said.

"Nothing," Kiki agreed.

Then they rushed away.

Why did they stop talking and run away from me? What were they hiding? I felt left out and alone.

Fatima has a conflict with the other kids.

Later, I saw Abdul and Cindy laughing and talking on the playground.

"What's going on?" I asked.

"Nothing, Fatima," Abdul said.

"Nothing," Cindy agreed.

Then they rushed away.

Why were the kids at school treating me weirdly? I felt like I had lost my friends. I almost cried.

After school, I was walking home alone. Rick caught up with me. "Come to my house," he said.

The setting is authentic.

I was glad I still had one friend.

When Rick opened his door, everyone yelled, "Surprise!" Jose and Kiki smiled at me. Cindy and Abdul hugged me. Rick's mom brought a cake from the kitchen. It had eight lit candles.

The characters are like the people you know in real life.

"Happy birthday, Fatima," my mom and dad said. "How do you like your surprise party?"

"I hate secrets!" I laughed.

Fatima's problem is solved.

Name _____   Date _____

The New Kid

The school bell rang for class to start. Everyone took their seats.

"We have a new **pupil**," Mrs. Hernandez said. "Who wants to show Maria around?"

Everyone put their hands up. Everyone wanted to help the new **student**.

"I'll show her the library," Reiko said.

"I'll show her the cafeteria," Frank said.

"I'll show her the gym," Alicia said.

"Problem solved," Mrs. Hernandez said. "Now open your history books."

Maria did not have a history book.

"I'll share mine," Evonna said.

"She can read with me," George said.

"You have lots of new friends, Maria," Mrs. Hernandez laughed.

At lunchtime, all the kids gathered around Maria. They told her where to get a tray. They even fought over which table she should sit at.

"I am glad everyone is getting along," Mrs. Hernandez said. "We will have another new student tomorrow."

"I will show the new student the cafeteria," Maria said.

Realistic Fiction 3

Name _____   Date _____

Analyze Story Elements

Reread a favorite realistic fiction story. Fill in the chart.

Story Title:	
Characters	
Setting	
Plot	
Problem/Solution	

Name _____ Date _____

Make Connections Across Texts

Realistic Fiction

	The Secret	The New Kid
Point of View		
Setting		
Main Characters		
Problem		
Solution		

Summarize and Synthesize/Analyze Story Elements

Reader's Theater

The Great Lemonade Standoff

by Ruth Romer • illustrated by Laurence Knighton

Unit 4/Week 3 at a Glance

Day	Mini-Lessons
ONE	• Introduce Fluency Skills: *Inflection/Intonation–Pitch* • Model the Skill
TWO	• Practice and Self-Assess Fluency Skills: *Inflection/ Intonation–Pitch* • Connect Fluency and Comprehension: *Analyze Author's Purpose*
THREE	• Apply Fluency Skills to Reader's Theater • Build Comprehension: *Analyze Author's Purpose*
FOUR	• Build Tier Two Vocabulary: *Multiple-Meaning Words*
FIVE	• Prepare for and Manage Student Performances: *Audience and Performer Expectations* • Show Time! • Assess and Reflect

Wishy-Washy Friend

Bert: Hi, Mert. Are you having a good day?
Mert: Well, yes and no. It's a day, but it's not good.
Bert: Did something bad happen?
Mert: Well, yes and no. It wasn't bad, but it wasn't good.
Bert: Is someone mad at you?
Mert: Well, yes and no. He's not mad, but he's not happy.
Bert: Are you going to do something about it?
Mert: Well, yes and no. I'm going to talk to him, but I'm not going to say anything.
Bert: Can you really talk without saying anything?
Mert: Well, yes and no. I'm talking to you, but do you know any more than you did when you came in?
Bert: Well, yes and no . . .
Mert: You're so wishy-washy!

Wishy-Washy Friend

Bert: Hi, Mert. Are you having a good day?
Mert: Well, yes and no. It's a day, but it's not good.
Bert: Did something bad happen?
Mert: Well, yes and no. It wasn't bad, but it wasn't good.
Bert: Is someone mad at you?
Mert: Well, yes and no. He's not mad, but he's not happy.
Bert: Are you going to do something about it?
Mert: Well, yes and no. I'm going to talk to him, but I'm not going to say anything.
Bert: Can you really talk without saying anything?
Mert: Well, yes and no. I'm talking to you, but do you know any more than you did when you come in?
Bert: Well, yes and no . . .
Mert: You're so wishy-washy!

Fluency Poster

Lesson Objectives

Students will:

- Make their voices rise at a question mark and fall at a period.

- Demonstrate understanding of the text through purposeful inflection and intonation.

- Use effective inflection and intonation to make their reading sound like talking.

Related Resources

- BenchmarkUniverse.com

Read-Aloud (10 MINUTES)

Select a favorite fiction read-aloud from your classroom or school library with which to model the metacognitive strategy "Summarize and Synthesize." Use the sample read-aloud lessons and suggested titles provided in the Getting Started Guide.

Mini-Lessons (20 MINUTES)

Introduce Fluency Skills: Inflection/Intonation—Pitch

Explain: *When we talk, we do not say every word the same. Instead we use different kinds of inflection and intonation. We say some words louder and some words softer. This is called* **volume**. *We emphasize some words. This is called* **stress**. *We also say some words at a higher* **pitch** *and some words at a lower pitch. When we read, how do we know when to make our voices rise or fall?* Allow responses.

Reinforce the idea that end punctuation helps us figure out when to use a higher or lower pitch. Demonstrate higher pitch (make your voice rise) and lower pitch (make your voice fall).

Ask:
- *Should we make our voices rise or fall when we see a question mark?*
    (rise)
- *Should we make our voices rise or fall when we see a period?*
    (fall)
- *What do you think we should do when we see an exclamation point?*
    (Our voices may rise or fall depending on what we are reading.)

Say: *Our voices should rise and fall many times as we read. We use ending punctuation to tell us when to change pitch.*

Model the Skill

Display the fluency poster "Wishy-Washy Friend" and read aloud the title.

Say: *This is a dialogue. The author uses question marks, periods, and exclamation points to show us when to make our voices rise and fall. Changing our pitch at each question mark, period, and exclamation point helps the sentences sound right and make sense. Changing our pitch makes our reading sound like talking.*

Ask students to listen and follow along as you read the dialogue aloud, making your voice rise at each question mark and fall at each period. Stop to experiment with a rising and falling pitch at the exclamation point and invite students to tell you which sounds better. (a falling pitch)

Say: *Now I will read the dialogue without making my voice rise and fall. Listen closely.*

Read the entire dialogue in a monotone.

Turn and talk. Have students turn to a neighbor and compare and evaluate your readings. Ask them to think about how each reading affected them as listeners. Then have pairs of students share their ideas with the whole class. Reinforce the idea that using inflection and intonation helps the sentences sound right and make sense.

Shared Writing. Invite students to help you create a class anchor chart to remind them how good readers use inflection and intonation. (See the example below.) When you are finished, ask students to echo-read the entire chart. Display the chart in the classroom for future reference.

Inflection/Intonation

- We do not read every word the same.
- We read some words louder and some words softer. This is called volume.
- We emphasize some words. This is called stress.
- We read some words higher and some words lower. This is called pitch.
- Ending punctuation helps us know when to make our voices rise or fall.
- Changing the way we read words helps our reading sound like talking.

Sample Anchor Chart

Make Content Comprehensible for ELLs

Beginning
Write simple statements and questions on chart paper. Read the sentences and demonstrate raising and lowering the pitch of your voice based on the ending punctuation. Invite students to echo-read, raising and lowering their voices, too.

Intermediate and Advanced
Engage ELLs in a discussion about why the last sentence of the dialogue is funny using the sentence frame: *The last sentence is funny because _____.* Record and reread students' responses.

All Levels
Before reading to model fluency, read to support comprehension of the term **wishy-washy**: unable to make a decision or choice. Use role-play and gestures around a simple idea such as, *Do you want to draw? I don't know. Yes. No. Maybe. Do you want to read? I don't know. Yes. No. Maybe.*

Support Special Needs Learners

Throughout the week, use the following strategies to help students who have learning disabilities access the content and focus on skills and strategies.

During partner reading practice, pair special needs students with more fluent readers who can model fluency and support their development.

Group students heterogeneously for small-group reading of the script so that struggling students benefit from working with more fluent readers.

Assign multiple students to specific reader's theater roles so that they can support each other.

Fluency and Comprehension Quick-Check

Throughout the week, refer to the Fluency Rubric provided in the Benchmark Literacy Assessments to help you informally assess where students are in their development of key areas of fluency.

The end goal of all fluency practice is increased comprehension. Use the following questions to check students' comprehension of the passage they have read:

- *Why did the author title this dialogue "Wishy-Washy Friend"?*

- *Who is the real wishy-washy friend? Why?*

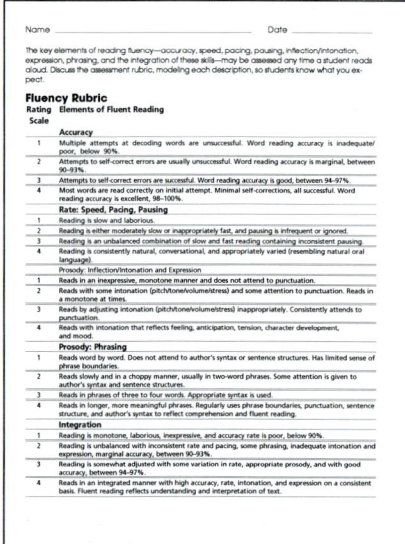

Fluency Rubric

Connect and transfer. Say: *Today during small-group reading, we will read a reader's theater script. As we read the script, we will practice making our voices rise and fall at ending punctuation so that our reading is easier to understand.*

Small-Group Reading Instruction (60 MINUTES)

Introduce and read *The Great Lemonade Standoff*. Use the before- and during-reading instruction in the Teacher's Guide for the script.

Individual Student Conferences (10 MINUTES)

Confer with individual students to discuss their understanding of the script. Use the Individual Reading Conference Form on page 32 of Informal Assessments for Reading Development to help guide your conferences.

Word Study Workshop (20 MINUTES)

Use the Day 1 instruction provided in Grade 3 Word Study Unit 12.

Read-Aloud (10 MINUTES)

Select a favorite fiction read-aloud from your classroom or school library with which to model the metacognitive strategy "Summarize and Synthesize." Use the sample read-aloud lessons and suggested titles provided in the Getting Started Guide.

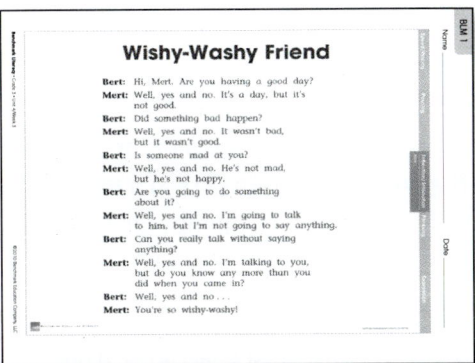

Wishy-Washy Friend (BLM 1)

Mini-Lessons (20 MINUTES)

Practice and Self-Assess Fluency Skills:
Inflection/Intonation—Pitch

Distribute copies of Wishy-Washy Friend (BLM 1).

Divide students into two groups and ask them to choral-read the dialogue with you one or more times.

Next, allow the groups to choral-read their parts without your assistance.

Distribute the Fluency Self-Assessment Master Checklist (BLM 2) and review the assessment criteria for inflection/intonation and integration. Ask students to give a thumbs-up or thumbs-down on each question based on the group's choral-reading. Discuss their responses.

Partner reading. Pair students and ask them to read "Wishy-Washy Friend" together one or more times.

Monitor students' partner rereading practice and provide responsive feedback using the prompts provided on page 6.

Ask students to rate themselves on specific fluency skills covered in this lesson using their Fluency Self-Assessment Master Checklist (BLM 2).

Connect and transfer. Ask students to reflect on their fluency practice, using the following prompts:
- *When did you make your voice rise? When did you make your voice fall?*
- *How did changing your pitch help you read and understand?*
- *Remember, you will need this skill as we practice and perform a reader's theater script this week.*

Lesson Objectives

Students will:
- Make their voices rise at a question mark and fall at a period.
- Demonstrate understanding of the text through purposeful inflection and intonation.
- Use effective inflection and intonation to make their reading sound like talking.

Related Resources
- Wishy-Washy Friend (BLM 1)
- Fluency Self-Assessment Master Checklist (BLM 2)
- BenchmarkUniverse.com

Make Content Comprehensible for ELLs

Beginning

Allow ELLs to participate through active listening while other students demonstrate changing pitch. Invite ELLs to track print with you and give a thumbs-up when they hear a rise or fall of the reader's voice.

All Levels

Pair ELLs with fluent English speakers during partner discussions and activities.

BLM 2

Name _____ Date _____

Fluency Self-Assessment Master Checklist

	Yes	No
Speed/Pacing		
Did my speed and pacing match the kind of text I was reading?		
Did my speed and pacing match what the character was saying?		
Did I read with a natural talking voice?		
Did I slow my reading down when appropriate?		
Did I pay attention to punctuation?		
Pausing		
Did I pause to keep from running all my words together?		
Did I pause in the correct locations?		
Did I pause for the appropriate length of time?		
Did I pause to help my reading make sense?		
Did I use punctuation to help me figure out when to pause?		
Inflection/Intonation		
Did I make my voice rise at a question mark?		
Did I make my voice fall at a period?		
Did I think about what the author was saying so I would know when to read louder or softer?		
Did I think about what the author was saying so I would know when to stress or emphasize words?		
Phrasing		
Did I notice the phrases?		
Did I read all the words in each phrase together?		
Did I think about what the words in the phrase mean when they are together?		
Expression		
Did I look for clues so I could anticipate the mood of the passage?		
Did I use my tone of voice, facial expressions, and body language to express what the author or characters were thinking or feeling?		
Did I change my reading when something new was about to happen?		
Integration		
Did I read the words right? (accuracy)		
Did I read the words at the right speed? (rate)		
Did I read with expression? (prosody)		
Did my reading sound like talking?		
Did I understand what I read?		

Benchmark Literacy • Grade 3 • Unit 4/Week 3   ©2010 Benchmark Education Company, LLC

Fluency Self-Assessment Master Checklist (BLM 2)

Responsive Prompts for Inflection/Intonation

As students work together, observe those who demonstrate understanding and those who struggle. Use appropriate responsive prompting to provide additional support or to validate students who demonstrate mastery.

Goal Oriented

- Listen to how I read this. Can you hear my voice go down at the period?
- Listen to how I read this. Can you hear my voice go up at the question mark?
- Listen to how my voice gets louder.
- Listen to how my voice gets softer.
- Emphasize the word _____ like this.

Directive and Corrective Feedback

- Make your voice go down at the period.
- Make your voice go up at the question mark.
- Read it louder.
- Read it softer.
- Stress the word _____ in this sentence.

Self-Monitoring and Reflection

- What should you do when you see a period?
- What should you do when you see a question mark?
- Should your voice go up or down at this exclamation point?
- How did you know to read louder?
- How did you know to read softer?

Validating and Confirming

- Good job at making your voice rise and fall.
- You read that part louder/softer—way to think like the author!
- You stressed exactly the right words in that sentence. Good thinking!

Connect Fluency and Comprehension:
Analyze Author's Purpose

Say: *Making your voice rise and fall in the correct places helps you make sense of the words and sentences you read. Understanding why an author wrote a passage can also help you. When you understand why an author wrote something, you can use your voice to help your audience understand what you are reading. Why do authors write? What purposes might an author have for writing?* **Allow responses.**

Say: *Now think about "Wishy-Washy Friend." Why do you think the author wrote this dialogue?* **Allow responses.**

Discuss with students how they know the primary purpose of "Wishy-Washy Friend" is to entertain. Is there any important information the author is sharing? Is the author trying to get the reader to agree with him about something?

Ask: *How does understanding the author's purpose of "Wishy-Washy Friend" change how you sound when you read it aloud? Do you try to make the dialogue sound serious and important? Or do you try to make the dialogue sound funny and lighthearted instead?*

Connect and transfer. Say: *Today during small-group reading, focus on understanding the purpose of the passage. This will help you read with the right inflection and intonation.*

Small-Group Reading Instruction (60 MINUTES)

Reread *The Great Lemonade Standoff* to build comprehension and critical thinking using the After Reading Interpret the Script questions. Assign roles to individual students.

Individual Student Conferences (10 MINUTES)

Confer with individual students to discuss their script roles and how they plan to rehearse and read their part. Use the Individual Reading Conference Form on page 32 of Informal Assessments for Reading Development to help guide your conferences.

Word Study Workshop (20 MINUTES)

Use the Day 2 instruction provided in Grade 3 Word Study Unit 12.

Oral Language Extension

Have pairs of students practice the fluency passage during independent workstation time.

Home/School Connection

Have students practice reading Wishy-Washy Friend (BLM 1) again with a family member. Ask students to focus on ending punctuation to know when to change pitch. Have them alternate roles with their family member so that they practice both sides of the dialogue.

Ask students to have their family member sign the page to indicate they have participated in the reading.

Day Three

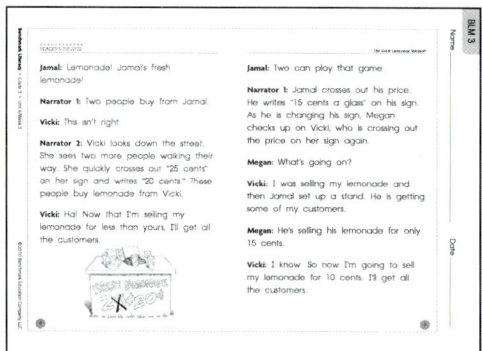

The Great Lemonade Standoff, pages 8–9 (BLM 3)

Lesson Objectives

Students will:

- Make their voices rise at a question mark and fall at a period.

- Demonstrate understanding of the text through purposeful inflection and intonation.

- Use effective inflection and intonation to make their reading sound like talking.

- Use metacognitive strategies to help them analyze the author's purpose.

- Build oral language and vocabulary through whole-group and partner discussion.

Related Resources

- *The Great Lemonade Standoff,* pages 8–9 (BLM 3)

- BenchmarkUniverse.com

Read-Aloud (10 MINUTES)

Select a favorite nonfiction read-aloud from your classroom or school library with which to model the metacognitive strategy "Summarize and Synthesize." Use the sample read-aloud lessons and suggested titles provided in the Getting Started Guide.

Mini-Lessons (20 MINUTES)

Apply Fluency Skills to Reader's Theater

Distribute pages 8–9 of *The Great Lemonade Standoff* (BLM 3), which students have completed during small-group reading time.

Say: *Yesterday you practiced making your voice rise and fall as you read a passage. Now I want you to apply what you learned to the script we will perform this week. Listen as I read these two pages to you.*

Read pages 8–9 of the script to model how you vary your pitch to make the dialogue sound natural. Use the suggestions below or interpret the text in your own way:
- Jamal: falling pitch on exclamations
- narrators: clearly, calmly
- Vicki: unhappy at first, then gloating
- Megan: emphasize **What's** and raise pitch at end

Ask students to comment on how your reading affected them as listeners. How did you use inflection and intonation to vary the characters' voices?

Partner reading. Have pairs of students practice reading these pages together. Monitor their practice and provide responsive prompting as needed to validate their efforts, give corrective feedback, or encourage them to self monitor. Use the responsive prompts provided on page 6.

Build Comprehension: Analyze Author's Purpose

Say: *Yesterday we discussed why the author of "Wishy-Washy Friend" wrote that passage. Today let's think about why the author of* The Great Lemonade Standoff *wrote about these events and characters. Understanding the author's purpose will help you interpret the script more effectively.*

Activate metacognitive strategies. Ask: *What strategies can we use to help ourselves understand the author's purpose?* Allow responses. If necessary, prompt students to use the following strategies:

Fix-up monitoring. Say: *If you are confused about something that has happened in the script, what can you do? Why is it important to have a clear understanding of what's happening in the story? How does rereading help you understand the author's purpose?*

Make inferences. Say: *What inference can you make about how Vicki feels when Jamal sets up his stand? How did you make that inference? Why is it important to think about the characters' feelings as you read? Does that fit in with the author's purpose?*

Support ELLs and struggling readers to participate in the discussion by providing the following sentence frames:

> When I am confused, I can _____.
> I can infer that Vicki feels _____.
> I made the inference by _____.
> It is important to think about the characters' feelings because _____.

Shared Writing. Make a list of students' ideas about the author's purpose. Post this on the wall.

Connect and transfer. Say: *Today, as you practice the script, think about what the author wants people to experience through the script. Use what you have learned about inflection and intonation to help you express her purpose.*

Small-Group Reading Instruction (60 MINUTES)

Have students rehearse their roles in *The Great Lemonade Standoff* together as a group. Offer suggestions for volume, expression, and pitch.

Individual Student Conferences (10 MINUTES)

Confer with individual students to discuss their script roles and their rehearsal progress. Use the Individual Reading Conference Form on page 32 of Informal Assessments for Reading Development to help guide your conferences.

Word Study Workshop (20 MINUTES)

Use the Day 3 instruction provided in Grade 3 Word Study Unit 12.

Make Content Comprehensible for ELLs

Beginning
Allow ELLs to participate through active listening while other students demonstrate varying pitch. Invite them to indicate when they hear a reader's voice rise or fall. Reinforce the connection between rising pitch and a question mark.

Intermediate and Advanced
Allow ELLs to read parts of the script chorally with you or other students as they demonstrate their use of pitch. Encourage students to highlight question marks and practice making their voices rise at those points in the script.

All Levels
Pair ELLs with fluent English speakers during partner reading practice.

Model the use of academic sentence frames to support ELLs' academic vocabulary and language development. (See suggested sentence frames provided.)

Home/School Connection

Have students take home *The Great Lemonade Standoff*, pages 8–9 (BLM 3) and read it with a family member to practice fluent reading. Ask students to have their family member sign the script page to indicate that they have participated in the reading.

Fluency Quick-Check

As students practice oral reading with a partner, note students who would benefit from additional repeated oral reading practice during independent workstation time.

Day Four

The Great Lemonade Standoff, pages 6–7 (BLM 5)

Lesson Objectives

Students will:

- Extend Tier Two Vocabulary by analyzing multiple-meaning words.
- Partner-read to build fluency.
- Build oral language and vocabulary through whole-group and partner discussion.

Related Resources

- Multiple-Meaning Words (BLM 4)
- *The Great Lemonade Standoff*, pages 6–7 (BLM 5)
- BenchmarkUniverse.com

Read-Aloud (10 MINUTES)

Select a favorite nonfiction read-aloud from your classroom or school library with which to model the metacognitive strategy "Summarize and Synthesize." Use the sample read-aloud lessons and suggested titles provided in the Getting Started Guide.

Mini-Lessons (20 MINUTES)

Build Tier Two Vocabulary: Multiple-Meaning Words

On chart paper, draw a graphic organizer like the one below (BLM 4). Write the word **stand** in the top box.

Think/Pair/Write/Share. Ask students to work with a partner and write down all the definitions they can think of for the word **stand**. Give students approximately three minutes, and then bring them back together to share their answers. If students are unable to come up with many definitions, prompt them with the following sentences:

- *What does it mean to stand up?*
- *If I say "My house stands on top of the hill," what does that mean?*
- *What do you call a table or rack that holds things like music or a lamp by your bed?*
- *If you sell cookies for a bake sale, what would you sell them from?*

Record students' definitions on the graphic organizer and reread them together to clarify their meaning and use the words in sentences. Ask students to identify which meanings of the word are verbs and which are nouns.

Distribute *The Great Lemonade Standoff*, pages 6–7 (BLM 5).

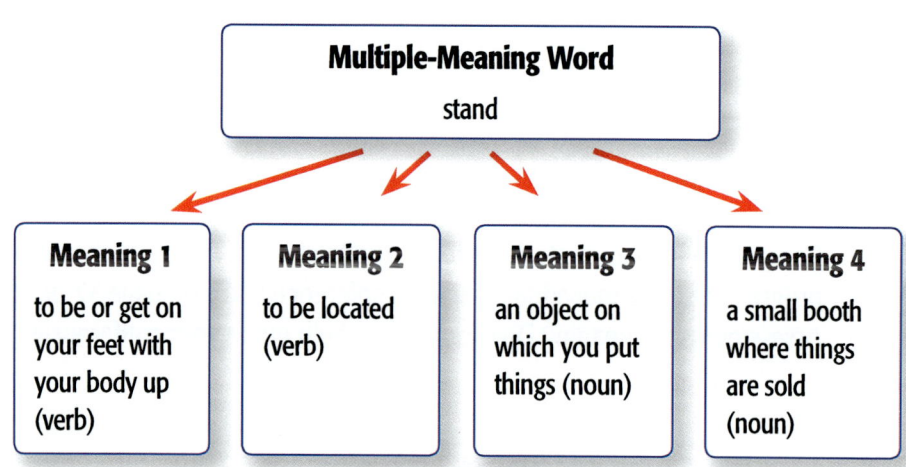

Sample Multiple-Meaning Words Annotations (BLM 4)

Say: *Read the text with a partner. Find the word **stand** in the script. Tell me the correct meaning of this word in the script. How can you tell?*

Have pairs share their answers and the context clues they used.

Then have partners find at least one more multiple-meaning word in the passage on BLM 5. Have them write multiple meanings for the word on the graphic organizer, choose the correct definition based on the script context, and share it with the class. Possible words include: **watch, pitcher, fair, sign, park**.

Discuss fix-up monitoring strategies. Ask students what they can do when they encounter a multiple-meaning word and are confused about the meaning. Generate discussion of the strategies that help good readers. For example, students can stop and think about which meaning fits the context. They can also reread and ask clarifying questions.

Connect and transfer. Say: *Several words in our script are multiple-meaning words. In order to understand your part, you need to think about which word meaning fits the context of the script. This will affect how you read.*

Small-Group Reading Instruction (60 MINUTES)

Have students continue to rehearse their roles in *The Great Lemonade Standoff* together as a group. Discuss and plan how students will stage their script performance tomorrow.

Individual Student Conferences (10 MINUTES)

Confer with individual students on sections of the script you would like them to work on before the performance. Use the Individual Reading Conference Form on page 32 of Informal Assessments for Reading Development to help guide your conferences.

Word Study Workshop (20 MINUTES)

Use the Day 4 instruction provided in Grade 3 Word Study Unit 12.

Make Content Comprehensible for ELLs

Beginning
Multiple-meaning words are particularly challenging for ELLs. Use gestures and props to help you convey the multiple meanings of each word you focus on.

Allow beginning ELLs to be active listeners during the multiple-meaning activity. Give them opportunities to hear and identify the multiple meanings once they have been clearly explained.

Intermediate and Advanced
Identify the multiple-meaning words in the script and invite students to generate definitions. Provide support. For example, **say:** *Yes, **watch** can be a verb that means to look at something. Now think about telling time. What does time have to do with the word **watch**?*

All Levels
Pair ELLs with fluent English speakers during partner discussions and activities.

Oral Language Extension

Write several glossary words from the reader's theater script on chart paper and display the list during independent workstation time. Challenge pairs of students to use each word in meaningful oral sentences. Ask students to write down at least five sentences to show you during independent student conference time.

Home/School Connection

Have students take home *The Great Lemonade Standoff*, pages 6–7 (BLM 5) and read it with a family member to practice fluency skills. Ask students to have their family member sign the script page to indicate that they have participated in the reading.

Day Five

The Great Lemonade Standoff

by Ruth Romer • illustrated by Laurence Knighton

Reader's Theater Script

Lesson Objectives

Students will:

• Demonstrate their level of fluency development through an oral reading interpretation of the script.

• Demonstrate active listening skills.

• Reflect on and assess their own fluency development.

Related Resources

• Reader's Theater Self-Assessment (BLM 6)

• BenchmarkUniverse.com

Read-Aloud (10 MINUTES)

Revisit the week's read-alouds to make text-to-text connections and to provide opportunities for reader response. Use the suggested activities in the Getting Started Guide, or implement ideas of your own.

Mini-Lessons (20 MINUTES)

Prepare for and Manage Student Performances: Audience and Performer Expectations

Prepare students for their reader's theater performances by sharing your expectations of audience members and performers.

Audience expectations. Say: *While you are listening to the other groups perform, I expect you to do the following:*

- Give your classmates your full attention.
- Do not speak to your neighbors or make any noise.
- Enjoy their performance and show your appreciation by clapping when they are finished.
- Be prepared to give your feedback on the script, and always remember to make your feedback constructive, or helpful.

Performer expectations. Say: *While you and your group are performing the script, remember to do these things:*

- Read in a loud, clear voice and act out your role.
- Use expression and fluency to help your listeners understand your character.
- Remember to use punctuation clues to make your voice rise and fall.
- When it is not your turn to read, follow along in the script so you know when to come in.
- If one of your group members gets lost or forgets to come in, prompt him or her quietly.
- Accept both suggestions and praise from your audience.

Show Time!

Invite students to perform the script for an audience such as members of the class, students from other classes, school staff members, or parents.

Continue your performances during small-group reading time, giving each group the opportunity to perform.

Assess and Reflect

After all groups have completed their performance, use the following self-assessment activity to help students reflect on their performance, identify how they have improved as readers and performers, and determine what they will focus on as they participate in future reader's theater experiences throughout the year.

Draw a three-column reflection chart on chart paper. Include a column for **Reflection Questions** and columns to answer **Yes** or **No** in response. Use the following questions to guide the group's assessment of their performance, or use the Reader's Theater Self-Assessment (BLM 6). Place a check mark in the appropriate column, noting their responses.

- Did we make our reading sound smooth like talking?
- Did we make our characters sound and feel like real people (or animals/objects) with feelings?
- Did we act out our parts with our voices and body language?
- Were our parts at "just right" reading levels?
- Did we practice our reading many times before performing?
- Did we make our voices rise and fall in the correct places to help our audience understand the characters and message of the script?

Connect and transfer. Discuss ways to improve future performances based on the self-assessment and reflections.

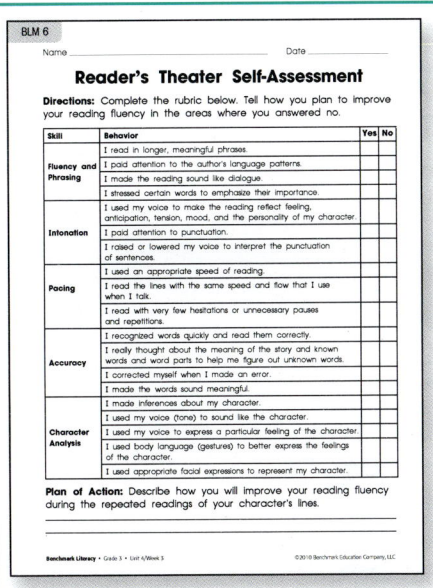

Reader's Theater Self-Assessment (BLM 6)

Make Content Comprehensible for ELLs

Beginning
Allow beginning ELLs to participate as active listeners. If students are ready for a speaking role, assign one or two shorter lines. Have students highlight their lines and work with fluent partners who can chorally read the lines with them.

Intermediate and Advanced
Pair ELLs with more fluent readers to chorally read their parts in the script. Encourage students to highlight places in their lines where they will raise their voices to a higher pitch.

Assessment Tip

During student performances, record anecdotal notes that focus on how students are developing fluency skills and how they are meeting performer and audience member expectations.

Small-Group Reading Instruction (60 MINUTES)

Use the small-group reading time to continue students' performances of *The Great Lemonade Standoff.*

After all groups have performed, use the Assess and Reflect activity above.

Individual Student Conferences (10 MINUTES)

Have students use their self-reflection to show how they would read differently next time. Discuss how students plan to apply what they learned to future performances and independent reading.

Word Study Workshop (20 MINUTES)

Use the Day 5 instruction provided in Grade 3 Word Study Unit 12.

Name _____   Date _____

Speed/Pacing	Pausing	Inflection/Intonation	Phrasing	Expression
		Pitch		

Wishy-Washy Friend

Bert: Hi, Mert. Are you having a good day?

Mert: Well, yes and no. It's a day, but it's not good.

Bert: Did something bad happen?

Mert: Well, yes and no. It wasn't bad, but it wasn't good.

Bert: Is someone mad at you?

Mert: Well, yes and no. He's not mad, but he's not happy.

Bert: Are you going to do something about it?

Mert: Well, yes and no. I'm going to talk to him, but I'm not going to say anything.

Bert: Can you really talk without saying anything?

Mert: Well, yes and no. I'm talking to you, but do you know any more than you did when you came in?

Bert: Well, yes and no . . . .

Mert: You're so wishy-washy!

Name _____ Date _____

Fluency Self-Assessment Master Checklist

	Yes	No
Speed/Pacing		
Did my speed and pacing match the kind of text I was reading?		
Did my speed and pacing match what the character was saying?		
Did I read with a natural talking voice?		
Did I slow my reading down when appropriate?		
Did I pay attention to punctuation?		
Pausing		
Did I pause to keep from running all my words together?		
Did I pause in the correct locations?		
Did I pause for the appropriate length of time?		
Did I pause to help my reading make sense?		
Did I use punctuation to help me figure out when to pause?		
Inflection/Intonation		
Did I make my voice rise at a question mark?		
Did I make my voice fall at a period?		
Did I think about what the author was saying so I would know when to read louder or softer?		
Did I think about what the author was saying so I would know when to stress or emphasize words?		
Phrasing		
Did I notice the phrases?		
Did I read all the words in each phrase together?		
Did I think about what the words in the phrase mean when they are together?		
Expression		
Did I look for clues so I could anticipate the mood of the passage?		
Did I use my tone of voice, facial expressions, and body language to express what the author or characters were thinking or feeling?		
Did I change my reading when something new was about to happen?		
Integration		
Did I read the words right? (accuracy)		
Did I read the words at the right speed? (rate)		
Did I read with expression? (prosody)		
Did my reading sound like talking?		
Did I understand what I read?		

Name _____ Date _____

Jamal: Two can play that game.

Narrator 1: Jamal crosses out his price. He writes "15 cents a glass" on his sign. As he is changing his sign, Megan checks up on Vicki, who is crossing out the price on her sign again.

Megan: What's going on?

Vicki: I was selling my lemonade and then Jamal set up a stand. He is getting some of my customers.

Megan: He's selling his lemonade for only 15 cents.

Vicki: I know. So now I'm going to sell my lemonade for 10 cents. I'll get all the customers.

9

Jamal: Lemonade! Jamal's fresh lemonade!

Narrator 1: Two people buy from Jamal.

Vicki: This isn't right.

Narrator 2: Vicki looks down the street. She sees two more people walking their way. She quickly crosses out "25 cents" on her sign and writes "20 cents." These people buy lemonade from Vicki.

Vicki: Ha! Now that I'm selling my lemonade for less than yours, I'll get all the customers.

8

Name _____ Date _____

Multiple-Meaning Words

Directions: Find a word with more than one meaning. Write the definitions of the word.

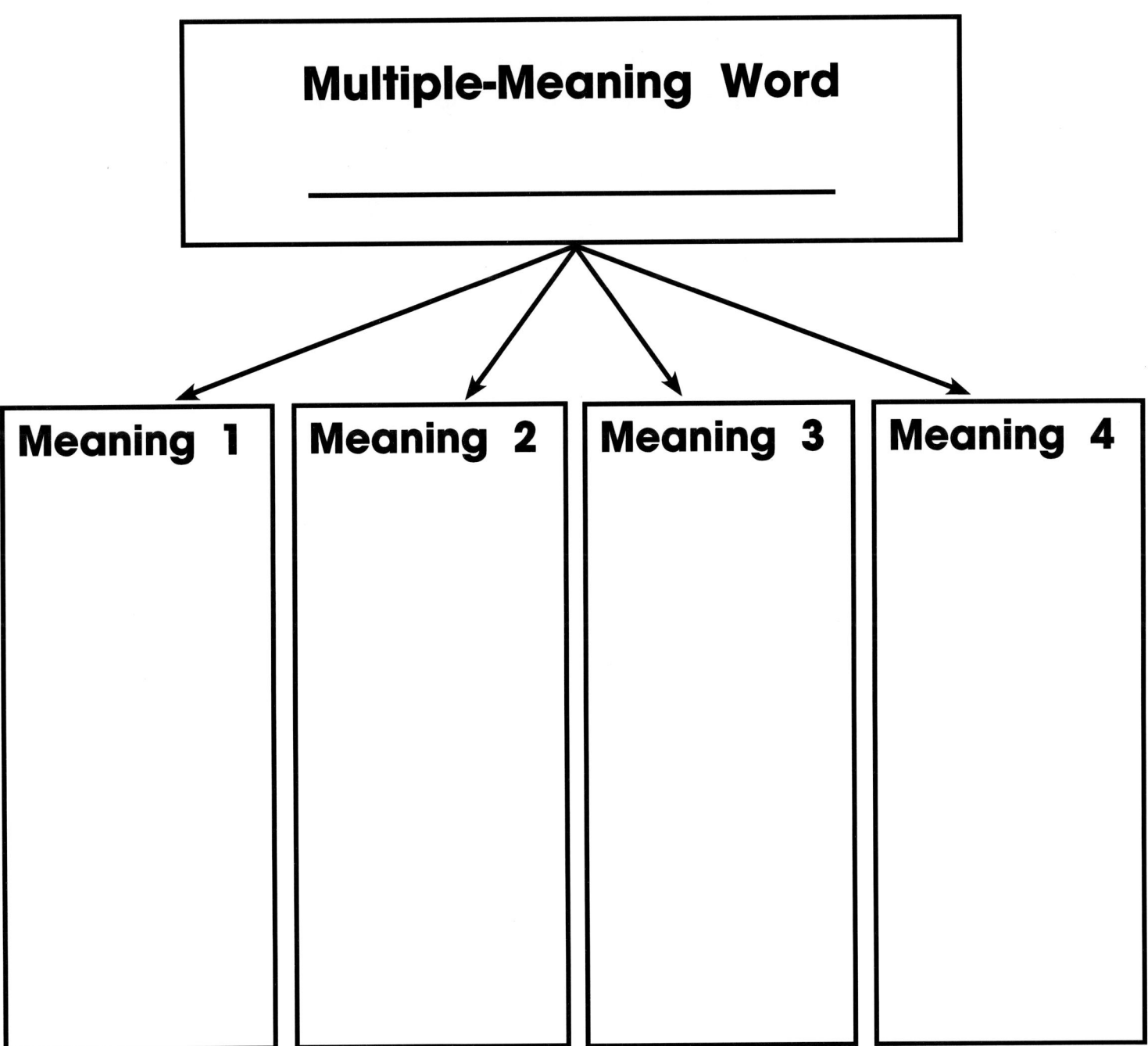

Name _____   Date _____

READER'S THEATER

Jamal: I could use some extra money. I'm saving for a remote-control car that spins and flips! I bet I could make more money than you.

Vicki: Bet not.

Jamal: Just watch me.

Narrator 1: Jamal goes inside his house and mixes up a pitcher of lemonade to sell. He makes a sign that says, "Even Better Lemonade, 25 cents a glass." He sets up his stand across the street from Vicki's stand.

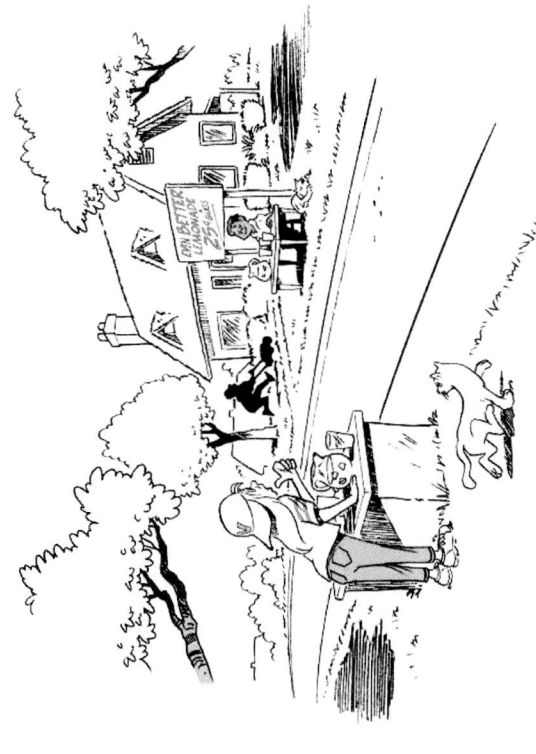

Vicki: You can't do that. I was selling my lemonade here first.

Jamal: It's a free country.

Vicki: That's not fair. If you sell lemonade here, it will take away my customers.

Jamal: I told you I'd sell more than you. Watch me.

Narrator 2: Jamal sees two people walking to the park.

6

7

Name _____   Date _____

Reader's Theater Self-Assessment

Directions: Complete the rubric below. Tell how you plan to improve your reading fluency in the areas where you answered no.

Skill	Behavior	Yes	No
Fluency and Phrasing	I read in longer, meaningful phrases.		
	I paid attention to the author's language patterns.		
	I made the reading sound like dialogue.		
	I stressed certain words to emphasize their importance.		
Intonation	I used my voice to make the reading reflect feeling, anticipation, tension, mood, and the personality of my character.		
	I paid attention to punctuation.		
	I raised or lowered my voice to interpret the punctuation of sentences.		
Pacing	I used an appropriate speed of reading.		
	I read the lines with the same speed and flow that I use when I talk.		
	I read with very few hesitations or unnecessary pauses and repetitions.		
Accuracy	I recognized words quickly and read them correctly.		
	I really thought about the meaning of the story and known words and word parts to help me figure out unknown words.		
	I corrected myself when I made an error.		
	I made the words sound meaningful.		
Character Analysis	I made inferences about my character.		
	I used my voice (tone) to sound like the character.		
	I used my voice to express a particular feeling of the character.		
	I used body language (gestures) to better express the feelings of the character.		
	I used appropriate facial expressions to represent my character.		

Plan of Action: Describe how you will improve your reading fluency during the repeated readings of your character's lines.

_____

_____

Make Connections/Make Inferences

Reader's Theater
Kanchil Outsmarts the Crocodile
A Folktale from Malaysia and Indonesia

by Carol Pugliano-Martin • illustrated by V.G. Myers

Unit 5/Week 3 at a Glance

Day	Mini-Lessons
ONE	• Introduce Fluency Skills: *Inflection/Intonation–Volume* • Model the Skill
TWO	• Practice and Self-Assess Fluency Skills: *Inflection/Intonation–Volume* • Connect Fluency and Comprehension: *Analyze Author's Purpose*
THREE	• Apply Fluency Skills to Reader's Theater • Build Comprehension: *Analyze Author's Purpose*
FOUR	• Build Tier Two Vocabulary: *Synonyms*
FIVE	• Prepare for and Manage Student Performances: *Audience and Performer Expectations* • Show Time! • Assess and Reflect

The Lion

Justin was traveling the back roads of Africa with his dad, a photographer, and their guide, Sandoa. "I've never been so bored in all my life!" Justin complained, but no one listened.

One day, Justin wandered away when his dad stopped to take photos. Suddenly, Justin saw a lion! Justin was getting ready to run away when he felt Sandoa's hand on his shoulder.

"Be still now," said Sandoa. "The lion is looking for his lunch. We don't want it to be us." Sandoa smiled slightly, but he kept his eyes on the lion.

Then Sandoa said, "If he comes at us, don't run. He'll catch you. Just stand behind me." Sandoa was so calm that Justin felt calmer. But it seemed like they waited forever, frozen, trying not to breathe.

The lion's tail began to twitch nervously. Sandoa continued to stare at the lion. Then Sandoa quietly stepped in front of Justin and lifted his spear in both hands. The lion turned and loped away into the brush.

"Awesome! You just scared away the lion!" said Justin.

Justin ran to his dad. "Africa is definitely NOT boring," he exclaimed.

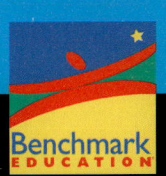

BENCHMARK EDUCATION COMPANY

The Lion

Justin was traveling the back roads of Africa with his dad, a photographer, and their guide, Sandoa. "I've never been so bored in all my life!" Justin complained, but no one listened.

One day, Justin wandered away when his dad stopped to take photos. Suddenly, Justin saw a lion! Justin was getting ready to run away when he felt Sandoa's hand on his shoulder.

"Be still now," said Sandoa. "The lion is looking for his lunch. We don't want it to be us." Sandoa smiled slightly, but he kept his eyes on the lion.

Then Sandoa said, "If he comes at us, don't run. He'll catch you. Just stand behind me." Sandoa was so calm that Justin felt calmer. But it seemed like they waited forever, frozen, trying not to breathe.

The lion's tail began to twitch nervously. Sandoa continued to stare at the lion. Then Sandoa quietly stepped in front of Justin and lifted his spear in both hands. The lion turned and loped away into the brush.

"Awesome! You just scared away the lion!" said Justin.

Justin ran to his dad. "Africa is definitely NOT boring," he exclaimed.

Fluency Poster

Lesson Objectives

Students will:

- Use a higher or lower volume to reflect what the author or the characters are saying.
- Demonstrate understanding of the text through purposeful inflection and intonation.
- Use effective inflection and intonation to make their reading sound like talking.

Related Resources

- BenchmarkUniverse.com

 ## Read-Aloud (10 MINUTES)

Select a favorite fiction read-aloud from your classroom or school library with which to model the metacognitive strategy "Make Connections." Use the sample read-aloud lessons and suggested titles provided in the Getting Started Guide.

Mini-Lessons (20 MINUTES)

Introduce Fluency Skills: Inflection/Intonation–Volume

Explain: *We have learned that we use different kinds of inflection and intonation when we read. We say some words higher and some words lower. This is called pitch. We emphasize, or stress, some words. We also say some words at a louder volume and some words at a softer volume. When do you think we would use a louder volume? A softer volume?* **Allow responses.**

Reinforce the idea that paying close attention to what the author or characters are saying helps us figure out when to use a louder volume (model with your voice) or a softer volume (model with your voice).

Ask:
- *How would we read if the author is saying something exciting or a character is calling out?*
  (louder)
- *How would we read if the author is saying something sad or a character is whispering?*
  (softer)

Say: *Our voices should change volume as we read. Paying close attention to what the author or the characters are saying helps us know when to use a louder or softer voice.*

Model the Skill

Display the fluency poster "The Lion" and read aloud the title.

Say: *This is a story about a boy visiting Africa. At the beginning he complains, and at the end he is amazed. I will read those parts at a louder volume, especially since the author uses exclamation points. In the middle, the boy's guide whispers to him to keep him calm, so I will read that part at a softer volume. Changing my volume helps the story sound right and make sense. Changing my volume makes my reading sound like talking, too.*

Ask students to listen and follow along as you read the story aloud, using a softer and louder volume as described previously.

Say: *Now I will read the part of the story using the same volume for every word. Listen closely.*

Read the first three paragraphs in a monotone.

Turn and talk. Have students turn to a neighbor and compare and evaluate your readings. Ask them to think about how each reading affected them as listeners. Then have pairs of students share their ideas with the whole class. Reinforce the idea that using inflection and intonation helps the sentences sound right and make sense.

Shared Writing. Invite students to help you create a class anchor chart (or use the one created in the previous lesson) to remind them how good readers use inflection and intonation. (See the example below.) When you are finished, ask students to echo-read the entire chart. Display the chart in the classroom for future reference.

Inflection/Intonation

- We do not read every word the same.

- We read some words louder and some words softer. This is called volume.

- We emphasize some words. This is called stress.

- We read some words higher and some words lower. This is called pitch.

- Ending punctuation helps us know when to make our voices rise or fall.

- Changing the way we read words helps our reading sound like talking.

Sample Anchor Chart

Make Content Comprehensible for ELLs

Beginning
Use role play to model louder and softer volumes with students. For example, **say:** *We are in the library. How do we speak? Right, we speak softly.* (model) *We are calling to friends on the playground. How do we speak? Right, we speak in a louder voice.* (model)

Beginning and Intermediate
Engage ELLs in a discussion about times when they have been bored, excited, and scared. Use the sentence frame: *I was bored/excited/scared when _____.* Have students show how they looked and tell how they sounded in those instances.

All Levels
Before reading to model fluency, read to support comprehension of unfamiliar Tier Two words through explanation, gestures, and role-play, or by using props. Difficult words may include: **photographer**, **guide**, **complained**, **wandered**, **slightly**, **calm**, **twitch**, **loped**, **exclaimed**.

Support Special Needs Learners

Throughout the week, use the following strategies to help students who have learning disabilities access the content and focus on skills and strategies.

During partner reading practice, pair special needs students with more fluent readers who can model fluency and support their development.

Group students heterogeneously for small-group reading of the script so that struggling students benefit from working with more fluent readers.

Assign multiple students to specific reader's theater roles so that they can support each other.

Fluency and Comprehension Quick-Check

Throughout the week, refer to the Fluency Rubric provided in the Benchmark Literacy Assessments to help you informally assess where students are in their development of key areas of fluency.

The end goal of all fluency practice is increased comprehension. Use the following questions to check students' comprehension of the passage they have read:

- *Summarize the story for me. What happened?*

- *How did Justin's ideas about Africa change?*

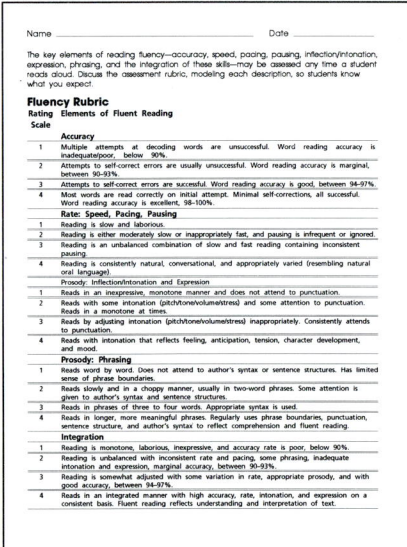

Fluency Rubric

Connect and transfer. Say: *Today during small-group reading, we will read a reader's theater script. As we read the script, one skill we will practice is changing our volume to make our reading sound like talking.*

Small-Group Reading Instruction (60 MINUTES)

Introduce and read *Kanchil Outsmarts the Crocodile*. Use the before- and during-reading instruction in the Teacher's Guide for the script.

Individual Student Conferences (10 MINUTES)

Confer with individual students to discuss their understanding of the script. Use the Individual Reading Conference Form on page 32 of Informal Assessments for Reading Development to help guide your conferences.

Word Study Workshop (20 MINUTES)

Use the Day 1 instruction provided in Grade 3 Word Study Unit 15.

Read-Aloud (10 MINUTES)

Select a favorite fiction read-aloud from your classroom or school library with which to model the metacognitive strategy "Make Connections." Use the sample read-aloud lessons and suggested titles provided in the Getting Started Guide.

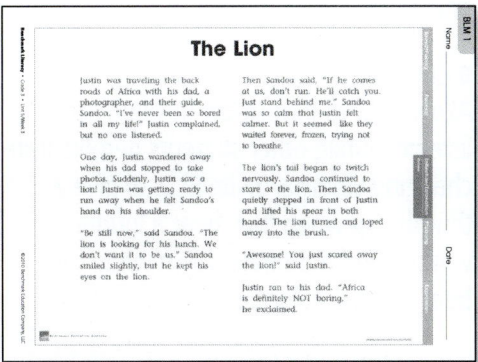

The Lion (BLM 1)

Mini-Lessons (20 MINUTES)

Practice and Self-Assess Fluency Skills:
Inflection/Intonation—Volume

Distribute copies of The Lion (BLM 1).

Invite students to choral-read the story with you one or more times.

Next, allow the group to choral-read the story without your assistance.

Distribute the Fluency Self-Assessment Master Checklist (BLM 2) and review the assessment criteria for inflection/intonation and integration. Ask students to give a thumbs-up or thumbs-down on each question based on the group's choral-reading. Discuss their responses.

Partner reading. Pair students and ask them to read "The Lion" together one or more times.

Monitor students' partner rereading practice and provide responsive feedback using the prompts provided on page 6.

Ask students to rate themselves on specific fluency skills covered in this lesson using their Fluency Self-Assessment Master Checklist (BLM 2).

Connect and transfer. Ask students to reflect on their fluency practice, using the following prompts:
- *When did you use a louder volume? When did you use a softer volume?*
- *How did changing your volume help you read and understand?*
- *Remember, you will need this skill as we practice and perform a reader's theater script this week.*

Lesson Objectives

Students will:
- Use a higher or lower volume to reflect what the author or characters are saying.
- Demonstrate understanding of the text through purposeful inflection and intonation.
- Use effective inflection and intonation to make their reading sound like talking.

Related Resources
- The Lion (BLM 1)
- Fluency Self-Assessment Master Checklist (BLM 2)
- BenchmarkUniverse.com

Make Content Comprehensible for ELLs

Beginning

Allow ELLs to participate through active listening while other students demonstrate changing volume. Invite ELLs to give a thumbs-up when they hear a louder volume and a thumbs-down when they hear a softer volume.

Intermediate and Advanced

Because this is a difficult text, allow ELLs to participate through active listening while other students demonstrate louder and softer volumes. Invite ELLs to track print with you and indicate when the volume changes.

All Levels

Pair ELLs with fluent English speakers during partner discussions and activities.

Fluency Self-Assessment Master Checklist (BLM 2)

Responsive Prompts for Inflection/Intonation

As students work together, observe those who demonstrate understanding and those who struggle. Use appropriate responsive prompting to provide additional support or to validate students who demonstrate mastery.

Goal Oriented
- Listen to how I read this. Can you hear my voice go down at the periods?
- Listen to how I read this. Can you hear my volume change at the exclamation points?
- Listen to how my voice gets louder.
- Listen to how my voice gets softer.
- Emphasize the word _____ like this.
- Notice what I do when I read the words in all uppercase letters.

Directive and Corrective Feedback
- Make your voice go down at the periods.
- Make your volume change at the exclamation points.
- Read it louder.
- Read it softer.
- Stress the word _____ in this sentence.
- Watch for words in all uppercase letters. Emphasize those words.

Self-Monitoring and Reflection
- What should you do when you see a period?
- What should you do when you see an exclamation point?
- Should your voice go up or down at this exclamation point?
- How did you know to read louder?
- How did you know to read softer?
- What made you emphasize the word _____?

Validating and Confirming
- Good job at making your voice rise and fall.
- You read that part louder/softer—way to think like the author!
- You stressed exactly the right words in that sentence. Good thinking!

Connect Fluency and Comprehension:
Analyze Author's Purpose

Say: *Using a louder or softer voice in the correct places helps you and your audience make sense of the words and sentences you read. Understanding the author's purpose for writing also helps you understand what you read. Why do authors write? What purposes might an author have for writing?* Allow responses.

Say: *Now think about "The Lion." Why do you think the author wrote this story?* Allow responses.

Discuss with students how they know the primary purpose of "The Lion" is to entertain. Ask students if an entertaining story always has to be funny. **Ask:** *Is this story funny? Is it exciting?* Point out that the secondary purpose of the story might be to provide a lesson. **Ask:** *What lesson does Justin learn?*

Ask: *How does understanding the author's purpose of "The Lion" change the way you use your voice when you read it aloud? How can you increase the excitement for your listeners?*

Connect and transfer. Say: *Today during small-group reading, focus on understanding the purpose of the script. This will help you read with the right inflection and intonation.*

Small-Group Reading Instruction (60 MINUTES)

Reread *Kanchil Outsmarts the Crocodile* to build comprehension and critical thinking using the After Reading Interpret the Script questions. Assign roles to individual students.

Individual Student Conferences (10 MINUTES)

Confer with individual students to discuss their script roles and how they plan to rehearse and read their part. Use the Individual Reading Conference Form on page 32 of *Informal Assessments for Reading Development* to help guide your conferences.

Word Study Workshop (20 MINUTES)

Use the Day 2 instruction provided in Grade 3 Word Study Unit 15.

Oral Language Extension

Have pairs of students practice the fluency passage during independent workstation time.

Home/School Connection

Have students practice reading The Lion (BLM 1) again with a family member. Ask students to focus on changing volume at the appropriate places.

Ask students to have their family member sign the page to indicate they have participated in the reading.

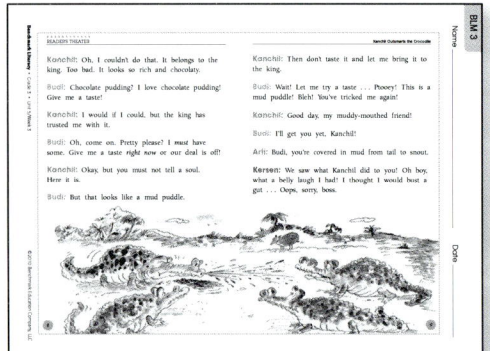

Kanchil Outsmarts the Crocodile, pages 8–9 (BLM 3)

Lesson Objectives

Students will:

- Use a higher or lower volume to reflect what the author or characters are saying.

- Demonstrate understanding of the text through purposeful inflection and intonation.

- Use effective inflection and intonation to make their reading sound like talking.

- Use metacognitive strategies to help them analyze the author's purpose.

- Build oral language and vocabulary through whole-group and partner discussion.

Related Resources

- *Kanchil Outsmarts the Crocodile*, pages 8–9 (BLM 3)

- BenchmarkUniverse.com

 Read-Aloud (10 MINUTES)

Select a favorite nonfiction read-aloud from your classroom or school library with which to model the metacognitive strategy "Make Connections." Use the sample read-aloud lessons and suggested titles provided in the Getting Started Guide.

 Mini-Lessons (20 MINUTES)

Apply Fluency Skills to Reader's Theater

Distribute the two pages of *Kanchil Outsmarts the Crocodile* (BLM 3), which students have completed during small-group reading time.

Say: *Yesterday you practiced making your voice louder and softer as you read a passage. Now I want you to apply what you learned to the script we will perform this week. Listen as I read these two pages to you. In this part, Budi has just asked Kanchil for a taste of the "chocolate pudding."*

Read pages 8–9 of the script to model how you vary your volume to make the dialogue sound natural. Use the suggestions below or interpret the text in your own way:

- Kanchil: neither loud nor soft at the beginning, then softer when he shows Budi the pudding, then loud and gloating as he leaves
- Budi: getting louder and louder until he is almost shouting as Kanchil leaves
- Kersen: laughing and loud, then much softer on "Oops, sorry, boss"

Ask students to comment on how your reading affected them as listeners. How did you use inflection and intonation to vary the characters' voices?

Partner reading. Have pairs of students practice reading these pages together. Monitor their practice and provide responsive prompting as needed to validate their efforts, give corrective feedback, or encourage them to self monitor. Use the responsive prompts provided on page 6.

Build Comprehension: Analyze Author's Purpose

Say: *Yesterday we discussed why the author of "The Lion" wrote that passage. Today let's think about why the author of Kanchil Outsmarts the Crocodile wrote about these events and characters. Understanding the author's purpose will help you interpret the script more effectively.*

Activate metacognitive strategies. Ask: *What strategies can we use to help ourselves understand the author's purpose?* Allow responses. If necessary, prompt students to use the following strategies:

Ask questions. Say: *There are a lot of characters in this script. That might get a little confusing. What questions can you ask and answer to help you remember who is who? How does knowing the characters help you understand the author's purpose?*

Summarize and synthesize. Say: *Think about what you would include in a summary of the story. How can summarizing it help you understand the story and the author's purpose?*

Support ELLs and struggling readers to participate in the discussion by providing the following sentence frames:

The two main characters are _____.
Kanchil is _____.
Knowing the characters is important because _____.
Summarizing the story helps me _____.
I think the author's purpose is to _____.

Shared Writing. Make a list of students' ideas about the author's purpose. Post this on the wall.

Connect and transfer. Say: *Today, as you practice the script, think about why the author wrote the script and what she wants people to experience through the script. Use what you have learned about inflection and intonation to help you express her purpose.*

 ## Small-Group Reading Instruction (60 MINUTES)

Have students rehearse their roles in *Kanchil Outsmarts the Crocodile* together as a group. Offer suggestions for voice, expression, and volume.

 ## Individual Student Conferences (10 MINUTES)

Confer with individual students to discuss their script roles and their rehearsal progress. Use the Individual Reading Conference Form on page 32 of *Informal Assessments for Reading Development* to help guide your conferences.

 ## Word Study Workshop (20 MINUTES)

Use the Day 3 instruction provided in Grade 3 Word Study Unit 15.

Make Content Comprehensible for ELLs

Beginning

Allow ELLs to participate through active listening while other students demonstrate varying volume. Invite them to indicate when they hear a reader's voice get louder or softer. Reinforce the connection between rising volume and rising emotion.

Intermediate and Advanced

Allow ELLs to read parts of the script chorally with you or other students as they demonstrate their use of volume. Encourage students to highlight exclamation points and practice making their voices louder at those points in the script.

All Levels

Pair ELLs with fluent English speakers during partner reading practice.

Model the use of academic sentence frames to support ELLs' academic vocabulary and language development. (See suggested sentence frames provided.)

Home/School Connection

Have students take home *Kanchil Outsmarts the Crocodile*, pages 8–9 (BLM 3) and read it with a family member to practice fluent reading. Ask students to have their family member sign the script page to indicate that they have participated in the reading.

Fluency Quick-Check

As students practice oral reading with a partner, note students who would benefit from additional repeated oral reading practice during independent workstation time.

Day Four

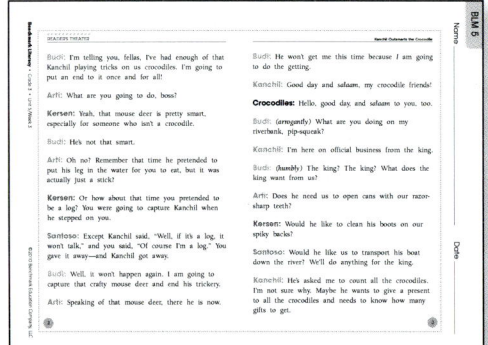

Kanchil Outsmarts the Crocodile, pages 2–3 (BLM 5)

Lesson Objectives

Students will:

- Extend Tier Two Vocabulary by analyzing synonyms.
- Partner-read to build fluency.
- Build oral language and vocabulary through whole-group and partner discussion.

Related Resources

- Synonyms (BLM 4)
- *Kanchil Outsmarts the Crocodile,* pages 2–3 (BLM 5)
- BenchmarkUniverse.com

 Read-Aloud (10 MINUTES)

Select a favorite nonfiction read-aloud from your classroom or school library with which to model the metacognitive strategy "Make Connections." Use the sample read-aloud lessons and suggested titles provided in the Getting Started Guide.

 Mini-Lessons (20 MINUTES)

Build Tier Two Vocabulary: Synonyms

On chart paper, draw a graphic organizer like the one below and distribute copies of the organizer (BLM 4). Write the word **smart** in the first column and ask students to write the word on their chart.

Think/Pair/Write/Share. Remind students that synonyms are words that mean the same or almost the same thing. Ask students to work with a partner to write synonyms for the word **smart**. Then ask them to write a sentence using one of the synonyms. Give students approximately three minutes, and then bring them back together to share their ideas. If students are unable to identify a synonym, prompt them with the following:

- *What does it mean to be smart?*
- *What would you call a person who is really, really smart?*
- *What would you call a person who can figure out puzzles and clues?*

Record students' responses on the chart and reread their sentences together.

Distribute *Kanchil Outsmarts the Crocodile,* pages 2–3 (BLM 5).

Word from Story	Synonyms	Sentence
smart	intelligent, brilliant, clever	My brilliant friend won first place in the science fair.

Sample Synonyms Annotations (BLM 4)

Say: *Now read the text with a partner. Find the word **smart** in the script. Then find a synonym for **smart** in the text. Replace the word you find with **smart**. Does the sentence still make sense?*

Have pairs share their responses. Add the synonym **crafty** to the chart if it has not already been listed.

Ask partners to write the story words **open, clean, transport,** and **present** on their chart and to find the words in the script. Then have them list at least one synonym for each word and use the synonym in a sentence. Let students use dictionaries if necessary. Discuss why a writer might use multiple words that mean the same thing instead of using the same word again and again. Do readers get a better picture of Kanchil when he is described as clever, crafty, *and* smart?

Discuss fix-up monitoring strategies. Ask students what they can do when they encounter an unfamiliar word. Generate discussion of the strategies that help good readers. For example, students can reread or read on to look for context clues that are familiar synonyms of the new word.

Connect and transfer. Say: *Synonyms are words that have basically the same meaning, but each word can have a slightly different meaning. As you read, pay attention to all the different ways a writer tells about a character or a situation. Each synonym gives you another clue about the character you are portraying.*

Small-Group Reading Instruction (60 MINUTES)

Have students continue to rehearse their roles in *Kanchil Outsmarts the Crocodile* together as a group. Discuss and plan how students will stage their script performance tomorrow.

Individual Student Conferences (10 MINUTES)

Confer with individual students on sections of the script you would like them to work on before the performance. Use the Individual Reading Conference Form on page 32 of Informal Assessments for Reading Development to help guide your conferences.

Word Study Workshop (20 MINUTES)

Use the Day 4 instruction provided in Grade 3 Word Study Unit 15.

Make Content Comprehensible for ELLs

Beginning
Allow beginning ELLs to be active listeners during the synonym activity. Provide simple pairs of synonyms to foster understanding of the concept: **big/large; little/small; story/tale; happy/glad**.

Intermediate and Advanced
Help students understand the concept of synonyms by saying a familiar word and prompting them to say a word that means the same thing. (little/small; big/large; fast/quick)

All Levels
Pair ELLs with fluent English speakers during partner discussions and activities.

Oral Language Extension

Write several glossary words from the reader's theater script on chart paper and display the list during independent workstation time. Challenge pairs of students to use each word in meaningful oral sentences. Ask students to write down at least five sentences to show you during independent student conference time.

Home/School Connection

Have students take home *Kanchil Outsmarts the Crocodile,* pages 2–3 (BLM 5) and read it with a family member to practice fluency skills. Ask students to have their family member sign the script page to indicate that they have participated in the reading.

Day Five

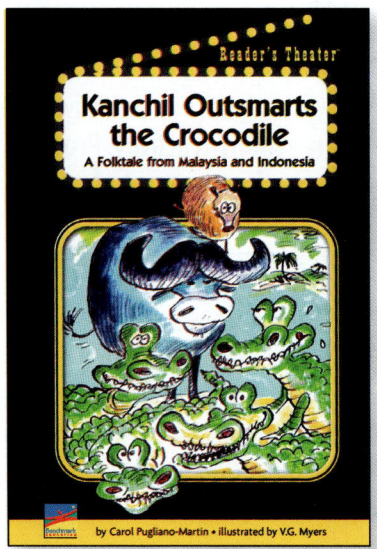

Reader's Theater Script

Lesson Objectives

Students will:

- Demonstrate their level of fluency development through an oral reading interpretation of the script.
- Demonstrate active listening skills.
- Reflect on and assess their own fluency development.

Related Resources

- Reader's Theater Self-Assessment (BLM 6)
- BenchmarkUniverse.com

Read-Aloud (10 MINUTES)

Revisit the week's read-alouds to make text-to-text connections and to provide opportunities for reader response. Use the suggested activities in the Getting Started Guide, or implement ideas of your own.

Mini-Lessons (20 MINUTES)

Prepare for and Manage Student Performances: Audience and Performer Expectations

Prepare students for their reader's theater performances by sharing your expectations of audience members and performers.

Audience expectations. Say: *While you are listening to the other groups perform, I expect you to do the following:*

- Give your classmates your full attention.
- Do not speak to your neighbors or make any noise.
- Enjoy their performance and show your appreciation by clapping when they are finished.
- Be prepared to give your feedback on the script, and always remember to make your feedback constructive, or helpful.

Performer expectations. Say: *While you and your group are performing the script, remember to do these things:*

- Read in a loud, clear voice and act out your role.
- Use expression and fluency to help everyone listening to understand your character.
- Remember to make your voice louder and softer depending on what your character is saying.
- When it is not your turn to read, follow along in the script so you know when to come in.
- If one of your group members gets lost or forgets to come in, prompt him or her quietly.
- Accept both suggestions and praise from your audience.

Show Time!

Invite students to perform the script for an audience such as members of the class, students from other classes, school staff members, or parents.

Continue your performances during small-group reading time, giving each group the opportunity to perform.

Assess and Reflect

After all groups have completed their performance, use the following self-assessment activity to help students reflect on their performance, identify how they have improved as readers and performers, and determine what they will focus on as they participate in future reader's theater experiences throughout the year.

Draw a three-column reflection chart on chart paper. Include a column for **Reflection Questions** and columns to answer **Yes** or **No** in response. Use the following questions to guide the group's assessment of their performance, or use the Reader's Theater Self-Assessment (BLM 6). Place a check mark in the appropriate column, noting their responses.

- Did we make our reading sound smooth like talking?
- Did we make our characters sound and feel like real people (or animals/objects) with feelings?
- Did we act out our parts with our voices and body language?
- Were our parts at "just right" reading levels?
- Did we practice our reading many times before performing?
- Did we make our voices louder and softer in the correct places to help our audience understand the characters and message of the script?

Connect and transfer. Discuss ways to improve future performances based on the self-assessment and reflections.

Small-Group Reading Instruction (60 MINUTES)

Use the small-group reading time to continue students' performances of *Kanchil Outsmarts the Crocodile*.

After all groups have performed, use the Assess and Reflect activity above.

Individual Student Conferences (10 MINUTES)

Have students use their self-reflection to show how they would read differently next time. Discuss how students plan to apply what they learned to future performances and independent reading.

Word Study Workshop (20 MINUTES)

Use the Day 5 instruction provided in Grade 3 Word Study Unit 15.

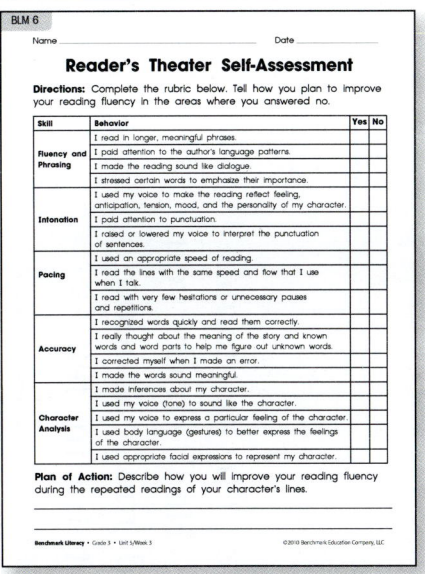

Reader's Theater Self-Assessment (BLM 6)

Make Content Comprehensible for ELLs

Beginning
Allow beginning ELLs to participate as active listeners. If students are ready for a speaking role, assign one or two shorter lines. Have students highlight their lines and work with fluent partners who can chorally read the lines with them.

Intermediate and Advanced
Pair ELLs with more fluent readers to chorally read their parts in the script. Encourage students to highlight places in their lines where they will use a louder/softer voice.

Assessment Tip

During student performances, record anecdotal notes that focus on how students are developing fluency skills and how they are meeting performer and audience member expectations.

Name _____   Date _____

Speed/Pacing	Pausing	Inflection/Intonation	Phrasing	Expression
		Volume		

The Lion

Justin was traveling the back roads of Africa with his dad, a photographer, and their guide, Sandoa. "I've never been so bored in all my life!" Justin complained, but no one listened.

One day, Justin wandered away when his dad stopped to take photos. Suddenly, Justin saw a lion! Justin was getting ready to run away when he felt Sandoa's hand on his shoulder.

"Be still now," said Sandoa. "The lion is looking for his lunch. We don't want it to be us." Sandoa smiled slightly, but he kept his eyes on the lion.

Then Sandoa said, "If he comes at us, don't run. He'll catch you. Just stand behind me." Sandoa was so calm that Justin felt calmer. But it seemed like they waited forever, frozen, trying not to breathe.

The lion's tail began to twitch nervously. Sandoa continued to stare at the lion. Then Sandoa quietly stepped in front of Justin and lifted his spear in both hands. The lion turned and loped away into the brush.

"Awesome! You just scared away the lion!" said Justin.

Justin ran to his dad. "Africa is definitely NOT boring," he exclaimed.

©2010 Benchmark Education Company, LLC • FLP052
BENCHMARK EDUCATION COMPANY

Name _____   Date _____

Fluency Self-Assessment Master Checklist

	Yes	No
Speed/Pacing		
Did my speed and pacing match the kind of text I was reading?		
Did my speed and pacing match what the character was saying?		
Did I read with a natural talking voice?		
Did I slow my reading down when appropriate?		
Did I pay attention to punctuation?		
Pausing		
Did I pause to keep from running all my words together?		
Did I pause in the correct locations?		
Did I pause for the appropriate length of time?		
Did I pause to help my reading make sense?		
Did I use punctuation to help me figure out when to pause?		
Inflection/Intonation		
Did I make my voice rise at a question mark?		
Did I make my voice fall at a period?		
Did I think about what the author was saying so I would know when to read louder or softer?		
Did I think about what the author was saying so I would know when to stress or emphasize words?		
Phrasing		
Did I notice the phrases?		
Did I read all the words in each phrase together?		
Did I think about what the words in the phrase mean when they are together?		
Expression		
Did I look for clues so I could anticipate the mood of the passage?		
Did I use my tone of voice, facial expressions, and body language to express what the author or characters were thinking or feeling?		
Did I change my reading when something new was about to happen?		
Integration		
Did I read the words right? (accuracy)		
Did I read the words at the right speed? (rate)		
Did I read with expression? (prosody)		
Did my reading sound like talking?		
Did I understand what I read?		

Name _____   Date _____

READER'S THEATER

Kanchil: Oh, I couldn't do that. It belongs to the king. Too bad. It looks so rich and chocolaty.

Budi: Chocolate pudding? I love chocolate pudding! Give me a taste!

Kanchil: I would if I could, but the king has trusted me with it.

Budi: Oh, come on. Pretty please? I *must* have some. Give me a taste *right now* or our deal is off!

Kanchil: Okay, but you must not tell a soul. Here it is.

Budi: But that looks like a mud puddle.

Kanchil: Then don't taste it and let me bring it to the king.

Budi: Wait! Let me try a taste . . . Ptooey! This is a mud puddle! Bleh! You've tricked me again!

Kanchil: Good day, my muddy-mouthed friend!

Budi: I'll get you yet, Kanchil!

Arti: Budi, you're covered in mud from tail to snout.

Kersen: We saw what Kanchil did to you! Oh boy, what a belly laugh I had! I thought I would bust a gut . . . Oops, sorry, boss.

8   9

Name _____   Date _____

Synonyms

Directions: Write the story words your teacher gives you. Write at least one synonym for each word. Write a sentence using the synonym.

Word from Story	Synonyms	Sentence

Name _____ Date _____

Budi: He won't get me this time because *I* am going to do the getting.

Kanchil: Good day and *salaam*, my crocodile friends!

Crocodiles: Hello, good day, and *salaam* to you, too.

Budi: (*arrogantly*) What are you doing on my riverbank, pip-squeak?

Kanchil: I'm here on official business from the king.

Budi: (*humbly*) The king? The king? What does the king want from us?

Arti: Does he need us to open cans with our razor-sharp teeth?

Kersen: Would he like to clean his boots on our spiky backs?

Santoso: Would he like us to transport his boat down the river? We'll do anything for the king.

Kanchil: He's asked me to count all the crocodiles. I'm not sure why. Maybe he wants to give a present to all the crocodiles and needs to know how many gifts to get.

③

Budi: I'm telling you, fellas, I've had enough of that Kanchil playing tricks on us crocodiles. I'm going to put an end to it once and for all!

Arti: What are you going to do, boss?

Kersen: Yeah, that mouse deer is pretty smart, especially for someone who isn't a crocodile.

Budi: He's not that smart.

Arti: Oh no? Remember that time he pretended to put his leg in the water for you to eat, but it was actually just a stick?

Kersen: Or how about that time you pretended to be a log? You were going to capture Kanchil when he stepped on you.

Santoso: Except Kanchil said, "Well, if it's a log, it won't talk," and you said, "Of course I'm a log." You gave it away—and Kanchil got away.

Budi: Well, it won't happen again. I am going to capture that crafty mouse deer and end his trickery.

Arti: Speaking of that mouse deer, there he is now.

②

Name _____   Date _____

Reader's Theater Self-Assessment

Directions: Complete the rubric below. Tell how you plan to improve your reading fluency in the areas where you answered no.

Skill	Behavior	Yes	No
Fluency and Phrasing	I read in longer, meaningful phrases.		
	I paid attention to the author's language patterns.		
	I made the reading sound like dialogue.		
	I stressed certain words to emphasize their importance.		
Intonation	I used my voice to make the reading reflect feeling, anticipation, tension, mood, and the personality of my character.		
	I paid attention to punctuation.		
	I raised or lowered my voice to interpret the punctuation of sentences.		
Pacing	I used an appropriate speed of reading.		
	I read the lines with the same speed and flow that I use when I talk.		
	I read with very few hesitations or unnecessary pauses and repetitions.		
Accuracy	I recognized words quickly and read them correctly.		
	I really thought about the meaning of the story and known words and word parts to help me figure out unknown words.		
	I corrected myself when I made an error.		
	I made the words sound meaningful.		
Character Analysis	I made inferences about my character.		
	I used my voice (tone) to sound like the character.		
	I used my voice to express a particular feeling of the character.		
	I used body language (gestures) to better express the feelings of the character.		
	I used appropriate facial expressions to represent my character.		

Plan of Action: Describe how you will improve your reading fluency during the repeated readings of your character's lines.

_____

_____

Program Planning References

Year at a Glance

Leveled Text Titles

Recommended Trade Book Read-Aloud Titles

Benchmark Literacy Scope and Sequence K–6

Bibliography

Benchmark Literacy Grade 3 Year at a Glance

Unit Strategies Focus	Unit. Week	Week	Suggested Interactive Trade Book Read-Aloud Focus (See recommended titles.)	Mini-Lessons for Comprehension, Vocabulary, and Fluency	Small-Group Reading (See list: Leveled Text Titles)	Word Study Workshop (Review and new skills)
• Ask Questions • Identify Main Idea & Supporting Details	1.1	1	Ask questions	• Comprehension Anchor Posters: Ask questions/ Identify stated main idea & supporting details	• Leveled Texts for Comprehension Instruction	Compound words
	1.2	2	Ask questions	• Genre Anchor Posters: Biography	• Leveled Texts for Comprehension Instruction • Leveled Texts for Genre Study	• Compound words • Adding -ing to words with VC and VCC patterns
	1.3	3	Ask questions	• Reader's Theater: *Harriet Tubman and the Underground Railroad* • Fluency Poster: Speed/ Pacing—Varied	• Reader's Theater Scripts	• Adding -ing to words with VC and VCC patterns • Adding -ing to words with VCe and VCC patterns
• Visualize • Analyze Character	2.1	4	Visualize	• Comprehension Anchor Posters: Visualize/Analyze character	• Leveled Texts for Comprehension Instruction	• Adding -ing to words with VCe and VCC patterns • Review of double, e-drop, and no change
	2.2	5	Visualize	• Genre Anchor Posters: Personal Narratives	• Leveled Texts for Comprehension Instruction • Leveled Texts for Genre Study	• Review of double, e-drop, and no change • Adding -ed to words
	2.3	6	Visualize/Ask questions	• Reader's Theater: *Our New Home* • Fluency Poster: Pausing— Short Pause	• Reader's Theater Scripts	• Adding -ed to words • Unusual past-tense words
• Determine Text Importance • Identify Sequence of Events	3.1	7	Determine text importance	• Comprehension Anchor Posters: Determine text importance/Identify sequence of events	• Leveled Texts for Comprehension Instruction	• Unusual past-tense words • Plural endings: adding -es, -ies
	3.2	8	Determine text importance	• Genre Anchor Posters: Historical Fiction	• Leveled Texts for Comprehension Instruction • Leveled Texts for Genre Study	• Plural endings: adding -es, -ies • Irregular plurals
	3.3	9	Determine text importance/ Visualize	• Reader's Theater: *Cesar Chavez Comes to Visit* • Fluency Poster: Pausing—Full Stop	• Reader's Theater Scripts	• Irregular plurals • y + inflectional endings
• Summarize & Synthesize • Analyze Story Elements	4.1	10	Summarize & synthesize	• Comprehension Anchor Posters: Summarize & synthesize/Analyze story elements	• Leveled Texts for Comprehension Instruction	• y + inflectional endings • Syllable juncture in VCV and VCCV patterns
	4.2	11	Summarize & synthesize	• Genre Anchor Posters: Realistic Fiction	• Leveled Texts for Comprehension Instruction • Leveled Texts for Genre Study	• Syllable juncture in VCV and VCCV patterns • More syllable juncture in VCV and VCCV patterns
	4.3	12	Summarize & synthesize/ Determine text importance	• Reader's Theater: *The Great Lemonade Standoff* • Fluency Poster: Inflection/ Intonation—Pitch	• Reader's Theater Scripts	• More syllable juncture in VCV and VCCV patterns • Syllable juncture in VCV and VVCV patterns
• Make Connections • Make Inferences	5.1	13	Make connections	• Comprehension Anchor Posters: Make connections/ Make inferences	• Leveled Texts for Comprehension Instruction	• Syllable juncture in VCV and VVCV patterns • Syllable juncture in VCCCV and VV patterns
	5.2	14	Make connections	• Genre Anchor Posters: Trickster Tales	• Leveled Texts for Comprehension Instruction • Leveled Texts for Genre Study	• Syllable juncture in VCCCV and VV patterns • Open and closed syllables and inflected endings
	5.3	15	Make connections/ Summarize & synthesize	• Reader's Theater: *Kanchil Outsmarts the Crocodile* • Fluency Poster: Inflection/ Intonation—Volume	• Reader's Theater Scripts	• Open and closed syllables and inflected endings • Long a patterns in accented syllables

Unit Strategies Focus	Unit. Week	Week	Suggested Interactive Trade Book Read-Aloud Focus (See recommended titles.)	Mini-Lessons for Comprehension, Vocabulary, and Fluency	Small-Group Reading (See list: Leveled Text Titles)	Word Study Workshop (Review and new skills)
• Fix-Up Monitoring • Distinguish & Evaluate Fact & Opinion	6.1	16	Fix-up monitoring	• Comprehension Anchor Posters: Fix-up monitoring/ Distinguish & evaluate fact & opinion	• Leveled Texts for Comprehension Instruction	• Long **a** patterns in accented syllables • Long **i** patterns in accented syllables
	6.2	17	Fix-up monitoring	• Genre Anchor Posters: Persuasive Letters	• Leveled Texts for Comprehension Instruction • Leveled Texts for Genre Study	• Long **i** patterns in accented syllables • Long **o** patterns in accented syllables
	6.3	18	Fix-up monitoring/Make connections	• Reader's Theater: *The Food Pyramid Disaster* • Fluency Poster: Inflection/ Intonation–Stress	• Reader's Theater Scripts	• Long **o** patterns in accented syllables • Long **u** patterns in accented syllables
• Make Inferences • Make Predictions	7.1	19	Make inferences	• Comprehension Anchor Posters: Make Inferences/ Make predictions	• Leveled Texts for Comprehension Instruction	• Long **u** patterns in accented syllables • Long **e** patterns in accented syllables
	7.2	20	Make inferences	• Genre Anchor Posters: Fairy Tales	• Leveled Texts for Comprehension Instruction • Leveled Texts for Genre Study	• Long **e** patterns in accented syllables • Unaccented final syllables (**le**)
	7.3	21	Make inferences/Fix-up monitoring	• Reader's Theater: *Rough-Face Girl* • Fluency Poster: Phrasing– High-Frequency Word Phrases	• Reader's Theater Scripts	• Unaccented final syllables (**le**) • Unaccented final syllables (**le, el, il, al**)
• Determine Text Importance • Compare & Contrast	8.1	22	Determine text importance	• Comprehension Anchor Posters: Determine text importance/Compare & contrast	• Leveled Texts for Comprehension Instruction	• Unaccented final syllables (**le, el, il, al**) • Unaccented final syllables (**er, ar, or**)
	8.2	23	Determine text importance	• Genre Anchor Posters: Tall Tales	• Leveled Texts for Comprehension Instruction • Leveled Texts for Genre Study	• Unaccented final syllables (**er, ar, or**) • Agents
	8.3	24	Determine text importance/ Make inferences	• Reader's Theater: *How Davy Crockett Moved the Sun* • Fluency Poster: Expression– Anticipation and Mood	• Reader's Theater Scripts	• Agents • Final **-y, -ey,** and **-ie**
• Make Connections • Identify Cause & Effect	9.1	25	Make connections	• Comprehension Anchor Posters: Make connections/ Identify cause & effect	• Leveled Texts for Comprehension Instruction	• Final **-y, -ey,** and **-ie** • Hard and soft **c**
	9.2	26	Make connections	• Genre Anchor Posters: Pourquoi Tales	• Leveled Texts for Comprehension Instruction • Leveled Texts for Genre Study	• Hard and soft **c** • Hard and soft **g**
	9.3	27	Make connections/ Determine text importance	• Reader's Theater: *Why the Sky Is Far Away* • Fluency Poster: Expression– Characterization and Feelings	• Reader's Theater Scripts	• Hard and soft **g** • The sound of **k** spelled **ck, ic,** and **x**
• Make Inferences • Draw Conclusions	10.1	28	Make inferences	• Comprehension Anchor Posters: Make inferences/Draw conclusions	• Leveled Texts for Comprehension Instruction	• The sound of **k** spelled **ck, ic,** and **x** • Prefixes (**re-, un-**)
	10.2	29	Make inferences	• Genre Anchor Posters: Fables	• Leveled Texts for Comprehension Instruction • Leveled Texts for Genre Study	• Prefixes (**re-, un-**) • Prefixes (**dis-, mis-, pre-**)
	10.3	30	Make inferences/Make connections	• Reader's Theater: *The Ant and Grasshopper Show* • Fluency Poster: Expression– Dramatic Expression	• Reader's Theater Scripts	• Prefixes (**dis-, mis-, pre-**) • Suffixes (**-y, -ly, -ily**)

Grade 3 Leveled Text Titles

Benchmark Literacy Unit	Level Letter	Level Number	Title	Comprehension Strategy	Genre/Content Area
Unit 1: Ask Questions/ Identify Main Idea & Supporting Details	P	38	George Washington & Abraham Lincoln	Identify main idea & supporting details	Genre: Biography
	M	28	Probability	Identify main idea & supporting details	Nonfiction/Math
	N	30	Our Solar System: The Sun	Identify main idea & supporting details	Nonfiction/Science
	O	34	Bridges: Chemistry in Medicine	Identify main idea & supporting details	Nonfiction/Science
	P	38	Bridges: Gold	Identify main idea & supporting details	Nonfiction/Science
	Q	40	The Southeast	Identify main idea & supporting details	Nonfiction/Social Studies
	R	40	Bridges: Ancient Greece	Identify main idea & supporting details	Nonfiction/Social Studies
Unit 2: Visualize/ Analyze Character	M	28	The Cooking Contest	Analyze character	Realistic Fiction
	N	30	The Three Little Pigs Wise Up, & The Princess, The Prince, and the Vegetables	Analyze character	Plays
	O	34	Sports Legends	Analyze character	Nonfiction/Science
	P	38	Max's Glasses	Analyze Character	Nonfiction/Math
	Q	40	Women Who Dared	Analyze Character	Nonfiction/Social Studies/ Biography
	R	40	Daniel Boone, Sal Fink, & Paul Bunyan	Analyze Character	Genre: Tall Tales
	P	38	Memorable Misadventures	Analyze Character	Genre: Personal Narratives
Unit 3: Determine Text Importance/ Identify Sequence of Events	O	34	From Broad Street to Beacon Hill: An Irish Immigrant Experience, & Rocket Girl: A Story of the Civil Rights Movement	Identify sequence of events	Genre: Historical Fiction
	M	28	Taking Photographs	Identify sequence of events	Nonfiction/Procedural Text
	N	30	Making Crafts From Around the World	Identify sequence of events	Nonfiction/Social Studies
	O	34	Bridges: The Voyages of Christopher Columbus	Identify sequence of events	Nonfiction/Social Studies
	P	38	Math in the Garden	Identify sequence of events	Nonfiction/Math
	Q	40	Being a Bug Scout	Identify sequence of events	Nonfiction/Science/ Procedural Text
	R	40	Gold Rush!	Identify sequence of events	Nonfiction/Social Studies
Unit 4: Summarize & Synthesize/ Analyze Story Elements	M	28	Environmentally Friendly World	Analyze story elements	Realistic Fiction
	N	30	The Thing in the Cave & Jamal's Secret	Analyze story elements	Genre: Realistic Fiction
	O	34	Storm Chasers	Analyze story elements	Realistic Fiction
	P	38	Sleeping Beauty & Puss in Boots	Analyze story elements	Genre: Fairy Tales
	Q	40	Rough-Face Girl & The Red Swan	Analyze story elements	Genre: Fairy Tales
	R	40	Why Mosquitoes Buzz in People's Ears, How Leopard Got His Spots, & How Giraffe Got Such a Long Neck	Analyze story elements	Genre: Pourquoi Tales
	N	30	The Writing on the Wall & Tia's Bad Day	Analyze story elements	Genre: Realistic Fiction
Unit 5: Make Connections/ Make Inferences	N	30	The Fox and the Raccoon, The Hodja and the Soup, & Loki Saves the Boy	Make inferences	Genre: Trickster Tales
	M	28	Samantha Saves the Stream	Make inferences	Realistic Fiction
	N	30	Math on the Moon	Make inferences	Nonfiction/Science, Math
	O	34	Daily Life Around the World	Make inferences	Nonfiction/Social Studies
	P	38	Three Historical Communities of North America	Make inferences	Nonfiction/Social Studies
	Q	40	Animals of North America	Make inferences	Nonfiction/Science/Math
	R	40	Math to Build On	Make inferences	Nonfiction/Math

Benchmark Literacy • Grade 3 • ©2011 Benchmark Education Company, LLC

Benchmark Literacy Unit	Level Letter	Level Number	Title	Comprehension Strategy	Genre/Content Area
Unit 6: Fix-Up Monitoring/ Distinguish & Evaluate Fact & Opinion	M	28	Birthdays Around the World	Distinguish & evaluate fact & opinion	Nonfiction/Social Studies
	N	30	Bridges: Diamonds	Distinguish & evaluate fact & opinion	Nonfiction/Science
	O	34	From Caves to Canvas	Distinguish & evaluate fact & opinion	Nonfiction/Social Studies
	P	38	My Running Log	Distinguish & evaluate fact & opinion	Genre: Journal
	Q	40	Letters to the Editor: Old Oak Park	Distinguish & evaluate fact & opinion	Genre: Persuasive Letters
	R	40	The Pacific Northwest	Distinguish & evaluate fact & opinion	Nonfiction/Social Studies
	N	30	Clean Up City Park!, Ride Bikes, Not Cars! & We Need New Playground Equipment!	Distinguish & evaluate fact & opinion	Genre: Persuasive Letters
Unit 7: Make Inferences/ Make Predictions	O	34	Yeh-shen & The Toad Bridegroom	Make predictions	Genre: Fairy Tales
	M	28	Pizza Parts	Make predictions	Nonfiction/Math
	N	30	Symbols of Our Country	Make Predictions	Nonfiction/Social Studies
	O	34	Animal Behaviorists	Make predictions	Nonfiction/Social Studies/ Biography
	P	38	Anansi and Sky King & Hare and Lion	Make predictions	Genre: Trickster Tales
	Q	40	The Dog Did My Homework & Bigger	Make predictions	Genre: Science Fiction
	R	40	The Magic Passport	Make predictions	Fantasy
Unit 8: Determine Text Importance/ Compare & Contrast	M	28	Polar Habitats	Compare & contrast	Nonfiction/Science
	N	30	Why Polar Bears Like Snow . . . and Flamingos Don't	Compare & contrast	Nonfiction/Science
	O	34	Habitats of South America	Compare & contrast	Nonfiction/Science
	P	38	Bridges: Body Systems: Human Cells	Compare & contrast	Nonfiction/Science
	Q	40	Our Solar System	Compare & contrast	Nonfiction/Science
	R	40	Pocahontas & Squanto	Compare & contrast	Genre: Biography
	O	34	Johnny Appleseed Gets His Name & Glooscap Makes the Seasons	Compare & contrast	Genre: Tall Tales
Unit 9: Make Connections/ Identify Cause & Effect	N	30	How Rabbit Lost His Tail, How Chipmunk Got Its Stripes, & Why Hummingbirds Drink Nectar	Identify cause & effect	Genre: Pourquoi Tales
	M	28	Move It!	Identify cause & effect	Nonfiction/Science
	N	30	Deadwood, South Dakota: A Frontier Community	Identify cause & effect	Nonfiction/Social Studies
	O	34	Habitat Rescue	Identify cause & effect	Nonfiction/Science
	P	38	Human Body Math	Identify cause & effect	Nonfiction/Science/Math
	Q	40	Earth: Fast Changes	Identify cause & effect	Nonfiction/Science
	R	40	Light and Sound Technology	Identify cause & effect	Nonfiction/Science
Unit 10: Make Inferences/ Draw Conclusions	M	28	The Cost of Dinner	Draw conclusions	Nonfiction/Social Studies
	N	30	The Seven Natural Wonders	Draw conclusions	Nonfiction/Social Studies
	O	34	A Whaling Community: New Bedford, Massachusetts	Draw conclusions	Nonfiction/Social Studies
	P	38	Three Immigrant Communities: New York City in 1900	Draw conclusions	Nonfiction/Social Studies
	Q	40	What Makes a Plant a Plant?	Draw conclusions	Nonfiction/Science
	R	40	Ponce de León and the True Fountain of Youth, & Sail On, Columbus!	Draw conclusions	Genre: Historical Fiction
	P	38	Town Mouse and Country Mouse, Belling the Cat, & The Dog and the Wolf	Draw conclusions	Genre: Fables

Grade 3 Recommended Trade Book Read-Aloud Titles*

Benchmark Literacy Unit	Suggested Metacognitive Strategy Focus	Title	Author	Genre
1	Ask questions	The Wreck of the *Zephyr*	Chris Van Allsburg	Fantasy
1	Ask questions	Cactus Hotel	Brenda Guiberson	Informational Nonfiction
1	Ask questions	Knots on a Counting Rope	John Archambault	Realistic Fiction
1	Ask questions	Insectiopedia	Douglas Florian	Informational Nonfiction
1	Ask questions	Casey Over There	Straton Rabin	Historical Fiction
1	Ask questions	Vision of Beauty: The Story of Sarah Breedlove Walker	Kathryn Lasky	Biography
2	Visualize	Something Permanent	Cynthia Rylant	Historical Fiction
2	Visualize	Mr. Williams	Karen Barbour	Historical Fiction
2	Visualize	Charlotte's Web	E. B. White	Realistic Fiction/Animal Fantasy
2	Visualize	Gone Again Ptarmigan	Jonathan London	Informational Nonfiction
2	Visualize	Mufaro's Beautiful Daughters	John Steptoe	Fantasy/Fables
2	Visualize	Charlotte	Janet Lunn	Historical Fiction
3	Determine text importance	Nothing Here But Trees	Jean Van Leeuwen	Historical Fiction
3	Determine text importance	Elisabeth	Claire Nivola	Historical Fiction
3	Determine text importance	Going West	Jean Van Leeuwen	Historical Fiction
3	Determine text importance	Richard Wright and the Library Card	William Miller	Historical Fiction/Biography
3	Determine text importance	Seven Blind Mice	Ed Young	Animal Fantasy
3	Determine text importance	Lou Gehrig: The Luckiest Man	David A. Adler	Biography
4	Summarize & synthesize	The Blizzard	Betty Ren Wright	Realistic Fiction
4	Summarize & synthesize	Great Black Heroes: Five Notable Inventors	Wade Hudson	Informational Nonfiction/Biography
4	Summarize & synthesize	The Wagon	Tony Johnston	Historical Fiction
4	Summarize & synthesize	Dinomummy: The Life, Death, and Discovery of Dakota, a Dinosaur From Hell Creek	Philip Manning	Informational Nonfiction
4	Summarize & synthesize	Cassie's Journey: Going West in the 1860s	Brett Harvey	Historical Fiction
4	Summarize & synthesize	Animals Nobody Loves	Seymour Simon	Informational Nonfiction
5	Make connections	Lon Po Po	Ed Young	Fairy Tales
5	Make connections	Thinking About Ants	Barbara Brenner	Informational Nonfiction
5	Make connections	Boundless Grace	Mary Ann Hoffman	Realistic Fiction
5	Make connections	Salt in His Shoes: Michael Jordan In Pursuit of a Dream	Deloris and Roslyn Jordan	Biography
5	Make connections	Freedom Summer	Deborah Wiles	Historical Fiction
5	Make connections	Sharks	Seymour Simon	Informational Nonfiction

*All titles are based on the recommended read-aloud lists of Linda Hoyt, Fountas & Pinnell, Stephanie Harvey, Making Meaning, and Booksource.

Benchmark Literacy Unit	Suggested Metacognitive Strategy Focus	Title	Author	Genre
6	Fix-up monitoring	My Rows and Piles of Coins	Tololwa M. Mollel	Historical Fiction/Realistic Fiction
6	Fix-up monitoring	Milton Hershey: Chocolate King, Town Builder	Charnan Simon	Biography
6	Fix-up monitoring	Follow the Drinking Gourd	Jeanette Winters	Historical Fiction
6	Fix-up monitoring	What Is the Animal Kingdom?	Bobbie Kalman	Informational Nonfiction
6	Fix-up monitoring	Plantzilla	Jerden Nolen	Fantasy
6	Fix-up monitoring	The Life Cycle of a Tree	Bobbie Kalman	Informational Nonfiction
7	Make inferences	Tight Times	Barbara Shook Hazen	Realistic Fiction
7	Make inferences	Welcome to the Green House	Jane Yolen	Informational Nonfiction
7	Make inferences	Katie's Trunk	Ann Turner	Historical Fiction
7	Make inferences	Levers	David Glover	Informational Nonfiction
7	Make inferences	Sweet Clara and the Freedom Quilt	Deborah Hopkinson	Historical Fiction
7	Make inferences	Mr. Lincoln's Whiskers	Karen Winnick	Informational Nonfiction
8	Determine text importance	Galimoto	Karen Lynn Williams	Realistic Fiction
8	Determine text importance	Teammates	Peter Golenbock	Informational Nonfiction/ Biography
8	Determine text importance	Now Let Me Fly	Dolores Johnson	Historical Fiction
8	Determine text importance	The Buried City of Pompeii	Shelley Tanaka	Informational Nonfiction
8	Determine text importance	Postcards From Pluto	Loreen Leedy	Science Fiction
8	Determine text importance	Tornado: Nature in Action	Stephen Kramer	Informational Nonfiction
9	Make connections	A. Lincoln and Me	Louise Borden	Realistic Fiction
9	Make connections	Baseball's Best: Five True Stories	Andre Gutelle	Informational Nonfiction
9	Make connections	Ira Sleeps Over	Bernard Waber	Realistic Fiction
9	Make connections	If I Only Had a Horn: Young Louis Armstrong	Roxanne Orgill	Historical Fiction
9	Make connections	I Hate English	Ellen Levine	Realistic Fiction
9	Make connections	Tomas and the Library Lady	Pat Mora	Historical Fiction/Biography
10	Make inferences	Star of Fear, Star of Hope	Jo Hoestlandt	Historical Fiction
10	Make inferences	Animals Eat the Weirdest Things	Diane Swanson	Informational Nonfiction
10	Make inferences	A Picnic in October	Eve Bunting	Realistic Fiction
10	Make inferences	Tea with Milk	Allen Say	Informational Nonfiction/ Biography
10	Make inferences	The Whispering Cloth	Pegi Dietz Shea	Realistic Fiction
10	Make inferences	Children of the Gold Rush	Claire Murphy	Nonfiction

Benchmark Literacy Program Scope and Sequence K–6

Skills and Strategies	K	1	2	3	4	5	6
Concepts About Print							
Identify the front of the book	●						
Identify the back of the book	●						
Know where to begin reading the story	●						
Know the direction in which to read (left to right)	●						
Know where to go next at the end of the line	●						
Identify the first word on the page	●						
Identify the last word on the page	●						
Identify one word/two words	●						
Identify the first letter in a word	●						
Identify the last letter in a word	●						
Identify one letter/two letters	●						
Point to and name letters on a page	●						
Recognize capital letters on the page	●						
Recognize small letters on the page	●						
Recognize the title	●	●					
Recognize the text	●	●					
Track words one-to-one as they are read	●	●					
Recognize a period (.)	●	●					
Recognize a question mark (?)	●	●					
Recognize an exclamation point (!)	●	●					
Recognize quotation marks (" ")	●	●					
Recognize a comma (,)	●	●					
Phonological & Phonemic Awareness							
Identify rhyme	●						
Listen for initial sounds	●						
Listen for medial sounds	●						
Differentiate initial sounds	●						
Discriminate medial sounds	●						
Produce rhyme	●						
Identify final sounds	●						
Segment onset and rime	●	●					
Blend phonemes	●	●					
Initial sound substitution	●	●					
Medial sound substitution	●	●					
Final sound substitution	●	●					
Segment phonemes		●					

Benchmark Literacy Program Scope and Sequence K–6

Skills and Strategies	K	1	2	3	4	5	6
Phonics and Word Study							
Letter recognition	•						
Letter formation	•						
Short vowels	•						
Consonants	•						
Long vowels		•					
Blends		•					
Digraphs		•					
Diphthongs		•					
Variant vowels		•					
Fluency and automaticity practice	•	•	•				
Syllable spelling patterns		•					
Multisyllabic word-solving strategies			•	•	•	•	•
Compound words			•	•	•		
Inflectional endings			•	•	•		
Open and closed syllables			•	•			
Vowel patterns in accented/stressed syllables				•	•		
Unaccented syllables				•	•		
Consonants				•	•		
Word study investigations				•	•	•	•
Prefixes			•	•	•	•	•
Suffixes			•	•	•	•	•
Vowel and consonant alternations						•	•
Greek and Latin word elements						•	•
Spelling	•	•	•	•	•	•	•
Metacognitive Strategies							
Ask questions	•	•	•	•	•	•	•
Determine text importance	•	•	•	•	•	•	•
Fix-up monitoring	•	•	•	•	•	•	•
Make connections	•	•	•	•	•	•	•
Make inferences	•	•	•	•	•	•	•
Summarize and synthesize	•	•	•	•	•	•	•
Visualize	•	•	•	•	•	•	•

Benchmark Literacy Program Scope and Sequence K–6

Skills and Strategies	K	1	2	3	4	5	6
Comprehension Skills/Strategies							
Make predictions	•	•	•	•	•	•	•
Identify sequence of events	•	•	•	•	•	•	•
Analyze story elements	•	•	•	•	•	•	•
Identify main idea and supporting details	•	•	•	•	•	•	•
Compare and contrast	•	•	•	•	•	•	•
Summarize information	•	•	•	•	•	•	•
Identify cause and effect	•	•	•	•	•	•	•
Make inferences	•	•	•	•	•	•	•
Analyze character	•	•	•	•	•	•	•
Draw conclusions	•	•	•	•	•	•	•
Use graphic features	•	•	•	•	•	•	•
Use text features	•	•	•	•	•	•	•
Text structure and organization	•	•	•	•	•	•	•
Evaluate author's purpose			•	•	•	•	•
Distinguish and evaluate fact and opinion				•	•	•	•
Make judgments					•	•	•
Nonfiction Text and Graphic Features							
Photographs	•	•	•	•	•	•	•
Illustrations	•	•	•	•	•	•	•
Title Page/Table of Contents	•	•	•	•	•	•	•
Glossary	•	•	•	•	•	•	•
Index	•	•	•	•	•	•	•
Captions	•	•	•	•	•	•	•
Labels	•	•	•	•	•	•	•
Maps	•	•	•	•	•	•	•
Sidebars	•	•	•	•	•	•	•
Diagrams	•	•	•	•	•	•	•
Chapter headings	•	•	•	•	•	•	•

Benchmark Literacy Program Scope and Sequence K–6

Skills and Strategies	K	1	2	3	4	5	6
Recognize and Analyze Literary Genres							
Animal Fantasy	●	●	●				
Biography	●	●	●	●	●	●	●
Fables				●	●		
Fairy Tales	●	●	●	●	●		
Historical Fiction	●	●	●	●	●	●	●
Informational Texts	●	●	●	●	●	●	●
Mystery						●	●
Myths						●	●
Personal Narratives				●	●		
Persuasive Essays						●	●
Persuasive Letters				●	●		
Plays						●	●
Pourquoi Tales				●	●		
Realistic Fiction	●	●	●	●	●	●	●
Reviews						●	●
Science Fiction						●	●
Tall Tales				●	●		
Trickster Tales			●	●	●		
Vocabulary							
Tier 1 High-Frequency and Sight Word Vocabulary	●	●	●				
Tier 2 Vocabulary	●	●	●	●	●	●	●
Tier 3 (Academic) Vocabulary	●	●	●	●	●	●	●
Vocabulary Strategies	●	●	●	●	●	●	●
Fluency							
Speed/pacing: fast	●	●	●	●	●	●	●
Speed/pacing: slow	●	●	●	●	●	●	●
Speed/pacing: varied	●	●	●	●	●	●	●
Pausing: short pause	●	●	●	●	●	●	●
Pausing: full stop	●	●	●	●	●	●	●
Inflection/intonation: pitch	●	●	●	●	●	●	●
Inflection/intonation: volume	●	●	●	●	●	●	●
Inflection/intonation: stress	●	●	●	●	●	●	●
Phrasing: high-frequency word phrases	●	●	●	●	●	●	●
Expression: anticipation/mood	●	●	●	●	●	●	●
Expression: characterization/feelings	●	●	●	●	●	●	●
Expression: dramatic expression	●	●	●	●	●	●	●

Bibliography

Adams, M. J. *Beginning to Read: Thinking and Learning About Print*. Cambridge, MA: MIT Press, 1990.

Allen, J. *Word, Words, Words: Teaching Vocabulary in Grades 4–12*. York, ME: Stenhouse, 1999.

Allen, J. *Yellow Brick Roads: Shared and Guided Paths to Independent Reading 4–12*. Stenhouse, 2000.

Allen, Janet. *On the Same Page*. Stenhouse, 2002.

Allington, R. L. "Fluency: The neglected goal of the reading program." The Reading Teacher 36 (1983): 556–561.

Allington, Richard L. "The Reading Instruction Provided Readers of Differing Reading Abilities." Elementary School Journal 18 (1983): 548–559.

Anderson, R. C., E. H. Hiebert, J. A. Scott, and I. A. G. Wilkinson. *"Becoming a nation of readers: The report of the commission on reading."* U. S. Department of Education (Champaign-Urbana, IL: Center for the Study of Reading), 1985.

Armbruster, B. B., F. Lehr, and J. Osborne. *Put Reading First: The Research Blocks for Teaching Children to Read*. The Partnership in Reading, 2001.

Armbruster, B. B. & W. E. Nagy. "Vocabulary in content area lessons." The Reading Teacher, Vol. 45, No. 7 (1992), p. 550.

Atwell, N. *In the Middle: New Understandings About Writing, Reading, and Learning*. Upper Montclair: Boynton/Cook, 1998.

Au, Kathryn H., et al. "Teaching English Language Learners." Handbook for English Language Learners. Boston: Houghton-Mifflin, 2003.

August, D. & M. Calderón. "Teacher beliefs and professional development." In D. August & T. Shanahan (Eds.), *Developing literacy in second-language learners: Report of the National Literacy Panel on Language-Minority Children and Youth*. Mahwah, NJ: Lawrence Erlbaum Associate, Publishers, 2006.

August, D., M. Carlo, M. Calderón, & P. Proctor. "Development of literacy in Spanish-speaking English-language learners: Findings from a longitudinal study of elementary school children." The International Dyslexia Association, Spring 2005, (31) 2, 17–19.

August, D., M. S. Carlo, M. Calderón, & M. Nuttall. *"Developing literacy in English-language learners: An examination of the impact of English-only versus bilingual instruction."* Childhood Bilingualism. Ed. P. McCardle and E. Hoff, Clevedon, England: Multilingual Matters, 2006.

August, D., M. Calderón, A. Cheung, D. Durán, N. Madden, and R. Slavin. "Bringing Words to Life in Classrooms with English Language Learners." Research and Development on Vocabulary, ed. A. Hiebert and M. Kamil. Lawrence Erlbaum, 2005.

August, D., M. Calderón, E. Duursma, P. Proctor, S. Romero-Contreras, C. Snow, & A. Szuber. *"The role of home literacy and language environment on bilinguals' English and Spanish vocabulary development."* Applied Linguistics 28 (2007), 171–190.

Baker, S., E. Kame'enui, and D. Simmons. "Vocabulary Acquisition: Synthesis of the Research." National Center to Improve the Tools of Educators, 1995.

Barone, Diane. "How Do We Teach Literacy to Children Who Are Learning English as a Second Language?" Children Achieving: Best Practices In Early Literacy. Ed. Susan Neuman et al. Newark, DE: International Reading Association, 1998.

Batalova, J., M. Fix, and J. Murray. "Measures of Change: Demography and Literacy of Adolescent English Learners." A Report to the Carnegie Corp. of New York. Migration Policy Institute, 2007.

Baumann, J., and E. Kame'enui. *Vocabulary Instruction: Research to Practice*. New York: Guilford Press, 2004.

Baumann, J. and E. Kame'enui. "Research on Vocabulary Instruction: Ode to Voltaire." Handbook on Teaching the English Language Arts, ed. J. Flood, J.M. Jensen, D. Lapp, and J.R. Squire. Stenhouse, 1999.

Baumann. J. & E. Kame'enui, "Research on Vocabulary Instruction: Ode to Voltaire." Baumann. J. and E. Kame'enui, Vocabulary Instruction: Research to Practice. New York: Guilford Press, 2004.

Baumann, J. F., E. C. Edwards, G. Font, C. A. Tereshinksi, E. J. Kame'enui, & S Olejnik. *Teaching morphemic and contextual analysis to fifth-grade students*. Reading Research Quarterly, 37 (2), 150–176.

Bear, D. B., M. Invernizzi, S. Templeton, & F. Johnson. *Words Their Way: A Developmental Approach to Phonics, Spelling, and Vocabulary K–8*. Columbus: Macmillan/Merrill, 1996.

Bear, D. R., et al. *Words Their Way: Word Study for Phonics, Vocabulary and Spelling Instruction*. Columbus: Merrill/Prentice Hall, 2000.

Bear, D., M. Invernizzi, S. Templeton, & F. Johnston. *Words Their Way: Word Study for Phonics, Spelling, and Vocabulary Instruction*. Columbus: Merrill/Macmillan, 2008.

Beaver, J. *Developmental Reading Assessment*. Parsippany: Celebration Press, 1997.

Beck, I. L., M. G. McKeown, and L. Kucan. *Bringing Words to Life: Robust Vocabulary Instruction*. New York, NY: The Guilford Press, 2002.

Beck, I. L., E. S. McCaslin, & M. G. McKeown. *The Rationale and Design of a Program to Teach Vocabulary to Fourth-Grade Students*. (ERDC Publication 1980/25). Pittsburgh University–Pittsburgh Learning Research and Development Center, Pittsburgh, 1980.

Beck, I. L. and M. G. McKeown. "Learning Vocabulary: Different Ways for Different Goals." Remedial and Special Education, 1988, 9, 16.

Beck, I. L., E. S. McCaslin & M. G. McKeown. *The Rationale and Design of a Program to Teach Vocabulary to Fourth-Grade Students*. (ERDC Publication 1980/25). Pittsburgh University-Pittsburgh Learning Research and Development Center, 1980.

Beers, K. *When Kids Can't Read: What Teachers Can Do*. Portsmouth: Heinemann, 2003.

Blachman, B. A. and James, S. L. *Metalinguistic abilities and reading achievement in first-grade children*. In J. Niles and R. Lalik (Eds.), *Issues in literacy: A research perspective* (pp. 280-286). Rochester, NY: National Reading Conference, 1985.

Blachowicz, C., and P. Fisher. *Teaching Vocabulary in All Classrooms*. Columbus, OH: Merrill Prentice Hall, 2002.

Blevins, W. *Teaching Phonics & Word Study in the Intermediate Grades*. New York: Scholastic, 2001.

Blevins, Wiley. *Building Fluency: Lessons and Strategies for Reading Success*. Scholastic, 2002.

Booth, D. *Guiding the Reading Process: Techniques and Strategies for Successful Instruction in K-8 Classrooms*. Portland: Stenhouse, 1998.

Booth, D., ed. *Literacy Techniques for Building Successful Readers and Writers*. Portland: Stenhouse, 1996.

Brechtel, Marcia. *Bringing the Whole Together*. San Diego: Dominie Press, 1992.

Buell, M. J., M.S. Burns, & A. Love. 2007. *"Writing: Empowering Literacy."* Young Children 62, no. 1: 12–16.

Burns, M.S., P. Griffin and C.F. Snow. *"Preventing Reading Difficulties in Young Children."* National Research Council. Washington, D.C.: National Academy Press, 1998.

Busching, B. A. *"Readers' Theatre: An education for language and life."* Language Arts 58, (1981): 330–338.

Caine, R. N., & G. Caine. *Making Connections: Teaching and the Human Brain*. Addison-Wesley, 1994.

Calderón, M. *"Adolescent literacy and English language learners: An urgent issue!"* ESL Magazine, March/April 2007, (56) p. 9–14.

Calderón, M. *"Adolescent sons and daughters of immigrants: How schools can respond."* The Adolescent Years: Social influences and educational challenges. Ninety-seventh Yearbook of the National Society for the Study of Education. Kathryn M. Borman and Barbara Schneider (eds.). Chicago: University of Chicago Press, 1998.

Calderón, M. *"Staff Development in Multilingual Multicultural Schools."* ERIC Digest. New York: ERIC Clearinghouse on Urban Education, 1998.

Calderón, M. *"Training teachers on effective literacy instruction for English language learners."* Training Teachers of Language Minority Students. ed. K. Telles & Hersh, Mahwah, NJ: Erlbaum, 2005.

Calderón, M. *"What Do We Mean By 'Quality Instruction' for English Language Learners?"* Voices in Urban Education. Annenberg Institute for School Reform, 2007.

Calderón, M. & R.E. Slavin. *"Building community through cooperative learning."* Special issue of Theory into Practice Journal. Columbus, OH: Ohio State University. Spring 1999, 38 (2).

Calderón, M. and L. Minaya-Rowe. *Raising the literacy achievement of English language learners: Facilitator's Guide*. Alexandria, VA: Association for Supervision and Curriculum Development, 2006.

Calderón, M. and M. McGroarty, *"Cooperative learning for second language learners: Models, applications and challenges."* Academic success for English language learners. Strategies for K–12 mainstream teachers. ed. P. A. Richard-Amato and M. A. Snow, White Plains, NY: Pearson Education, Inc., 2005, (pp. 174–194).

Calderón, M. and R.E. Slavin. *Effective programs for Latino children*. Nahwah, NJ: Lawrence Erlbaum, 2001.

Calderón, M. E., *Teaching reading to English language learners*, Grades 6–12: A framework for improving achievement in the content areas. Thousand Oaks, CA: Corwin Press, 2007.

Calderón, M. *National Trends of Staff Development for Bilingual Teachers*. Mid-Atlantic Regional Educational Laboratory, 2005.

Calderón, M. *National trends of staff development for bilingual teachers*. Philadelphia, PA: Mid-Atlantic Regional Educational Laboratory, 2005.

Calderón, M. *No teacher left behind: Teaching English language learners*. Washington, DC: National Clearinghouse for English language learners/George Washington University, 2004.

Calderón, M. *Teaching English Language Learners: Instructional tools for mainstream teachers*. web site for WETA/AFT joint project: www.colorincolorado. net, 2005.

Calderón, M. *Teaching Reading to English Language Learners*, Grades 6-12: A Framework for Improving Achievement in the Content Areas. Corwin Press, 2007.

Calderón, M. *Writing for English Language Learners in secondary schools*. Downey, CA: Southern California Comprehensive Assistance Center.

Calderón, M., A. Carreón and L. Minaya-Rowe. *"Professional development for teachers of English language learners and striving readers,"* Handbook of Literacy and Research on Literacy Instruction: Issues of Diversity, Policy and Equity. ed. L. Mandel-Morrow, R. Rueda & D. Lapp. Gilford Press.

Calderón, M., and L. Minaya-Rowe. *Raising the Literacy Achievement of English Language Learners: Facilitator's Guide. Association for Supervision and Curriculum Development*, 2006.

Calderón, M., and R. Wasden. *"Preparing Secondary School Teachers to Teach Reading, Language and Content to English Language Learners."* English Learners: Reaching the Highest Level of English Literacy, ed. J. Coppola and E. Primas. International Reading Association. California Department of Education. Basic Principles for the Education of Language Minority Students: An Overview. California Department of Education, 1982.

Calderón, M., D. Durán & L. Minaya-Rowe. *Colorín Colorado AFT toolkit for Teachers: Reaching out to parents of English language learners*. Washington, D.C.: American Federation of Teachers, 2005.

Calderón, M., *No Teacher Left Behind: Teaching English Language Learners*. National Clearinghouse for English Language Learners, George Washington University, 2004.

Calderón, M., R. Hertz-Lazarowitz & R. E. Slavin. *"Effects of Bilingual Cooperative Integrated Reading and Composition on students making the transition from Spanish to English reading."* The Elementary School Journal, 1998, 99, 2, 153–165.

Calderón, M., *Reading Instructional Goals for Older Readers: RIGOR for Students with Interrupted Formal Education*. Benchmark Education Company, 2007.

Calderón, M.E., *Reading Instructional Goals for Older Readers: RIGOR for Students with Interrupted Formal Education*. Pelham, NY: Benchmark Education Company, 2007.

California Department of Education. *Basic Principles for the Education of Language Minority Students: An Overview. Sacramento: California Department of Education*, 1982.

Calkings, I. *The Art of Teaching Writing*. Heinemann, 1994.

Cappellini, Mary. *Balancing Reading and Language Learning: A Resource For Teaching English Language Learners*, K–5. Portland, Maine: Stenhouse Publishers, 2005.

Carey, Stephen. *Working With Second Language Learners; Answers to Teachers' Top Ten Questions*. Portsmouth, NH: Heinemann, 2000.

Carroll, J. and E. Wilson. *Acts of Teaching: How to Teach Writing*. Teacher Ideas Press, 1993.

Chambers, A. *Tell Me: Children, Reading, and Talk*. Stenhouse, 1996.

Chard, D.J., S. Vaughn, and B. Tyler. *"A synthesis of research on effective interventions for building fluency with elementary students with learning disabilities."* Journal of Learning Disabilities, 35, (2002): 386–406.

Clay, Marie. 2005. *Literacy Lessons Designed for Individuals (Part One: Why? When? and How?)*. Portsmouth, NH: Heinemann.

Clay, Marie. 2005. *Literacy Lessons Designed for Individuals (Part Two: Teaching Procedures)*. Portsmouth, NH: Heinemann.

Clemens, J., E. Patterson, & M. Schaller. 2008. *"A Closer Look at Interactive Writing."* The Reading Teacher 61: 496–497.

Coelho, Elizabeth. *Adding English: A Guide to Teaching in Multilingual Classrooms*. Toronto, Ontario: Pippin Publishing, 2004.

Cole, A. 2006. *"Scaffolding beginning readers: Micro and macro cues teachers use during student oral reading."* The Reading Teacher 59: 450–459.

Cole, Ardith Davis. *When Reading Begins: The Teacher's Role in Decoding, Comprehension, and Fluency*. Heinemann, 2004.

Collier, V. and Thomas W. *"How Quickly Can Immigrants Become Proficient In School English?"* Journal of Educational Issues of Language Minority Students 5 (1989): 26–38.

Cummins, J. *"The Role of Primary Language Development in Promoting Educational Success for Language Minority Students."* Schooling and Language Minority Students: A Theoretical Framework. Los Angeles: California State University, Los Angeles, 1990.

Cunningham, A. E., and K. E. Stanovich. *"What reading does for the mind."* American Educator 22, (1998): 8–15.

Cunningham, P. *Phonics they use: words for reading and writing*. Boston: Allyn & Bacon. 2005.

Cunningham, Patricia A., and Dorothy P. Hall. *Making Words*. Torrance, CA: Good Apple, 1994.

Diaz-Rico, Lynne, and Kathryn Z. Weed. The *Crosscultural, Language, and Academic Development Handbook: A Complete K–12 Reference Guide*. *Needham Heights*, MA: Allyn and Bacon, 1995.

Diller, D. 2007. *Making the Most of Small Groups: Differentiation for All*. Portland, ME: Stenhouse.

Dixon, N., A. Davies, & C. Politano. *Learning with Readers Theatre*. Winnipeg, AB: Peguis, 1996.

Dixon, N., A. Davies, and C. Politano. *Learning with Reader's Theatre*. Winnipeg, AB: Peguis, 1996.

Dorn, L., C. French, & T. Jones. *Apprenticeship in Literacy: Transitions Across Reading and Writing*. Stenhouse, 1998.

Dowhower, S. L. *"Effects of repeated reading on second-grade transitional readers' fluency and comprehension."* Reading Research Quarterly 22 (1987): 389–406.

Dowhower, S. L. *"Repeated reading revisited: Research into practice."* Reading and Writing Quarterly, 10, (1994): 343–358.

Dowhower, S. L. *"Repeated reading: Research into practice."* The Reading Teacher 42 (1989): 502–507.

Dutro, Susana, and Kristen Prestridge. *Language Arts Functions, Target Forms & Classroom-based Examples*. California Reading & Literature Project, 2001.

Dutro, Susana. *A Teacher's Handbook: A Focused Approach for English Language Instruction*. California Reading & Literature Project, 2002.

Echevarria, Jana, and Deborah Short. *"Teacher Skills to Support English Language Learners."* Educational Leadership. (December 2004/January 2005): 9–13.

Echevarria, Jana, Deborah Short, and MaryEllen Vogt. *Making Content Comprehensible for English Language Learners: The SIOP Model*. Needham Heights, MA: Allyn and Bacon, 2000.

Ehri, L. C. & Rosenthal, J. *Spelling of words: A neglected facilitator of vocabulary learning*. Journal of Literacy Research, 39 (4), 389–409. 2007.

ESCORT. The Help! Kit, *A Resource Guide for Secondary Teachers of Migrant English Language Learners*. Oneonta: State University of New York at Oneonta, 2001.Fairbanks, M.M. and S.A. Stahl. *"The effects of vocabulary instruction: A model-based meta analysis."* Review of Educational Research, 56(1), 72–110.

Fairbanks, M.M., and S.A. Stahl. *"The Effects of Vocabulary Instruction: A Model-Based Meta Analysis."* Review of Educational Research, 56(1),(1985): 72–110.

Farstrup, A., Samuels, S. J. (eds.) *What Research Has to Say About Vocabulary Instruction*. IRA. 2008

Fletcher, J.M., B.R. Foorman, D.J. Francis, P. Mehta and C. Schatsschneider. *"The Role of Instruction in Learning to Read: Preventing Reading Failure in At-Risk Children."* Journal of Educational Psychology 90 (1998): 1–15.

Fletcher, R., & J. Portalupi. *Craft Lessons: Teaching Writing K–8*. Stenhouse, 1998.

Fletcher, R., & J. Portalupi. *Nonfiction Craft Lessons: Teaching Information Writing K–8*. Stenhouse, 2001.

Fletcher, R., & J. Portalupi. *Writing Workshop: The Essential Guide*. Heinemann, 2001.

Flood, J., D. Lapp, S. Flood, & G. Nagel. *"Am I allowed to group? Using flexible patterns for effective instruction."* The Reading Teacher 45 (1992): 608–615.

Flood, J., D. Lapp, S. Flood, and G. Nagel. *"Am I allowed to group? Using flexible patterns for effective instruction."* The Reading Teacher 45, (1992): 608–615.

Foorman, B.R., Francis, D.J., Fletcher, J.M., Schatsschneider, C., and Mehta, P. (1998).

Fountas, I. C., & G. S. Pinnell. 2006. *Teaching for Comprehending and Fluency: Thinking, Talking, and Writing About Reading K–8*. Portsmouth, NH: Heinemann.

Fountas, I. C., & G. S. Pinnell. 2007. *The Continuum of Literacy Learning*, Grades K–2: A Guide to Teaching. Portsmouth, NH: Heinemann.

Fountas, I., & G. Pinnell. *Guided Readers and Writers Grades 3–6: Teaching Comprehension, Genre, and Content Literacy*. Heinemann, 2001.

Fountas, I., & G. Pinnell. *Matching Text to Readers*. Heinemann, 1998.

Fountas, I.C., and G.S. Pinnell. *Guiding Readers and Writers Grades 3-6: Teaching Comprehension, Genre, and Content Literacy*. Heinemann, 2001.

Fountas, I.C., and G.S. Pinnell. *Leveled Books K-8: Matching Texts to Readers for Effective Teaching*. Heinemann, 2005.

Fountas, Irene C., and Gay Su Pinnell. *Guided Reading; Good First Teaching for All Children*. Portsmouth, NH: Heinemann, 1996.

Freeman, D., and Y. Freeman. *ESL/EFL Teaching: Principles for Success*. Heinemann, 1998.

Freeman, D., and Y. Freeman. *Teaching Reading in Multilingual Classrooms*. Heinemann, 2000.

Freeman, David E., & Yvonne S. Freeman. *Essential Linguistics: What You Need to Know to Teach Reading*. Heinemann, 2004.

Freeman, David, and Yvonne Freeman. *Between Worlds: Access to Second Language Acquisition*. Portsmouth, NH: Heinemann, 2001.

Fry, E., J. Kress, & D. L. Fountoukidis. *The Reading Teacher's Book of Lists*. 3rd edition. Prentice Hall, 1993.

Ganske, K. *Mindful of Words: Spelling and Vocabulary Explorations 4-8*. New York: Guilford Press (2008).

Ganske, K. *Word Journeys: Assessment-guided Phonics, Spelling, and Vocabulary Instruction*. New York: Guilford Press (2000).

Ganske, K. *Word Sorts and More: Sound, Pattern, and Meaning Explorations K-3*. New York: Guilford Press, (2006).

Gibbons, P. *Scaffolding Language, Scaffolding Learning*. Heinemann, 1991.

Gibbons, Pauline. *Learning to Learn in a Second Language*. Portsmouth, NH: Heinemann, 2002.

Gill, S. 2006. *"Teaching rimes with shared reading."* The Reading Teacher 60: 191–193.

Glazer, S.M. Assessment Is Instruction: Reading, Writing, Spelling and Phonics for All Learners. Christopher-Gordon, 1998.

Glazer, S.M., and C.S. Brown. *Portfolios and Beyond: Collaborative Assessment in Reading and Writing*. Christopher-Gordon, 1993.

Good, T.L., and S. Marshall. *"Do Students Learn More in Heterogeneous or Homogeneous Groups?"* In The Social Context of Instruction, ed. P.L. Peterson, et al. Academic Press, 1984.

Gove, M., R. Vacca. and J. Vacca. *Reading and Learning to Read, Second Edition*. New York: Harper Collins Publishers, 1991.

Griffith, L. W., and T. V. Rasinski. *"A focus on fluency: How one teacher incorporated fluency with her reading curriculum."* The Reading Teacher, 58, (2004): 126–137.

Harvey, S. *Nonfiction Matters: Reading, Writing, and Research in Grades 3–8*. Stenhouse, 1998.

Harvey, S., & A. Goudvis. *Strategies That Work: Teaching Comprehension to Enhance Understanding*. Stenhouse, 2000.

Hasbrouck, J. E., and G. Tindal. *"Curriculum-based oral reading fluency norms for students in Grades 2 through 5."* Teaching Exceptional Children, 24, (1992): 41–44.

Hasbrouck, J. E., C. Ihnot, & G. H. Rogers. *"'Read Naturally': A strategy to increase oral reading fluency."* Reading Research and Instruction 39(1) (1999): 18–27.

Hasbrouck, J. E., C. Ihnot, and G. H. Rogers *"'Read Naturally': A strategy to increase oral reading fluency."* Reading Research and Instruction 39, (1999): 27–28.

Heckelman, R. G. *"A neurological impress method of reading instruction."* Academic Therapy, 4, (1969): 277–282.

Heibert, E.H. *"An Examination of Ability Grouping for Reading Instruction."* Reading Research Quarterly 18 (1983): 231–255.

Herman, P. A. *"The effect of repeated readings on reading rate, speech pauses, and word recognition accuracy."* Reading Research Quarterly, 20, (1985): 553–564.

Herrell, Adrienne. *Fifty Strategies for Teaching English Language Learners*. New Jersey: Prentice Hall, 2000.

Hindley, J. *In the Company of Children*. Stenhouse, 1996.

Hoffman, J. V., and S. Crone. *"The oral recitation lesson: A research-derived strategy for reading in basal texts."* In J. A. Niles & R. V. Lalik (Eds.), *Issues in Literacy: A Research Perspective, 34th Yearbook of the National Reading Conference* (pp. 76–83). Rockfort, NY: National Reading Conference, 1985.

Hollingsworth, P. M. *"An experimental approach to the impress method of teaching reading."* The Reading Teacher, 31, (1978): 624–626.

Horn, M., & M. E. Giocobbe. 2007. *Talking, Drawing, Writing: Lessons for Our Youngest Writers*. Portland, ME: Stenhouse.

Hoskisson, K. *"The many facets of assisted reading."* Elementary English, 52, (1975a): 312–315.

Howard, Sandy, et al. *"Facilitating Language in Early Elementary Classrooms."* Young Children (May), 1998.

Hoyt, Linda. *Make It Real: Strategies for Success with Informational Texts*. Portsmouth, NH: Heinemann, 2002.

Johns, J., and R. Berglund. *Fluency: Questions, Answers, Evidence-Based Strategies*. Dubuque, IA: Kendall Hunt, 2002.

Juel, C. *"Beginning reading."* In R. Barr, M. L. Kamil, P. B. Mosenthal, and P. D. Pearson (Eds.), Handbook of Reading Research (pp. 759–788). New York: Longman, 1991.

Juel, C. *"Learning to Read and Write: A Longitudinal Study of 54 Children From First Through Fourth Grades."* Journal of Educational Psychology 80, no. 4 (1998): 437–447.

Juel, C. 1991. *"Beginning Reading."* Handbook of Reading Research: 759–788. New York: Longman.

Juel, C., Griffith, P.L. and Gough, P.B. (1986). *Acquisition of literacy: A longitudinal study of children in first and second grade*. Journal of Educational Psychology, 78, 243-255 Learning First Alliance (1998). Every child reading: An action plan of the Learning First Alliance. Washington, D.C.

Kagen, Spencer. *Cooperative Learning*. San Juan Capistrano, CA: Resources for Teachers, 1994.

Kame'enui, E. J., and D. C. Simmons, (Ed.). *"The role of fluency in reading competence, assessment, and instruction: Fluency at the intersection of accuracy and speed."* Scientific Studies of Reading, [Special issue] 5(3), 2001.

Kame'enui, E. J., D. C. Simmons, S. Baker, D. J. Chard, S. V. Dickson, B. Gunn, S. B. Smith, M. Sprick, & S. J. Lin. 1997. *"Effective strategies for teaching beginning reading."* Effective Teaching Strategies That Accommodate Diverse Learners. Columbus, OH: Merrill.

Kame'enui, E. J., D. W. Carnine, R. C. Dixon, D. C. Simmons, & M. D. Coyne. 2001. *Effective Teaching Strategies That Accommodate Diverse Learners*. 2nd ed. Upper Saddle River, NJ: Prentice Hall.

Kame'enui, E. J., D. W. Carnine, R. C. Dixon, D. C. Simmons, and M. D. Coyne. *Effective Teaching Strategies that Accommodate Diverse Learners (2nd ed.)*. Upper Saddle River, NJ: Prentice Hall, 2002.

Kame'enui, E. J., et al. *"Effective Strategies for Teaching Beginning Reading."* In E. J. Kame'enui and D. W. Carnine (Eds.), *Effective Teaching Strategies That Accommodate Diverse Learners*. Columbus, OH: Merrill, 1997.

Keene, E., & S. Zimmerman. *Mosaic of Thought: Teaching Comprehension in a Reader's Workshop*. Heinemann, 1999.

Keene, E., and S. Zimmerman. *Mosaic of Thought: Teaching Comprehension in a Reader's Workshop*. Heinemann, 1999

Keene, Ellin, and Susan Zimmerman. *Mosaic of Thought: Teaching Comprehension in a Reader's Workshop*. Portsmouth, NH: Heinemann Publishers, 1997.

Knox, Charlotte, et al. *"Questioning Techniques for English Language Learners."* The Strategic Schooling Project. Point Richmond, CA: 2001.

Kohn, A. *The Schools Our Children Deserve: Moving Beyond Traditional Classrooms and "Tougher Standards."* Houghton Mifflin, 1999.

Koskinen, P. S. and I. H. Blum. *"Paired repeated reading: A classroom strategy for developing fluent reading."* The Reading Teacher 40, (1986): 70–75.

Koskinen, P. S., & I. H. Blum. 1986. *"Paired repeated reading: A classroom strategy for developing fluent reading."* The Reading Teacher 40: 70–75.

Koskinen, P. S., and I. H. Blum. *"Repeated oral reading and acquisition of fluency."* In J. A. Niles and L. A. Harris (Eds.), *Changing Perspectives on Research in Reading/Language Processing and Instruction*, 33rd Yearbook of the National Reading Conference (pp. 183-187). Rochester, NY: National Reading Conference, 1984.

Koskinen, P. S., I. H. Blum, S. A. Bisson, S. M. Phillips, T. S Creamer, and T. K. Baker. *"Book access, shared reading, and audio models: The effects of supporting the literacy learning of linguistically diverse students in home and school."* Journal of Educational Psychology, 92(1), 23–36, 2000.

Krashen, Stephen. *"Bilingual Education and Second Language Acquisition Theory."* Schooling and Language Minority Students: A Theoretical Framework. Los Angeles: California State University, Los Angeles, 1990.

Kroon, K. A. 2005. *"Using Reader's Theater in a Kindergarten Classroom."* Reader's Theatre Digest 8.

Kuhn, M. R., L. M. Morrow, & P. J. Schwanenflugel. 2007. *"The Family Fluency Program."* The Reading Teacher 60: 322–333.

Kuhn, M.R., and S. A. Stahl. *"Fluency: A review of developmental and remedial practices."* (CIERA Rep. No. 2-008). Ann Arbor, MI: Center for the Improvement of Early Reading Achievement, 2000.

LaBerge, D., & S. A. Samuels. *Toward a theory of automatic information processing in reading*. Cognitive Psychology, 6, (1974): 293–323.

Learning First Alliance. *Every Child Reading: An Action Plan of the Learning First Alliance*. Washington, D.C., 1998.

Lundberg, I., Olofsson, A. and Wall, S. (1980). *Reading and spelling skills in the first school years, predicted from phonemic awareness skills in kindergarten*. Scandinavian Journal of Psychology, 21, 159-73.

Martinez, M., N. Roser, and S. Strecker. *"'I never thought I could be a star': A Reader's Theatre ticket to reading fluency."* The Reading Teacher, 52, (1999): 326–334.

Marzano, R.J. *What Works in Schools: Translating Reasearch into Action*. ASCD, 2003.

Marzano, R.J., and D. Pickering. *Building Academic Vocabulary: Teacher's Manual*. ASCD, 2005.

Marzano, R.J., D. Pickering, and J. McTighe. *Assessing Student Outcomes*. ASCD, 1993.

Marzano, R.J., Pickering, D. J. *Building Academic Vocabulary: Teacher's Manual*. Alexandria, VA. Association for Supervision and Curriculum Development, 2005.

Marzano, Robert J. B*uilding Background Knowledge for Academic Achievement: Research on What Works In Schools. Alexandria*, VA: Association for Supervision and Curriculum Development, 2004.

Mayer, K. 2007. *"Emerging Knowledge about Emergent Writing."* Young Children 62, no. 1: 34–40.

McCall, J. *"Frontloading for ELLs: Building Concepts and Vocabulary Before Reading."* Spotlight on Comprehension: Building a Literacy of Thoughtfulness, ed. Linda Hoyt et al. Heinemann, 2005.

McGee, L. M., & J. A. Schickendanz. 2007. *"Repeated interactive read-alouds in preschool and kindergarten."* The Reading Teacher 60: 742–751.

McKeown, M. G. & Beck, I. L. *"Learning Vocabulary: Different Ways for Different Goals."* Remedial and Special Education 9, 16, 1988.

McVicker, C. 2007. *"Young Readers Respond: The Importance of Child Participation in Emerging Literacy."* Young Children 62, no. 3: 18–22.

Mercer, C. C., K. U. Campbell, M. D. Miller, K. D Mercer, and H. B. Lane . *"Effects of a reading fluency intervention for middle schoolers with specific learning disabilities."* Learning Disabilities: Research and Practice, 15(4), (2000): 179–189.

Meyer, M. S., amd R. H. Felton. *"Repeated reading to enhance fluency: Old approaches and new directions."* Annals of Dyslexia, 49, (1999): 283–306.

Millin, S. K., amd S. D. Rinehart. *"Some of the benefits of reader's theater participation for second-grade Title I readers."* Reading Research and Instruction, 39, (1999): 71–88.

Moats, L. *How spelling supports reading: and why it is more regular and predictable than you may think*. American Educator, 12-16, 20-22, 42-43, (2005/2006 Winter).

Moats, L.C. *"Teaching Decoding."* American Educator Spring/Summer (1998): 42–49.

Morrison, P. *"Flexible Grouping Strategies for Management of Differentiated ELD Instruction."* Eleventh Annual National Conference: Two-Way Bilingual Immersion. Burlingame, CA, July 23, 2003.

Nagy, W.E. *Teaching Vocabulary to Improve Reading Comprehension*. ERIC Clearinghouse on Reading and Communication Skills, 1998.

Nagy, W.E. & Scott, J. A. Vocabulary processes. In M. Kamil, P. Mosenthal, P. D. Pearson, & R. Barr (eds.), *The handbook of reading research* (Vol. 3, pp. 269-284). New York: Longman.

National Association of State Boards of Education (NASBE). *Reading at Risk: How States Can Respond to the Crisis in Adolescent Literacy*, 2005.

National Center on Education and the Economy. *Reading and Writing Grade by Grade: Primary Literacy Standards*. Smith Lithograph, 1999.

National Institute for Literacy. *Put Reading First: The Research Building Blocks for Teaching Children to Read*. National Institute for Literacy at ED Pubs, 2001.

National Institute of Child Health and Human Development (2000). Report of the National Reading Panel. *Teaching Children to Read: An Evidence-Based Assessment of the Scientific Research Literature on Reading and Its Implications for Reading Instruction* (NIH Publication No. 00-4769). Washington, D.C.: U.S. Government Printing Office.

National Reading Panel (2000). *"Teaching children to read: An evidence-based assessment of the scientific research literature on reading and its implications for reading instruction"* [on-line]. Available at: http://www.nichd.nih.gov/publications/.

Neill, K. *"Turn kids on with repeated reading."* Teaching Exceptional Children, 12, (1980): 63–64.

Opitz, M. F., and T. V. Rasinski. *Good-bye Round Robin: 25 Effective Oral Reading Strategies.* Portsmouth, NH: Heinemann, 1998.

Opitz, M.F. *Literacy Instruction for Culturally and Linguistically Diverse Students.* International Reading Association, 2003.

Padak, N., & T. Rasinski. *Evidenced Based Instruction in Reading: A Professional Development Guide to Fluency.* Pearson, 2008.

Peck, S. M., & A. Virkler. 2006. *"Reading in the shadows: Extending literacy skills through shadow-puppet theater."* The Reading Teacher 59: 786–795.

Pinnell, G. S., J. J. Pikulski, K. K. Wixson, J. R. Campbell, P. B. Gough, and A. S. Beatty. *"Listening to children read aloud."* Washington, DC: U. S. Department of Education, Office of Educational Research and Improvement, 1995.

Pluck, M. *"Rainbow Reading Programme: Using Taped Stories."* Reading Forum, 1, (1995): 25–29.

Prescott-Griffin, M. L., & N. L. Witherell. 2004. *Fluency in Focus: Comprehension Strategies for All Young Readers.* Portsmouth, NH: Heinemann.

Prescott, J. O. *"The power of reader's theater."* Instructor, 112(5), (2003): 22–26+.

Rasinski, T .V. *"Effects of repeated reading ad listening-while-reading on reading fluency."* Journal of Educational Research, 83, (1990): 147–150.

Rasinski, T. V. *"Fluency for everyone: Incorporating fluency in the classroom."* The Reading Teacher, 42, (1989): 690–693.

Rasinski, T. V. *"Reading fluency instruction: Moving beyond accuracy, automaticity, and prosody."* The Reading Teacher, 59, (2006): 704–706.

Rasinski, T. V. *"Speed does matter in reading."* The Reading Teacher 54 (2000): 146–151.

Rasinski, T. V. 2003. *The Fluent Reader: Oral Reading Strategies for Building Word Recognition, Fluency, and Comprehension.* New York: Scholastic.

Rasinski, T. V. *Assessing Reading Fluency. Honolulu: Pacific Resources for Education and Learning,* 2004. Available at www.prel.org.

Rasinski, T. V. *The Fluent Reader: Oral Reading Strategies for Building Word Recognition, Fluency, and Comprehension.* New York: Scholastic, 2003.

Rasinski, T. V., and J. V. Hoffman. *"Theory and research into practice: Oral reading in the school literacy curriculum."* Reading Research Quarterly, 38, (2003): 510–522.

Rasinski, T. V., and N. D. Padak. *"Fluency beyond the primary grades: Helping adolescent readers."* Voices from the Middle, 13, (2005): 34–41

Rasinski, T. V., and N. D. Padak. *"How elementary students referred for compensatory reading instruction perform on school-based measures of word recognition, fluency, and comprehension."* Reading Psychology: An International Quarterly, 19, (1998): 185–216.

Rasinski, T. V., and N. D. Padak. *From Phonics to Fluency: Effective Teaching of Decoding and Reading Fluency in the Elementary School.* New York: Longman, 2001.

Rasinski, T. V., and N. Padak. *Effective Reading Strategies: Teaching Children Who Find Reading Difficult (3rd Ed.).* Columbus, OH: Merrill/Prentice Hall, 2004.

Rasinski, T. V., and N. Padak. *Three Minute Reading Assessments: Word Recognition, Fluency, and Comprehesnion for Grades 5–8.* New York: Scholastic, 2005.

Rasinski, T. V., N. Padak, W. Line., and E. Sturtevant. *"The effects of fluency development instruction on urban second graders readers."* Journal of Educational Research, 87, (1994): 158–164.

Rasinski, T. V., S. Johnston, and A. Rikli. *"Analysis of fluency and reading comprehension scores among third, fifth, and seventh grade students."* Unpublished manuscript, 2007.

Rasinski, T., and B. Stevenson. *"The effects of fast start reading, a fluency based home involvement reading program, on the reading achievement of beginning readers."* Reading Psychology: An International Quarterly, 26, (2005): 109–125.

Rasinski, T., C. Blachowicz, & K. Lems. 2005. *Fluency Instruction: Research-Based Best Practices.* New York: Guilford Press.

Rasinski, T., C. Blachowicz, and K. Lems. *Fluency Instruction: Research-Based Best Practices.* New York: Guilford, 2006.

Rasinski, T., N. Padak, C. McKeon, L. Krug,-Wilfong, J. Friedauer, and P. Heim. *"Is reading fluency a key for successful high school reading?"* Journal of Adolescent and Adult Literacy, 49, (2005): 22–27.

Rasinski, Timothy. *From Phonics to Fluency: Effective Teaching of Decoding and Reading Fluency in the Elementary School.* Allyn and Bacon, 2000.

Rasinski, Timothy. *The Fluent Reader: Oral Reading Strategies for Building Word Recognition, Fluency, and Comprehension.* Teaching Resources, 2003.

Reitsma, P. *"Reading practice for beginners: Effects of guided reading, reading-while-listening, and independent reading with computer-based speech."* Reading Research Quarterly, 23, (1988): 219–235.

Reutzel, D. R., and P. M. Hollingsworth. *"Effects of fluency training on second graders' reading comprehension."* Journal of Educational Research, 86, (1993): 325–331.

Reutzel, D. R., P. M. Hollingsworth, and L. Eldredge. *"Oral reading instruction: The impact on student reading achievement."* Reading Research Quarterly, 29, (1994): 40–62.

Rinehart, S. D. *"'Don't think for a minute that I'm getting up there': Opportunities for reader's theater in a tutorial for children with reading problems."* Reading Psychology: An International Quarterly, 20, (1999): 71–89.

Routman, R. *Conversations.* Heinemann, 2000.

Routman, R. *Invitations.* Heinemann, 1991.

Samuels, S. J. *"Automaticity and repeated reading."* Foundations for a Literate America. (pp. 215–230). Lexington, MA: Lexington Books, 1985.

Samuels, S. J. 1985. *"Automaticity and repeated reading."* Foundations for a Literate America: 215, 230. Lexington, MA: Lexington Books.

Sanacore, J. *"Genuine caring and literacy learning for African American children."* The Reading Teacher, May 2004.

Schreiber, P .A. *"Prosody and structure in children's syntactic processing."* In R. Horowitz & S. J. Samuels (Eds.), Comprehending Oral and Written Language (pp. 243-270). New York: Academic Press, 1987.

Schreiber, P .A., and C. Read. *"Children's use of phonetic cues in spelling, parsing, and–maybe–reading."* Bulletin of the Orton Society, 30, (1980): 209–224.

Schreiber, P. A. "*On the acquisition of reading fluency.*" Journal of Reading Behavior, 12, (1980): 177–186.

Schreiber, P. A. "*Understanding prosody's role in reading acquisition.*" Theory into Practice, 30, (1991): 158–164.

Schwartz, R. "*Learning to Learn: Vocabulary in Content Area Textbooks.*" Journal of Reading, November (1988): IRA.

Schwartz, R. "*Learning to Learn: Vocabulary in Content Area Textbooks*". Journal of Reading, November 1988, IRA.

Slavin, R.E. *Cooperative Learning: Theory, Research and Practice.* Prentice Hall, 1970.

Snow, C.F., Burns, M. S., and Griffin, P. (1998) *Preventing Reading Difficulties in Young Children.* National Research Council. National Academy Press. Washington, D.C.

Stahl, S. A., K. Heubach, and B. Cramond. "*Fluency-oriented reading instruction.*" Reading Research Report No. 79. Athens, GA and College Park, MD: National Reading Research Center, 1997.

Stahl, S., and K. Heubach. "*Fluency-oriented reading instruction.*" Journal of Literacy Research, 37, (2005): 25–60.

Stahl, S. A. & Nagy, W. *Teaching word meanings.* Mahwah, NJ Lawrence Erlbaum Associates. 2006.

Stahl, S.A., & Fairbanks, M.M. "*The effects of vocabulary instruction: A model-based meta analysis.*" Review of Educational Research, 56(1), 72-110.

Stevenson, B. "*The efficacy of the Fast Start parent tutoring program in the development of reading skills of first grade students.*" Unpublished doctoral dissertation, The Ohio State University, Columbus, 2002.

Strecker, S., N. Roser, and N. Martinez. "*Toward an understanding of oral reading fluency.*" In T. Shanahan & F. Rodriguez-Brown (Eds.), 47th Yearbook of the National Reading Conference (pp. 295–310). Chicago: National Reading Conference, 1998.

Strickland, Kathleen. *What's After Assessment?: Follow-Up Instruction for Phonics, Fluency, and Comprehension.* Heinemann, 2005.

Taba, H. *Teacher's Handbook for Elementary Social Studies.* MA: Addison-Wesley, 1967.

The role of instruction in learning to read: Preventing reading failure in at-risk children. Journal of Educational Psychology, 90, 1-15.

Tovani, C. *I Read It, But I Don't Get It: Comprehension Strategies for Adolescent Readers.* Stenhouse, 2000.

Trelease, J. 2006. *The Read-Aloud Handbook.* 6th ed. New York: Penguin Books.

Tunmer, W.E. and Nesdale, A. R. (1985). *Phonemic segmentation skill and beginning reading.* Journal of Educational Psychology, 77, 417-427.

Tyler, B. J. & D. Chard. "*Using reader's theater to foster fluency in struggling readers: A twist on the repeated reading strategy.*" Reading and Writing Quarterly, 16, (2000): 163–168.

Vacca, J., Vacca, R., Gove, M. *Reading and Learning to Read, Second Edition.* New York: Harper Collins Publishers, 1991. Chapter 7.

Vacca, R., and J. Vacca. *Content Area Reading: Literacy and Learning Across the Curriculum.* Eighth Edition. Pearson, 2005.

Valentino, C. "*Flexible Grouping.*" 2000. http://www.eduplace.com/science/profdev/articles/valentino.html.

Walker, Lois. *Reader's Theater in the Elementary Classroom.* Take Part Productions, 1990.

Wilhem, J. D. *Improving comprehension with think-aloud strategies.* New York: Scholastic, 2001.

Wilkinson, I., J. L. Wardrop, and R. C. Anderson. "*Silent reading reconsidered: Reinterpreting reading instruction and its effects.*" American Educational Research Journal, 25, (1988): 127–144.

Worthy, J. and K. Prater. "*I thought about it all night: Reader's Theater for reading fluency and motivation.*" The Reading Teacher, November 2002.

Worthy, J., and K. Broaddus. "*Fluency beyond the primary grades: From group performance to silent, independent reading.*" The Reading Teacher, 55, (2002): 334–343.

Zemelman, S., H. Daniels, & A. Hyde. *Best Practices: New Standards for Teaching and Learning in American Schools.* Heinemann, 1998.

Zutell, J., and T. V. Rasinski. "*Training teachers to attend to their students' oral reading fluency.*" Theory into Practice 30, (1991): 211–217.

Zutell, J. *Word sorting: A developmental spelling approach to word study for delayed readers.* Reading & Writing Quarterly, 14, 219-238. 1998